Microsoft®

Office 2000

Professional Edition

Illustrated Brief

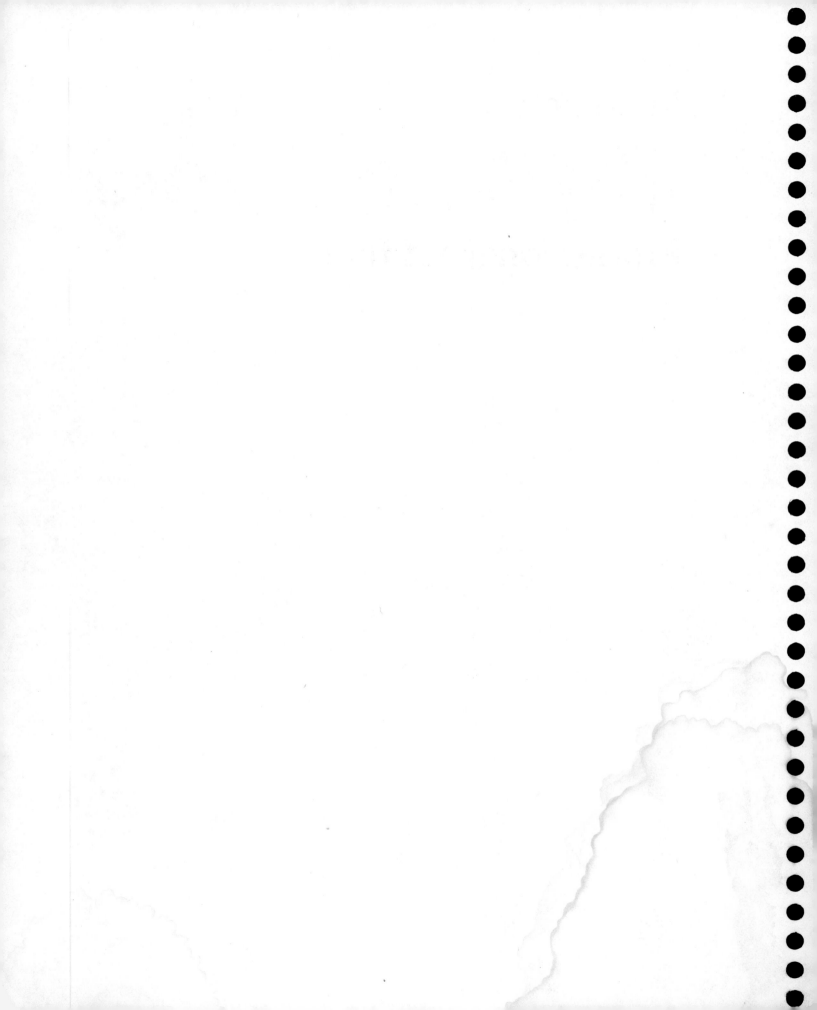

Microsoft®
Office 2000
Professional Edition

Illustrated Brief

Michael Halvorson

COURSE
TECHNOLOGY

Thomson Learning™

ONE MAIN STREET, CAMBRIDGE, MA 02142

Microsoft® Office 2000 Professional Edition—Illustrated Brief

is published by Course Technology

Senior Product Manager:	Kathryn Schooling
Product Manager:	Rebecca VanEsselstine
Contributing Authors:	Mary-Terese Cozzola
Production Editor:	Christine Spillett
Developmental Editor:	Mary A. Kemper
Composition House:	GEX, Inc.
QA Manuscript Reviewers:	Nicole Ashton, John Freitas, Jeff Schwartz, Alex White
Text Designer:	Joseph Lee, Joseph Lee Designs
Cover Designer:	Doug Goodman, Doug Goodman Designs

For more information contact:

Course Technology
One Main Street
Cambridge, MA 02142
or find us on the World Wide Web at: www.course.com

ISBN 0-7600-6155-6

Printed in the United States of America

10 11 12 13 14 15 16 17 18 19 20 BM 09 08 07 06 05 04 03

Exciting New Products

Enhance Any Illustrated Text with these Exciting Products!

Course CBT

Enhance your students' Office 2000 classroom learning experience with self-paced computer-based training (CBT) on CD-ROM. Course CBT engages students with interactive multimedia and hands-on simulations that reinforce and complement the concepts and skills covered in the textbook. All the content is aligned with the MOUS (Microsoft Office User Specialist) program, making it a great preparation tool for the certification exams. Course CBT also includes extensive pre- and post-assessments that test students' mastery of skills. These pre- and post-assessments automatically generate a "custom learning path" through the course that highlights only the topics students need to practice.

Course Assessment

How well do your students *really* know Microsoft Office? Course Assessment is a performance-based testing program that measures students' proficiency in Microsoft Office 2000. Previously known as SAM, Course Assessment is available for Office 2000 in either a live or simulated environment. You can use Course Assessment to place students into or out of courses, monitor their performance throughout a course, and help prepare them for the MOUS certification exams.

Create Your Ideal Course Package with CourseKits™

If one book doesn't offer all the coverage you need, create a course package that does. With Course Technology's CourseKits—our mix-and-match approach to selecting texts—you have the freedom to combine products from more than one series. When you choose any two or more Course Technology products for one course, we'll discount the price and package them together so your students can pick up one convenient bundle at the bookstore.

For more information about any of these offerings or other Course Technology products, contact your sales representative or visit our web site at:

www.course.com

Preface

Welcome to *Microsoft Office 2000 Professional Edition – Illustrated Brief Edition*. This highly visual book offers users a hands-on introduction to Microsoft Office 2000 and also serves as an excellent reference for future use.

▶ Organization and Coverage

This text is organized into six sections as illustrated by the brightly colored tabs on the sides and tops of the pages. There are sections for Microsoft Windows 98, Microsoft Word 2000, Microsoft Excel 2000, Microsoft Access 2000, Microsoft PowerPoint 2000, and one unit on integrating Microsoft Office 2000 applications.

▶ About this Approach

What makes the Illustrated approach so effective at teaching software skills? It's quite simple. Each skill is presented on two facing pages, with the step-by-step instructions on the left page, and large screen illustrations on the right. Students can focus on a single skill without having to turn the page. This unique design makes information extremely accessible and easy to absorb, and provides a great reference for after the course is over. This hands-on approach also makes it ideal for both self-paced or instructor-led classes.

Each lesson, or "information display," contains the following elements:

Each 2-page spread focuses on a single skill.

Concise text that introduces the basic principles discussed in the lesson. Procedures are easier to learn when concepts fit into a framework.

Entering Data Into a Database

Access 2000

To enter information in a database field, you select the record and the field, then type the appropriate data. The field properties sometimes limit what you can enter in a field to help with accuracy and integrity in your database. For example, if you typed "Mass" in the state field, which you formatted as two characters, the form would only accept the first two letters, "Ma." ◀──── To test the form, you enter a record in the Outdoor Designs database for the company Cambridge Kite Supplies in Form view.

Steps

1. Click the **Field list button** 📋 on the Form Design toolbar to close this window, then click the **Toolbox button** 🧰 to close the Toolbox

2. Click the **Form View button** 📄 on the Form Design toolbar
   The data entry portion of the Customer ID field is highlighted. This part of the field is called the **field value**. The first part of the field (the words "Customer ID") is called the field name. The Customer ID field is the primary key field for this database. It is an **AutoNumber** field, a unique number that is assigned to each record in sequence, so you do not have to enter anything in it. Pressing the [Tab] key confirms your entry and moves you to the next field. See Table A-2 for keyboard shortcuts for working with database fields in a form.

   QuickTip
   You can determine the sequence, whether random or incremental, of numbers in an AutoNumber field by changing the field property for that field.

3. Press [Tab], then type **Cambridge Kite Supplies** in the Company field
   Cambridge Kite Supplies appears in the Company field, the number "1" is assigned as the Customer ID for the record, and the insertion point is in the next field.

4. Type **Jennifer**, press [Tab], type **Heller**, press [Tab], type **1437 Main Street**, press [Tab], type **Cambridge**, press [Tab], type **MA**, then press [Tab]
   The contact name, street address, city, and state are entered in the appropriate fields. See Figure A-16.

5. Type **021421225**, press [Tab], type **6175552323**, press [Tab], type **6175552424**, press [Tab], then press [Tab]
   The input masks you created when modifying the field properties determine the format for data entry for the Postal Code field in the xxxxx-xxxx format, and the Phone Number fields in the (area) xxx-xxxx format.

6. Type **94/1/9**, then press [Tab]
   Access converted the entry to 1/9/94 because you set the field properties for this field to accept only valid dates. If you had entered an invalid date, you would have received a warning box.

7. Click the **Active check box**
   A check mark appears in the box. The Yes/No field can be displayed as either a checkbox or a yes/no field, depending on the field property. The first record is complete, as shown in Figure A-17.

8. Click the **Customer Data Entry Form Close Window button**
   Data edited in forms is automatically saved, so you can close the form without saving first. The Customer Data Entry Form appears as an object on the Forms tab in the Outdoor Designs database window.

▶ 230 **BUILDING A DATABASE WITH ACCESS 2000**

QuickTips as well as troubleshooting advice right where you need it – next to the step itself.

Clear step-by-step directions, with what students are to type in green. When students follow the numbered steps, they quickly learn how each procedure is performed and what the results will be.

Every lesson features large-size, full-color representations of what the students' screen should look like after completing the numbered steps.

Brightly colored tabs indicate which section of the book you are in. Useful for finding your place within the book and for referencing information from the index.

Additional Features

The two-page lesson format featured in this book provides the new user with a powerful learning experience. Additionally, this book contains the following features:

▶ **Windows Overview**
The Microsoft Windows 98 section provides an overview so students can begin working in the Windows environment right away.

▶ **Real-World Case**
The case study used throughout the textbook, a fictitious company called Outdoor Designs, is designed to be "real-world" in nature and introduces the kinds of activities that students will encounter when working with Microsoft Office. With a real-world case, the process of solving problems will be more meaningful to students.

▶ **Integration Unit**
The integration unit provides hands-on instruction and meaningful examples for using Word, Excel, Access, PowerPoint, and the Internet together. This integration unit also reinforces the skills and concepts learned in the program sections.

▶ **End of Unit Material**
Each unit concludes with a Concepts Review that tests students' understanding of what they learned in the unit. The Concepts Review is followed by a Skills Review, which provides students with additional hands-on practice of the skills they learned in the unit. The Skills Review is followed by Independent Challenges, which pose case problems for students to solve. The Independent Challenges allow students to learn by exploring and to develop critical thinking skills. At least one Independent Challenge in each unit asks students to use the World Wide Web to solve the problem as indicated by a Web Work icon. Visual Workshops that follow the Independent Challenges in the later units help students to develop critical thinking skills. Students are shown completed documents and are asked to recreate them from scratch.

FIGURE A-16: Entering the first record

Indicates editing current record

This field value determined based on AutoNumber field

Record number indicates this is the first record in database

FIGURE A-17: Completed record

Checkmark indicates yes

Selected field

Field name description appears on status bar to help user input data

Input masks control formatting

CLUES TO USE

Changing tab order

When you set up a form, the order in which you advance when you press [Tab] to enter data into the form is determined by the order of the fields in the table that the form is based on. If you want to change this for any reason, open the form in Design View, then click View on the menu bar to open the Tab Order dialog box. Drag the field selectors to reorder the listed fields, then click OK.

TABLE A-2: Keyboard shortcuts for working with database fields in a form

key	function
[Tab]	Moves to the next field in the database
[Shift][Tab]	Moves to the previous field in the database
[F2]	Selects the entry in the selected field in the form
[Delete]	Deletes the contents of the selected field

BUILDING A DATABASE WITH ACCESS 2000   231

Access 2000

Quickly accessible summaries of key terms, toolbar buttons, or keyboard alternatives connected with the lesson material. Students can refer easily to this information when working on their own projects at a later time.

Clues to Use boxes provide concise information that either expands on one component of the major lesson skill or describes an independent task that is in some way related to the major lesson skill.

Instructor's Resource Kit

The Instructor's Resource Kit is Course Technology's way of putting the resources and information needed to teach and learn effectively into your hands. With an integrated array of teaching and learning tools that offers you and your students a broad range of technology-based instructional options, we believe this kit represents the highest quality and most cutting edge resources available to instructors today. Many of these resources are available at www.course.com. The resources available with this book are:

Course Test Manager Designed by Course Technology, this Windows-based software helps instructors design, administer, and print tests and pre-tests. A full-featured program, Course Test Manager also has an online testing component that allows students to take tests at the computer and have their exams automatically graded.

Instructor's Manual Available as an electronic file, the Instructor's Manual is quality-assurance tested and includes unit overviews, detailed lecture topics for each unit with teaching tips, an Upgrader's Guide, solutions to all lessons and end-of-unit material, and extra Independent Challenges. The Instructor's Manual is available on the Instructor's Resource Kit CD-ROM or you can download it from www.course.com.

Course Faculty Online Companion You can browse this textbook's password-protected site to obtain the Instructor's Manual, Solution Files, Project Files, and any updates to the text. Contact your Customer Service Representative for the site address and password.

Project Files Project Files contain all of the data that students will use to complete the lessons and end-of-unit material. A Readme file includes instructions for using the files. Adopters of this text are granted the right to install the Project Files on any standalone computer or network. The Project Files are available on the Instructor's Resource Kit CD-ROM, the Review Pack, and can also be downloaded from www.course.com.

Solution Files Solution Files contain every file students are asked to create or modify in the lessons and end-of-unit material. A Help file on the Instructor's Resource Kit includes information for using the Solution Files.

Figure Files The figures in the text are provided on the Instructor's Resourse Kit CD to help illustrate key topics or concepts. Instructors can create traditional overhead transparencies by printing the figure files. Or they can create electronic slide shows by using the figures in a presentation program such as PowerPoint.

Student Online Companion This book features its own Online Companion where students can go to access Web sites that will help them complete the Webwork Independent Challenges. Because the Web is constantly changing, the Student Online Companion will provide the reader with current updates regarding links referenced in the book

WebCT WebCT is a tool used to create Web-based educational environments and also uses WWW browsers as the interface for the course-building environment. The site is hosted on your school campus, allowing complete control over the information. WebCT has its own internal communication system, offering internal e-mail, a Bulletin Board, and a Chat room.

Course Technology offers pre-existing supplemental information to help in your WebCT class creation, such as a suggested Syllabus, Lecture Notes, Figures in the Book/Course Presenter, Student Downloads, and Test Banks in which you can schedule an exam, create reports, and more.

Contents

From the Illustrated Series™ Team   III

Preface   IV

Windows 98

Getting Started with Windows 98   1

Starting Windows and Viewing the Active Desktop 2

Accessing the Internet from the Active Desktop 2

Using the Mouse 4

More about the mouse: Classic style and Internet style 5

Starting a Program 6

Moving and Resizing Windows 8

More about sizing windows 9

Using Menus, Keyboard Shortcuts, and Toolbars 10

Using Dialog Boxes 12

Using Scroll Bars 14

Getting Help 16

Context-sensitive help 17

Closing a Program and Shutting Down Windows 18

The Log Off command 19

Concepts Review 20

Skills Review 21

Independent Challenges 23

Visual Workshop 24

Working with Programs, Files, and Folders   25

Creating and Saving a WordPad File 26

Opening, Editing, and Saving an Existing Paint File.............................28

Working with Multiple Programs..30

Understanding File Management 32

Viewing Files and Creating Folders with My Computer........................34

Moving and Copying Files Using My Computer 36

Managing Files with Windows Explorer 38

Deleting and Restoring Files 40

Customizing your Recycle Bin 40

Creating a Shortcut on the Desktop...42

Adding shortcuts to the Start menu 43

Concepts Review 44

Skills Review 45

Independent Challenges 47

Visual Workshop 48

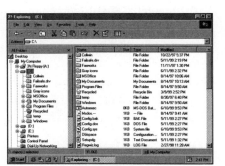

Contents

Office 2000

Getting Started with Office 2000   49

Understanding Office 2000 Professional 50
Starting an Office Program 52
   Starting an Office program with the New Office Document dialog box .. 53
Using Menus and Toolbars 54
Using Help 56
   Using the Office Assistant 57
Creating a New File with a Wizard 58
Saving a File 60
   Naming Files 61
Closing a File and Exiting an Office Program 62
Concepts Review 64
Skills Review 67
Independent Challenges 69
Visual Workshop 72

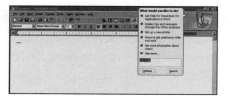

Word 2000

Creating a Document with Word 2000   73

Planning a Document 74
Opening a File and Saving it with a New Name 76
Entering Text in a Document 78
   Using AutoCorrect 79
Editing a Document 80
   Using Click and Type 81
Moving Text in a Document 82
   Using the Office Clipboard 83
Using the Spelling and Grammar Checker 84
Viewing a Document 86
   Using the View buttons 87
Printing a Document 88
Concepts Review 90
Skills Review 92
Independent Challenges 94
Visual Workshop 96

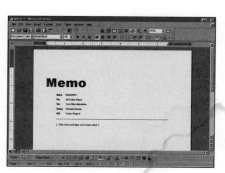

Enhancing a Document   97

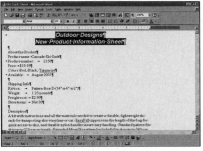

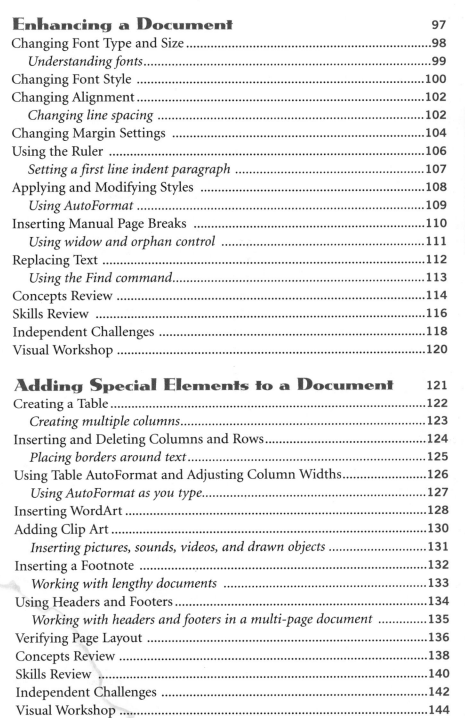

Changing Font Type and Size 98
   Understanding fonts..99
Changing Font Style 100
Changing Alignment 102
   Changing line spacing 102
Changing Margin Settings 104
Using the Ruler 106
   Setting a first line indent paragraph 107
Applying and Modifying Styles 108
   Using AutoFormat 109
Inserting Manual Page Breaks 110
   Using widow and orphan control 111
Replacing Text 112
   Using the Find command..113
Concepts Review 114
Skills Review 116
Independent Challenges 118
Visual Workshop 120

Adding Special Elements to a Document   121

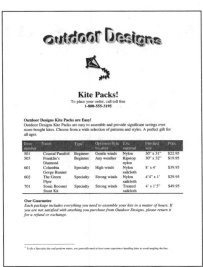

Creating a Table 122
   Creating multiple columns..123
Inserting and Deleting Columns and Rows..124
   Placing borders around text..125
Using Table AutoFormat and Adjusting Column Widths..126
   Using AutoFormat as you type..127
Inserting WordArt 128
Adding Clip Art 130
   Inserting pictures, sounds, videos, and drawn objects 131
Inserting a Footnote 132
   Working with lengthy documents 133
Using Headers and Footers 134
   Working with headers and footers in a multi-page document 135
Verifying Page Layout 136
Concepts Review 138
Skills Review 140
Independent Challenges 142
Visual Workshop 144

Contents

Excel 2000

Creating and Enhancing a Worksheet with Excel 2000   145

Navigating a Workbook **146**
Entering Numbers and Labels **148**
Changing Column Width and Row Height **150**
Using Formulas **152**
   Calculating formulas in Excel **153**
Editing a Worksheet **154**
   Understanding relative and absolute cell references **155**
Changing Alignment and Number Format **156**
   Changing the number format **157**
Changing Font Type and Font Style and Adding Borders **158**
   Adding shading to cells..**159**
Previewing and Printing a Worksheet **160**
   Adding headers and footers **161**
Concepts Review **162**
Skills Review **163**
Independent Challenges **165**
Visual Workshop **168**

Working with Excel Functions   169

Understanding Functions **170**
   Planning to use functions...**171**
Using the SUM Function **172**
Using Date and Time Functions...**174**
   How dates are calculated using serial numbers **175**
Using Statistical Functions **176**
   Mathematical functions **177**
Using Financial Functions **178**
   Using Excel templates..**179**
Using Goal Seek...**180**
   Using Solver to solve complex problems **181**
Sorting Rows **182**
   Sorting by more than one column **183**
Filtering Data and Printing...**184**
   Customizing a filter **185**
Concepts Review **186**
Skills Review **188**
Independent Challenges **189**
Visual Workshop **192**

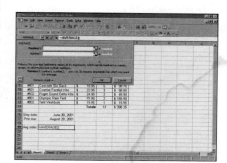

Creating Excel Charts

Creating Excel Charts   193

Planning a Chart 194
Creating a Chart 196
Moving and Resizing a Chart and Chart Objects 198
Changing the Chart Type 200
Adding Axis Labels and Gridlines 202
Changing Fonts and Colors 204
Enhancing a Chart...206
   Adding enhancements to a chart 206
Previewing and Printing a Chart 208
Concepts Review 210
Skills Review 212
Independent Challenges 214
Visual Workshop 216

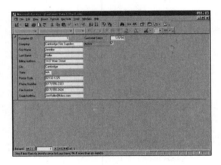

Access 2000

Building a Database with Access 2000

Building a Database with Access 2000   217

Planning a Database 218
Starting Access 2000 220
Creating a Database...222
Modifying a Table 224
Building a Data Entry Form 226
   Working in Datasheet view 226
Entering Data Into a Database 228
   Changing tab order 229
Adding and Editing Records in a Database 230
Printing a Database and Exiting Access 232
Concepts Review 234
Skills Review 235
Independent Challenges 237
Visual Workshop 240

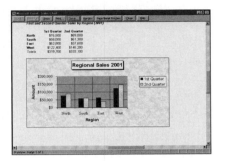

Contents

Enhancing a Database   241

Opening an Existing Database 242
  Opening more than one database file at a time 242
Modifying a Form's Layout 244
  Parts of the form...245
Changing Fonts and Styles on a Form 246
  Formatting controls using the property sheet......................247
Adding Clip Art to a Form 248
  Working with clip art 249
Filtering a Database..250
  Filtering by selection 251
Sorting Database Records 252
Creating a Query 254
Protecting a Database 256
Concepts Review 258
Skills Review 260
Independent Challenges 261
Visual Workshop 264

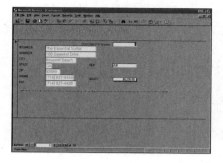

Creating Database Reports   265

Creating a Report 266
Modifying a Report 268
Creating a Report from a Query..270
Adding Summary Information to a Report 272
Adding an Expression to a Report 274
Viewing a Report in Print Preview..276
Adding Clip Art to a Report 278
  Inserting Pictures 279
Creating Mailing Labels 280
  Modifying labels in Design view 281
Concepts Review 282
Skills Review 284
Independent Challenges 286
Visual Workshop 288

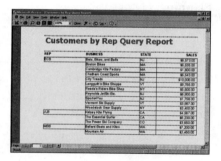

PowerPoint

Creating and Modifying a Presentation 289

Creating a Presentation 290
   Working with PowerPoint templates 291
Navigating a Presentation 292
   Working with PowerPoint views 293
Entering Text in Outline View 294
   Working with text in Outline view 295
Entering Text in Slide View...296
Formatting Text 298
Using the Drawing Toolbar..300
Adding Text Boxes 302
   Working with stacked objects 303
Checking Spelling and Previewing the Presentation......................304
   Working with the Spelling Checker 305
Concepts Review 306
Skills Review 308
Independent Challenges 310
Visual Workshop 312

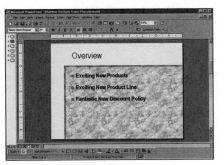

Polishing and Running a Presentation 313

Changing the Color Scheme of an Existing Presentation.....................314
   Designing your presentation 315
Using Clip Art 316
   Inserting other types of pictures 316
Working with Pictures...318
Running an Online Slide Show 320
   Using PowerPoint Viewer when PowerPoint isn't installed 321
Setting Preset Timing and Transitions...322
Setting Animation Effects 324
Creating Speaker's Notes and Printed Materials 326
   Preparing for an off-site presentation 327
Concepts Review 328
Skills Review 330
Independent Challenges 333
Visual Workshop 336

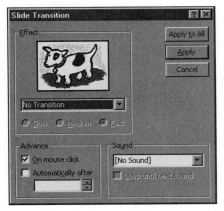

Contents

Integration

Integrating Office 2000 Programs — 337

Embedding an Excel Chart into a PowerPoint Slide 338
Sending a PowerPoint Presentation to Word 340
Inserting Word text into a PowerPoint slide presentation 341
Inserting a File in a Word Document 342
Using Drag and Drop to Insert an Access table into Word 342
Inserting Excel data in a Word file 343
Linking an Excel Worksheet to a Word Document 344
Updating a Linked Excel Worksheet 346
Unlinking files 347
Inserting Access Fields into a Word Form Letter 348
Merging Access Data with a Word Form Letter 350
Saving a Word Document as a Web Page 352
Understanding the World Wide Web 353
Concepts Review 354
Skills Review 355
Independent Challenges 357
Visual Workshop 360

Glossary — 361
Index — 369

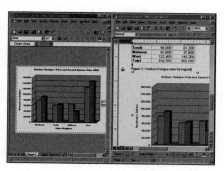

Unit
A

Getting
Started with Windows 98

Objectives

- ▶ **Start Windows and view the Active Desktop**
- ▶ **Use the mouse**
- ▶ **Start a program**
- ▶ **Move and resize windows**
- ▶ **Use menus, keyboard shortcuts, and toolbars**
- ▶ **Use dialog boxes**
- ▶ **Use scroll bars**
- ▶ **Get Help**
- ▶ **Close a program and shut down Windows**

Microsoft Windows 98 is an **operating system**, a computer program that controls how the computer carries out basic tasks such as displaying information on your computer screen and running programs. Windows 98 helps you save and organize the results of your work (such as a resume or a list of addresses) as **files**, which are electronic collections of data. Windows 98 also coordinates the flow of information among the programs, printers, storage devices, and other components of your computer system. When you work with Windows 98, you will notice many **icons**, small pictures intended to be meaningful symbols of the items they represent. You will also notice rectangular-shaped work areas known as **windows**, thus the name of the operating system. This use of icons and windows is called a **graphical user interface** (**GUI**, pronounced "gooey"), which means that you interact with the computer through the use of graphics such as windows, icons, and other meaningful words and symbols. ✐ This unit introduces you to basic skills that you can use in all Windows programs.

Unit A

Windows 98

Starting Windows and Viewing the Active Desktop

When you turn on your computer, Windows 98 automatically starts and the Active Desktop appears. The **Active Desktop**, shown in Figure A-1, is where you organize all the information and tools you need to accomplish your computer tasks. From the desktop, you can access, store, share, and explore information seamlessly, whether it resides on your computer, a network, or the Internet. The **Internet** is a worldwide collection of over 40 million computers linked together to share information. The desktop is called "active" because, unlike in other versions of Windows, it allows you to access the Internet. When you start Windows for the first time, the desktop appears with the **default** settings, those preset by the operating system. For example, the default color of the desktop is green. If any of the default settings have been changed on your computer, your desktop will look different than in the figures, but you should be able to locate all the items you need. The bar at the bottom of your screen is called the **taskbar**, which shows what programs are currently running. Use the **Start button** at the left end of the taskbar to start programs, find and open files, access Windows Help and so on. The **Quick Launch toolbar** is next to the Start button; it contains buttons you use to quickly start Internet-related programs and show the desktop when it is not currently displayed. The bar on the right side of your screen is called the **Channel Bar**, which contains buttons you use to access the Internet. Table A-1 identifies the icons and other elements you see on your desktop. If Windows 98 is not currently running, follow the steps below to start it now.

Steps

1. **Turn on your computer and monitor**

   Windows automatically starts and the desktop appears, as shown in Figure A-1. If you are working on a network at school or at an office, you might see a password dialog box. If so, continue to Step 2. If not, continue to the next lesson.

Trouble?

If you don't know your password, see your instructor or technical support person.

2. **Type your password, then press [Enter]**

   Once the password is accepted, the Windows desktop appears on your screen.

CLUES TO USE

Accessing the Internet from the Active Desktop

One of the important differences between Windows 98 and previous versions of Windows is that Windows 98 allows you to access the Internet from the desktop using Internet Explorer, a program that is integrated into the Windows 98 operating system. Internet Explorer is an example of a **browser,** a program designed to access the **World Wide Web (WWW, the Web)**. One feature of Internet Explorer is that you can use the Favorites command on the Start menu to access places on the Internet that you visit frequently. Also, you can use the Quick Launch toolbar to launch Internet-related programs and the Channel Bar to view Internet channels, which are like those on television but display Internet content. The integration of a browser into the operating system provides a seamless connection between your desktop and the Internet.

FIGURE A-1: Windows Active Desktop

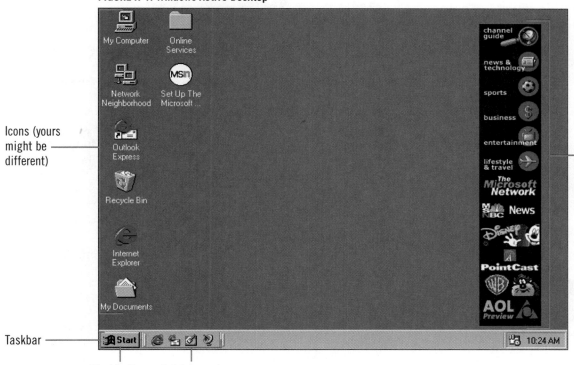

Icons (yours
might be
different)

Channel Bar
(yours might not
be showing)

Taskbar

Start button   Quick Launch
toolbar

TABLE A-1: Elements of the Windows desktop

desktop element	allows you to
My Computer	Work with different disk drives and printers on your computer
Network Neighborhood	Work with different disk drives and printers on a network
Outlook Express	Start Outlook Express, an electronic mail program
Recycle Bin	Delete and restore files
Internet Explorer	Start Internet Explorer, a program you use to access the Internet
My Documents folder	Store programs, documents, graphics, or other files
Taskbar	Start programs and switch among open programs
Start button	Start programs, open documents, find a file, and more
Channel Bar	Start Internet Explorer and open channels
Quick Launch toolbar	Start Internet Explorer, start Outlook Express, show the desktop, and view channels

Windows 98

Using the Mouse

A **mouse** is a hand-held **input device** that you use to interact with your computer. Input devices come in many shapes and sizes; some, like a mouse, are directly attached to your computer with a cable; others function like a TV remote control and allow you to access your computer without being right next to it. Figure A-2 shows examples of common pointing devices. Because the most common pointing device is a mouse, this book uses that term. If you are using a different pointing device substitute that device whenever you see the term "mouse." When you move the mouse, the **mouse pointer** on the screen moves in the same direction. The **mouse buttons** are used to select icons and commands, which is how you communicate with the computer. Table A-2 shows some common mouse pointer shapes that indicate different activities. Table A-3 lists the five basic mouse actions.  Begin by experimenting with the mouse now.

1. **Locate the mouse pointer on the desktop, then move the mouse across your desk or mousepad**
   Watch how the mouse pointer moves on the desktop in response to your movements. Practice moving the mouse pointer in circles, then back and forth in straight lines.

Trouble?

If the My Computer window opens, your mouse isn't set with the Windows 98 default mouse settings. See your instructor or technical support person for assistance. This book assumes your computer is set to all Windows 98 default settings

2. **Position the mouse pointer over the My Computer icon**
   Positioning the mouse pointer over an item is called **pointing**.

3. **With the pointer over the My Computer icon, press and release the left mouse button**
   Pressing and releasing the left mouse button is called **clicking** or single-clicking, to distinguish it from double-clicking, which you'll do in Step 7. When you position the mouse pointer over an icon or any item and click, you select that item. When an item is **selected**, it is **highlighted** (shaded differently than other items), and any action you take will be performed on that item.

4. **With the icon selected, press and hold down the left mouse button, then move the mouse down and to the right and release the mouse button**
   The icon becomes dimmed and moves with the mouse pointer; this is called **dragging**, which you use to move icons and other Windows elements. When you release the mouse button, the icon is moved to a new location.

5. **Position the mouse pointer over the My Computer icon, then press and release the right mouse button**
   Clicking the right mouse button is known as **right-clicking**. Right-clicking an item on the desktop displays a **pop-up menu**, as shown in Figure A-3. This menu lists the commands most commonly used for the item you have clicked. A **command** is a directive that provides access to a program's features.

QuickTip

When a step tells you to "click," use the left mouse button. If it says "right-click", use the right mouse button.

6. **Click anywhere outside the menu to close the pop-up menu**

7. **Position the mouse pointer over the My Computer icon, then press and release the left mouse button twice quickly**
   Clicking the mouse button twice quickly is known as **double-clicking**, which, in this case, opens the My Computer window. The **My Computer** window contains additional icons that represent the drives and system components that are installed on your computer.

8. **Click the Close button ⊠ in the upper-right corner of the My Computer window**

TABLE A-2: Common mouse pointer shapes

shape	used to
⩤	Select items, choose commands, start programs, and work in programs
I	Position mouse pointer for editing or inserting text; called the insertion point
⧖	Indicate Windows is busy processing a command
↔	Change the size of a window; appears when mouse pointer is on the border of a window
⬈	Select and open Web-based data

FIGURE A-2: Common pointing devices

Right mouse button

Left mouse button

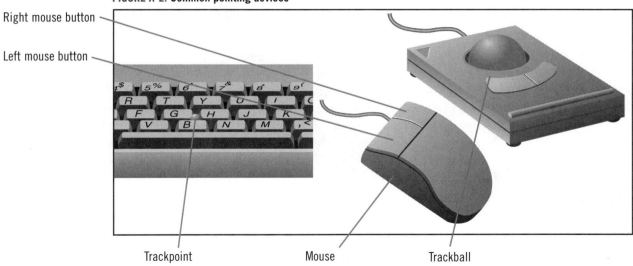

Trackpoint   Mouse   Trackball

FIGURE A-3: Displaying a pop-up menu

Selected icon

Pop-up menu

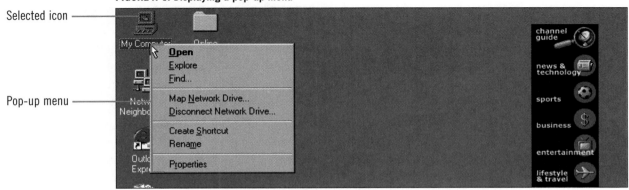

TABLE A-3: Basic mouse techniques

technique	what to do
Pointing	Move the mouse to position the mouse pointer over an item on the desktop
Clicking	Press and release the left mouse button
Double-clicking	Press and release the left mouse button twice quickly
Dragging	Point to an item, press and hold the left mouse button, move the mouse to a new location, then release the mouse button
Right-clicking	Point to an item, then press and release the right mouse button

More about the mouse: Classic style and Internet style

Because Windows 98 integrates the use of the Internet with its other functions, it allows you to choose whether you want to extend the way you click on the Internet to the rest of your computer work. With previous versions of the Windows operating system, and with the default Windows 98 settings, you click an item to select it and double-click an item to open it. When you use the Internet, however, you point to an item to select it and single-click to open it. Therefore, Windows 98 gives you two choices for using the mouse buttons: with the **Classic style**, you double-click to open items, and with the **Internet style** or **Web style**, you single-click to open items. To change from one style to another, click the Start button, point to Settings, click Folder Options, then click the Web style, Classic style, or Custom option.

Windows 98

Starting a Program

To start a program in Windows 98, click the Start button, which lists categories for a variety of tasks described in Table A-4. As you become familiar with Windows, you might want to customize the Start menu to include additional items that you use most often. To start a program from the Start menu, you click the Start menu, point to Programs to open the Programs submenu, then click the program you want to start. Windows 98 comes with several built-in programs, called **accessories**. Although not as feature-rich as many programs sold separately, Windows accessories are useful for completing basic tasks. ✐ In this lesson, you start a Windows accessory called **WordPad**, which is a word processing program you can use to create and edit simple documents. Table A-5 describes other popular Windows Accessories.

1. **Click the Start button on the taskbar**
   The Start menu opens.

2. **Point to Programs**
   The Programs submenu opens, listing the programs and categories for programs installed on your computer. WordPad is in the category called Accessories.

3. **Point to Accessories**
   The Accessories menu, shown in Figure A-4, contains several programs to help you complete common tasks. You want to start WordPad, which is probably at the bottom of the list.

4. **Click WordPad**
   WordPad opens and a blank document window opens, as shown in Figure A-5. Note that a **program button** appears on the taskbar, indicating that WordPad is open.

TABLE A-4: Start menu categories

category	description
Windows Update	Connects to a Microsoft Web site and updates your Windows 98 files as necessary
Programs	Opens programs included on the Start menu
Favorites	Connects to favorite Web sites or opens folders and documents that you previously selected
Documents	Opens the most recently opened and saved documents
Settings	Opens tools for selecting settings for your system, including the Control Panel, printers, taskbar and Start menu, folders, icons, and the Active Desktop
Find	Locates programs, files, folders, or computers on your computer network, or finds information and people on the Internet
Help	Provides Windows Help information by topic, alphabetical index, or search criteria
Run	Opens a program or file based on a location and filename that you type or select
Log Off	Allows you to log off the system and log on as a different user
Shut Down	Provides options to shut down the computer, restart the computer in Windows mode, or restart the computer in MS-DOS mode

FIGURE A-4: Cascading menus

Cascading menus (also called submenus)

Arrow indicates submenu

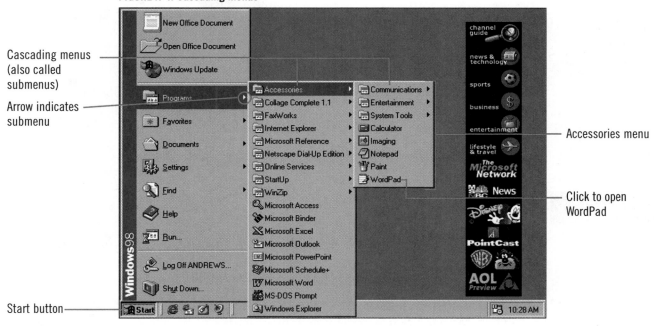

Accessories menu

Click to open WordPad

Start button

FIGURE A-5: WordPad window

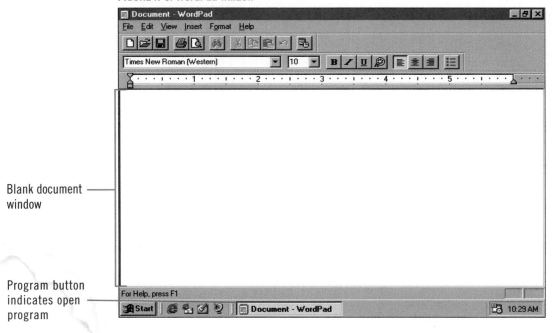

Blank document window

Program button indicates open program

TABLE A-5: Common Windows Accessories on the Accessories menu

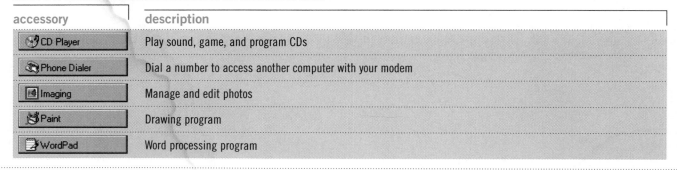

accessory	description
CD Player	Play sound, game, and program CDs
Phone Dialer	Dial a number to access another computer with your modem
Imaging	Manage and edit photos
Paint	Drawing program
WordPad	Word processing program

Windows 98

Moving and Resizing Windows

One of the powerful features of Windows is the ability to open more than one window or program at once. This means, however, that the desktop can get cluttered with the various programs and files you are using. One of the ways to keep your desktop organized is by changing the size of a window or moving it. You can do this using the standard borders and sizing buttons that are part of each window. ✒ Practice sizing and moving the WordPad window now.

Steps

1. **If the WordPad window does not already fill the screen, click the Maximize button** in the WordPad window.
   When a window is **maximized**, it takes up the whole screen.

2. **Click the Restore button** in the WordPad window
   To **restore** a window is to return it to its previous size, as shown in Figure A-6. The Restore button only appears when a window is maximized. In addition to minimizing, maximizing, and restoring windows, you can also change the dimensions of any window.

3. **Position the pointer on the right edge of the WordPad window until the pointer changes to ↔, then drag the border to the right**
   The width of the window increases. You can size the height and width of a window by dragging any of the four sides individually. You can also size the height and width of the window simultaneously by dragging the corner of the window.

QuickTip

You can resize windows by dragging any corner, not just the lower left. You can also drag any border to make the window taller, shorter, wider, or narrower.

4. **Position the pointer in the lower-right corner of the WordPad window until the pointer changes to ↘, as shown in Figure A-6, then drag down and to the right**
   The height and width of the window increase at the same time. You can also position a restored window wherever you wish on the desktop by dragging its title bar.

5. **Click the title bar on the WordPad window, as shown in Figure A-6, then drag the window up and to the left**
   The window is repositioned on the desktop. The **title bar** is the area along the top of the window that displays the file name and program used to create it. At times, you might wish to close a program window, yet keep the program running and easily accessible. You can accomplish this by minimizing a window.

QuickTip

If you have more than one window open and you want to access something on the desktop, you can click the Show Desktop button on the Quick Launch toolbar. All open windows are minimized so the desktop is visible.

6. **In the WordPad window, click the Minimize button**
   When you **minimize** a window, it shrinks to a program button on the taskbar, as shown in Figure A-7. WordPad is still running, but it is out of your way.

7. **Click the WordPad program button on the taskbar to reopen the window**
   The WordPad program window reopens.

8. **Click the Maximize button** in the upper-right corner of the WordPad window
   The window fills the screen.

FIGURE A-6: Restored WordPad window

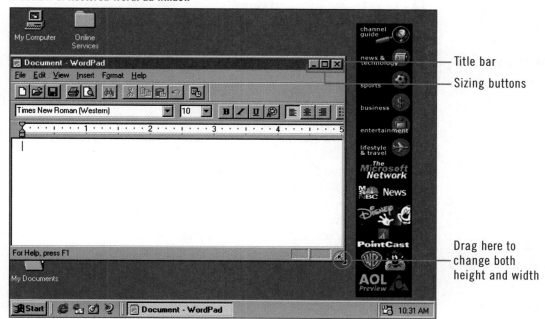

— Title bar
— Sizing buttons

Drag here to change both height and width

FIGURE A-7: Minimized WordPad window

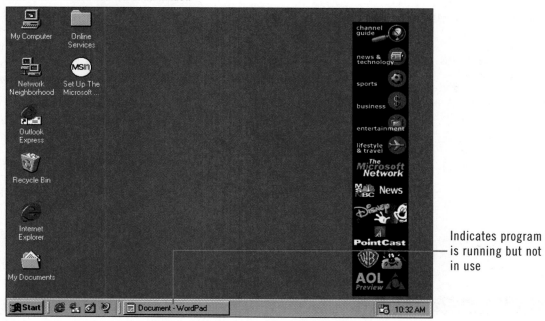

Indicates program is running but not in use

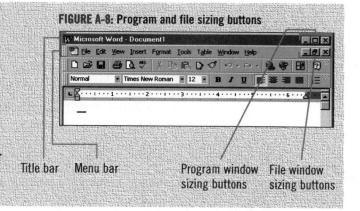

More about sizing windows

Many programs contain two sets of sizing buttons: one that controls the program window itself and another that controls the window for the file with which you are working. The program sizing buttons are located in the title bar and the file sizing buttons are located below them. See Figure A-8. When you minimize a file window within a program, the file window is reduced to an icon in the lower-left corner of the program window, but the size of the program window remains intact.

FIGURE A-8: Program and file sizing buttons

Title bar Menu bar   Program window sizing buttons   File window sizing buttons

Using Menus, Keyboard Shortcuts, and Toolbars

A **menu** is a list of commands that you use to accomplish certain tasks. You've already used the Start menu to start WordPad. Each Windows program also has its own set of menus, which are located on the **menu bar** under the title bar. The menus organize commands into groups of related operations. See Table A-6 for examples of what you might see on a typical menu. A **toolbar** is a series of buttons, located under the menu bar, that you click to accomplish certain tasks. Buttons are another method for executing menu commands. You will open the Control Panel, then use a menu and toolbar button to change how the contents of the window appear.

Steps 1 2 3 4

1. **Click the Start button on the taskbar, point to Settings, then click Control Panel**
   The Control Panel window opens over the WordPad window. The **Control Panel** contains icons for various programs that allow you to specify how your computer looks and performs. You use the Control Panel to practice using menus and toolbars.

2. **Click View on the menu bar**
   The View menu appears, listing the View commands, as shown in Figure A-9. On a menu, a **check mark** identifies a feature that is currently enabled or "on." To disable, or turn "off" the feature, click the command again to remove the check mark. A **bullet mark** can also indicate that an option is enabled. To disable a bulleted option, you must select another option in its place.

3. **Click Small Icons**
   The icons are now smaller than they were before, taking up less room in the window.

4. **Press [Alt][V] to open the View menu**
   The View menu appears again; this time you opened it using the keyboard. Notice that a letter in each command on the View menu is underlined. You can select these commands by pressing the underlined letter. Executing a command using the keyboard is called a **keyboard shortcut**. You might find that you prefer keyboard shortcuts to the mouse if you find it cumbersome to reposition your hands at the keyboard each time you use the mouse.

5. **Press [T] to select the Toolbars command**
   The Toolbars submenu appears with check marks next to the commands that are currently selected.

6. **Press [T] to deselect the Text Labels command**
   The buttons appear without labels below each one; now you can see the entire toolbar.

7. **On the Control Panel toolbar, position the pointer over the Views button** 🖳 **but do not click yet**
   When you position the mouse pointer over a button (and other items), a **ScreenTip** appears, showing the name of the item, as shown in Figure A-10. ScreenTips help you learn the names of the various elements in Windows programs.

8. **Click the Views button list arrow** 🖳▾
   Some toolbar buttons have an arrow, which indicates the button contains several choices. Clicking the arrow shows the choices; clicking the button itself automatically selects the command below the one that was previously selected.

9. **In the list of View choices, click Details**
   The Details view includes a description of each program in the Control Panel.

FIGURE A-9: Opening a menu

Menu bar ————————

Commands in View menu ————

Status bar displays description of menu ————

Arrow indicates submenu

Check mark

Bullet

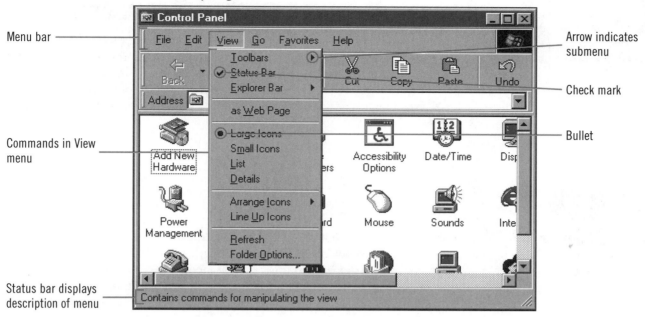

FIGURE A-10: ScreenTip in Control Panel

Toolbar ————

Position pointer over button to display ScreenTip

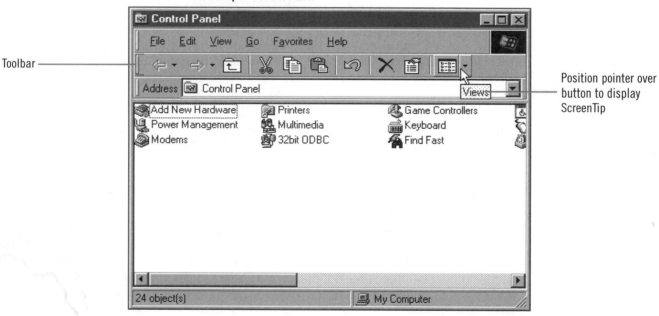

TABLE A-6: Typical items on a menu

item	description	example
Dimmed command	A menu command that is not currently available	Undo Ctrl+Z
Ellipsis	Opens a dialog box that allows you to select different or additional options	Save As...
Triangle	Opens a cascading menu containing an additional list of commands	Zoom ▶
Keyboard shortcut	A keyboard alternative to using the mouse for executing a command	Paste Ctrl+V
Underlined letter	Indicates the letter to press for the keyboard shortcut	Print Preview

Windows 98

Using Dialog Boxes

A **dialog box** is a window that opens when you choose a menu command that is followed by an ellipsis (…), or any command that needs more information before the program can carry out the command you selected. Dialog boxes open in other situations as well, such as when you open a program in the Control Panel. See Figure A-11 and Table A-7 for some of the typical elements of a dialog box. Practice using a dialog box to control your mouse settings.

Trouble?

If you can't see the Mouse icon, resize the Control Panel window.

1. In the Control Panel window, double-click the **Mouse icon** 🖱

The Mouse Properties dialog box opens, as shown in Figure A-12. **Properties** are characteristic of a specific computer element (in this case, the mouse) that you can customize. The options in this dialog box allow you to control the way the mouse buttons are configured, select the types of pointers that appear, choose the speed of the mouse movement on the screen, and specify what type of mouse you are using. **Tabs** at the top of the dialog box separate these options into related categories.

2. Click the **Motion tab** if it is not already the frontmost tab

This tab has two boxes. The first, Pointer speed, has a slider for you to set how fast the pointer moves on the screen in relation to how you move the mouse in your hand. The second, **Pointer trail**, has a check box you can select to add a "trail" or shadow to the pointer on your screen, making it easier to see. The slider in the Pointer trail box lets you determine the degree to which the option is in effect—in this case, the length of the pointer trail.

3. In the Pointer trail box, click the **Show pointer trails check box** to select it

4. Drag the **slider** below the check box all the way to the right, then move the mouse pointer across your screen

As you move the mouse, notice the pointer trails.

5. Click the other tabs in the Mouse Properties dialog box and experiment with the options that are available in each category

After you select the options you want in a dialog box, you need to select a **command button**, which carries out the options you've selected. The two most common command buttons are OK and Cancel. Clicking OK accepts your changes and closes the dialog box; clicking Cancel leaves the original settings intact and closes the dialog box. The third command button in this dialog box is Apply. Clicking the Apply button accepts the changes you've made and keeps the dialog box open so that you can select additional options. Because you might share this computer with others, it's important to return the dialog box options back to the original settings.

QuickTip

You can also use the keyboard to carry out commands in a dialog box. Pressing [Enter] is the same as clicking OK; pressing [Esc] is the same as clicking Cancel.

6. Click **Cancel** to leave the original settings intact and close the dialog box

FIGURE A-11: Elements of a typical dialog box

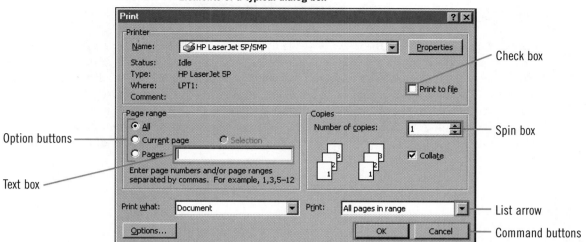

Option buttons

Text box

Check box

Spin box

List arrow

Command buttons

FIGURE A-12: Mouse Properties dialog box

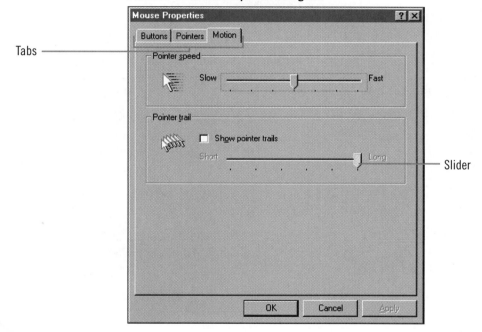

Tabs

Slider

TABLE A-7: Typical items in a dialog box

item	description	item	description
Check box	A box that turns an option on (when the box is checked) and off (when it is blank)	**List box**	A box containing a list of items; to choose an item, click the list arrow, then click the desired item
Text box	A box in which you type text	**Spin box**	A box with two arrows and a text box; allows you to scroll numerical increments or type a number
Option button	A small circle that selects a single dialog box option; you cannot check more than one option button in a list	**Slider**	A shape that you drag to set the degree to which an option is in effect
Command button	A rectangular button in a dialog box with the name of the command on it	**Tab**	A place in a dialog box where related commands and options are organized

Windows 98

Using Scroll Bars

When you cannot see all of the items available in a window, scroll bars appear on the right and/or bottom edges of the window. **Scroll bars** allow you to display the additional contents of the window. There are several ways you can scroll in a window. When you need to scroll only a short distance, you can use the scroll arrows. To scroll the window in larger increments, click in the scroll bar above or below the scroll box. Dragging the scroll box moves you quickly to a new part of the window. See Table A-8 for a summary of the different ways to use scroll bars. ✒ With the Control Panel window in Details view, you can use the scroll bars to view all of the items in this window.

Steps

Trouble?

If you can't see the scroll bars, resize the window until both the horizontal and vertical scroll bars appear. Scroll bars don't appear when the window is large enough to include all the information.

QuickTip

The size of the scroll box changes to reflect how many items or the amount of text that does not fit in a window. A larger scroll box indicates that a relatively small amount of the window's contents is not currently visible; you need to scroll only a short distance to see the remaining items. A smaller scroll box indicates that a relatively large amount of information is currently not visible.

1. In the Control Panel window, click the **down scroll arrow**, as shown in Figure A-13
   Clicking this arrow moves the view down one line. Clicking the up arrow moves the view up one line.

2. Click the **up scroll arrow** in the vertical scroll bar
   The screen moves up one line.

3. Click anywhere in the area below the scroll box in the vertical scroll bar
   The view moves down one window's height. Similarly, you can click in the scroll bar above the scroll box to move up one window's height.

4. Drag the **scroll box** all the way down to the bottom of the vertical scrollbar
   The view now includes the items that appear at the very bottom of the window. Similarly, you can drag the scroll box to the top of the scroll bar to view the information that appears at the top of the window.

5. Drag the **scroll box** all the way up to the top of the vertical scroll bar
   This view shows the items that appear at the top of the window.

6. Click the area to the right of the scroll box in the horizontal scroll bar
   The far right edge of the window comes into view. The horizontal scroll bar works the same as the vertical scroll bar.

7. Click the area to the left of the scroll box in the horizontal scroll bar
   You should return the Control Panel to its original settings.

8. On the Control Panel toolbar, click the **Views button list arrow** ⊞▾ , click **Large Icons**, then maximize the Control Panel window

FIGURE A-13: Scroll bars in the Control Panel

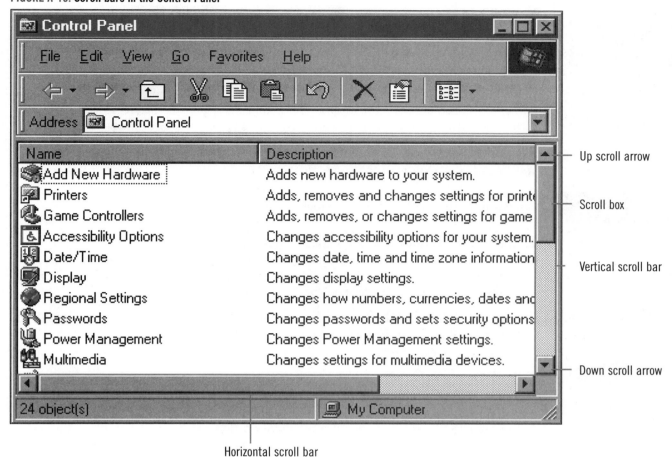

Up scroll arrow

Scroll box

Vertical scroll bar

Down scroll arrow

Horizontal scroll bar

TABLE A-8: Using scroll bars in a window

to	do this
Move down one line	Click the down arrow at the bottom of the vertical scroll bar
Move up one line	Click the up arrow at the top of the vertical scroll bar
Move down one window height	Click in the area below the scroll box in the vertical scroll bar
Move up one window height	Click in the area above the scroll box in the vertical scroll bar
Move up a large distance in the window	Drag the scroll box up in the vertical scroll bar
Move down a large distance in the window	Drag the scroll box down in the vertical scroll bar
Move a short distance side-to-side in a window	Click the left or right arrows in the horizontal scroll bar
Move to the right one window width	Click in the area to the right of the scroll box in the horizontal scroll bar
Move to the left one window width	Click in the area to the left of the scroll box in the horizontal scroll bar
Move left or right a large distance in the window	Drag the scroll box in the horizontal scroll bar

Getting Help

When you have a question about how to do something in Windows 98, you can usually find the answer with a few clicks of your mouse. **Windows Help** works like a book stored on your computer, with a table of contents and an index to make finding information easier. Help provides guidance on many Windows features, including detailed steps for completing a procedure, definitions of terms, lists of related topics, and search capabilities. To open the main Windows 98 Help system, click Help on the Start menu. From here you can browse the Help "book," or you can connect to a Microsoft Web site on the Internet for the latest technical support on Windows 98. To get help on a specific Windows program, click Help on the program's menu bar. You can also access **context-sensitive help,** help specifically related to what you are doing, using a variety of methods such as right-clicking an object or using the question mark button in a dialog box. In this lesson, you get Help on how to start a program. You also get information on the taskbar.

Steps

1. **Click the Start button on the taskbar, then click Help**
   The Windows Help dialog box opens with the Contents tab in front, as shown in Figure A-14. The Contents tab provides you with a list of Help categories. Each "book" has several "chapters" that you can see by clicking the book or the name next to the book.

2. **Click the Contents tab if it isn't the frontmost tab, click Exploring Your Computer, then click Work with Programs to view the Help categories**
   The Help window contains a selection of topics related to running programs.

3. **Click Start a Program**
   The Help window appears in the right pane, as shown in Figure A-15. **Panes** divide a window into two or more sections. At the bottom of the right pane, you can click Related Topics to view a list of topics that may also be of interest. Some Help topics also allow you to view additional information about important words; these words are underlined.

4. **Click the underlined word taskbar**
   A pop-up window appears with a definition of the underlined word.

5. **Read the definition, then press [Enter] or click anywhere outside the pop-up window to close it**

6. **In the left pane, click the Index tab**
   The Index tab provides an alphabetical list of all the available Help topics, like an index at the end of a book. You can enter a topic in the text box at the top of the pane. As you type, the list of topics automatically scrolls to try to match the word or phrase you type. You can also scroll down to the topic. In either case, the topic appears in the right pane, as usual.

7. **In the left pane, click the Search tab**
   You can use the Search tab to locate a Help topic using keywords. You enter a word or phrase in the text box and click List Topics; a list of matching topics appears below the text box. To view a topic, double-click it or select the topic, then click Display.

8. **Click the Web Help button ▣ on the toolbar**
   Information on the Web page for Windows 98 Help appears in the right pane (a **Web page** is a document that contains highlighted words, phrases, and graphics that link to other pages on the Internet). You could access this Web page by clicking the "Support Online" underlined text.

9. **In the Windows Help window, click the Close button ☒ in the upper-right corner of the window**
   Clicking the Close button closes the active window.

FIGURE A-14: Windows Help dialog box

Help toolbar ——

Help tabs ——

Click to view alphabetical list of Help topics

Click to search for words and phrases used in Help topics

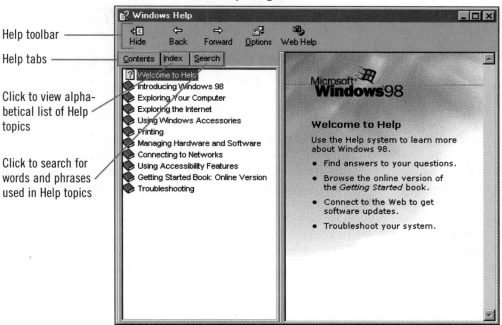

FIGURE A-15: Viewing Help on starting a program

Help topic ——

Hand pointer ——

Left pane contains Help categories and topics

Right pane contains help on the topic you select

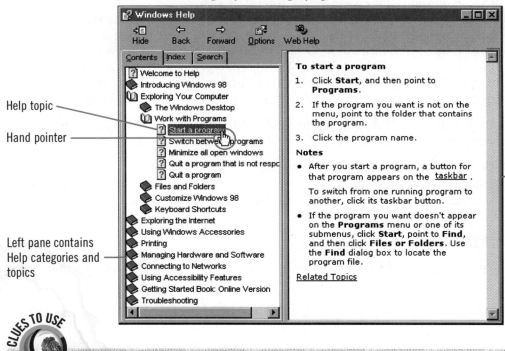

Context-sensitive help

To receive help in a dialog box, click the Help button ? in the upper-right corner of the dialog box; the mouse pointer changes to ?. Click the Help pointer on the item for which you need additional information. A pop-up window provides a brief explanation of the selected feature. You can also click the right mouse button on an item in a dialog box, then click the What's This? button to display the Help explanation. In addition, when you click the right mouse button in a Help topic window, you can choose commands to annotate, copy, and print the contents of the topic window. From the Help pop-up menu, you can also choose to have topic windows always appear on top of the currently active window, so you can see Help topics while you work.

Windows 98

Closing a Program and Shutting Down Windows

When you are finished working on your computer, you need to make sure you shut it down properly. This involves several steps: saving and closing all open files, closing all the open programs and windows, shutting down Windows, and finally, turning off the computer. If you turn off the computer while Windows is running, you could lose important data. To **close** programs, you can click the Close button in the window's upper-right corner or click File on the menu bar and choose either Close or Exit. To shut down Windows after all your files and programs are closed, click Shut Down from the Start menu, then select the desired option from the Shut Down dialog box, shown in Figure A-16. See Table A-9 for a description of shutdown options. Close all your open files, windows, and programs, then exit Windows.

1. In the Control Panel window, click the **Close button** ✕ in the upper-right corner of the window
The Control Panel window closes.

2. Click **File** on the WordPad menu bar, then click **Exit**
If you have made any changes to the open file, you will be prompted to save your changes before the program quits. Some programs also give you the option of choosing the Close command on the File menu in order to close the active file but leave the program open, so you can continue to work in it with a different file. Also, if there is a second set of sizing buttons in the window, the Close button on the menu bar will close the active file only, leaving the program open for continued use.

3. If you see a message asking you to save changes to the document, click **No**
WordPad closes and you return to the desktop.

QuickTip

Complete the remaining steps to shut down Windows and your computer only if you have been told to do so by your instructor or technical support person.

4. Click the **Start button** on the taskbar, then click **Shut Down**
The Shut Down Windows dialog box opens, as shown in Figure A-16. In this dialog box, you have the option to shut down the computer, restart the computer in Windows mode or restart the computer in MS-DOS mode.

5. Click the **Shut down option button**, if necessary

6. If you are working in a lab, click **Cancel** to leave the computer running and return to the Windows desktop
If you are working on your own machine or if your instructor told you to shut down Windows, click **OK** to exit Windows.

7. When you see the message **It's now safe to turn off your computer**, turn off your computer and monitor

FIGURE A-16: **Shut Down Windows dialog box**

Click to shut down Windows

Click to restart computer in Windows mode

Click to restart computer in MS-DOS mode

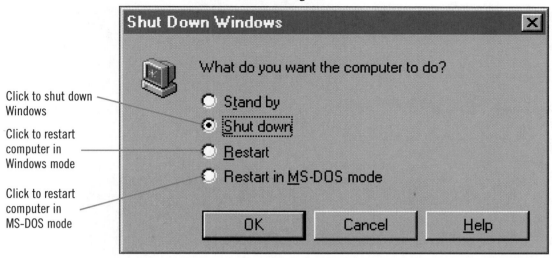

TABLE A-9: **Shut down options**

shut down option	function	when to use it
Shut down	Prepares the computer to be turned off	When you are finished working with Windows and you want to shut off your computer
Restart	Restarts the computer and reloads Windows	When you want to restart the computer and begin working with Windows again (your programs might have frozen or stopped working).
Restart in MS-DOS mode	Starts the computer in the MS-DOS mode	When you want to run programs under MS-DOS or use DOS commands to work with files

The Log Off command

To change users on the same computer quickly, you can choose the Log Off command from the Start menu. This command identifies the name of the current user. When you choose this command, Windows 98 shuts down and automatically restarts, stopping at the point where you need to enter a password. When the new user enters a user name and password, Windows restarts and the desktop appears as usual.

Practice

► Concepts Review

Identify each of the items labeled in Figure A-17.

FIGURE A-17

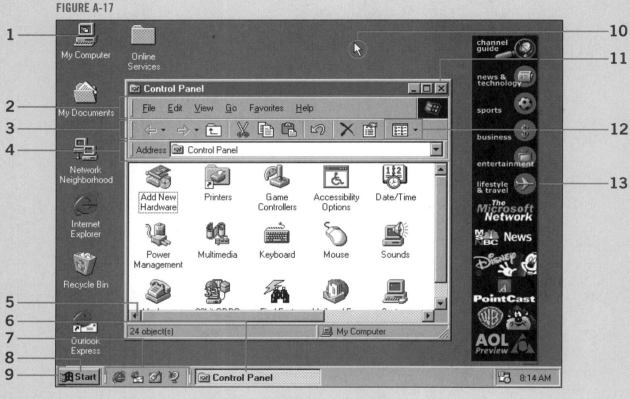

Match each of the statements with the term it describes.

14. Shrinks a window to a button on the taskbar
15. Shows the name of the window or program
16. The item you first click to start a program
17. Requests more information that you supply before carrying out command
18. Shows the Start button, Quick Launch toolbar, and any currently open programs
19. An input device that lets you point to and make selections
20. Graphic representation of program

a. Taskbar
b. Dialog box
c. Start button
d. Mouse
e. Title bar
f. Minimize button
g. Icon

Select the best answer from the list of choices.

21. The acronym GUI means
    a. Grayed user information.
    b. Group user icons.
    c. Graphical user interface.
    d. Group user interconnect.

22. **Which of the following is NOT provided by an operating system?**
   a. Programs for organizing files
   b. Instructions to coordinate the flow of information among the programs, files, printers, storage devices, and other components of your computer system
   c. Programs that allow you to specify the operation of the mouse
   d. Spell checker for your documents

23. **All of the following are examples of using a mouse, EXCEPT**
   a. Clicking the Maximize button.
   c. Double-clicking to start a program.
   b. Pressing [Enter].
   d. Dragging the My Computer icon.

24. **The term for moving an item to a new location on the desktop is**
   a. Pointing.
   b. Clicking.
   c. Dragging.
   d. Restoring.

25. **The Maximize button is used to**
   a. Return a window to its previous size.
   c. Scroll slowly through a window.
   b. Expand a window to fill the computer screen.
   d. Run programs from the Start menu.

26. **What appears if a window contains more information than can be displayed in the window?**
   a. Program icon
   b. Cascading menu
   c. Scroll bars
   d. Check box

27. **A window is active when**
   a. You see its program button on the taskbar.
   c. It is open and you are currently using it.
   b. Its title bar is dimmed.
   d. It is listed in the Programs submenu.

28. **You can exit Windows by**
   a. Double-clicking the Control Panel application.
   b. Double-clicking the Program Manager control menu box.
   c. Clicking File, then clicking Exit.
   d. Selecting the Shut Down command from the Start menu.

► Skills Review

1. **Start Windows and view the Active Desktop**
   a. Turn on the computer, if necessary.
   b. After Windows starts, identify as many items on the desktop as you can, without referring to the lesson material.
   c. Compare your results to Figure A-1.

2. **Use the mouse**
   a. Double-click the Recycle Bin icon.
   b. Drag the Recycle Bin window to the upper-right corner of the desktop.
   c. Right-click the title bar of the Recycle Bin, then click Close.

3. **Start a program.**
   a. Click the Start button on the taskbar, then point to Programs.
   b. Point to Accessories, then click Calculator.
   c. Minimize the Calculator window.

4. **Practice dragging, maximizing, restoring, sizing, and minimizing windows.**
   a. Drag the Recycle Bin icon to the bottom of the desktop.
   b. Double-click the My Computer icon to open the My Computer window.
   c. Maximize the window, if it is not already maximized.
   d. Restore the window to its previous size.
   e. Resize the window until you see both horizontal and vertical scroll bars.
   f. Resize the window until the horizontal scroll bar no longer appears.

g. Click the Minimize button.

h. Drag the Recycle Bin back to the top of the desktop.

5. **Use menus, keyboard shortcuts, and toolbars**

a. Click the Start button on the taskbar, point to Settings, then click Control Panel.

b. Click View on the menu bar, point to Toolbars, then click Standard Buttons to hide the toolbar.

c. Redisplay the toolbar.

d. Press [Alt][V] to show the View menu, then press [W] to view the Control Panel as a Web page.

e. Note the change, then use the same keyboard shortcuts to change the view back.

f. Click the Up One Level button to view My Computer.

g. Click the Back button to return to the Control Panel.

h. Double-click the Display icon.

6. **Use dialog boxes.**

a. Click the Screen Saver tab.

b. Click the Screen Saver list arrow, select a screen saver, and preview the change but do not click OK.

c. Click the Effects tab.

d. In the Visual effects section, click the Use large icons check box to select it, then click Apply.

e. Note the change in the icons on the desktop and in the Control Panel window.

f. Click the Use large icons check box to deselect it, Click the Screen Saver tab, return the scrren saver to its original setting, then click Apply.

g. Click the Close button in the Display Properties dialog box, but leave the Control Panel open.

7. **Use scroll bars**

a. Click View on the Control Panel toolbar, then click Details.

b. Resize the Control Panel window, if necessary, so that both scroll bars are visible.

c. Drag the vertical scroll box down all the way.

d. Click anywhere in the area above the vertical scroll box.

e. Click the up scroll arrow until the scroll box is back at the top of the scroll bar.

f. Drag the horizontal scroll box so you can read the descriptions for the icons.

8. **Get Help**

a. Click the Start button on the taskbar, then click Help.

b. Click the Contents tab, then click Introducing Windows 98.

c. Click Exploring Your Computer, click Customize Windows 98, then click How the Screen Looks.

d. Click each of the topics and read them in the right pane.

9. **Close a program and shut down Windows.**

a. Click the Close button to close the Help topic window.

b. Click File on the menu bar, then click Close to close the Control Panel window.

c. Click the Calculator program button on the taskbar to restore the window.

d. Click the Close button in the Calculator window to close the Calculator program.

e. Click the My Computer program button on the taskbar, then click the Close button to close the window.

f. If you are instructed to do so, shut down your computer.

► Independent Challenges

1. Windows 98 has an extensive help system. In this independent challenge, you will use Help to learn about more Windows 98 features and explore the help that's available on the Internet.

   a. Open Windows Help and locate help topics on: adjusting the double-click speed of your mouse; using Print; and, displaying Web content on your desktop.

If you have a printer, print a Help topic for each subject. If you do not have a printer, write a summary of each topic.

   b. Follow these steps below to access help on the Internet. If you don't have Internet access, you can't do this step.

      i. Click the Web Help button on the toolbar.

      ii. Read the introduction, then click the link Support Online. A browser will open and prompt you to connect to the Internet. Once you are connected, a Web site called Support Online will appear.

      iii. Click the View Popular Topics link. Write a summary of what you find.

      iv. Click the Close button in the title bar of your browser, then disconnect from the Internet and close Windows Help.

2. You may need to change the format of the clock and date on your computer. For example, if you work with international clients it might be easier to show the time in military (24-hour) time and the date with the day before the month. You can also change the actual time and date on your computer, such as when you change time zones.

   a. Open the Control Panel window, then double-click the Regional Settings icon.

   b. Click the Time tab to change the time to show a 24-hour clock rather than a 12-hour clock.

   c. Click the Date tab to change the date to show the day before the month (e.g., 30/3/99).

   d. Change the time to one hour later using the Date/Time icon in the Control Panel window.

   e. Return the settings to the original time and format and close all open windows.

3. Calculator is a Windows program on the Accessories menu that you can use for calculations you need to perform while using the computer. Follow these guidelines to explore the Calculator and the Help that comes with it:

   a. Start the Calculator from the Accessories menu.

   b. Click Help on the menu bar, then click Help topics. The Calculator Help window opens, showing several Help topics.

   c. View the Help topic on how to perform simple calculations, then print it if you have a printer connected.

   d. Open the Tips and Tricks category, then view the Help topic on how to find out what a calculator button does.

   e. View the Help topic (under Tips and Tricks) on how to use keyboard equivalents of calculator buttons, then print the topic if you have a printer connected to your computer.

   f. Determine how many months you have to work to earn an additional week of vacation if you work for a company that provides one additional day of paid vacation for every 560 hours you work. (*Hint*: First multiply 560 times 5 days, then divide the answer by the number of hours you work in a month.)

   g. Close all open windows.

4. You can customize many Windows features to suit your needs and preferences. One way you do this is to change the appearance of the taskbar on the desktop. In this challenge, try the guidelines described to explore the different ways you can customize the appearance of the taskbar.

   a. Position the pointer over the top border of the taskbar. When the pointer changes shape, drag up an inch.

   b. Resize the taskbar back to its original size.

   c. Click the Start button on the taskbar, then point to Settings, and click Taskbar & Start Menu.

   d. In the upper-right corner of the Taskbar Properties window, click the Help button, then click each option to view the pop-up window describing the option. You need to click the Help button before clicking each option.

   e. Click each option and observe the effect in the preview area. (*Note:* Do not click OK.)

   f. Return the options to their original settings or click Cancel.

▶ Visual Workshop

Use the skills you have learned in this unit to create a desktop that looks like the one in Figure A-18. Make sure you include the following:

- Calculator program minimized
- Scroll bars in Control Panel window
- Details view in Control Panel window
- Rearranged icons on desktop; your icons may be different (*Hint:* If the icons "snap" back to where they were, they are set to be automatically arranged. Right-click a blank area of the desktop, point to Arrange Icons, then click Auto Arrange to deselect it.)
- Channel Bar closed

Use the Print Screen key to make a copy of the screen and then print it from the Paint program (see your instructor or technical support person for assistance.) Be sure to return your settings and desktop back to their original arrangement when you complete this exercise.

FIGURE A-18

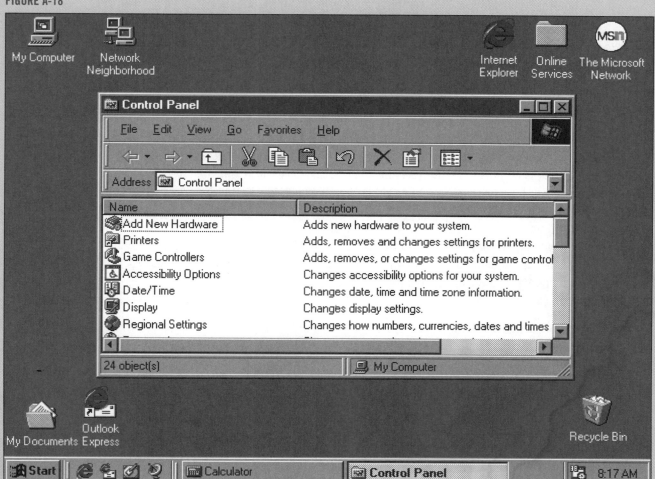

Working

with Programs, Files, and Folders

Objectives

- ► **Create and save a WordPad file**
- ► **Open, edit, and save an existing Paint file**
- ► **Work with multiple programs**
- ► **Understand file management**
- ► **View files and create folders with My Computer**
- ► **Move and copy files using My Computer**
- ► **Manage files with Windows Explorer**
- ► **Delete and restore files**
- ► **Create a shortcut on the desktop**

Most of your work on a computer involves creating files in programs. For example, you might use WordPad to create a resume or Microsoft Excel to create a budget. The resume and the budget are examples of **files**, electronic collections of data that you create and save on a computer. In this unit, you learn how to work with files and the programs you use to create them. You create new files, open and edit an existing file, and use the Clipboard to copy and paste data from one file to another. You also explore the file management features of Windows 98, using My Computer and Windows Explorer. Finally, you learn how to work more efficiently by managing files directly on your desktop.

Creating and Saving a WordPad File

As with most programs, when you start WordPad a new, blank **document** (or file) opens. To create a new file, such as a memo, you simply begin typing. Your work is automatically stored in your computer's **random access memory (RAM)** until you turn off your computer, at which point the computer's RAM is erased. To store your work permanently, you must save your work as a file on a disk. You can save files either on an internal **hard disk**, which is built into your computer, usually drive C, or on a removable 3.5" or 5.25" **floppy disk**, which you insert into a drive on your computer, usually drive A or B. Before you can save a file on a floppy disk, the disk must be formatted. See the Appendix, "Formatting a Disk," or your instructor or technical support person for more information. When you name a file, you can use up to 255 characters including spaces and punctuation in the File Name box, using either upper or lowercase letters. In this unit, you save your files to your Project Disk. If you do not have a Project Disk, see your instructor or technical support person for assistance. First, you start WordPad and create a file that contains the text shown in Figure B-1. Then you save the file to your Project Disk.

Steps

1. Click the **Start button** on the taskbar, point to **Programs**, point to **Accessories**, click **WordPad**, then click the **Maximize button** if the window does not fill your screen
   The WordPad program window opens with a new, blank document. The blinking **insertion point** | indicates where the text you type will appear.

2. Type **Memo**, then press **[Enter]** to move the insertion point to the next line

3. Type the remaining text shown in Figure B-1, pressing **[Enter]** at the end of each line to move to the next line and to insert blank lines
   Now that the text is entered, you can format it. **Formatting** changes the appearance of text to make it more readable or attractive.

4. Click in front of the word **Memo**, then drag the mouse to the right to select the word
   The text is now **selected** and any action you make will be performed on the text.

5. Click the **Center button** 🔳 on the Formatting toolbar, then click the **Bold button** 🔳 on the Formatting toolbar
   The text is centered and bold.

6. Click the **Font Size list arrow** 🔟 ▾, then click **16**
   A **font** is a particular shape and size of type. The text is enlarged to 16 point. One **point** is 1/72 of an inch in height. Now that your memo is complete, you are ready to save it to your Project Disk.

7. Click **File** on the menu bar, then click **Save As**
   The Save As dialog box opens, as shown in Figure B-2. In this dialog box, you specify where you want your file saved and also give your document a name.

8. Click the **Save in list arrow**, then click **3½ Floppy (A:)** or whichever drive contains your Project Disk
   The drive containing your Project Disk is now active, meaning that any files currently on the disk are displayed in the list of folders and files and that the file you save now will be saved on the disk in this drive.

9. Double-click the **text** in the File name text box, type **Memo**, then click **Save**
   Your memo is now saved as a WordPad file with the name "Memo" on your Project Disk. Notice that the WordPad title bar contains the name of the file.

FIGURE B-1: Text to enter in WordPad

Bold button

Center button

Press [Enter]
three times
to insert
blank lines

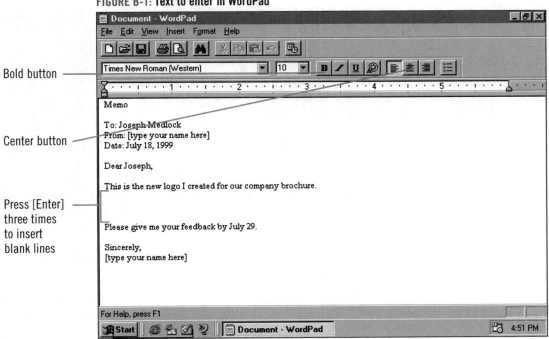

FIGURE B-2: Save As dialog box

Click to select
where to save file

Type new
filename here

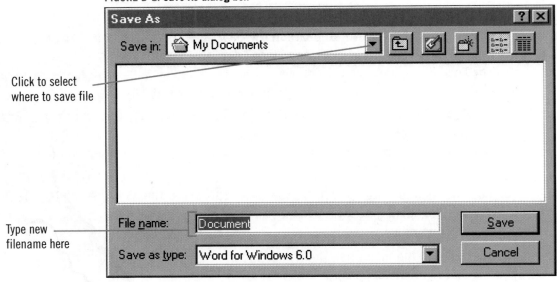

Opening, Editing, and Saving an Existing Paint File

Sometimes you create files from scratch, but often you may want to reopen a file you or someone else has already created. Once you open a file, you can **edit** it, or make changes to it, such as adding or deleting text. After editing a file, you can save it with the same filename, which means that you no longer will have the file in its original form, or you can save it with a different filename, so that the original file remains unchanged. In this lesson, you use **Paint**, a drawing program that comes with Windows 98, to open a file, edit it by changing a color, then save the file with a new filename to leave the original file unchanged.

Steps

1. Click the **Start button** on the taskbar, point to **Programs**, point to **Accessories**, click **Paint**, then click the **Maximize button** if the window doesn't fill the screen
   The Paint program opens with a blank work area. If you wanted to create a file from scratch, you would begin working now.

2. Click **File** on the menu bar, then click **Open**
   The Open dialog box works similarly to the Save As dialog box.

3. Click the **Look in list arrow**, then click **3½ Floppy (A:)**
   The Paint files on your Project Disk are displayed in the Open dialog box, as shown in Figure B-3.

QuickTip

You can also open a file by double-clicking it in the Open dialog box.

4. Click **Win B-1** in the list of files, then click **Open**
   The Open dialog box closes and the file named Win B-1 opens. Before you make any changes to the file, you decide to save it with a new filename, so that the original file is unchanged.

5. Click **File** on the menu bar, then click **Save As**

6. Make sure **3½ Floppy (A:)** appears in the Save in text box, select the text **Win B-1** in the File name text box if necessary, type **Logo**, then click **Save**
   The Logo file appears in the Paint window, as shown in Figure B-4. Because you saved the file with a new name, you can edit it without changing the original file.

7. Click the **Fill With Color button** 🪣 in the Toolbox, click the **Blue color box**, which is the fourth from the right in the first row
   Now when you click an area in the image, it will be filled with the color you selected. See Table B-1 for a description of the tools in the Toolbox.

8. Move the pointer into the **white area that represents the sky**, the pointer changes to 🪣, then click
   The sky is now blue.

9. Click **File** on the menu bar, then click **Save**
   The change you made is saved.

FIGURE B-3: **Open dialog box**

List of files

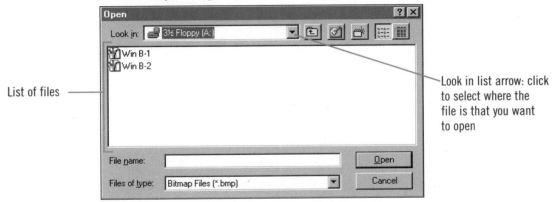

Look in list arrow: click
to select where the
file is that you want
to open

FIGURE B-4: **Paint file saved with new filename**

Name of file
displayed in title bar

Fill With Color button

Choose this blue color

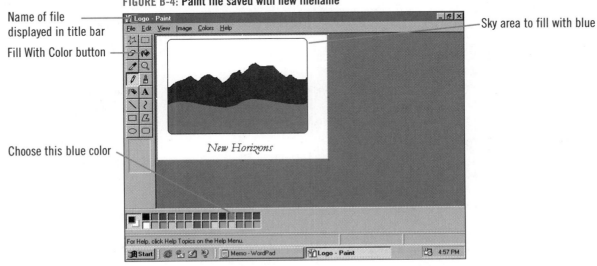

Sky area to fill with blue

TABLE B-1: **Paint Toolbox buttons**

tool	description	tool	description
Free-Form Select button	Selects a free-form section of the picture to move, copy, or edit	**Airbrush button**	Produces a circular spray of dots
Select button	Selects a rectangular section of the picture to move, copy, or edit	**Text button**	Inserts text into the picture
Eraser button	Erases a portion of the picture using the selected eraser size and foreground color	**Line button**	Draws a straight line with the selected width and foreground color
Fill With Color button	Fills closed shape or area with the current drawing color	**Curve button**	Draws a wavy line with the selected width and foreground color
Pick Color button	Picks up a color off the picture to use for drawing	**Rectangle button**	Draws a rectangle with the selected fill style; also used to draw squares by holding down [Shift] while drawing
Magnifier button	Changes the magnification; lists magnifications under the toolbar	**Polygon button**	Draws polygons from connected straight-line segments
Pencil button	Draws a free-form line one pixel wide	**Ellipse button**	Draws an ellipse with the selected fill style; also used to draw circles by holding down [Shift] while drawing
Brush button	Draws using a brush with the selected shape and size	**Rounded Rectangle button**	Draws rectangles with rounded corners using the selected fill style; also used to draw rounded squares by holding down [Shift] while drawing

Working with Multiple Programs

A powerful feature of Windows is that you can use more than one program at a time. For example, you might be working with a file in WordPad and want to search the Internet to find the answer to a question. You can start your **browser**, a program designed to access information on the Internet, without closing WordPad. When you find the information, you can leave your browser open and switch back to WordPad. Each program that you have open is represented by a program button on the taskbar that you click to switch between programs. You can also copy data from one file to another, whether the files were created with the same program or not, using the **Clipboard**, a temporary area in your computer's memory, and the Cut, Copy, and Paste commands. See Table B-2 for a description of these commands. In this lesson, you copy the logo graphic you worked with in the previous lesson into the memo you created in WordPad.

Trouble?

If some parts of the image or text are outside the dotted rectangle, click anywhere outside the image, then select the image again, making sure you include everything.

QuickTip

To switch between programs using the keyboard, press and hold down [Alt], press [Tab] until the program you want is selected, then release [Alt].

1. Click the **Select button** ▫ on the Toolbox, then drag a rectangle around the entire graphic, including the text
   When you release the mouse button, the dotted rectangle indicates the contents of the selection, as shown in Figure B-5. Make sure the entire image and all the text is inside the rectangle. The next action you take affects the entire selection.

2. Click **Edit** on the menu bar, then click **Copy**
   The logo is copied to the Clipboard. When you **copy** an object onto the Clipboard, the object remains in its original location and is also available to be pasted into another location.

3. Click the **WordPad program button** on the taskbar
   WordPad becomes the active program.

4. Click in the **second line** below the line that ends "for our company brochure."
   The insertion point indicates where the logo will be pasted.

5. Click the **Paste button** 📋 on the WordPad toolbar
   The contents of the Clipboard, in this case the logo, are pasted into the WordPad file, as shown in Figure B-6.

6. Click the **Save button** 💾 on the toolbar
   The Memo file is saved with the logo inserted.

7. Click the **Close buttons** in both the WordPad and Paint programs to close all open files and exit both programs
   You return to the desktop.

TABLE B-2: **Overview of cutting, copying, and pasting**

toolbar button	function	keyboard shortcut
✂ **Cut**	Removes selected information from a file and places it on the Clipboard	[Ctrl][X]
📋 **Copy**	Places a copy of selected information on the Clipboard, leaving the file intact	[Ctrl][C]
📋 **Paste**	Inserts whatever is currently on the Clipboard into another location within the same file or in a different file	[Ctrl][V]

FIGURE B-5: Selecting the logo to copy and paste into the Memo file

Select button

Dotted line indicates
selected area

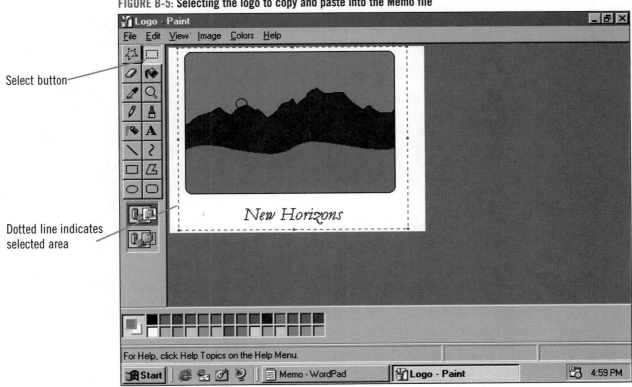

FIGURE B-6: Memo with pasted logo

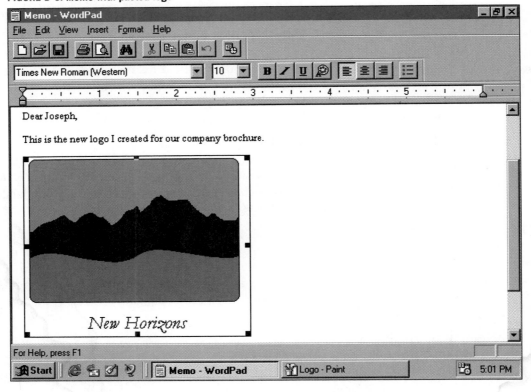

Understanding File Management

After you have created and saved numerous files using various programs, **file management**, the process of organizing and keeping track of all of your files can be a challenge. Fortunately, Windows 98 provides tools to keep everything organized so you can easily locate the files you need. There are two main tools for managing your files: My Computer and Windows Explorer. ✐ In this lesson, you preview the ways you can use My Computer and Windows Explorer to manage your files.

Details

Windows 98 gives you the ability to:

Create folders in which you can save your files

Folders are areas on a floppy disk or hard disk in which you can store files. For example, you might create a folder for your documents and another folder for your graphic files. Folders can also contain additional folders, which creates a more complex structure of folders and files, called a **file hierarchy**. See Figure B-7 for an example of how you could organize the files on your Project Disk.

QuickTip

To browse My Computer using multiple windows, click View on the menu bar, then click Folder Options. In the Folder Options dialog box, click the General tab, click Settings, then under Browse folders as follows, click the second option button. Each time you open a new folder, a new window opens, leaving the previous folder's window open so that you can view both at the same time.

Examine and organize the hierarchy of files and folders

When you want to see the overall structure of your files and folders, you can use either My Computer or Windows Explorer. By examining your file hierarchy with these tools, you can better organize the contents of your computer and adjust the hierarchy to meet your needs. Figures B-8 and B-9 illustrate how My Computer and Windows Explorer display folders and files.

Copy, move, and rename files and folders

If you decide that a file belongs in a different folder, you can move it to another folder. You can also rename a file if you decide a new name is more descriptive. If you want to keep a copy of a file in more than one folder, you can copy it to new folders.

Delete files and folders you no longer need, as well as restore files you delete accidentally

Deleting files and folders you are sure you don't need frees up disk space and keeps your file hierarchy more organized. Using the **Recycle Bin**, a space on your computer's hard disk that stores deleted files, you can restore files you deleted by accident. To free up disk space, you should occasionally empty the Recycle Bin by deleting the files permanently from your hard drive.

Locate files quickly with the Windows 98 Find feature

As you create more files and folders, you may forget where you placed a certain file or you may forget what name you used when you saved a file. With Find, you can locate files by providing only partial names or other factors, such as the file type (for example, a WordPad document, a Paint graphic, or a program) or the date the file was created or modified.

Trouble?

If the Quick View command does not appear on the pop-up menu, it means that this feature was not installed on your computer. See your instructor or technical support person for assistance.

Preview the contents of a file without opening the file in its program

After locating a particular file, use Quick View to look at the file to verify that it is the one you want. This saves time because you do not need to open the program to open the file; however, if you decide that you want to edit the file, you can open the program right from Quick View. To preview a file, right-click the selected file in My Computer or Windows Explorer, then click Quick View on the pop-up menu. A preview of the file appears in the Quick View window.

Use shortcuts

If a file or folder you use often is located several levels down in your file hierarchy, in a folder within a folder, within a folder, it might take you several steps to access it. To save time accessing the files and programs you use frequently, you can create shortcuts to them. A **shortcut** is a link that gives you quick access to a particular file, folder, or program.

FIGURE B-7: Example of file hierarchy for Project Disk files

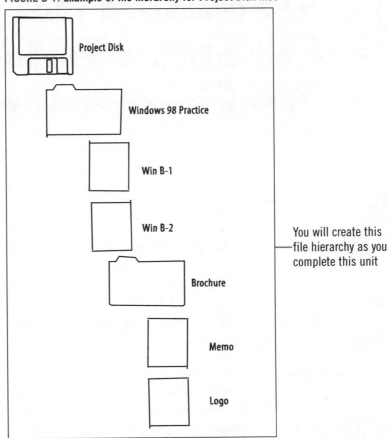

Project Disk

Windows 98 Practice

Win B-1

Win B-2

Brochure

You will create this file hierarchy as you complete this unit

Memo

Logo

FIGURE B-8: Brochure folder shown in My Computer

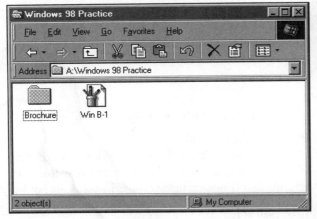

FIGURE B-9: Brochure folder shown in Windows Explorer

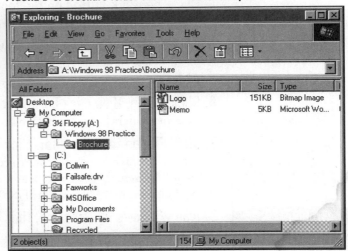

Viewing Files and Creating Folders with My Computer

My Computer shows the contents of your computer, including files, folders, programs, disk drives, and printers. You can click the icons representing these various parts of your computer to view their contents. You can manage your files using the My Computer menu bar and toolbar. See Table B-3 for a description of the toolbar buttons. ✒ In this lesson, you begin by using My Computer to move around in your computer's file hierarchy, then you create two new folders on your Project Disk that contain the files you created.

Steps 1 2 3 4

Trouble?

If you do not see the toolbar, click View on the menu bar, point to Toolbars, then click Standard Buttons. If you do not see the Address Bar, click View, point to Toolbar, then click the Address Bar.

1. **Double-click the My Computer icon** on your desktop, then click the **Maximize button** if the My Computer window does not fill the screen

   My Computer opens and displays the contents of your computer, as shown in Figure B-10. Your window may contain icons for different folders, drives, printers, and so on.

2. **Make sure your Project Disk is in the floppy disk drive, then double-click the 3½ Floppy (A:) icon**

   The contents of your Project Disk are displayed in the window. These are the project files and the files you created using WordPad and Paint. Each file is represented by an icon, which indicates the program that was used to create the file. If Microsoft Word is installed on your computer, the Word icon appears for the WordPad files; if not, the WordPad icon appears.

Trouble?

This book assumes that your hard drive is drive C. If yours differs, substitute the appropriate drive for drive C wherever it is referenced. See your instructor or technical support person for assistance.

3. **Click the Address list arrow** on the Address Bar, as shown in Figure B-10, then click **(C:)**, or the letter for the main hard drive on your computer

   The window changes to show the contents of your hard drive. The **Address Bar** allows you to open and display a drive, folder, or even a Web page. You can also type in the Address Bar to go to a different drive, folder, or Web page. For example, typing "C:\" will display drive C; typing "E:\Personal Letters" will display the Personal Letters folder on drive E, and typing "http://www.microsoft.com" opens Microsoft's Web site if your computer is connected to the Internet.

4. **Click the Back button** on the toolbar

   The Back button displays the previous location, in this case, your Project Disk.

5. **Click the Views button list arrow** ▦▾ on the toolbar, then click **Details**

   Details view shows not only the files and folders, but also the size of the file; the type of file, folder, or drive; and the date the file was last modified.

6. **Click** ▦▾ , then click **Large Icons**

   This view offers less information but provides a large, clear view of the contents of the disk.

7. **Click File on the menu bar, click New, then click Folder**

   A new folder is created on your Project Disk, as shown in Figure B-11. The folder is called "New Folder" by default. It is selected and ready to be renamed. You can also create a new folder by right-clicking in the blank area of the My Computer window, clicking New, then clicking Folder.

Trouble?

To rename a folder, click the folder to select it, click the folder name so it is surrounded by a rectangle, type the new folder name, then press [Enter].

8. **Type Windows 98 Practice, then press [Enter]**

   Choosing descriptive names for your folders helps you remember their contents.

9. **Double-click the Windows 98 Practice folder**, repeat Step 7 to create a new folder in the Windows 98 Practice folder, type **Brochure** for the folder name, then press **[Enter]**

10. **Click the Back button** ⇦ to return to your Project Disk

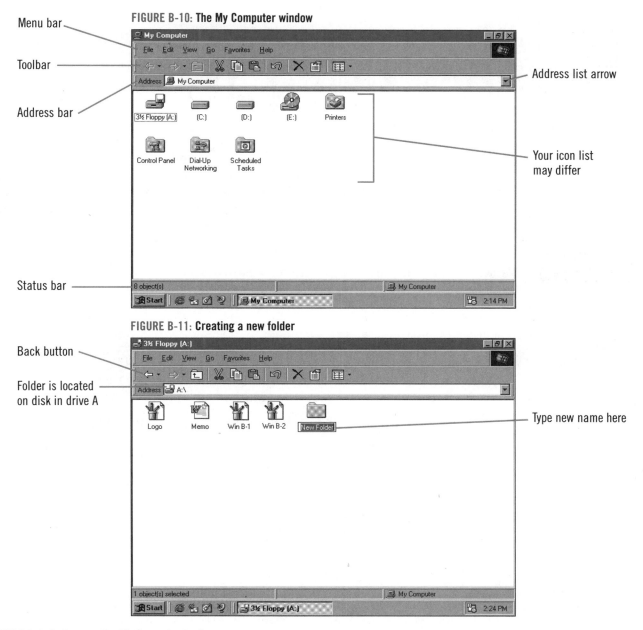

FIGURE B-10: **The My Computer window**

Menu bar

Toolbar

Address bar

Address list arrow

Your icon list may differ

Status bar

FIGURE B-11: **Creating a new folder**

Back button

Folder is located on disk in drive A

Type new name here

TABLE B-3: **Buttons on the My Computer toolbar**

button	function
⇐	Moves back to the previous location you have already visited
⇒	Moves forward to the previous location you have already visited
▣	Moves up one level in the file hierarchy
✂	Deletes a folder or file and places it on the clipboard
▤	Copies a folder or file
▥	Pastes a folder or file
↶	Undoes the most recent My Computer operation
✕	Deletes a folder or file permanently
▦	Shows the properties of a folder or file
▦	Lists the contents of My Computer using different views

Moving and Copying Files Using My Computer

You can move a file or folder from one location to another using a variety of methods in My Computer or Windows Explorer. If the file or folder and the location to which you want to move it are both visible on the desktop, you can simply drag the item from one location to the other. You can also use the cut, copy and paste commands on the Edit menu or the corresponding buttons on the toolbar. You can also right-click the file or folder and choose the Send to command to "send" it to another location—most often a floppy disk for **backing up** files. Backup copies are made in case you have computer trouble, which may cause you to lose files. In this lesson, you move your files into the folder you created in the last lesson.

QuickTip
To copy a file so that it appears in two locations, press and hold [Shift] while you drag the file to its new location.

1. Click **View**, click **Arrange Icons**, then click **By Name**
   In this view, folders are listed first in alphabetical order, followed by files, also in alphabetical order.

2. Click the **Win B-1 file**, hold down the mouse button and drag the file onto the **Windows 98 Practice folder**, as shown in Figure B-12, then release the mouse button
   Win B-1 is moved into the Windows 98 Practice folder.

3. Double-click the **Windows 98 Practice folder** and confirm that it contains the Win B-1 file as well as the Brochure folder

4. Click the **Up button** 🗀 on the My Computer toolbar, as shown in Figure B–12
   You return to your Project Disk. The Up button displays the next level up in the folder hierarchy.

QuickTip
It is easy to confuse the Back button with the Up One Level button. The Back button returns you to the last location you visited, no matter where it is in your folder hierarchy. The Up One Level button displays the next level up in the folder hierarchy, no matter where you last visited.

5. Click the **Logo file**, press and hold [Shift], then click the **Memo file**
   Both files are selected. Table B-4 describes methods for selecting multiple files and folders.

6. Click the **Cut button** ✂ on the 3½ Floppy (A:) toolbar
   The icons for the files are gray, as shown in Figure B-13. This indicates that they've been cut and placed on the Clipboard, to be pasted somewhere else. Instead of dragging items to a new location, you can use the Cut, Copy, and Paste toolbar buttons or the cut, copy, and paste commands on the Edit menu.

7. Click the **Back button** ⬅ to return to the Windows 98 Practice folder, then double-click the **Brochure folder**
   The Brochure folder is currently empty.

8. Click the **Paste button** 📋 on the toolbar
   The two files are pasted into the Brochure folder.

9. Click the **Address list arrow**, then click **3½ Floppy (A:)** and confirm that the Memo and Logo files are no longer listed there and that only the Windows 98 Practice folder and the Win B-2 file remain

10. Click the **Close button** in the 3½ Floppy (A:) window

FIGURE B-12: Dragging a file from one folder to another

Up One Level
button

Drag file here

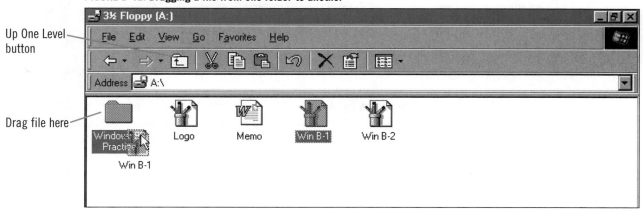

FIGURE B-13: Cutting files to move them

Gray icons
indicate files
have been cut

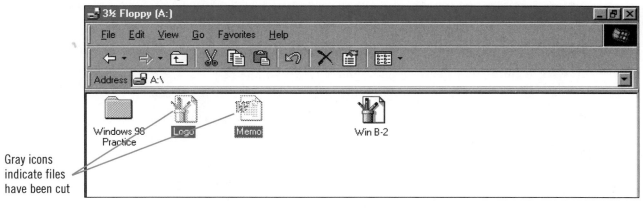

TABLE B-4: Techniques for selecting multiple files and folders

to select	use this technique
Individual objects not grouped together	Click the first object you want to select, then press [Ctrl] as you click each additional object you want to add to the selection
Objects grouped together	Click the first object you want to select, then press [Shift] as you click the last object in the list of objects you want to select; all the objects listed between the first and last objects are selected

Managing Files with Windows Explorer

As with My Computer, you can use Windows Explorer to copy, move, delete, and rename files and folders. However, **Windows Explorer** is more powerful than My Computer: it allows you to see the overall structure of the contents of your computer or network, the file hierarchy, while you work with individual files and folders within that structure. This means you can work with more than one computer, folder, or file at once. ◣ In this lesson, you copy a folder from your Project Disk onto the hard drive, then rename the folder.

Steps 1 2 3 4

1. **Click the Start button, point to Programs, point to Windows Explorer, then click the Maximize button if the Windows Explorer window doesn't already fill the screen**
   Windows Explorer opens, as shown in Figure B-14. The window is divided into two sides called **panes**. The left pane, also known as the **Explorer Bar**, displays the drives and folders on your computer in a hierarchy. The right pane displays the contents of whatever drive or folder is currently selected in the left pane. Each pane has its own set of scroll bars, so that changing what you can see in one pane won't affect what you can see in the other. Like My Computer, Windows Explorer has a menu bar, toolbar, and Address Bar.

2. **Click View on the menu bar, then click Details if it is not already selected**

3. **In the left pane, scroll to and click 3½ Floppy (A:)**
   The contents of your Project Disk are displayed in the right pane.

4. **In the left pane, click the plus sign (+) next to 3½ Floppy (A:)**
   You can use the plus signs (+) and minus signs (-) next to items in the left pane to show or hide the different levels of the file hierarchy, so that you don't always have to look at the entire structure of your computer or network. A plus sign (+) next to a computer, drive, or folder indicates there are additional folders within that object. A minus sign (-) indicates that all the folders of the next level of hierarchy are shown. Clicking the + displays (or "expands") the next level; clicking the – hides (or "collapses") them.

5. **In the left pane, double-click the Windows 98 Practice folder**
   The contents of the Windows 98 Practice folder appear in the right pane of Windows Explorer, as shown in Figure B-15. Double-clicking an item in the left pane that has a + next to it displays its contents in the right pane and also expands the next level in the hierarchy in the left pane.

6. **In the left pane, drag the Windows 98 Practice folder on top of the C: drive icon, then release the mouse button**
   The Windows 98 Practice folder and the files in it are copied to the hard disk.

7. **In the left pane, click the C: drive icon**
   The Windows 98 Practice folder should now appear in the list of folders in the right pane. Now you should rename the folder so you can distinguish the original folder from the copy.

8. **Right-click the Windows 98 Practice folder in the right pane, click Rename in the pop-up menu, type Practice Copy, then press [Enter]**

FIGURE B-14: The Windows Explorer window

Contents of C drive

Left pane, also known as Explorer bar

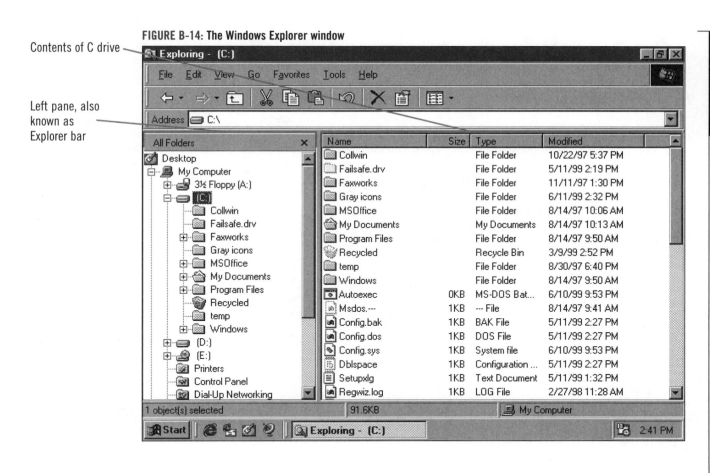

FIGURE B-15: Contents of Windows 98 Practice folder

Contents of Windows 98 Practice folder

Windows 98 Practice folder is selected in left pane

Windows 98

Deleting and Restoring Files

To save disk space and manage your files more effectively, you should **delete** (or remove) files you no longer need. Because files deleted from your hard drive are stored in the Recycle Bin until you remove them permanently by emptying the Recycle Bin, you can restore any files you might have deleted accidentally. However, if you delete a file from your floppy disk it will not be stored in the Recycle Bin—it will be permanently deleted. See Table B-5 for an overview of deleting and restoring files. There are many ways to delete files in Windows 98. In this lesson, you use two different methods for removing files you no longer need. Then, you learn how to restore a deleted file.

1. Click the **Restore button** on the Windows Explorer title bar
   You should be able to see the Recycle Bin icon on your desktop. If you can't see it, resize or move the Windows Explorer window until it is visible. See Figure B-16.

QuickTip

If you are unable to delete the file, it might be because your Recycle Bin is full, or too small, or the properties have been changed so that files are not stored in the Recycle Bin but are deleted instead. See your instructor or technical support person for assistance.

2. Drag the **Practice Copy** folder from the right pane to the **Recycle Bin** on the desktop, as shown in Figure B-16, then click **Yes** to confirm the deletion
   The folder no longer appears in Windows Explorer because you have moved it to the Recycle Bin. Next, you will examine the contents of the Recycle Bin.

3. Double-click the **Recycle Bin icon** on the desktop
   The Recycle Bin window opens, as shown in Figure B-17. Depending on the number of files already deleted on your computer, your window might look different. Use the scroll bar if you can't see the files.

4. Click **Edit** on the Recycle Bin menu bar, then click **Undo Delete**
   The Practice Copy folder is restored and should now appear in the Windows Explorer window. You might need to minimize your Recycle Bin window if it blocks your view of Windows Explorer, and you might need to scroll the right pane to find the restored folder. Now you should delete the Practice Copy folder from your hard drive.

5. Click the **Practice Copy** folder in the right pane, click the **Delete button** ☒ on the Windows Explorer toolbar, resizing the window as necessary to see the button, then click **Yes**
   When you are sure you no longer need files you've moved into the Recycle Bin, you can empty the Recycle Bin. You won't do this now, in case you are working on a computer that you share with other people. But, when you're working on your own machine, simply right-click the Recycle Bin icon, then click Empty Recycle Bin in the pop-up menu.

Customizing your Recycle Bin

You can set your Recycle Bin according to how you like to delete and restore files. For example, if you do not want files to go to the Recycle Bin but rather want them to be immediately and permanently deleted, right-click the Recycle Bin, click Properties, then click the Do Not Move Files to the Recycle Bin check box. If you find that the Recycle Bin fills up too fast and you are not ready to delete the files permanently, you can increase the amount of disk space devoted to the Recycle Bin by moving the Maximum Size of Recycle Bin slider to the right. This, of course, reduces the amount of disk space you have available for other things. Also, you can choose not to have the Confirm File Delete dialog box open when you send files to the Recycle Bin. See your instructor or technical support person before changing any of the Recycle Bin settings.

FIGURE B-16: Dragging a folder to delete it

Drag the folder here ——

Folder located on drive C

FIGURE B-17: The Recycle Bin window

Deleted folder ——

TABLE B-5: Methods for deleting and restoring files

ways to delete a file	ways to restore a file from the Recycle Bin
Select the file, then click the Delete button on the toolbar	Click the Undo button on the toolbar
Select the file, then press [Delete]	Select the file, click File, then click Restore
Right-click the file, then click Delete on the pop-up menu	Right-click the file, then click Restore
Drag the file to the Recycle Bin	Drag the file from the Recycle Bin to any other location

Creating a Shortcut on the Desktop

When you use a file, folder, or program frequently, it can be cumbersome to open it if it is located several levels down in the file hierarchy. You can create a shortcut to an object and place the icon for the shortcut on the desktop or any other location you find convenient. To open the file, folder, or program using the shortcut, double-click the icon. A **shortcut** is a link between the original file, folder, or program you want to access and the icon you create. In this lesson, you create a shortcut to the Memo file on your desktop.

Steps

1. **In the left pane of the Windows Explorer window, click the Brochure folder**
   The contents of the Brochure folder appear in the right pane.

2. **In the right pane, right-click the Memo file**
   A pop-up menu appears, as shown in Figure B-18.

3. **Click Create Shortcut in the pop-up menu**
   The file named Shortcut to Memo file appears in the right pane. Now you need to move it to the desktop so that it will be accessible whenever you need it.

4. **Click the Shortcut to Memo file with the right-mouse button, then drag the shortcut to an empty area of the desktop**
   Dragging an icon using the left mouse button copies it. Dragging an icon using the right mouse button gives you the option to copy or move it. When you release the mouse button a pop-up menu appears.

5. **Click Move Here in the pop-up menu**
   A shortcut to the Memo file now appears on the desktop, as shown in Figure B-19. You might have to move or resize the Windows Explorer window to see it.

6. **Double-click the Shortcut to Memo file icon**
   WordPad starts and the Memo file opens (if you have Microsoft Word installed on your computer, it will start and open the file instead). Using a shortcut eliminates the many steps involved in starting a program and locating and opening a file.

7. **Click the Close button in the WordPad or Word title bar**
   Now you should delete the shortcut icon in case you are working in a lab and share the computer with others. Deleting a shortcut does not delete the original file or folder to which it points.

8. **On the desktop, click the Shortcut to Memo file if necessary, press [Delete], then click Yes to confirm the deletion**
   The shortcut is removed from the desktop and is now in the Recycle Bin.

9. **Close all windows**

> **QuickTip**
> Make sure to use the *right* mouse button in Step 4. If you used the left mouse button by accident, right-click the Shortcut to Memo file in the right pane of Windows Explorer, then click Delete.

> **QuickTip**
> Deleting a shortcut deletes only the link; it does not delete the original file or folder to which it points.

FIGURE B-18: **Creating a shortcut**

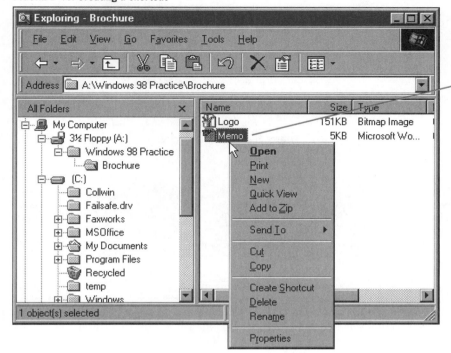

Right-click icon or filename to display pop-up menu. Your menu items may differ.

FIGURE B-19: **Shortcut on desktop**

Double-click to open file

Original file located in Brochure folder

CLUES TO USE

Adding shortcuts to the Start menu

If you do not want your desktop to get cluttered with icons but you would still like easy access to certain files, programs, and folders, you can create a shortcut on the Start menu. Drag the file, program, or folder that you want to add to the Start menu from the Windows Explorer window to the Start button. The file, program, or folder will appear on the first level of the Start menu.

Practice

► Concepts Review

Label each of the elements of the Windows Explorer window shown in Figure B-20.

FIGURE B-20

Match each of the statements with the term it describes.

6. Electronic collections of data
7. Your computer's temporary storage area
8. Temporary location of information you wish to paste into another program
9. Storage areas on your hard drive for files, folders, and programs
10. Structure of files and folders

a. RAM
b. Folders
c. Files
d. File hierarchy
e. Clipboard

Select the best answer from the list of choices.

11. To prepare a floppy disk to save your files, you must first do which of the following?
    a. Copy work files to the disk
    b. Format the disk
    c. Erase all the files that might be on the disk
    d. Place the files on the Clipboard

12. You can use My Computer to
    a. Create a drawing of your computer.
    b. View the contents of a folder.
    c. Change the appearance of your desktop.
    d. Add text to a WordPad file.

13. Which of the following best describes WordPad?
    a. A program for organizing files
    b. A program for performing financial analysis
    c. A program for creating basic text documents
    d. A program for creating graphics

14. **Which of the following is NOT a way to move files from one folder to another?**
    a. Open the file and use the Save As command to save the file in a new location.
    b. In My Computer or the Windows Explorer, drag the selected file to the new folder.
    c. Use the Cut and Paste commands on the Edit menu while in the My Computer or the Windows Explorer windows.
    d. Use the [Ctrl][X] and [Ctrl][V] keyboard shortcuts while in the My Computer or the Windows Explorer windows.

15. **In which of the following can you view the hierarchy of drives, folders, and files in a split pane window?**
    a. Windows Explorer
    b. Programs
    c. My Computer
    d. WordPad

16. **To restore files that you have sent to the Recycle Bin:**
    a. Click File, then click Empty Recycle Bin.
    b. Click Edit, then click Undo Delete.
    c. Click File, then click Undo.
    d. You cannot retrieve files sent to the Recycle Bin.

17. **To copy instead of move a file from one folder to another, drag while pressing**
    a. [Shift].
    b. [Alt].
    c. [Tab].
    d. [Ctrl].

18. **To select files that are not grouped together, select the first file, then**
    a. Press [Shift] while selecting the second file.
    b. Press [Alt] while selecting the second file.
    c. Press [Ctrl] while selecting the second file.
    d. Click on the second file.

19. **Pressing [Backspace]**
    a. Deletes the character to the right of the cursor.
    b. Deletes the character to the left of the cursor.
    c. Moves the insertion point one character to the right.
    d. Moves the insertion point one character to the left.

20. **The size of a font is measured in**
    a. Centimeters.
    b. Points.
    c. Places.
    d. Millimeters.

21. **The Back button on the My Computer toolbar:**
    a. Starts the last program you used.
    b. Displays the next level of the file hierarchy.
    c. Backs up the currently selected file.
    d. Displays the last location you visited.

▶ Skills Review

If you are doing all of the exercises in this unit, you may run out of space on your Project Disk. Use a blank, formatted disk to complete the exercise if this happens.

1. **Create and save a WordPad file.**
    a. Start Windows, then start WordPad.
    b. Type a short description of your artistic abilities, pressing [Enter] several times to insert blank lines between the text and the graphic you are about to create.
    c. Save the document as "Drawing Ability" to the Windows 98 Practice folder on your Project Disk.

2. **Open and save a Paint file.**
    a. Start Paint and open the file Win B-2 from your Project Disk.
    b. Inside the picture frame, create your own unique, colorful design using several colors. Use a variety of tools. For example, create a filled circle and then place a filled square inside the circle.
    c. Save the picture as "First Unique Art" to the Windows 98 Practice folder on your Project Disk.

3. **Work with multiple programs.**
    a. Select the entire graphic and copy it to the Clipboard, then switch to WordPad.
    b. Place the insertion point in the last blank line, then paste the graphic into your document.
    c. Save the changes to your WordPad document using the same filename.
    d. Switch to Paint.
    e. Using the Fill With Color button, change the color of a filled area of your graphic.

   f. Save the revised graphic with the new name, "Second Unique Art," to the Windows 98 Practice folder.

   g. Select the entire graphic and copy it to the Clipboard.

   h. Switch to WordPad and type "This is another version of my graphic." below the first picture, then press [Enter]. (*Hint:* To move the insertion point to the line below the graphic, click below the graphic, then press [Enter].)

   i. Paste the second graphic under the text you just typed.

   j. Save the changed WordPad document as "Two Drawing Examples" to the Windows 98 Practice folder.

   k. Close Paint and WordPad.

4. View files and create folders with My Computer.

   a. Open My Computer, then insert your Project Disk in the appropriate drive if necessary.

   b. Double-click the drive that contains your Project Disk.

   c. Create a new folder on your Project Disk by clicking File, New, then Folder, and name the new folder "Review."

   d. Open the folder to display its contents (it is empty).

   e. Use the Address Bar to view your hard drive, usually (C:).

   f. Create a folder on the hard drive called "Temporary" then use the Back button to view the Review folder. (*Note:* You may not be able to add items to your hard drive.)

   g. Create two new folders in the Review folder. Name one "Documents" and the other "Artwork."

   h. Use the Forward button as many times as necessary to view the hard drive.

5. Move and copy files using My Computer.

   a. Use the Address Bar to view your Project Disk, then open the Windows 98 Practice folder.

   b. Select the two Paint files, then cut and paste them into the Artwork folder.

   c. Use the Back button as many times as necessary to view the Windows 98 Practice folder.

   d. Select the two WordPad files, then move them into the Documents folder.

   e. Close My Computer.

6. View, move and copy files.

   a. Open Windows Explorer and display the contents of the Artwork folder in the right pane.

   b. Select the two Paint files.

   c. Drag the two Paint files from the Artwork folder to the Temporary folder on the hard drive to copy them.

   d. Display the contents of the Documents folder in the right pane.

   e. Select the two WordPad files.

   f. Repeat Step c to copy the files to the Temporary folder on the hard drive.

   g. Display the contents of the Temporary folder in the right pane to verify that the four files are there.

7. Delete and restore files and folders.

   a. Resize the Windows Explorer window so you can see the Recycle Bin icon on the desktop, then scroll in Windows Explorer so you can see the Temporary folder in the left pane.

   b. Delete the Temporary folder from the hard drive by dragging it to the Recycle Bin.

   c. Select the Review folder in the left pane, then press [Delete]. Click Yes if necessary to confirm the deletion.

   d. Open the Recycle Bin, restore the Review folder and its files to your Project Disk, then close the Recycle Bin. (*Note:* If your Recycle Bin is empty, your computer is set to automatically delete items in the Recycle Bin.)

8. Create a shortcut on the desktop.

   a. Use the left pane of Windows Explorer to locate the Windows folder on your hard drive. Select the folder to display its contents in the right pane. (*Note:* If you are in a lab setting, you may not have access to the Windows folder.)

   b. In the right pane, scroll through the list of objects until you see a file called Explorer.

   c. Drag the Explorer file to the desktop to create a shortcut.

   d. Close Windows Explorer.

   e. Double-click the new shortcut to make sure it starts Windows Explorer. Then close Windows Explorer again.

   f. Delete the shortcut for Windows Explorer and exit Windows.

▶ Independent Challenges

If you are doing all of the Independent Challenges, you will need to use a new floppy disk.

1. You have decided to start a bakery business and you want to use Windows 98 to organize the files for the business.

   a. Create two new folders on your Project Disk named "Advertising" and "Customers".

   b. Use WordPad to create a form letter inviting new customers to the open house for the new bakery, then save it as "Open House Letter" and place it in the Customers folder.

   c. Use WordPad to create a list of five tasks that need to get done before the business opens, then save it as "Business Plan" to your Project Disk, but don't place it in a folder.

   d. Use Paint to create a simple logo for the bakery, save it as "Bakery Logo", then place it in the Advertising folder.

   e. On a piece of paper, draw out the new organization of all the folders and files on your Project Disk, close all open programs, then exit Windows.

2. On your computer's hard drive, create a folder called "IC3". Follow the guidelines listed here to create the file hierarchy shown in Figure B-21.

   a. Start WordPad, create a new file that contains a list. Save the file as "To Do List" to your Project Disk.

   b. Start My Computer and copy the Memo file on your Project Disk to the IC3 folder. Rename the file "Article."

   c. Copy the Memo file again to the IC3 folder on your hard drive and rename the second copy of the file "Article Two."

   d. Use My Computer to copy any Paint file to the IC3 folder and rename the file "Sample Logo."

   e. Copy the To Do List from your Project Disk to the IC3 folder and rename the file "Important List."

   f. Move the files into the folders shown in Figure B-21.

FIGURE B-21

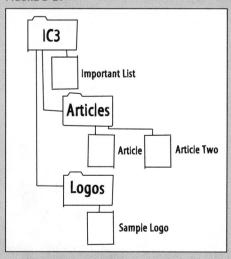

   g. Copy the IC3 folder to your Project Disk. Then delete the IC3 folder on your hard drive. Using the Recycle Bin, restore the file called IC3. To remove all your work on the hard drive, delete this folder again.

3. With Windows 98, you can access the Web from My Computer and Windows Explorer, allowing you to search for information located not only on your computer or network, but also on any computer connected to the Internet.

   a. Start Windows Explorer, then click in the Address Bar so the current location (probably your hard drive) is selected, then type "www.microsoft.com"

   b. Connect to the Internet if necessary. The Microsoft Web page displays in the right pane of Windows Explorer.

c. Click in the Address Bar, then type "www.course.com", then wait a moment while the Course Technology Web page opens.

d. Make sure your Project Disk is in the floppy disk drive, then click 3½ Floppy (A:) in the left pane.

e. Click the Back button list arrow, then click Welcome to Microsoft Homepage.

f. Capture a picture of your desktop by using [Print Screen]. Save the file as "Microsoft", then print it. See Independent Challenge 4 for instructions.

g. Click the Close button on the Explorer Bar.

h. Close Windows Explorer and disconnect from the Internet.

► Visual Workshop

Recreate the screen shown in Figure B-22, which contains the Brochure window in My Computer, two shortcuts on the desktop, and two files open. Press [Print Screen] to make a copy of the screen, then print it from Paint. See your instructor or technical support person for assistance.

FIGURE B-22

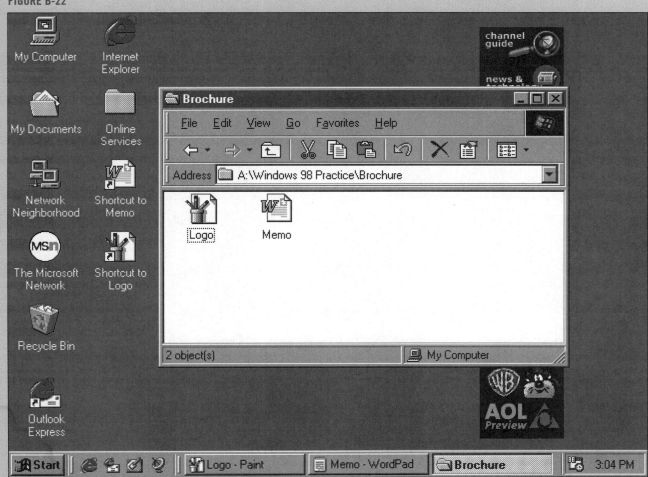

Unit A

Getting
Started with Office 2000

► **Understand Office 2000 Professional**
► **Start an Office program**
► **Use menus and toolbars**
► **Use Help**
► **Create a new file with a wizard**
► **Save a file**
► **Close a file and exit an Office program**

Microsoft Office 2000, often referred to as simply "Office," is a collection (or **suite**) of programs that you can use to produce a wide variety of documents and to communicate on the Internet. Office comes in several **editions**, or versions. The Professional Edition includes Word, Excel, PowerPoint, Access, Outlook, and Small Business Tools. Other editions include the Standard Edition, which does not include Access or Small Business Tools, and the Small Business Edition, which does not include Access but does include Publisher 2000. ✐ The staff at Outdoor Designs, a company that sells kits for recreational products, uses Office 2000 Professional to write memos and reports, manage inventory and sales data, track customers, and create business presentations. Sue Ellen Monteiro, the sales manager, has asked you to begin preparing a memo to the sales force using Office 2000.

Understanding Office 2000 Professional

Microsoft Office 2000 Professional Edition comes with a variety of programs and tools you can use to create documents, analyze data, and complete almost any business task. The programs you learn about in this book include Word, Excel, Access, and PowerPoint. Sue Ellen suggests that you familiarize yourself with the programs and tools in Office 2000 Professional before starting work on your memo.

Details

 Microsoft Word is a word processing program you use to create text-based documents, such as letters, term papers, and reports (see Figure O-1). You also can use Word to add pictures, drawings, tables, and other graphical elements to your documents. At Outdoor Designs, you'll create memos, letters, flyers, and reports in Word to communicate with staff, customers, and distributors.

 Microsoft Excel is a spreadsheet program you use to manipulate, analyze, and chart quantitative data, particularly financial information (see Figure O-2). In your work at Outdoor Designs, you'll use Excel to create product order worksheets, shipping tickets, sales reports, and charts to help the sales and marketing departments track sales and make informed business decisions.

 Microsoft Access is a database management program you use to store, organize, and display information, such as names and addresses, product inventories, and employee data (see Figure O-3). At Outdoor Designs, you'll use Access to create customer and product databases, data entry forms that others can use to input additional data, and reports the staff can use to spot important trends in the data.

 Microsoft PowerPoint is a presentation graphics program you use to develop materials for presentations, including slide shows, computer-based presentations, speaker's notes, and handouts. The staff at Outdoor Designs is preparing for the fall season, so you'll use PowerPoint to create a sales presentation for the sales department and an informational presentation for the fall company meeting.

 Microsoft Outlook is an e-mail and information manager you use to send and receive e-mail, schedule appointments, maintain to-do lists, and store contact information.

 Microsoft Small Business Tools are accessories that help you plan and run a small business. The tools include **Microsoft Business Planner**, which provides information and guidance on planning, starting, and running a business, **Microsoft Direct Mail Manager**, which leads you through the process of producing a direct mail campaign, **Microsoft Small Business Customer Manager**, which helps you track customer and sales information, and **Microsoft Small Business Financial Manager**, which you use to maintain and analyze financial data, such as income statements and balance sheets.

 Microsoft Office Tools are tools that facilitate working with the Office suite. The tools include **Microsoft Access Snapshot Viewer**, which you can use to view and transmit Microsoft Access reports using less disk space, **Microsoft Office Language Settings**, which you can use to enable editing and related tools for working in other languages in Office documents, **Microsoft Office Shortcut Bar**, a toolbar that contains buttons for starting Office programs and performing other common Office tasks, and **Server Extensions Administrator**, a tool for network administrators managing Office on a network.

FIGURE O-1: Document created using Microsoft Word

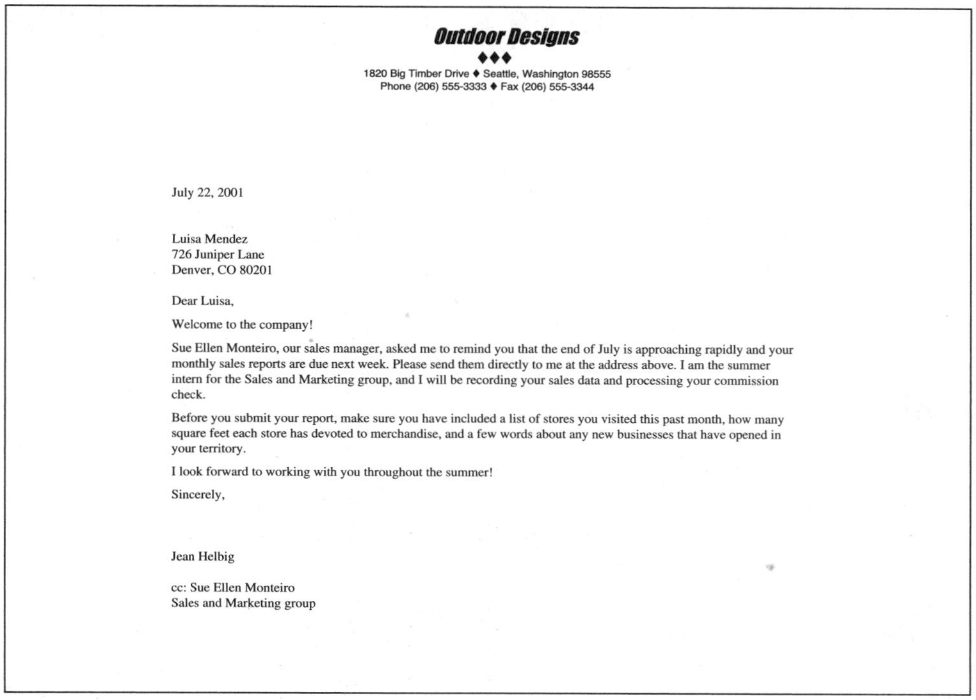

Outdoor Designs

♦♦♦

1820 Big Timber Drive ♦ Seattle, Washington 98555
Phone (206) 555-3333 ♦ Fax (206) 555-3344

July 22, 2001

Luisa Mendez
726 Juniper Lane
Denver, CO 80201

Dear Luisa,

Welcome to the company!

Sue Ellen Monteiro, our sales manager, asked me to remind you that the end of July is approaching rapidly and your monthly sales reports are due next week. Please send them directly to me at the address above. I am the summer intern for the Sales and Marketing group, and I will be recording your sales data and processing your commission check.

Before you submit your report, make sure you have included a list of stores you visited this past month, how many square feet each store has devoted to merchandise, and a few words about any new businesses that have opened in your territory.

I look forward to working with you throughout the summer!

Sincerely,

Jean Helbig

cc: Sue Ellen Monteiro
Sales and Marketing group

FIGURE O-2: Worksheet with a chart in Microsoft Excel

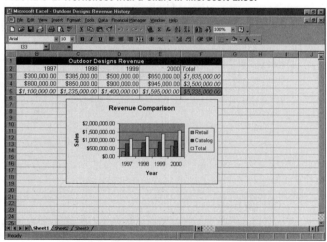

FIGURE O-3: Database table in Microsoft Access

Microsoft Access - [Inventory : Table]

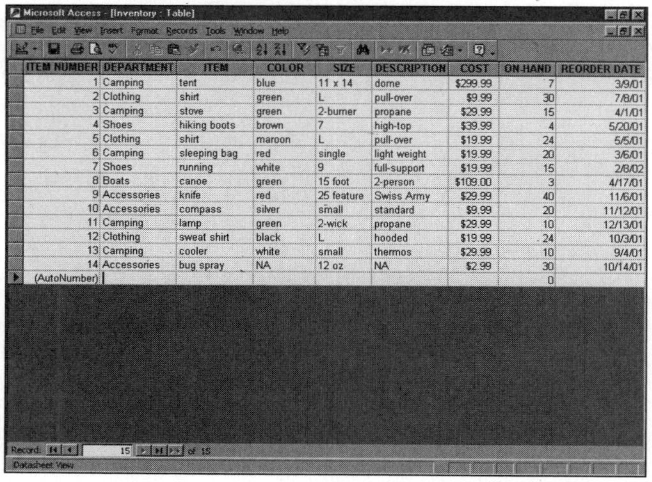

ITEM NUMBER	DEPARTMENT	ITEM	COLOR	SIZE	DESCRIPTION	COST	ON HAND	REORDER DATE
1	Camping	tent	blue	11 x 14	dome	$299.99	7	3/9/01
2	Clothing	shirt	green	L	pull-over	$9.99	30	7/8/01
3	Camping	stove	green	2-burner	propane	$29.99	15	4/1/01
4	Shoes	hiking boots	brown	7	high-top	$39.99	4	5/20/01
5	Clothing	shirt	maroon	L	pull-over	$19.99	24	5/5/01
6	Camping	sleeping bag	red	single	light weight	$19.99	20	3/6/01
7	Shoes	running	white	9	full-support	$19.99	15	2/8/02
8	Boats	canoe	green	15 foot	2-person	$109.00	3	4/17/01
9	Accessories	knife	red	25 feature	Swiss Army	$29.99	40	11/6/01
10	Accessories	compass	silver	small	standard	$9.99	20	11/12/01
11	Camping	lamp	green	2-wick	propane	$29.99	10	12/13/01
12	Clothing	sweat shirt	black	L	hooded	$19.99	24	10/3/01
13	Camping	cooler	white	small	thermos	$29.99	10	9/4/01
14	Accessories	bug spray	NA	12 oz	NA	$2.99	30	10/14/01
(AutoNumber)							0	

Record: 15 of 15

Starting an Office Program

As with many tasks you perform in Office, there are several ways you can start an Office program. One of the more basic methods is using the Start menu on the taskbar. You decide to familiarize yourself with Office. You will use Microsoft Word to create the memo Sue Ellen asked you to prepare, so you decide to start this program now.

Steps

1. **Click the Start button on the taskbar**

   A menu similar to the one shown in Figure O-4 opens above the Start button. (Your list of options may vary.) The Programs folder contains commands for starting each program installed on your system.

   Trouble?

   If this is the first time you are using Word, click the Start button using the Microsoft Word option button in the Welcome to Microsoft Word dialog box, then close the Office Assistant.

2. **Point to Programs, then click Microsoft Word**

   Microsoft Word starts and displays a blank document on the screen, as shown in Figure O-5. The Word program window contains several elements common to all Office programs. Use Figure O-5 to familiarize yourself with these elements.

FIGURE O-4: Start menu

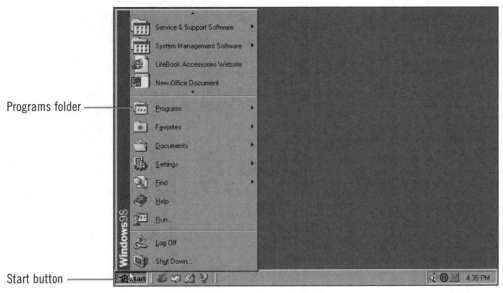

Programs folder

Start button

FIGURE O-5: Word program window

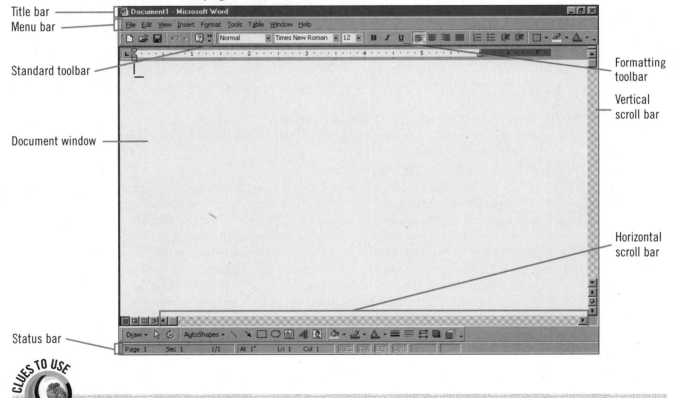

Title bar

Menu bar

Standard toolbar

Document window

Formatting toolbar

Vertical scroll bar

Horizontal scroll bar

Status bar

Starting an Office program with the New Office Document dialog box

If you prefer to work in a more **docucentric** environment, meaning that you like to focus on documents rather than the programs used to create them, you might prefer to start an Office program using the New Office Document dialog box. To use the New Office Document dialog box, click the Start button on the taskbar, then click New Office Document. The New Office Document dialog box opens, containing tabs for different types of documents. Depending on the type of document you click, Office starts the necessary program. If the Office Shortcut Bar is installed on your system, you can open the New Office Document dialog box by clicking the New Office Document button on the Shortcut Bar.

Office 2000

Using Menus and Toolbars

In all the Office programs, you choose commands from menus to perform tasks. If Office needs more information in order to carry out the command, it displays a dialog box that presents available options. A **toolbar** is a customizable set of buttons and list boxes, usually located below the menu bar of an Office program, that provides rapid access to the most commonly used commands in the program. Buttons on a toolbar are often easier to remember than menu and keyboard commands because the buttons graphically represent the tasks they accomplish. Table O-1 lists some common toolbar buttons found in many Office programs. You'll use menus and toolbars often in your work at Outdoor Designs, so practice using them now.

Steps

1. **Click View on the menu bar**

   The View menu opens. It includes commands for changing your view of the program window and hiding or displaying different elements such as toolbars. Office program menus are **personalized** to suit the way you work. When you first use an Office program, the menus display the most commonly used commands. Other commands are available on the full menu, which you can see by clicking the arrows ⤓ at the bottom of a menu or by simply waiting a moment. When you use commands from the long menu, they are added to the short menu (and commands you don't use on the short menu are "demoted" to the long menu). This personalization helps reduce clutter in the program window.

2. **Click the arrows ⤓ at the bottom of the menu if necessary**

   The full View menu opens, as shown in Figure O-6. Notice that the commands from the short menu appear against a darker gray background than the commands from the full menu.

QuickTip

To see what toolbars are available in an Office program, right-click a blank area of any toolbar. A short-cut menu opens, listing the available toolbars. A check mark next to a toolbar name means the toolbar is already displayed. To display or hide a toolbar, click its check box to add or remove the check mark.

3. **Point to Toolbars, then click Customize**

   This dialog box contains options for customizing toolbars and menu commands to suit your work preferences.

4. **Click the Options tab if necessary**

   The Options tab of the Customize dialog box opens, as shown in Figure O-7. Here you can customize several elements in the program window, including toolbar and menu settings. By default, Word displays two toolbars side by side: the **Formatting toolbar**, which contains buttons and list boxes for formatting commands such as changing font style, applying and removing italics, and aligning text, and the **Standard toolbar**, which contains buttons for common general tasks such as opening a file and printing a document. Displaying the toolbars on one row leaves more room on your screen for the document window.

5. **Click the Standard and Formatting toolbars share one row check box to deselect it if necessary**

   Now the two most common toolbars will appear each on its own row, so that you can see more buttons as you work.

6. **Click the Reset my usage data button**

   An information box opens, informing you that this selection will restore the default set of menus and toolbar buttons to the program window. Clicking this button before you begin working in Office is a good idea if you are working on a system that others share; it ensures that you will see the most common menus and toolbar buttons when you begin working. Office will then personalize the menus and toolbar buttons based on your actions.

7. **Click OK in the information box, then click Close in the Customize dialog box**

   The dialog box closes, and you are returned to the document window.

FIGURE O-6: View menu

Commands on the short menu appear on a dark gray background

Commands on the full menu appear on a light gray background

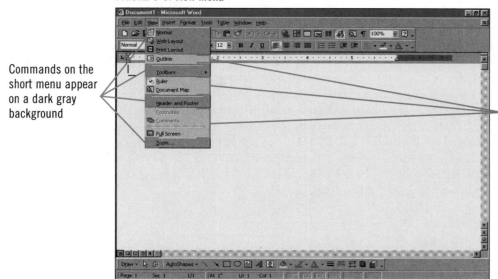

FIGURE O-7: Options tab of Customize dialog box

Make sure this check box is deselected

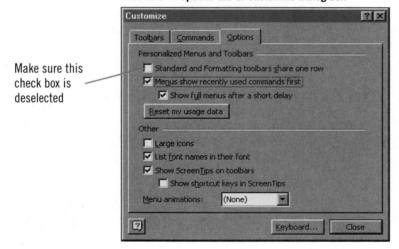

TABLE O-1: Commonly used toolbar buttons

button	button name	description
	New	Start a new document
	Open	Open a file
	Save	Save the current file under the current name
	Print	Print the current document using the default settings
	Spelling and Grammar	Check the spelling of the current document
	Insert Hyperlink	Insert a hyperlink at the insertion point
	Microsoft Word Help	View Help information
	Format Painter	Copy the formatting style of the selected text and "paint" it to a different selection
	Bold	Turn on the Bold formatting style
	Italic	Turn on the Italic formatting style
	Underline	Turn on the Underline formatting style

Using Help

Office has an extensive Help system you can use to guide you through using almost any feature or completing any procedure. It has both step-by-step instructions and explanations of difficult concepts. The variety of Help tools available suits many different situations and work styles. You can access Help using an index or a table of contents; you can ask a question of the animated Office Assistant, which searches the Help database for keywords related to the question you type; you can get a quick explanation of almost any screen element by pointing to it with the What's This? pointer ▶?, available through the Help menu; and you can obtain assistance and information on the World Wide Web. ✐ Familiarize yourself with the Help system now by learning about some formatting features in preparation for the documents you will be creating in Word.

Steps

1. Click Help on the menu bar
This menu contains commands for the major Help options in this program.

2. Click What's This?
The pointer changes to ▶?. When this pointer is active and you click a screen element or command for which a ScreenTip is available, the ScreenTip opens in a shaded box. A **ScreenTip** is a concise explanation of the selected screen element. You can also click the What's This? pointer on text in your documents to view the text's current formatting.

3. Click the Font Size list box on the Formatting toolbar
A ScreenTip opens.

4. Click anywhere on the screen to close the ScreenTip

5. Click Help on the menu bar, then click Show the Office Assistant
The Office Assistant appears on your screen. It may look like the paper clip shown in Figure O-8 or it may be a different character.

6. Click the Assistant, type Use Help in the text box at the bottom of the Help bubble, then press [Enter]
The Assistant displays a list of Help topics, as shown in Figure O-8.

7. Click Ways to get assistance while you work
The Microsoft Word Help window opens, as shown in Figure O-9. The left pane serves as a navigation center, the right pane displays the contents of the selected item, and the buttons along the top facilitate your work. In the left pane, tabs let you look for help by browsing in the Contents tab, entering a term or scrolling through a list in the Index tab, or by asking a question of the Answer Wizard. When you select a topic, detailed information is displayed in the right pane.

8. In the right pane, click Getting Help from the Help menu
A Help window opens, displaying information on this topic. Underlined text in Help indicates a **link**, which you can click to get more information about the topic.

9. After reading the information, click the Help window's Close button ☒
Help closes, and the Office Assistant remains open on your screen.

QuickTip
Many dialog boxes also contain a Help button ? on the right side of the title bar that you can click to activate the What's This? pointer. Using this pointer to click the elements of the dialog box helps you learn about the options available and when to use them.

QuickTip
You can also press [Esc] to close a ScreenTip and to turn off the What's This? pointer.

Trouble?
If you do not see the left pane, click the Show button ⧉ to display it.

QuickTip
To see more text of the left pane, drag the border between the two panes to the right; to see more of the right pane, drag the border to the left.

FIGURE O-8: Asking for help from the Office Assistant

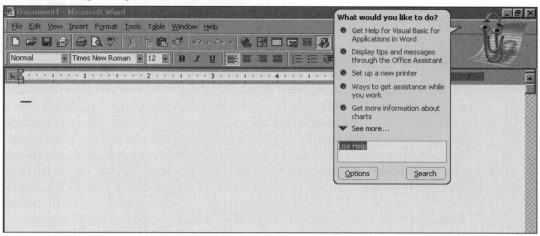

FIGURE O-9: Microsoft Word Help window

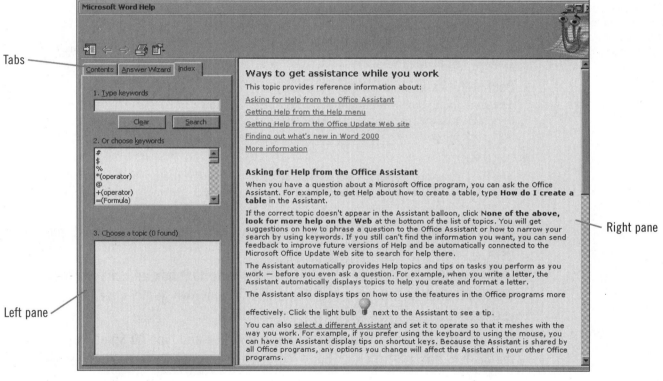

Tabs

Left pane

Right pane

Using the Office Assistant

Using the Office Assistant is a fun and easy way to find information. You can ask it questions or set it to provide tips and guidance while you work. You can also customize how the Assistant looks, to suit your personality (there's an Einstein, a cat and dog, a smiley face, and other graphics). To change the way the Office Assistant works, display the Office Assistant if necessary, right-click it, then click Options and choose the appropriate settings. Clicking outside the Assistant window closes the window, but the Assistant stays on your screen. To reopen the window, just click the Assistant and type your question. You can drag the Assistant to a new location if it's in the way (it also moves automatically when you enter data near it). To move the Assistant off your screen entirely, right-click the Assistant and then click Hide.

Office 2000

Creating a New File with a Wizard

A **wizard** is a series of dialog boxes that guides you step by step through the process of creating a new document or completing a task. A **template** is a special file that contains predesigned formatting, text, and other tools for creating common business documents, such as letters, business presentations, and invoices. By creating a new document using a wizard or template, you can save formatting time and be assured that the finished document will look professional. When you start a new document using a wizard, you first supply specific information, usually using dialog boxes, so that Office can prepare the initial document for your review and modification. When you start a new document using a template, the document opens immediately on your screen, ready for you to customize and save. Sue Ellen asks you to create a memo to company employees. You'll begin creating the memo with the Memo Wizard.

Steps

QuickTip
To see all the templates and wizards available in all of your installed Office programs, open the New Office Document dialog box using the Start menu.

1. **Click File on the menu bar, then click New**
   The New dialog box opens. The New dialog box organizes the templates and wizards available in the current Office program into tabs.

2. **Click the Memos tab**
   By default, Word contains four memo templates and wizards (you may have more or fewer), as shown in Figure O-10.

3. **Double-click the Memo Wizard icon**
   The first dialog box in the Memo Wizard opens, as shown in Figure O-11. The dialog boxes in a wizard are easy to navigate; after you finish reading or completing the current dialog box, click Next. To return to a previous dialog box to change information, click Back.

4. **Click Next**
   The next dialog box opens, where you choose a style for the memo. Notice that the chart on the left side of the wizard dialog box tracks your progress through the document creation process, so you know how many steps are left to complete.

5. **In the Style dialog box, accept the default style (Professional), click Next, then click Next in the Title dialog box**

6. **In the Heading Fields dialog box, click in the Date text box and change the date to 6/9/2001; click in the From text box and type your own name; click in the Subject text box and type Sales Reports; then click Next**

7. **In the Recipient dialog box, click in the To text box and type All Sales Reps; click in the CC text box and type Sue Ellen Monteiro; then click Next**

8. **Click Next two more times to accept the defaults in the Closing Fields and Header/Footer dialog boxes, then click Finish**

QuickTip
You can turn off the Office Assistant by clicking the Assistant, clicking Options, then in the Office Assistant dialog box clicking the Options tab, clicking the Use the Office Assistant check box to deselect it, then clicking OK.

9. **Right-click the Office Assistant, then click Hide**
   The completed memo appears in the document window, as shown in Figure O-12, ready for you to customize it further.

FIGURE O-10: Memos tab of the New dialog box

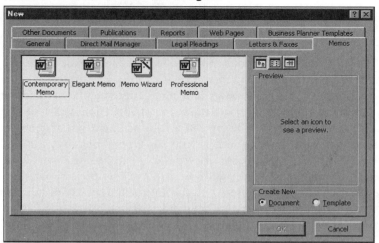

FIGURE O-11: Memo Wizard dialog box

Click to move to the next dialog box

FIGURE O-12: Completed document ready for customization

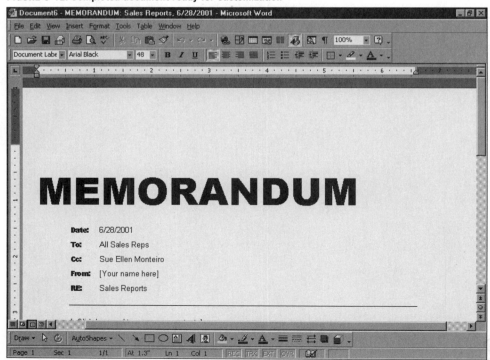

Office 2000

Saving a File

When you enter data into a computer, it is stored in the computer's **random access memory (RAM)** until you turn off your computer, at which point the computer's RAM is erased. To store your work permanently, you must save it as a **file** (an electronic collection of data). When you save a document, you must assign it a unique **filename** so you can identify it later. You must also specify where you want to save the document (on a floppy disk or on the computer's hard disk, and in what folder, if any). Before you save a document, it is assigned a temporary filename, such as Document1 or Book1, which reflects the type of document it is (the number is assigned in case you create more than one unsaved document during a work session). If the document was created based on a template or wizard, a more descriptive designation is added, such as Memo, plus additional information such as the date or the subject of the memo, if you designated this information when creating the document. ✐ You decide to save the memo you are working on so you can complete it later.

Steps

1. Click **File** on the menu bar, then click **Save As**
   The Save As dialog box opens, as shown in Figure O-13. Take a moment now to identify the elements of the dialog box, using the figure for guidance. A filename based on the first text in a document is always suggested as the default. The suggested filename appears in the File name text box.

2. Type **Memo to Sales Reps** in the File name text box
   The filename Memo to Sales Reps appears in the File name text box.

3. Click the **Save in list box**, then click the letter of the drive and the folder where you plan to store your files for this book

QuickTip

You can save most Office documents as a Web page by clicking Web Page in the Save as type list box. If necessary, Office will open a dialog box showing what formatting elements will not display in this file format.

4. If the Save as type list box does not display Word Document, click the **list arrow**, scroll if necessary, then click **Word Document**

5. Click **Save**
   The Save As dialog box closes, and your memo is saved to the location you specified in Step 3. Note that the title bar now displays the new filename.

FIGURE O-13: Save As dialog box

Current folder location

List of files in the current folder and drive location

Enter the filename here

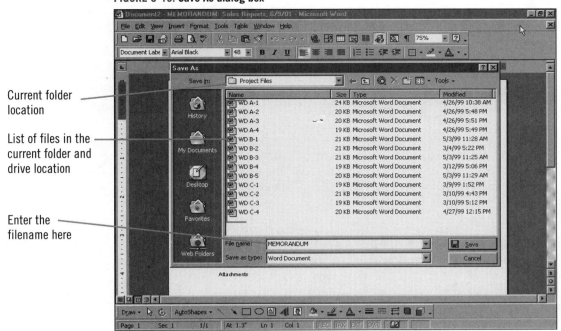

Naming files

A valid filename in an Office file can be up to 255 characters, but descriptive titles with fewer than 20 characters are easier to work with. You can use uppercase and lowercase letters in a filename, plus spaces and most symbols you can type on your keyboard. When you save your file, the proper program type is automatically associated with it so that even if you open it later using the Document menu on the Start menu, Windows Explorer, or some other means, the proper program will start and open the file. When you name your files, try to use precise names that you'll remember later. Make sure you know in what drive and folder you are saving your files so that you can quickly find them when you need them.

Closing a File and Exiting an Office Program

After you save a document, you can safely close it and exit the program. To close a file, use the File menu or the Close button on the document window. When you complete all the work you want to get done in a given session, you exit the program. ◀━━━ You're ready to close your memo and exit Word because your day at Outdoor Designs is finished.

Steps

QuickTip
You can also close a file by clicking the Close button in the top-right corner of the document window.

1. Click **File** on the menu bar

The File menu opens, as shown in Figure O-14.

2. Click **Close**

The memo file closes. If you made changes to the file since you saved it, Word opens a dialog box prompting you to save the changes. (You can save changes to a document at any time by clicking File on the menu bar, then clicking Save, or by clicking the Save button 🖫 on the Standard toolbar.)

QuickTip
You can also exit a program by clicking File on the menu bar, then clicking Exit.

3. Click the program window's **Close button** ☒, as shown in Figure O-15

The Word program closes.

FIGURE O-14: Closing a file

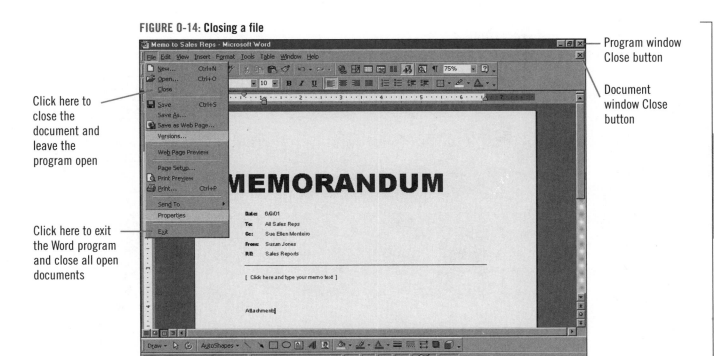

Click here to close the document and leave the program open

Click here to exit the Word program and close all open documents

Program window Close button

Document window Close button

FIGURE O-15: Exiting a program

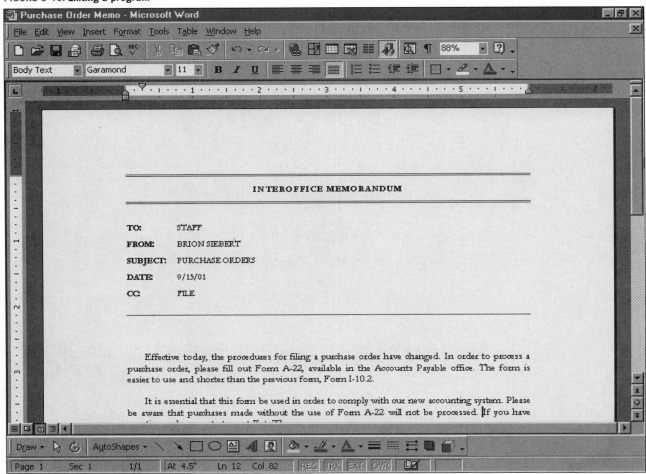

Practice

▶ Concepts Review

Label each of the elements shown in Figure O-16.

FIGURE O-16

Match each of the following programs with the task for which it is most useful.

8. Access
9. Outlook
10. Word
11. Excel
12. PowerPoint

a. Develop materials for presentations, such as transparencies and handouts
b. Manipulate and analyze spreadsheet data
c. Schedule appointments, maintain to-do lists, store contact information, and send e-mail
d. Organize databases of information
e. Create text-based documents, such as memos and letters

Select the best answer from the list of choices.

13. The phrase "Microsoft Office is a suite of programs" means that

a. Microsoft Office consists of one program that contains many features.

b. You cannot use one Office program unless all the programs are open.

c. The programs in Office must be installed on a network.

d. The programs in Office function independently but work together when needed.

14. In the New Office Document dialog box, you can

a. Start a new Word document.

b. Start a new Excel spreadsheet.

c. Start a new PowerPoint presentation.

d. All of the above.

15. Word is used primarily to

a. Create text-based documents such as letters, memos, and reports.

b. Track phone numbers and addresses.

c. Maintain spreadsheet information.

d. Surf the World Wide Web.

16. To get online help, you can

a. Use the Help menu.

b. Click the Help button on the toolbar.

c. Press [F10].

d. Either a or b.

17. Toolbars provide rapid access to

   a. Office programs

   b. Commonly used commands.

   c. Template designs.

   d. None of the above.

18. A wizard is a

   a. Shortcut file that is available only in Microsoft Word.

   b. An animated Office Assistant character.

   c. A Help file that teaches you about different Office programs.

   d. A series of dialog boxes that guides you through completing a task or creating a document.

19. The Office Assistant is a feature that

   a. Answers specific questions you ask about using an Office program.

   b. Displays an animated assistant to make learning more fun.

   c. Offers tips on using an Office program.

   d. All of the above.

► Skills Review

1. Start an Office program.
a. Click the Start button.
b. Point to Programs, then click Microsoft Word.

2. Use menus and toolbars.
a. Click Format on the menu bar, then click Font.
b. In the Font dialog box, click Tahoma in the Font list.
c. Click OK.
d. In the document, type the sentence, "This is a test."

3. Use Help.
a. Click Help on the menu bar, then click Show the Office Assistant.
b. Type "How do I Print?" and then click Search.
c. Click the Print a document option button.
d. Maximize the right pane if necessary.
e. Read the topics in the window, clicking any additional topics that interest you.
f. When you are finished, close the Help window.
g. Click the What's This? command on the Help menu, then click the Bullets button ▤ on the Formatting toolbar.
h. After reading the ScreenTip, click anywhere on the screen.
i. Right-click the Assistant icon, then click Hide.

4. Use a wizard.

a. Open the New dialog box.

b. Display the Letters & Faxes tab.

c. Click the Fax Wizard icon, then click OK.

d. In the Document to Fax dialog box, designate the following document without a cover sheet as the document to fax.

e. In the Fax Software dialog box, choose the option to print your document so that you can send it from a separate fax machine, and click the With a cover sheet option button if necessary to select it.

f. In the Recipients dialog box, enter Sue Ellen Monteiro at fax number 555-4646 as the recipient.

g. In the Cover Sheet dialog box, choose the Contemporary cover sheet style.

h. Enter your name as the sender.

i. When you reach the Finish dialog box, click Cancel.

5. Save a document.

a. Open the Save As dialog box.

b. Name the current document "Office Skills Review."

c. Display the drive and folder that contains your project files.

d. Save the document.

e. Click after the period (.) in the sentence "This is a test."

f. Press [Enter]. Click the Font list arrow on the Formatting toolbar, then click Times New Roman.

g. Type "Outdoor Designs encourages all employees to gain fluency in all Office programs."

h. Save your changes to the document.

i. If you have access to a printer, click the Print button 🖨 on the Standard toolbar.

6. Close a file and exit a program.

a. Close the Office Skills Review document.

b. Exit Word.

► Independent Challenges

1. Throughout this unit, you used Microsoft Word to learn about many features that are common to all Office programs, including screen elements such as toolbars. Use what you have learned to explore another Office program and see the similarities for yourself.

To complete this independent challenge:

a. Start Microsoft Excel.

b. Compare the Excel program screen with your knowledge of the Word program screen. The grid-like structure of the Excel worksheet window is different from the blank document screen of Word, but many of the screen elements, such as scroll bars, commands, and buttons, are the same.

c. Experiment with entering text in this window by typing your name and then pressing [Enter].

d. Use familiar buttons on the Standard and Formatting toolbars to see their effects in Excel.

e. To select text in Excel, click the cell that contains the text you entered. How does this selection process compare to working in Word? Try entering text or numbers in other cells of the worksheet, and then formatting them with a toolbar button.

f. When you are finished, use the File menu to exit the program. When prompted, do not save changes to the file.

2. The Office Help system offers a variety of tools for learning about Office programs. You've used the Contents tab in the Help topics window, but you might not be familiar with the Index tab. Some people prefer working with the Index tab because when you type in a term, all topics pertaining to that term are immediately displayed. Explore the Index tab now.

To complete this independent challenge:

a. Start any Office program.

b. Open the Help window. (To open the Help window if the Office Assistant is active, click the Office Assistant, type a phrase such as "Use Office" in the text box, click Search, then click any options that display.)

c. In the left pane of the Help window, click the Index tab.

d. In the text box, type the first few letters of a term you would like to learn more about, such as "AutoFormat," "File formats," or "Toolbars."

e. Display information about the term, and click as directed to read additional information.

f. If you have access to a printer, use the Print command on the Options menu to print the contents of the topic you have chosen.

g. When you are finished, close the Help window.

3. Microsoft offers a wealth of guidance on the World Wide Web for getting the most from Microsoft Office. If you have access to the Web, go online to explore a variety of resources including advice, information updates, and free software from Microsoft.

To complete this independent challenge:

a. Start any Office program.

b. Open the Help menu, then click Office on the Web.

c. If necessary, connect to the Internet. When you are connected to the Microsoft Office Update Home Page, scroll through the table of contents to familiarize yourself with it.

d. Click a program that interests you.

e. When the program page opens, click Assistance.

f. In the Assistance page, click a topic or category that interests you.

g. If necessary, enter a user profile.

h. Progress through the Help available for each page of the tour, clicking links that interest you, and clicking Back to return to a page when necessary. When you are finished, disconnect from the Internet.

4. Increase your familiarity with wizards by creating a letter using the Letter Wizard in Word. Write a letter to a friend about your progress in learning Microsoft Office, or about another topic that interests you. The Letter Wizard works a little differently from the Memo Wizard; there is no chart mapping your progress through the dialog boxes, but in addition to displaying the dialog boxes, the Office Assistant provides additional guidance.

To complete this independent challenge:

a. Open the New Office Document dialog box.

b. Click the Letters & Faxes tab.

c. Click the Letter Wizard icon.

d. When the new document opens, read the information provided by the Office Assistant, and then make the following selections: choose to create one letter; use today's date; use the contemporary letter page design; use the full block letter style; enter your friend's name and your friend's address as the recipient information; designate an informal salutation; and specify an appropriate subject in the Subject text box.

e. In the body of the letter, delete the paragraph that begins "Type your letter here" by selecting the text (dragging over it with the mouse) and pressing [Delete].

f. Type a paragraph about your progress in using Office or about the topic you have chosen.

g. Save the document as "Letter to Friend" to your Project Disk, then close the document and exit Word.

▶ Visual Workshop

Start Microsoft Word and then use the skills you have learned in this unit to create the document shown in Figure O-16. (*Hint: It was created using a wizard in the New dialog box.*) When you have finished, save the document to your Project Disk as Co-Marketing Proposal and exit Word.

FIGURE O-16

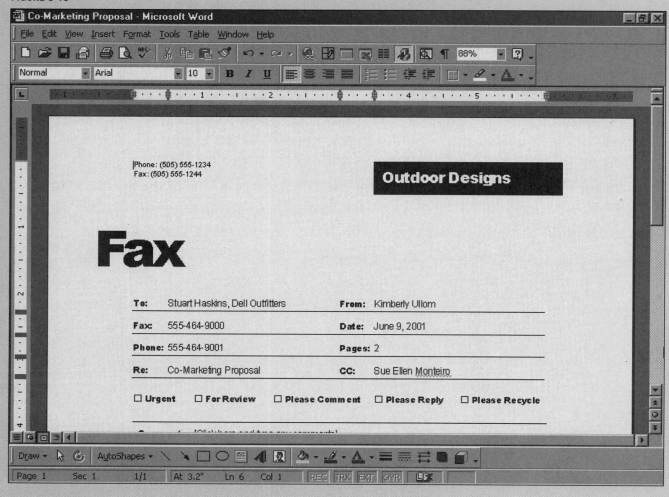

Creating
a Document with Word 2000

Objectives

- ► **Plan a document**
- ► **Open a file and save it with a new name**
- ► **Enter text in a document**
- ► **Edit a document**
- ► **Move text in a document**
- ► **Use the Spelling and Grammar Checker**
- ► **View a document**
- ► **Print a document**

In this unit you learn some basic skills for using Microsoft Word 2000, the word processor program included with Office 2000.  Sue Ellen Monteiro, the sales manager for Outdoor Designs, asks you to write a memo to send to the sales representatives reminding them that their monthly sales reports are due. She suggests that you use the memo you created in the last unit using the Memo Wizard. As you work on the memo, you'll learn word-processing skills that will help you each time you use Word.

Word 2000

Planning a Document

Before you begin to write any document, even a memo, you should outline its content and plan how you want it to look. You should consider who will read your document and what type of presentation will get your message across most clearly. ✐ Before you begin typing your memo to the sales representatives, you should plan what you want to accomplish and how you'll accomplish it. Figure A-1 shows a sample plan.

Details

 Determine the document's purpose
The purpose of your memo is twofold. Sue Ellen wants to remind sales representatives to send in their monthly sales reports on time, and you want to introduce yourself to them.

 Determine the document's content
You need to remind sales representatives of the date their reports are due to you. You also tell them who you are and describe some of your job responsibilities.

 Determine the document's length
You decide to keep the memo short, no more than two paragraphs, to keep from boring the representatives and to make sure they obtain the information they need quickly.

 Determine the document's organization
A standard business memo format is a professional way to introduce yourself to the representatives. You'll include the typical "To:" and "From:" lines at the top of the memo, followed by the main content, a closing, and your name.

 Determine how to create the document—from scratch or with a template
The templates and wizards provided in Word can help you create many types of documents, including memos. You already used the Memo Wizard to create the memo heading for this memo, so you will open and add to that file.

 Determine the document's format and adjust it if necessary
Your short and simple memo doesn't need a lot of formatting to make it attractive and readable.

1. Purpose

    Get sales reps to send their sales reports on time.

    Introduce myself.

2. Content

    Remind the reps that sales reports are due next week.

    Tell them that I'm responsible for processing their commission checks.

3. Length

    A two-paragraph memo

4. Organization

    Standard business memo

5. Create document

    Add to the Outdoor Designs memo.

6. Formatting

    Standard business memo format

Word 2000

Opening a File and Saving it with a New Name

There are several ways to open a file in Word: you can choose the Open Office Document command on the Start menu, you can choose the Open command on the File menu, or you can click the Open button on the Standard toolbar. ✎ You plan to continue creating the memo you started in the last unit. You'll open the memo file, save it with a different name, and enter the text. Saving a file with a different name keeps the original file intact in case you want to use it again.

Steps 1234

1. Start Word, then click the **Maximize button** in the upper-right corner of the program window if necessary

2. Click **View** on the menu bar, click **Toolbars**, click **Customize**, click to deselect the **Standard and Formatting toolbars share one row checkbox** if necessary, click the **Reset My Usage data button**, click **Yes**, then click **Close**
   Now the Standard and Formatting toolbars are displayed each on its own row, so that more buttons can be displayed and the toolbars and menus are reset to their default configuration.

QuickTip

To quickly return to the last location you displayed, click the Back button ⬅ on the toolbar in the Open dialog box.

3. Click the **Open button** 🖝 on the Standard toolbar
   The Open dialog box opens, similar to Figure A-2. It contains a Look in list box and buttons in the Places Bar for navigating to the folder and file you want, a toolbar for performing common tasks in this dialog box, a list of files in the folder currently selected in the Look in box, and text boxes for specifying the name, folder location, and type of file you want to open.

4. Insert your Project Disk in the appropriate drive if necessary, click the **Look in list arrow**, click the name of the drive that contains the Project files provided with this text, then, if necessary, double-click the folder containing your Project files
   All the files on the selected drive or folder, including WD A-1, appear in the list of files.

QuickTip

If you don't see the ruler, click View on the menu bar, then click Ruler. By default, the Drawing toolbar is displayed; if it is not open on your screen and you would like to see it, you can click the Drawing button 🖉 on the Standard toolbar.

5. Double-click **WD A-1**
   Double-clicking accomplishes the same thing as clicking WD A-1 then clicking the Open button. After a moment the memo document opens in the document window, as shown in Figure A-3. The document window contains several visual elements and controls to help you with word processing as listed in Table A-1.

6. Click **File** on the menu bar, then click **Save As**
   The Save As dialog box opens. It contains many of the same elements as the Open dialog box, so that you can navigate to the correct folder location, and specify the filename and type of file you want to save.

7. Make sure the drive and folder where you want to save your files is listed in the Save in list box, double-click in the **File name text box** to select the current filename if necessary, type **Sales Rep Memo** in the File name text box, then press **[Enter]**
   Word saves the new file, Sales Rep Memo, to the drive and folder you specified. The title bar changes to reflect the new name. The file WD A-1 is closed and left unchanged.

Trouble?

If your screen is already at 100% view, you will not see any changes.

8. Click **View** on the menu bar, click **Zoom**, click the **100% option button** in the Zoom dialog box, then click OK
   Changing the **zoom**, the percentage of normal size that you view a document on-screen, makes the text easier to read on-screen.

FIGURE A-2: Open dialog box

Look in list box ⎯

Places Bar ⎯

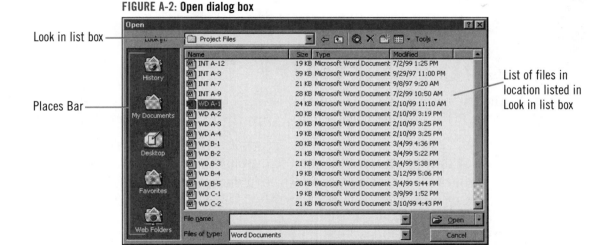

List of files in location listed in Look in list box

FIGURE A-3: Word program window with file WD A-1 opened

Standard toolbar
Formatting toolbar
Save button
Ruler

Scroll bar

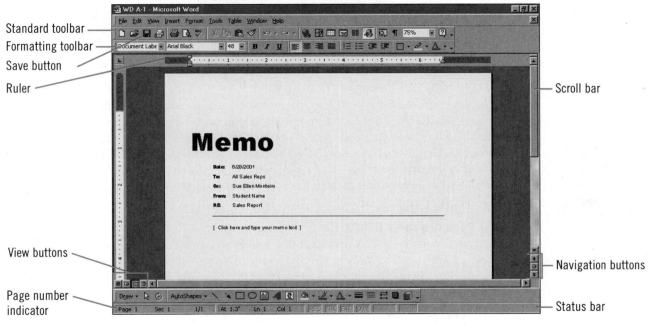

View buttons

Navigation buttons

Page number indicator

Status bar

TABLE A-1: Elements in Word document window

element	description
Standard toolbar	Contains buttons for frequently used commands
Formatting toolbar	Contains buttons for frequently used formatting commands
Ruler	Measures the body of the document in inches (can be changed to other units)
Scroll box	Use to display other parts of the document (also shows approximate position in the document)
View buttons	Used to display documents in different ways
Drawing toolbar	Contains buttons for inserting and modifying graphics in the document
Page number indicator	Indicates the current page and the total number of pages in the document
Navigation buttons	Use to move through the document one or more pages at a time (can be changed to move by specific text, graphics, and other objects)
Status bar	Displays information about the current document

Word 2000

Entering Text in a Document

The first step in creating a document is to **enter**, or type, the text that is the content of your document in the Word document window. ✦━━ You're ready to enter the text of the memo.

1. **Drag the vertical scroll box down so the word "Memo" is at the top of the screen, then position the mouse pointer anywhere in the document window**
The mouse pointer changes to Ĩ or Ĩ ☰. The mouse pointer changes shape depending on where it appears on-screen.

2. **Click anywhere in the text "Click here and type your memo text"**
"Click here and type your memo text" is a **placeholder** created by the Memo Wizard for the body of your memo, prompting you to enter appropriate information to complete the memo. When you click in the placeholder, the entire line becomes highlighted, or **selected**. See Figure A-4. Any text you enter automatically replaces selected text. Next you will enter the first two sentences in your memo. Watch the screen as you type.

3. **Type Greetings from the Seattle office!, press [Enter], then type I look forward to working with you throughout the summer!**
As soon as you started typing, the characters you typed replaced the placeholder text. The blinking, vertical line on the screen is the **insertion point**. The insertion point indicates where text will be inserted when you type, as opposed to the mouse pointer, which you use to click the various elements of the Word window (and to select text, move the insertion point, and other tasks). When you press [Enter], the insertion point moves down one line and to the left margin, just as a typewriter carriage does when you press the Return key.

Trouble?

The line wraps may not exactly match the figures in this book. Line wraps vary depending on the printer driver your particular machine uses.

4. **Press [Enter], then type the following, but do not press [Enter] when you reach the right edge of your screen**
The end of June is rapidly approaching, and I have been asked by Sue Ellen Monteiro, our sales manager, to remind you that your monthly reports are due next week.
At some point before the words "to remind you," the word you were typing jumped down, or wrapped to the next line on the screen. This is known as **word wrap**.

5. **Press [Enter], then continue typing the rest of the memo, making sure to type errors as shown (type "the" twice and don't correct the misspelled words)**
Please send them directly to me at the Seattle office. I have been hired as the the simmer intern for the Outdoor Designs Sales and Marketing group, and I will be recording your sales data and processing your commission chevks.
If you see red, wavy lines under the misspelled words on your screen, this indicates that automatic spell checking is on and these words have been flagged as possible misspellings. Green wavy lines indicate that automatic grammar checking is on.

6. **Click Tools on the menu bar, click Options, click to select the All checkbox under Formatting marks to select it, if necessary, then click OK**
Showing paragraph marks makes it easier to identify unintended spaces, paragraph returns, and other punctuation errors in a document. Dots appear between words to indicate spaces, and a ¶ appears at the end of paragraphs. Your screen should now look like Figure A-5.

7. **Click the Save button 🖫 on the Standard toolbar**

FIGURE A-4: Placeholder text selected

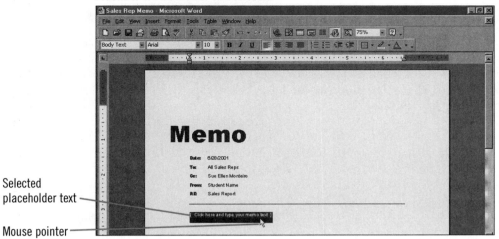

Selected placeholder text

Mouse pointer

FIGURE A-5: Screen after entering text

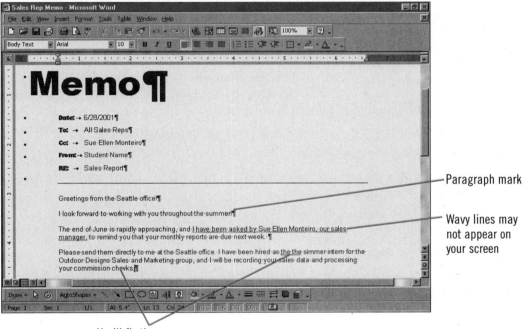

Paragraph mark

Wavy lines may not appear on your screen

You'll fix these errors

Using AutoCorrect

The AutoCorrect feature makes corrections to certain words as you type. For example, if you type "comapny" instead of "company," as soon as you press the [Spacebar] Word corrects the misspelling. You can turn AutoCorrect on and off and customize it in the AutoCorrect dialog box. To open this dialog box, click Tools on the menu bar, then click AutoCorrect. See Figure A-6. You can turn any of the options on or off by clicking the check boxes. If there is a word you mistype frequently, you can add it to the replacement list by typing it with the error in the Replace text box, then typing the correct version in the With text box.

FIGURE A-6: AutoCorrect dialog box

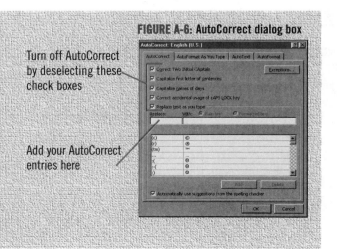

Turn off AutoCorrect by deselecting these check boxes

Add your AutoCorrect entries here

Word 2000

Editing a Document

After you enter text in a Word document, you can **edit**, or modify, the text in several ways. To delete individual letters, you can press [Backspace] or [Delete]. You can also select a block of unwanted text entirely, then press [Delete] to delete the selection or type new text to replace the selected text. As you read the letter, you decide to make some changes. First you will correct one of the misspellings.

Steps 1234

1. Press [↑], then press and hold [←] or [→] as long as necessary to position the insertion point between the letters **i** and **m** in the word **simmer**
The arrow keys are some of the keys you can press to move the insertion point around the document. Table A-2 describes these keys.

2. Press **[Backspace]**, then type **u**
When you pressed [Backspace], the "i" was deleted. Pressing [Backspace] deletes the character to the left of the insertion point. Pressing [Delete] deletes the character to the right of the insertion point. You can also move the insertion point around the document by positioning the mouse pointer and then clicking the left mouse button.

3. Click to the left of the letter **O** in Outdoor Designs
The insertion point blinks before the word "Outdoor."

QuickTip

To extend the selection only one character at a time, press only [Shift] while pressing the right or left arrow key.

4. Press and hold down **[Ctrl]** and **[Shift]** and press [→] twice to select the words Outdoor Designs and the blank space following them, then release the keys
"Outdoor Designs" is selected, as shown in Figure A-7.

5. Press **[Delete]**
The words "Outdoor Designs" are removed from the document. Notice that the text after the deleted words wraps back to fill the empty space.

6. Double-click the word **them** in the second line of the fourth paragraph
When you double-click a word, the entire word becomes selected.

7. Type **these**
The characters you type replace the selected text.

QuickTip

To undo just the most recent action more quickly, click the Undo button instead of the list arrow next to it.

8. Click the **list arrow** next to the **Undo button** 🔄 on the Standard toolbar, then click **Typing "these"** (the first entry in the list) as shown in Figure A-8
The replaced text reappears in the document exactly how and where it was before you changed it. You can select as many actions from the Undo list as you want; the most recent action is listed first.

9. Click the **Save button** 💾 on the Standard toolbar to save your changes

FIGURE A-7: Two words selected

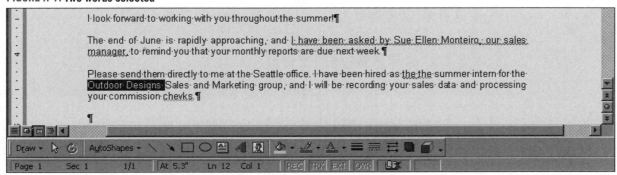

I·look·forward·to·working·with·you·throughout·the·summer!¶

The· end· of· June· is· rapidly· approaching,· and· I·have· been· asked· by· Sue·Ellen·Monteiro,· our·sales· manager,·to·remind·you·that·your·monthly·reports·are·due·next·week.¶

Please·send·them·directly·to·me·at·the·Seattle·office.·I·have·been·hired·as·the·the·summer·intern·for·the· Outdoor· Designs· Sales· and· Marketing· group,· and· I· will· be· recording· your· sales· data· and· processing· your·commission·chevks.¶

¶

Page 1   Sec 1   1/1   At 5.3"   Ln 12   Col 1   REC TRK EXT OVR   LEX

FIGURE A-8: Undo list

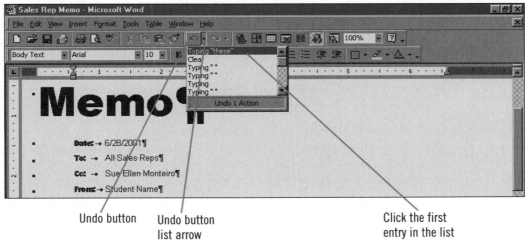

Undo button   Undo button list arrow   Click the first entry in the list

Using Click and Type

Click and Type is a feature that allows you to begin typing in almost any blank area of a document without pressing [Enter], [Tab], or [Spacebar] to move the insertion point to that location. Instead, you simply double-click where you want to begin typing. Click and Type is available only in Print Layout view and only in areas that do not contain a bulleted or numbered list, a left or right indent, a picture with text wrapping, or

multiple columns. To see if this feature is available, point to the area where you'd like to type; if the pointer changes to I≡ Click and Type is available and you can double-click to start typing there. To disable this feature (or to turn it on if it has been disabled), click Tools on the menu bar, click Options, click the Edit tab, then click the Enable click and type checkbox to deselect it (or to select it to turn this feature on).

TABLE A-2: Useful keys for moving the insertion point around a document

keyboard key	moves insertion point
[Backspace]	Back one space deleting previous character
[↑], [↓]	Up or down one line
[Ctrl] [←], [Ctrl] [→]	One word to the right or left
[Home]	To the beginning of the line
[End]	To the end of the line
[Ctrl][Home]	To the beginning of the document
[Ctrl][End]	To the end of the document

Word 2000

Moving Text in a Document

Sometimes you want to move text from one part of your document to another. The Cut and Paste commands make this easy. You can **cut** (remove) selected text from your document, place it on the **Windows Clipboard** (a temporary storage area), and then **paste** (insert) it in a new location. You can paste the same text as many times as you want without having to cut it again. You can also use a technique called **drag and drop**, in which you select the text you want to move, then use the mouse to drag it to a new location. You can **copy** (duplicate) text also, using methods similar to cutting. ◢ While checking your memo, you decide that you want to move the second paragraph to the end of the memo.

Steps 1234

1. **Position the mouse pointer to the left of the second paragraph so that it changes to ↗, then click**

   The entire line, including the paragraph mark, is selected. See Figure A-9. The area to the left of the margin is the **selection bar**. When the mouse pointer moves onto the selection bar, it changes to ↗, which you use to select entire lines.

QuickTip

To display a button that is not visible on a toolbar, click the More Buttons button » on the right side of the appropriate toolbar, then click the button you need. If the button you want is still not visible, click Add or Remove buttons, click the desired button, click outside the list, then click the button that was added to the toolbar.

2. **Click the Cut button ✄ on the Standard toolbar**

   The line is removed from the document and placed on the Clipboard. To cut selected text using the keyboard, press [Ctrl][X]; to copy selected text, press [Ctrl][C]; to paste text from the Clipboard, press [Ctrl][V].

3. **Click on the paragraph mark below the last paragraph, then click the Paste button 📋 on the Standard toolbar**

   The line of text is inserted from the Clipboard into the document at the new location. You can also use the Cut and Paste commands on the Edit menu to produce identical results. Note that pressing [Delete] or [Backspace] only deletes text; it does *not* place the text on the Clipboard.

4. **In the second paragraph, click to the left of Sue, then click and drag the mouse to the right to select Sue Ellen Monteiro and the comma and space after it**

QuickTip

To copy (rather than move text) using the drag and drop method, press and hold [Ctrl] while you are dragging.

5. **Position the mouse pointer over the selected text, and then click and drag the pointer after the word manager (and the comma), and just before the word to, then release the mouse button**

   As you drag, the pointer changes to ↖, and an indicator line shows you where the text will be pasted. See Figure A-10. The name is moved to the new location.

QuickTip

If the Clipboard toolbar opens, click its Close button to close it.

6. **In the third line of the second paragraph, select summer intern, then click the Copy button 📋 on the Standard toolbar**

   A copy of the selected text is placed on the Clipboard.

7. **Click after Student Name in the From line, type , (a comma), then press [Spacebar]**

8. **Click 📋**

   The words "summer intern" are pasted in the document from the Clipboard.

FIGURE A-9: Line of text selected

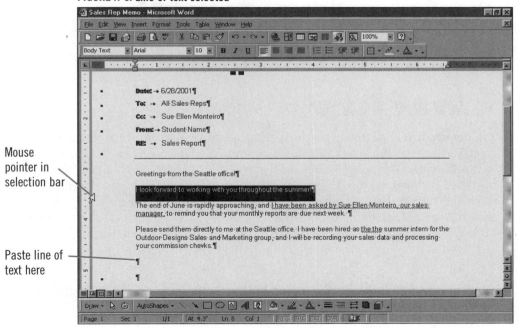

Mouse pointer in selection bar

Paste line of text here

FIGURE A-10: Dragging text

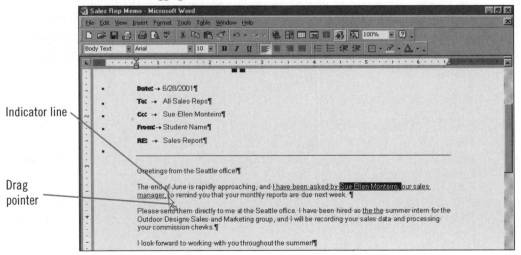

Indicator line

Drag pointer

Using the Office Clipboard

If you need to cut or copy multiple items before you're ready to paste them, you can use the Office Clipboard to store them. The Office Clipboard can hold up to 12 items at once and is accessible from any Office program, making it easy to paste multiple items among multiple documents throughout Office programs. To use the Office Clipboard, open the Office Clipboard toolbar by clicking View on the menu bar, pointing to Toolbars, then clicking Clipboard (if you cut or copy a selection, then cut or copy a second selection without pasting the first, the Office Clipboard toolbar opens automatically). Point to any item on the Clipboard toolbar to see a ScreenTip that displays the contents of the selection. Click any item to paste it at the insertion point. The Windows Clipboard works like the Office Clipboard, except that it can hold only one selection at a time; when you cut or copy a selection, then cut or copy another selection without pasting the first, the first selection is cleared and the second is stored on the Clipboard. This means that when you cut or copy a selection of multiple items to the Office Clipboard, the last item is the one copied to the Windows Clipboard. When you clear all items from the Office Clipboard, the Windows Clipboard is also cleared.

Using the Spelling and Grammar Checker

You can check your document for words that are misspelled, incorrectly hyphenated, incorrectly capitalized, repeated (such as "the the"), or not in the Word standard dictionary. When you run the Spelling and Grammar Checker and it encounters one of these words, the word is selected and suggested spellings are listed. You can also check for some grammatical errors such as passive voice and subject-verb agreement. Note that you should not rely on any spelling or grammar checker to ensure that your documents are error-free; always proofread your documents carefully, before printing. ✎ You decide to check the spelling and grammar in your letter.

Steps

QuickTip

You can add your own words to AutoCorrect at any time by clicking Tools on the menu bar, clicking AutoCorrect, then clicking the AutoCorrect tab.

1. Click the **Spelling and Grammar button** 📝 on the Standard toolbar, then ensure that the **Check grammar check box** is selected

The spelling and grammar check starts at the insertion point. The first possible error identified is Sue Ellen's last name, Monteiro, in the second paragraph. See Figure A-11. This is not an error. You need to choose one of the buttons in the dialog box. You can accept the suggested spelling if one is offered by clicking Change or Change All (if more than one spelling is suggested, first highlight the spelling you want to use), you can ignore the error by clicking Ignore or Ignore All, you can add the word to the dictionary so that Word no longer flags it as an error by clicking Add, and you can highlight a correction and then add the entry to AutoCorrect, a feature that corrects misspellings as you type. Table A-3 explains the buttons in the dialog box.

QuickTip

If you did not type the intentional errors as instructed in the Entering Text in a Document lesson, or if you made unintentional errors, follow the prompts in the dialog box, correcting errors as appropriate; then skip to Step 6.

2. Click **Ignore All**

The Spelling Checker will skip this word every time it appears in the document. The next error identified is a possible grammatical error. See Figure A-12. An alternative construction is suggested for the phrase in the passive voice in the second paragraph.

3. Click **Change**

The sentence is changed in the document, and the next possible error is identified. The word "the" appears twice in a row.

4. Click **Delete**

The next error is the misspelled word "chevks." This word is misspelled, so you want to change it. You will choose one of the words in the list of suggestions. If the correct spelling did not appear in the list of suggestions, you would correct the spelling by typing it in the top section of the dialog box.

5. Click **checks** in the list of suggestions if necessary, then click **Change**

6. Click **OK** in the message box indicating that the spelling and grammar check is complete

The message box closes.

FIGURE A-11: Possible spelling error identified

Possible error identified here →

Suggested spellings listed here →

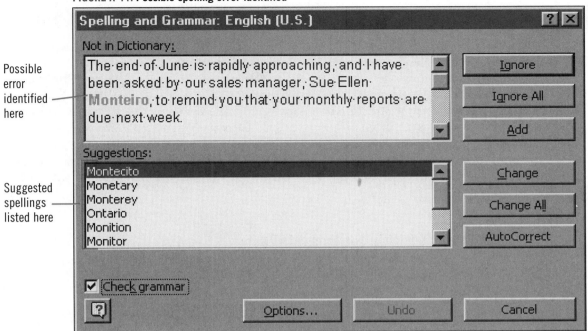

FIGURE A-12: Possible grammatical error identified

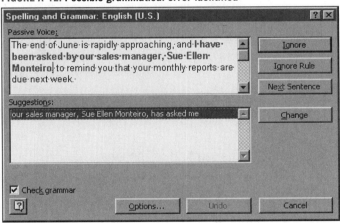

TABLE A-3: Buttons in the Spelling and Grammar dialog box

button	action
Ignore	Skips this instance of the word
Ignore All	Skips all instances of this word in the current document
Add	Adds the word to the standard dictionary so it is not marked as a possible error in other documents
Change	Changes this instance of the word to the selected suggestion
Change All	Changes all instances of the word in the current document to the selected suggestion
AutoCorrect	Adds the misspelled word and the corrected spelling to the AutoCorrect list

Word 2000

Viewing a Document

While you work on a document you can look at it in several views. **Normal view** shows a document with only some page elements visible, and not always where and how they'll be printed; **Web Layout view** shows how the document will look if you save it as a Web page; **Print Layout view** shows all page elements, including margins, and where and how they'll be printed; **Outline view** shows the structure of a document in selected levels. **Print Preview** shows the document exactly as it will appear on the printed page, so that you can easily check page margins and your document's overall appearance. In any view, you can change the zoom to increase or shrink your view of the document. Before you print the memo, you want to make sure it looks exactly like you want. You're currently viewing the memo in Print Layout view.

Steps 1 2 3 4

1. Click **View** on the menu bar, then click **Zoom**

The Zoom dialog box opens and should look similar to Figure A-13. The current zoom is 100%.

2. Click the **Page width option button**

The Preview box changes to reflect the new zoom. Now the document fits width-wise on the screen so you don't have to scroll horizontally to see any of the page.

3. Click **OK**

The document window changes to show the document so that you can see the left and right margins without scrolling.

QuickTip

The One Page 🔲 and Multiple Pages 🔳 buttons on the Print Preview toolbar change the view so that you can see up to 24 pages of a document at a time.

▶ **4.** Click the **Print Preview button** 🔍 on the Standard toolbar

The Print Preview window opens, showing the memo as it will appear when printed. See Figure A-14. The Print Preview toolbar is at the top of the window. In Print Preview, you can use the mouse pointer (rather than the Zoom command) to zoom in on your document.

5. Move the mouse pointer over the document page

The pointer changes to ⊕, which you use to zoom in to examine parts of your letter more closely in Print Preview.

6. Click anywhere in the top half of the memo

The document enlarges to 100% in the Print Preview window, and the pointer changes to ⊖.

7. Click the Magnifier button 🔍 on the toolbar

8. Select the text **Student Name** and replace it with your name, then click 🔍 again

9. Click on the memo again to return the document to the smaller view, then click **Close** on the Print Preview toolbar

FIGURE A-13: Zoom dialog box

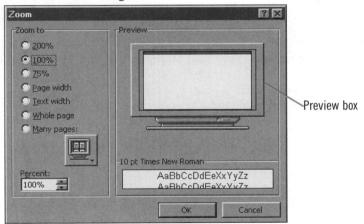

Preview box

FIGURE A-14: Print Preview window

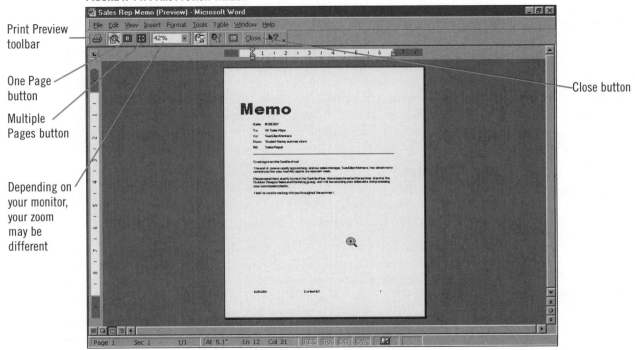

Print Preview toolbar

One Page button

Multiple Pages button

Depending on your monitor, your zoom may be different

Close button

Using the View buttons

The four view buttons to the left of the horizontal scroll bar correspond to four commands on the View menu. You can use these buttons to quickly change the way your document is displayed. Clicking the Normal View button ▤ displays the document without showing the margins, headers, footers, and columns. It is useful for quickly entering and editing text. Clicking the Web Page Layout View button 🖼 displays the document as it would appear if saved as a Web page (to be viewed in a Web browser), with document headings (if any) on the left, and the text of the document in a window on the right. Clicking the Print Layout View button 🗐 opens Print Layout View. This view is similar to Print Preview—it shows the actual page you're working on, including margins, headers, footers, columns, and graphical elements (such as Clip Art, WordArt, and text boxes). You typed the sales memo in Print Layout View. Clicking the Outline View button 🗒 displays the headings in a document so that you can see the flow of ideas and reorganize the document easily. You can collapse the headings to view only the main headings, or any level you choose.

Word 2000

Printing a Document

After you preview your document with Print Preview, you can print it with the Print command. Ask your instructor or technical support person for specific instructions on how to print using your classroom printer. ◢◣◣ The completed memo is ready to print. After you print it, you're finished working for the day and can close the document and exit Word.

Steps

1. Take a moment to verify that your printer is turned on, and is properly connected to your computer

2. Click **File** on the menu bar, then click **Print**
   The Print dialog box shown in Figure A-15 opens. The Print dialog box lets you specify many things related to printing, such as the range of pages you want to print (if you don't want to print an entire document), the number of copies you want to print, and print scaling (which you use to fit your document on a specified number of pages). You can also configure the settings of the default printer by clicking the Properties button and changing the settings in the Properties dialog box. Figure A-15 shows the default printer as a Canon Bubble-Jet BJ-200 connected to the LPT1 printer port. Your system's default printer is probably different.

QuickTip

You can print a document on fewer sheets of paper (for example, a four-page document on 2 pages per sheet) by clicking the Pages per sheet list arrow in the Print dialog box, then clicking the number of pages you want to fit on each sheet. Word adjusts the scaling for this print job without changing the document's formatting.

3. Click **Properties**
   The Properties dialog box for your printer opens. Here you can change paper size, orientation, graphics resolution, and other special options your printer supports. Your instructor will tell you if you need to adjust any settings.

4. Click **OK** to close the Properties dialog box, then click **OK** to print the memo
   The Print dialog box closes, and after a few moments the completed letter emerges from your printer. Congratulations! You've completed your first word processing session and your first assignment at Outdoor Designs. Compare your letter to Figure A-16.

QuickTip

To print the document without having to open the Print dialog box, click the Print button 🖨 on the Standard toolbar. This will print the document directly, with whatever the current settings are in the Print dialog box.

5. Click the **Save button** 💾 on the Standard toolbar to save your changes

6. Click **File** on the menu bar, then click **Exit**
   The memo document and the Word program close.

FIGURE A-15: Print dialog box

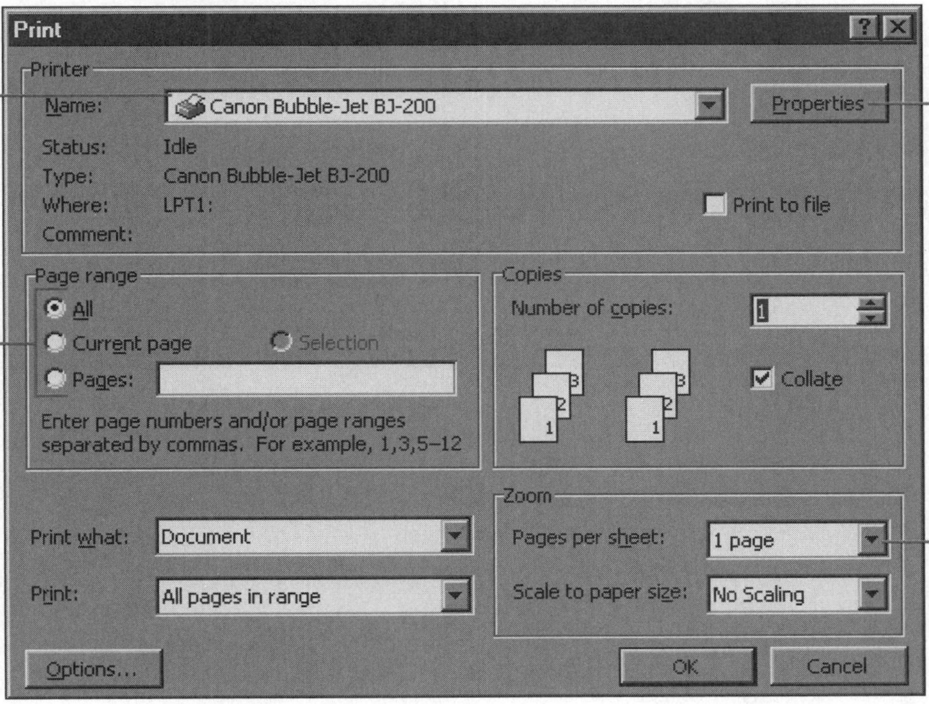

Your printer will probably be different

Click here to display your printer's properties

Choose the page range here

Change the print scaling here

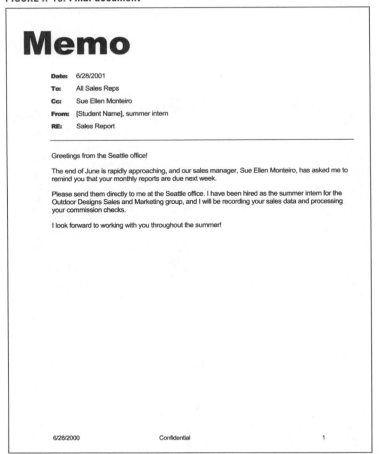

FIGURE A-16: Final document

Word 2000

Practice

► Concepts Review

Label the Word window elements shown in Figure A-17.

(handwritten) new blank doc.

FIGURE A-17

(handwritten) 7 paste

(handwritten) doc. label

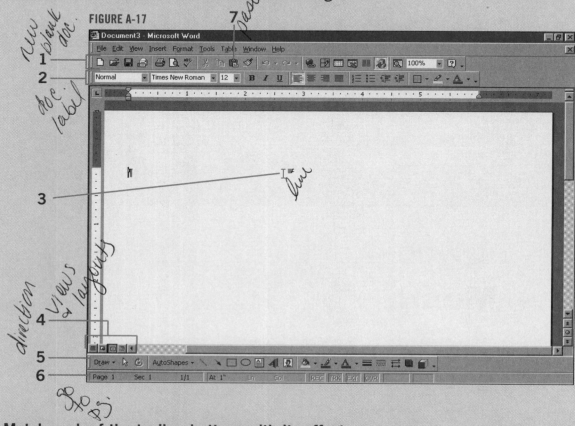

(handwritten) direction — views & layouts

1
2
3
4
5
6

(handwritten) 880 ps;

Match each of the toolbar buttons with its effect.

8. ▣ *B*
9. ▣ *C*
10. ▣ *E D A*
11. ▣ *D A*
12. ▣ *A*

a. Saves the current document to disk
b. Displays the document in Print Preview
c. Copies the selected text to the Clipboard
d. Cuts the selected text and places it on the Windows Clipboard
e. Checks the spelling and grammar in the document

Select the best answer from the list of choices.

13. **The Click and Type feature allows you to begin typing almost anywhere in a document without:**
    a. Starting Word
    b. Pressing any keys
    c. Moving the mouse to the desired location
    d. Moving the insertion point to the desired location

14. **Which keyboard key moves the insertion point to the end of the current line in a document?**
    a. [Page Up]
    b. [Page Down]
    c. [Home]
    d. [End]

15. **Which of these techniques cannot be used to move text from one location to another in Word?**
    a. The [Del] and [Ins] keys
    b. Cut and Paste commands on the Edit menu
    c. The drag and drop technique
    d. The Cut and Paste buttons on the toolbar

16. **What is the purpose of the magnifying glass mouse pointer ⊕ in Print Preview?**
    a. Adding page numbers to the document
    b. Printing the document
    c. Magnifying the page
    d. Speeding the editing process

17. **What is the purpose of the Add button in the Spelling dialog box?**
    a. Adds a corrected word to the document
    b. Adds a word to your personal dictionary
    c. Adds a synonym to the Thesaurus
    d. Activates the Always suggest check box

18. **Which view is most useful for viewing and editing text in a document?**
    a. Normal view
    b. Screen view
    c. Page width view
    d. Print view

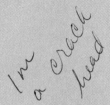

▶ Skills Review

1. **Open a file and save it with a new name.**
   a. Start Microsoft Word.
   b. Click the Open button ☞ on the Standard toolbar.
   c. Click the Look in list arrow, click the drive that contains your Project Files, then if necessary, double-click the folder containing your Project Files.
   d. Double-click WD A-2 to open the document.
   e. Click File on the menu bar, click Save As, make sure the drive and folder where you want to save your files is listed in the Save in list box, double-click in the File name text box to select the current filename if necessary, type "Welcome" in the File name text box, then click Save.
   f. Identify as many elements in the document window as you can without referring to the lesson.

2. **Enter text in a document.**
   a. If paragraph marks are not visible, click Tools on the menu bar, click Options, click the View tab and then click to select the All check box under Formatting marks.
   b. Move the insertion point to the paragraph marker in the blank line following the first paragraph in the body of the letter.
   c. Type the following text: "Before you submit your report, make sure you have included a list of stores you visited this past month and how many square feet each store has devoted to merchandise. Also include a few words about any new businesses that have opened in your territory."
   d. Using the arrow keys, move the insertion point to the end of the document.
   e. Select the text "Your Name" below the closing, then type your name.
   f. Click the Save button 🖫 on the Standard toolbar.

3. **Edit a document.**
   a. Use the arrow keys to move the insertion point to the paragraph you inserted and locate any misspelled words.
   b. Use [Backspace] or [Delete] to delete the mistakes, then type the corrections.
   c. Use the mouse to select the phrase "have been hired as" in the first paragraph.
   d. Type the word "am" so the sentence begins "I am the summer intern."
   e. Using the keyboard, select the phrase "a few words" in the second paragraph.
   f. Delete the selected phrase.
   g. Click the Undo button ↺ on the Standard toolbar.
   h. Save your changes.

4. **Move text in a document.**
   a. Position the insertion point at the beginning of the sentence "Welcome to the company!" in the beginning of the third paragraph, press and hold [Ctrl][Shift], and then press [→] five times to select the sentence.
   b. Press [Ctrl][X] to place the selected text on the Clipboard.
   c. Position the insertion point in the empty paragraph below the salutation "Dear Luisa."
   d. Press [Ctrl][V] to paste the sentence from the Clipboard so it is the first sentence of the letter.
   e. Position the mouse pointer in front of the "S" in "Sales and Marketing group" in the first paragraph, then drag the mouse pointer over the phrase to select it. (Do not select the comma.)
   f. Click Edit on the menu bar, then click Copy. (If the Clipboard toolbar appears, click its Close button to close it.)

g. Move the insertion point to the end of the document so it is after the name "Sue Ellen Monteiro" in the cc: line.

h. Type a comma and a space, click Edit on the menu bar, then click Paste to paste the text after the space.

i. Select the word "rapidly" in the second paragraph.

j. Drag the text so it follows the word "approaching."

k. Save your changes.

5. Use the Spelling and Grammar Checker.

a. If necessary, scroll left until you can see the left margin of the second paragraph.

b. Move the mouse pointer onto the selection bar to change the insertion pointer to the line pointer.

c. Select the entire second paragraph by dragging the line pointer over all lines in the paragraph.

d. Click the Spelling and Grammar Checker button on the Standard toolbar.

e. Correct any errors.

f. Click Yes to check the spelling in the rest of the document.

g. Close the message box that opens when the spelling and grammar check is complete.

h. Save your changes.

6. View a document.

a. Click the Print Preview button on the Standard toolbar.

b. Click the magnifying glass pointer on the second paragraph, and examine that paragraph.

c. Click Close on the Print Preview toolbar to return the document to Normal view.

d. Scroll to the top of the document; notice that the margins are not visible on the page.

e. Click the Print Layout View button to the left of the horizontal scroll bar to switch to Print Layout view.

f. Click View on the menu bar, then click Zoom.

g. Double-click in the Percent text box, type "70", click OK; then examine the layout of the letter.

h. Click View on the menu bar, click Zoom, click the 200% option button, then click OK.

i. Switch the document to Page Width zoom.

7. Print a document.

a. Save any changes you made to the letter.

b. Verify that your printer is on and is properly connected to your computer.

c. Click File on the menu bar, then click Print.

d. Click Properties, and examine your printer's settings.

e. Click the Number of copies up spin arrow once to change the number of copies to 2.

f. Click OK.

g. Click the Close button in the document window to close the document.

h. Click the Close button in the program window to exit Word.

▶ Independent Challenges

1. You're in charge of organizing a sales conference for the sales department of Wacky Words, a company that produces comic greeting cards. You need to prepare a letter welcoming the sales department and field sales representatives to the semi-annual Wacky Words Sales Conference on August 16. The conference will take place in Orange, New Jersey, at the Bosco Convention Center, from 10:00 a.m. until 5:00 p.m. Afterward, there will be an awards ceremony and banquet, featuring speaker Pierre Maury, a noted French cartoonist, who frequently contributes art to Wacky Words. The president of the company has asked that attendees confirm their travel plans with you within the next three weeks.

To complete this independent challenge:

a. Open the file WD A-3, and save it as "Sales Conference Letter."

b. Remove the destination name and address so one copy can be sent to all conference attendees.

c. Delete the placeholder text "SUBJECT OF THE LETTER IN UPPERCASE," then type the subject of your letter in uppercase.

d. Delete the placeholder text "START TYPING YOUR LETTER HERE," then write a short letter inviting everyone to the conference; include all information listed in the paragraph describing this exercise. Make sure you tell them to confirm their travel plans with you.

e. At the bottom of the page, delete the placeholder text "YOUR NAME GOES HERE," and replace it with your name in uppercase.

f. After you enter all the text, check the spelling and grammar.

g. Save your changes.

h. Use Print Preview to see how the printed letter will look. When you're satisfied, print a copy, and sign it beneath your name.

2. You provide office help to Joel Rubin, who runs a small steakhouse in Austin, Texas. He wants to attend a trade show displaying the latest in grill pits, smoke ventilators, and other equipment he uses in his restaurant. He asked you to write a letter of inquiry to the coordinator of the trade show, which is held each fall in Denver, Colorado. He wants you to find out when the trade show is, the cost of admission, how many people attend, and who the typical exhibitors are. In addition, he wants you to request any general literature distributed for the show, such as hotel information, past experiences, airline discounts, and so on. The letter should use the company letterhead and fit on one page.

To complete this independent challenge:

a. Open the file WD A-4, and save it as "Denver Show Inquiry."

b. Address the letter to the trade show coordinator: Maria Burgos, Grills and More Trade Show Coordinator, 4433 High Bluff Road, Denver, CO 80201. Remember to delete the placeholder text.

c. Write a short letter to the trade show coordinator, asking Joel's questions as listed in the paragraph describing this exercise.

d. Check the spelling and grammar.

e. Save your changes.

f. Use Print Preview to see how the printed letter will look. When you're satisfied, print a copy of the letter.

3. The Literary Loft, a small bookstore, plans to start selling gift certificates. Kristine Moscallo, the owner, has asked you to send a letter to an advertising agency containing information about the gift certificates so that they can create a flyer to publicize the new policy.

To complete this independent challenge:

a. Start Word and open a new, blank document.

b. Insert fictional addresses at the top of the letter, the date, and an appropriate salutation.

c. Write the body of the letter using the information provided in the paragraph describing this exercise. Use fictitious information for the following items: the amounts the certificates will be available in; the length of time the certificates will be valid; and the policy on whether a lost certificate can be replaced.

d. Check the spelling and grammar in your letter.

e. Save the file as "Gift Certificates."

f. Use Print Preview to verify the layout of the letter.

g. Print the letter.

4. You are a sales representative for a wholesale pet supply store, Stuff for Pets. This morning, you received a letter from Seth Lightfoot, owner of a small pet store in Livingston, Montana. Seth wants the Stuff for Pets product catalog and an opportunity to talk with a sales representative about prices of gourmet cat and dog foods. You need to compose a letter to Seth telling him briefly about your products and prices. You also need to show him how your prices are competitive. You will get information on your competition from the World Wide Web (WWW).

To complete this independent challenge:

a. Start Word, click File on the menu bar, then click New.

b. Click the Letters and Faxes tab, then double-click the Elegant Letter icon to open a new document based on this template.

c. Click the company name placeholder, then type "Stuff for Pets."

d. Scroll to the bottom of the page, click each of the placeholders in turn, and enter a fictional address, phone, and fax number.

e. Replace the recipient address placeholder with Seth Lightfoot's name and the following address: 7788 Sawmill Gulch Road, Livingston, Montana, 59047.

f. Replace "Sir or Madam" in the salutation with "Mr. Lightfoot".

g. Select the two lines acting as a placeholder in the body of the letter (but not the paragraph mark), delete them, then type your letter using the information listed in the paragraph describing this exercise.

h. Log on to the Internet, and use your browser to go to http://www.course.com. From there, click the link Student Online Companions, click the link for this textbook, then click the Word link for Unit A. Use the links there as a starting point to find information about other companies' gourmet pet foods. You can also use any search engine to find information about other companies. Make sure your prices are competitive. Add information about competitors' prices (as presented in the Web pages you found) to your letter.

i. Add your name and job title at the end of the letter.

j. Check the spelling and grammar of this letter.

k. Save the letter as "Montana Sales Letter."

l. Preview, then print the document.

Visual Workshop

Use the Memo Wizard to create the document shown in Figure A-18. When you finish, save it as "Client Followup," and print the letter.

FIGURE A-18

MEMORANDUM

DATE:	5/15/2001
TO:	ALL SALES REPS
CC:	SUE ELLEN MONTEIRO
FROM:	DONELLE FRANKLIN, SALES MANAGER
RE:	FOLLOWING UP ON SALES CALLS

All sales reps need to be much more vigilant about following up on sales calls with a letter. In the letter, thank the client for taking time of his or her busy schedule to talk to you. Next, you should reap you conversation and include any information you said you would get for the client.

If you have any questions, call me at the Seattle office, x3027.

Enhancing

a Document

Objectives

- ► **Change font type and size**
- ► **Change font style**
- ► **Change alignment**
- ► **Change margin settings**
- ► **Use the ruler**
- ► **Apply and modify styles**
- ► **Insert manual page breaks**
- ► **Replace text**

In addition to letters and memos, you can use Word to prepare brochures, flyers, and newsletters. To make these documents effective, you can use Word to **format**, or enhance, the way the document looks. In this unit, you will use several methods to change the way characters and paragraphs look. You will also learn how to control where pages begin and end in a multiple-page document. ✎— Derek Hofbauer, marketing manager for Outdoor Designs, gives you a product information sheet on the Cascade Ski Pack the company's newest product, and asks you to format it so that it is readable and attractive. Sales representatives will refer to the product information sheet to promote the ski sack when they call stores that carry their products. The more clearly the sheet is formatted, the easier it will be for the sales representatives to find information when they need it.

Changing Font Type and Size

A **font type** is a set of characters in a particular design. **Font size** refers to the size of the characters in a font. The unit for measuring font size is points. A **point** is ½ of an inch; for example, so the common font size of 12 is ⅙ of an inch tall. When you change the way characters look, you change the **font style**. Table B-1 shows some examples of font types with varying font sizes and font styles. You can access many commands related to fonts from the Formatting toolbar. To format characters, you select them first. ➤ After you open the product information sheet, you see that all text is the same font type (Times New Roman) and size (12-point). First you decide to change the title's font type and increase the size so it stands out from the rest of the document.

Steps

1. Start Word, then click the **Open button** 📂 on the Standard toolbar
   The Open dialog box opens.

2. In the **Look in list box**, select the drive that contains your Project Disk, double-click the name of the folder containing your Project Files if necessary, then double-click **WD B-1**
   The unformatted product information sheet opens in Normal view.

3. Click **File** on the menu bar, click **Save As**, type **Ski Sack Sheet** in the File name text box, then click **Save**
   Word saves a copy of the file with a new name in the same location as your other Project Files.

4. Select **Outdoor Designs** and **New Product Information Sheet**, the first two lines of the Ski Sack Sheet document
   The lines are selected; now you can format them. See Figure B-1.

5. Click the **Font list arrow** on the Formatting toolbar, then click **Arial** (you may have to scroll the list to find this)
   The selected text changes to the Arial font type; Arial appears in the Font list box and will remain there as long as the insertion point remains in any text with the Arial font type.

6. Click the **Font Size list arrow** on the Formatting toolbar, then click **18**
   The font size of the selected text increases to 18, and 18 appears in the Font Size list box.

7. Click anywhere in the document window to deselect the text
   See Figure B-2. Depending on where you clicked to deselect the text, the Font and Font Size list boxes may display different information than what is shown in the figure.

8. Click the **Save button** 💾 on the Standard toolbar to save your changes

TABLE B-1: Font type, size, and style samples

font formats	samples
Type	Arial, Courier, Times New Roman, **Impact**
Size	eight point, twelve point, fourteen point, eighteen point
Style	**Bold**, *italic*, underline

FIGURE B-1: Text selected

Selected text formatted as 12-point Times New Roman

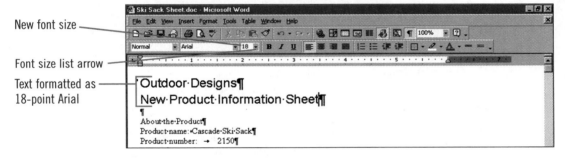

FIGURE B-2: Selected text formatted with 18-point Arial

New font size

Font size list arrow

Text formatted as 18-point Arial

Understanding fonts

Font creation, or **fontography**, is an old business. In ancient times, scribes concerned with the uniformity of letters and symbols wrote in standard forms so future generations could easily understand their writing. Some of today's fonts are descended from these earlier type styles; other type styles were developed in modern times.

Before you can use fonts on a computer, they must be installed. The Windows operating system comes with several **TrueType fonts**, such as Arial and Times New Roman. TrueType fonts look the same on your screen as they do on your printed page. The symbol **TT** that appears in the Font list identifies which fonts are TrueType fonts. Your system might include other fonts supplied by the manufacturer of your printer or another company. Ask your instructor or technical support person for a list of fonts on your system, or click the Font list arrow on the Formatting toolbar and scroll through the list to see for yourself.

Word 2000

Changing Font Style

In many documents, you'll want to emphasize certain words, phrases, or lines of text to show readers their importance. To add emphasis, you can use font styles, such as **bold** (darker type), *italics* (slanted type), and <u>underlining</u>. Use these styles selectively. Too much emphasis has the same effect as too little emphasis—nothing stands out. ▰ You've just made the title of the product information sheet stand out from the rest of the document by changing the font type and size. Now you decide to change the font style to make it even more distinctive. Also, the document includes two magazine names, which you'll italicize to indicate that they're publication titles.

Steps

1. Select the first two lines of the Ski Sack Sheet document

2. Click the **Bold button** **B** on the Formatting toolbar, and then press [←] to deselect the text
   The Bold button appears indented and the selected text is formatted as bold. See Figure B-3.

3. Select the first two lines of the document again, then click the **Italic button** **I** on the Formatting toolbar
   The selected text is now formatted as bold *and* italic.

QuickTip

You can also use the keyboard shortcuts [Ctrl][B], [Ctrl][I], and [Ctrl][U] to format selected text in boldface, italic, and underline, respectively.

4. Click the **Underline button** **U** on the Formatting toolbar, then press [←]
   The first two lines are now underlined, in addition to being bold and italicized.

5. Click the **Undo button** ↺ on the Standard toolbar
   Word removes the underlining from the first two lines of the document, and the Underline button is no longer indented.

6. Click the **down scroll arrow** until the line starting with the word **"Advertising"** is visible, select the words **Profitable Craft Merchandising**, then click **I**

7. Italicize the other magazine title, **Outside Magazine**, and then deselect the text
   See Figure B-4.

8. Save your changes

FIGURE B-3: Formatted product sheet title

Bold button
(toggle on)

Underline
button
(toggle off)

Italic button
(toggle off)

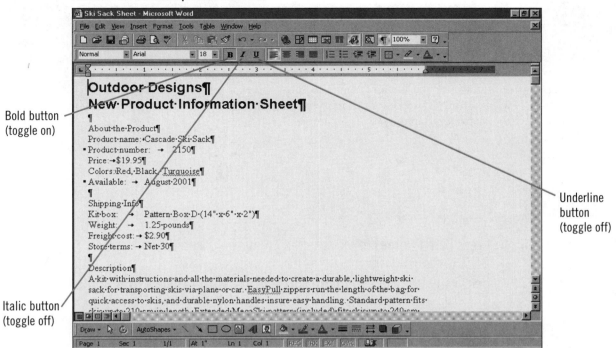

FIGURE B-4: Font style changes in product sheet

Formatting
toolbar always
shows formatting
at location of
insertion point,
so it may not
reflect the last
text you formatted

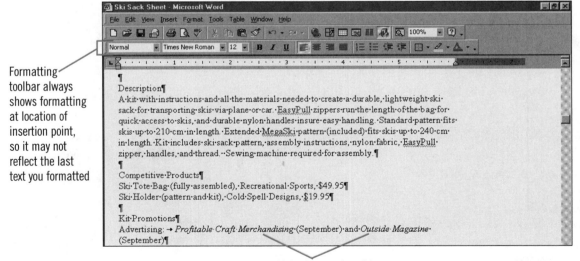

Italicized magazine titles

Changing Alignment

You can change the **alignment**, or position of text in relation to a document's margins, with the alignment buttons on the toolbar. For example, titles are often centered, headings left-aligned, and paragraphs justified (aligned equally between the left and right margins). The product information sheet contains lots of important information that is all aligned along the left margin. You decide to change the alignment of the different types of information to make the document look more professional.

Steps

1. **Press [Ctrl][Home] to move to the top of the document**
   The insertion point moves to the top of the document.

2. **Select the title lines, Outdoor Designs and New Product Information Sheet**
   The first two lines (formatted with Arial, bold, and italic) are selected.

3. **Click the Center button ▤ on the Formatting toolbar**
   The text is centered between the two margins. See Figure B-6.

4. **Scroll down until you see the paragraph under the heading "Description," then click anywhere in the paragraph**
   Although you need to select text to change character formats such as font size or font style, you can change most paragraph formatting, such as alignment, just by positioning the insertion point anywhere in the paragraph.

5. **Click the Justify button ▤ on the Formatting toolbar**
   The Description paragraph's alignment changes to justified. See Figure B-7. Notice that the paragraph is aligned at both margins. When you select Justified alignment, Word adds or reduces the space between each word so that the text is aligned along both the right and left margins. This is different from centering text, which does not adjust spacing but merely places the text equally between the margins.

6. **Click the Save button ▣ on the Standard toolbar to save your changes**

CLUES TO USE

Changing line spacing

Word's default **line spacing**, or distance between lines, is one line, or **single spaced**. You can adjust line spacing in a paragraph, in multiple paragraphs, or in an entire document by using the Indents and Spacing tab in the Paragraph dialog box, shown in Figure B-5. For example, to double-space a single paragraph, click anywhere within the paragraph, click Format on the menu bar, click Paragraph, click the Line spacing list arrow, click Double, then click OK. You can also use the Indents and Spacing tab to set spacing before and after paragraphs so that, for example, you don't have to press [ENTER] twice after a paragraph to have space between it and the following paragraph.

FIGURE B-5: Margin tab in Page Setup dialog box

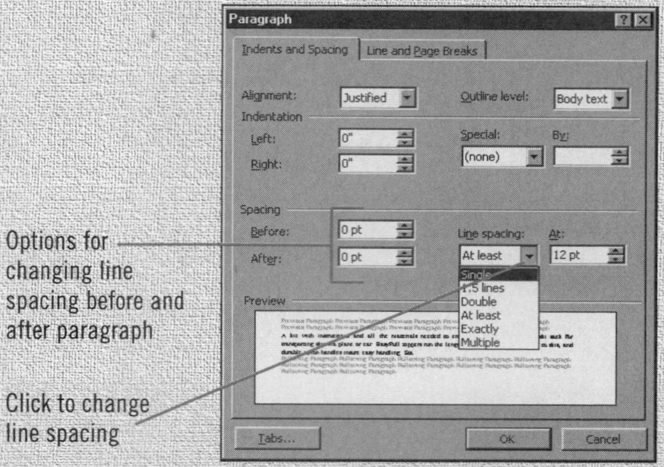

Options for changing line spacing before and after paragraph

Click to change line spacing

FIGURE B-6: Title centered

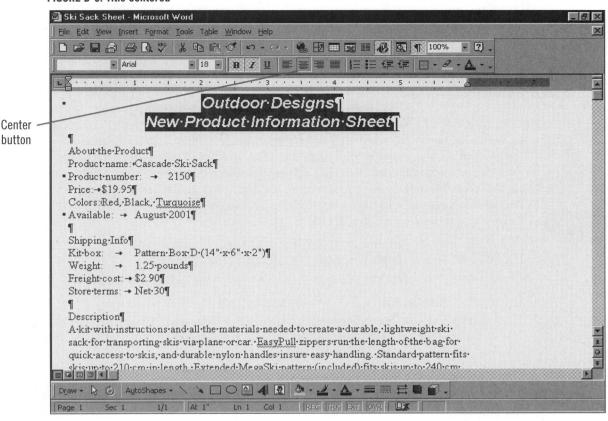

Center button

FIGURE B-7: Justified product description paragraph

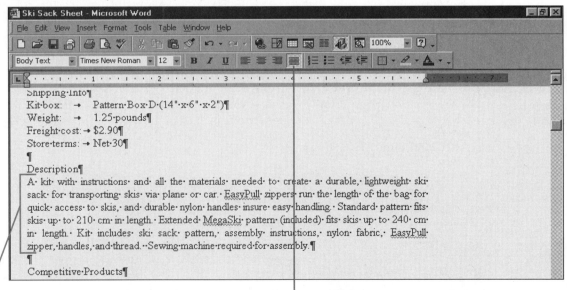

Justified alignment forces increased space between words to distribute text evenly between margins

Justify button

Changing Margin Settings

Word sets default page margins at one inch from the top and bottom of the page, and 1.25" from the left and right sides of the page. You can change the margin settings in Page Layout view, in Print Preview, or any view using the Page Setup dialog box. When you change the margins, Word automatically adjusts line wrapping and **repaginates** (renumbers) your document. To evaluate what margin settings to use in a specific document, switch to Page Layout view or Print Preview to see the actual margins on the page. ⟍⟍⟍ The margins on the Ski Sack product information sheet are the default margins. Outdoor Designs' style guidelines indicate that all product information sheets should have one-inch margins around the whole document. You need to change the margins on your document.

Steps

1. Click **File** on the menu bar, then click **Page Setup**
   The Page Setup dialog box opens with options for changing page formatting. See Table B-2.

2. Click the **Margins tab** if it is not already in front
   See Figure B-8. The Margins tab contains margin text boxes, a Preview box, two command buttons, and a Default button (to restore default settings). The first text box, Top, is currently selected.

3. Press **[Tab]** twice
   The Left text box is selected. Pressing [Tab] moves the insertion point from one text box to the next.

QuickTip

For mechanical reasons, most printers require at least a ¼" margin around the page.

4. Type **1** in the Left text box, then press **[Tab]**
   The Left text box shows 1 and the Right text box is selected. The inch symbol is added when you close the Page Setup dialog box. The Preview box shows the new left margin.

5. Type **1** in the Right text box, then click **OK**
   The Page Setup dialog box closes, and the left and right margins in the product information sheet change to one inch.

QuickTip

To see the margins, you must be in Print Layout view or Print Preview.

6. Click the **Print Layout View button** ▣ to the left of the horizontal scroll bar
   The view switches to Print Layout, and you can see the document margins. Use the ruler to verify that the left and right margins are one inch from the edges of the page. See Figure B-9.

7. Save your changes

TABLE B-2: Options in the Page Setup dialog box

tab	use to...
Margins	Set top, bottom, left, and right margins; set mirror margins (for binding a document); print on two pages per sheet; set gutter position (space between margin and inside edge of paper in a mirror margin document); apply settings to whole document, selected text, or insertion point forward
Paper size	Set paper size; change orientation (**portrait** prints down longer size of paper; **landscape** prints along width); apply settings to whole document or insertion point forward
Paper Source	Set printer tray location of first page (use if using different paper stock for first page) and following pages in a document; apply settings to whole document or insertion point forward
Layout	Set how new sections begin (as new page or continuous in document); change vertical alignment (as opposed to horizontal alignment); set line numbering; add page borders; apply settings to whole document or insertion point forward

FIGURE B-8: Margins tab in Page Setup dialog box

Set margins here ——

Preview box

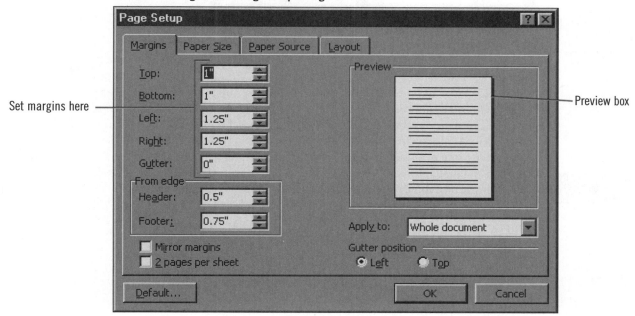

FIGURE B-9: Document in Print Layout view

1-inch margins

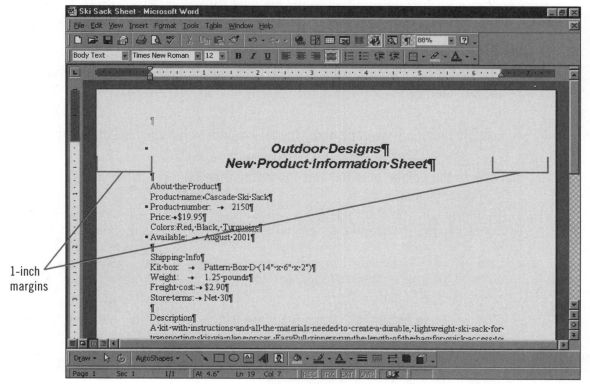

Word 2000

Using the Ruler

Tabs and indents are two important tools for positioning and aligning text to improve the appearance of a document. A **tab** is a set position where text following a tab character is aligned. An **indent** is a set amount of space between the edge of a paragraph and the right or left margin. The ruler makes it easy to set **tab stops** (locations the insertion point moves to when you press [Tab]) and indents and see immediately how they affect your document. The default ruler is marked in inches and contains symbols for left margins, right margins, indents, and tab stops. There is a tab character following each colon in the product information sheet, but the tab stops are not all set at the same position. Also, the first paragraph under the Kit Promotions heading contains two lines, and would look neater if the second line of this paragraph were aligned under the first word after the tab. You decide to use the ruler to modify these two elements.

Steps

1. Press **[Ctrl][Home]**

   The insertion point moves to the beginning of the document.

QuickTip

Press [Ctrl][A] to select all the text in the document quickly.

2. Click **Edit** on the menu bar, then click **Select All**

   The entire document is selected.

Trouble?

If you click the wrong place, make sure the text is selected, then either drag the tab to the correct position, or drag it off the ruler and try again.

3. Click the **1.25" mark** on the ruler, as shown in Figure B-10

   As long as you hold the mouse button, a vertical line appears on the document so that you can see (and move) the location of the tab stop in the document. See Figure B-10. The text after existing tabs in each line is automatically aligned at the new tab stop position. Any text without tabs is left unchanged.

QuickTip

To change the tab type using the ruler, click the icon at the left end of the ruler until it changes to the type of tab you want.

4. Point to the tab stop you just set until the Screen Tip "Left Tab" appears to verify that you set a left tab

5. Scroll to the first paragraph under the Kit Promotions heading and click anywhere in it

6. Position the pointer over the **Left Indent marker** ▢, then drag the ▢ to the one-inch position on the ruler

   The paragraph indents at the 1-inch position. Instead of indenting an entire paragraph from the left margin, you drag the markers on the ruler to set a **hanging indent**, where the first line in the paragraph is set off, or hangs, from the lines of text that wrap below it. A **First Line indent** is where only the first line indents. A **Right Indent** is where the paragraph is indented from the right margin. See Figure B-11.

7. Click the **Undo button** ↺ on the Standard toolbar to undo this paragraph indent

QuickTip

You can remove the ruler if you don't use it and want to make more room for the document in the window by clicking View on the menu bar, then clicking Ruler.

8. Position the pointer over the **Hanging Indent marker** △ on the ruler, as shown in Figure B-11, then click and hold the △

   Make sure the ScreenTip identifies the marker as Hanging Indent and not First Line Indent or Left Indent. A dotted vertical line appears.

9. Drag the △ to the right until the dotted line is next to the **P** in **Profitable** and the Hanging Indent marker is on top of the tab marker

   See Figure B-12. The second line of the paragraph now "hangs" under the word "Profitable." Be sure to save your work.

FIGURE B-10: Setting a tab stop on the ruler

Left tab marker at 1.25"

Vertical line indicates tab position

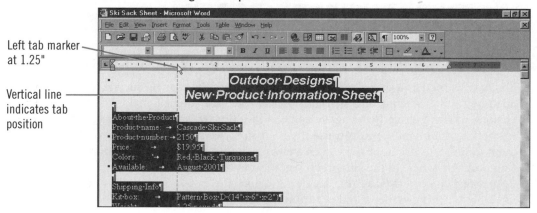

FIGURE B-11: Dragging to create a hanging indent

First Line Indent marker

Hanging Indent marker

Left Indent marker

Right Indent marker

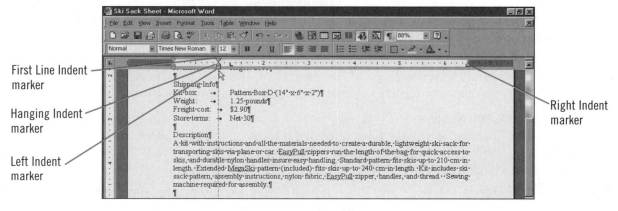

FIGURE B-12: Paragraph formatted with hanging indent

Second line is indented at hanging indent and change is reflected in the ruler

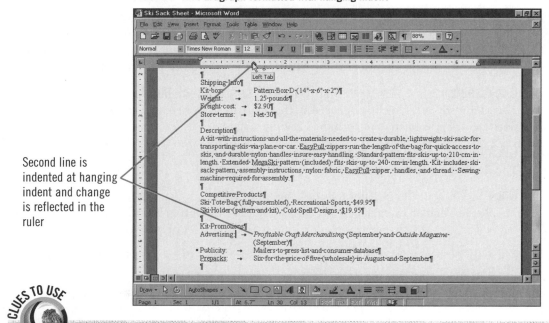

CLUES TO USE

Setting a first line indent paragraph

You can also use the ruler to indent the first line of a paragraph. Select the paragraphs you want to indent, then drag the First Line Indent marker, shown in Figure B-11, to the indent position you want.

Alternatively, you can click Format on the menu bar, then click Paragraph to open the Paragraph dialog box. Click the Special list arrow, then click First line. Set the indent position in the By text box.

Applying and Modifying Styles

You have learned how to make many individual formatting changes such as font style, paragraph alignment, line spacing, and margins. When you find yourself making the same formatting changes to text over and over again, you can save time by applying paragraph **styles**, or sets of formatting commands. You can use the built-in styles that come with Word, you can modify them to suit your needs, or you can create your own. To apply a style, you first position the insertion point anywhere in the paragraph you want to format and then you use the Style list on the Formatting toolbar. ◢◣◥◤ You decide to format the title and other headings in the product information sheet so they stand out from the rest of the text.

Steps

1. Press **[Ctrl][Home]**, then click anywhere in the heading **About the Product**

2. Click the **Style list arrow** on the Formatting toolbar

   The list of styles available in this document opens. See Figure B-13. It includes a variety of pre-defined formatting styles. The current style is Normal. The style names in the list are shown with their corresponding formatting so that you can see what changes you are applying.

3. Click **Heading 1**

   The list closes, and the selected text is formatted with Heading 1 style, which is 14-point Arial boldface. You can see that using a style requires fewer steps than making each formatting change individually.

QuickTip

To view style names in a document, you can expand the style area along the left edge of the document window. Click Tools on the menu bar, click Options, then in the Style area width text box, enter a positive value.

4. Repeat Steps 2 and 3 for the headings **Shipping Info**, **Description**, **Competitive Products**, and **Kit Promotions**

5. Click **Format** on the menu bar, then click **Style**

   The Style dialog box opens. You can use this dialog box to modify existing styles to suit your needs and to create entirely new styles. It doesn't matter where the insertion point is when you modify a style; all of the text formatted with that style will be changed.

6. Click **Heading 1** in the Styles list if necessary, then click **Modify**

   The Modify Style dialog box opens. Any changes you make here will affect all the text in this document that is formatted with the Heading 1 style.

7. Click **Format**, then click **Border**

   The Borders and Shading dialog box opens.

8. Click **Shadow** in the Setting column, then click **OK**

   The Borders and Shading dialog box closes, and the Description box in the Modify Style dialog box reflects the change you made to the style as shown in Figure B-14.

9. Click **OK** to close the Modify Style dialog box, then click **Close** to close the Style dialog box, then save your changes

   The headings are all reformatted to include a shadow box around them.

FIGURE B-13: Style list on the Formatting toolbar

Style at current location of insertion point

Each style name is formatted in the style shown

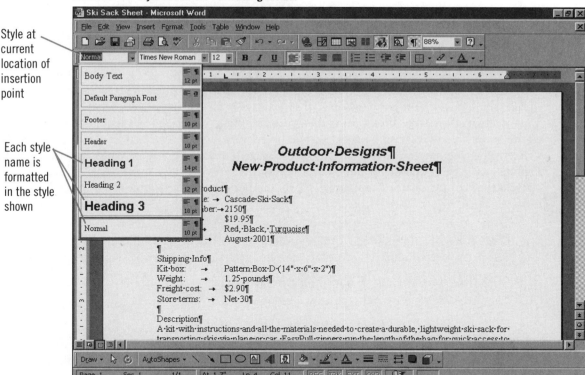

FIGURE B-14: Modify Style dialog box

Preview box shows formatting of the style being modified (Heading 1)

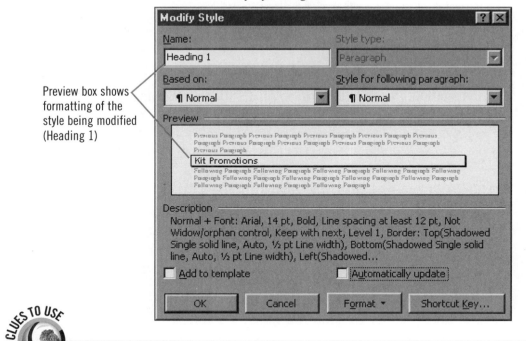

CLUES TO USE

Using AutoFormat

The AutoFormat feature in Word formats certain elements of your documents automatically. You can control which features are formatted automatically by clicking Format on the menu bar, then clicking AutoCorrect. The AutoCorrect dialog box contains two tabs relating to AutoFormatting. When options on the AutoFormat tab are selected, Word automatically formats those elements when you click Format on the menu bar, then click AutoFormat. When options on the AutoFormat As You Type tab are selected, Word formats these elements as you type. By default, AutoFormat is turned on.

Inserting Manual Page Breaks

Word automatically wraps text in a document to the next page when the last line of the current page is full. If you want text to go on to the next page before the current page is full, you can also manually insert a **page break** using the Break command on the Insert menu. Before you print a document that has several pages you should preview it with the Print Preview command to determine whether you need to insert manual page breaks. The Outdoor Designs style guidelines suggest dividing product information sheets into two or more pages to separate different types of information and make information easier for salespeople to find.

Steps

1. **Click the insertion point at the beginning of the Description heading**
   The insertion point blinks at the left margin, just before the word "Description".

2. **Click Insert on the menu bar, then click Break**
   The Break dialog box opens, as shown in Figure B-15.

3. **Make sure the Page break option button is selected, then click OK**
   A page break is inserted into the document before the Description heading, as shown in Figure B-16. In Normal view, the dotted line across the page marks the page break, and the words "Page Break" in the middle of the line indicate a manual page break.

4. **Click the insertion point at the beginning of the Competitive Products heading, then press [Ctrl][Enter]**
   This key combination is a quick way to insert a manual page break. The document is now three pages, with the Competitive Products and the Kit Promotional sections on the third page.

5. **Click the Print Preview button ⊡ on the Standard toolbar**

6. **Click the Multiple Pages button ⊞ on the Print Preview toolbar, drag the pointer to select 1 x 3 Pages, then release the mouse button**
   The three pages of the document appear side-by-side in Print Preview. See Figure B-17. The page number indicator in the status bar of the screen tells that the insertion point is on the third of three pages.

7. **Click Close on the Print Preview toolbar**
   The product information sheet returns to Normal view.

8. **Click the page break above Competitive Products, then press [Delete]**
   The dotted line disappears from the document. Save your work.

FIGURE B-15: Break dialog box

FIGURE B-16: Page break inserted in the document

Page break
inserted here

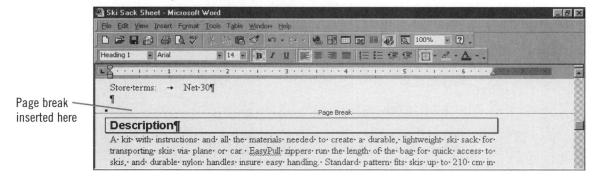

FIGURE B-17: Three-page product information sheet in Print Preview

Multiple
Pages button

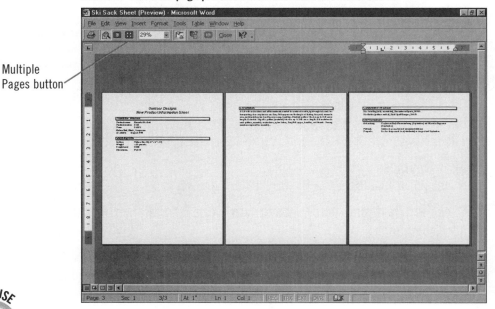

Using widow and orphan control

A **widow** is the last line of a paragraph that appears by itself on top of a page. An **orphan** is the first line of a paragraph that appears by itself on the bottom of a page. Both are undesirable in documents, because of appearance and readability. You can prevent them with Word by using the Paragraph dialog box (clicking Format on the menu bar, then Paragraph). Click the Line and Page Breaks tab, then click the Widow/Orphan control check box to select it. Word will automatically increase the length of a page by one line to prevent a widow, and it will force a page break one line sooner to prevent an orphan.

Replacing Text

The **Replace command** helps you quickly and easily substitute one or more occurrences of a particular word or phrase in a document. First you tell Word the text to search for, then you tell Word what you want to replace it with. You can replace every occurrence of the text in one action or you can review each occurrence and choose to replace or keep the text. ✐ You have just learned that the name of the "Cascade Ski Sack" product has changed to "Cascade Mobile Sack". You need to update this in the product information sheet. You decide to use the Replace command to speed up the process.

Steps

1. Press **[Ctrl][Home]** to move to the beginning of the document, click **Edit** on the menu bar, then click **Replace**

   The Find and Replace dialog box opens, as shown in Figure B-18.

2. Type **ski** in the Find what text box, press **[Tab]**, then type **mobile** in the Replace with text box

   The text you want to find or insert can be one or more characters.

3. Click **Replace All**

   Word searches the document from the insertion point and replaces all instances of the word "ski" with the word "mobile". An alert box opens telling you that 10 replacements were made.

4. Click **OK** to close the alert box, click **Close** to close the Find and Replace dialog box, then scroll through the document to see the changes

   As you scroll through the document, you notice that there are many instances of the word "ski" that should not have been replaced with the word "mobile." For example, in the paragraph under the "Description" heading, the sentence now reads "for transporting mobiles via plane" instead of "for transporting skis via plane".

QuickTip

The More button in the Find and Replace dialog box offers options for customizing the Find and Replace commands, such as matching the case or format of a word.

5. Click the **Undo button** 🔄 on the Standard toolbar, press **[Ctrl][Home]**, click **Edit** on the menu bar, click **Replace**, then click **Find Next**

   The first instance of the word "ski" is selected. See Figure B-19.

6. Click **Replace**

   Next, "ski" is highlighted in the text "lightweight ski sack".

7. Click **Find Next** nine more times to skip over each instance of "ski" (which you do not need to change)

   An alert box opens telling you that Word has finished searching the document.

8. Click **OK** to close the alert box, then click **Close** to close the Find and Replace dialog box

   Save your work.

9. Save your changes

FIGURE B-18: Find and Replace dialog box

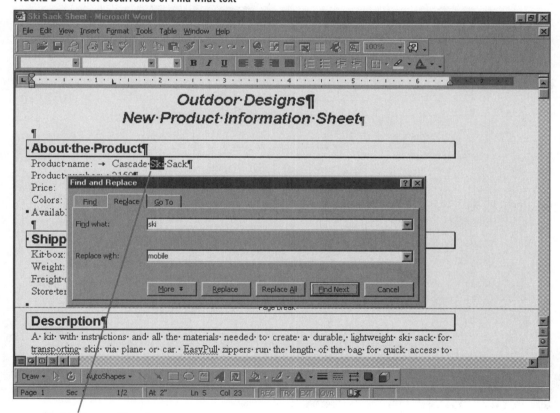

FIGURE B-19: First occurrence of Find what text

First instance of found
text is highlighted

Using the Find command

The Find command on the Edit menu opens the Find and Replace dialog box with the Find tab on top. It is similar to the Replace command, but the Find command searches for text without replacing it. The Find command is useful when you want to locate a particular word or phrase in a document but you don't know where it is. To use the Find command, type the word you're looking for in the Find what text box (for example, "nylon"), then click Find Next. If the word is found, Word scrolls to its location and the word is selected. To search for the next occurrence of the word in the document, click Find Next again.

Practice

► Concepts Review

Label the Word window elements shown in Figure B-20.

FIGURE B-20

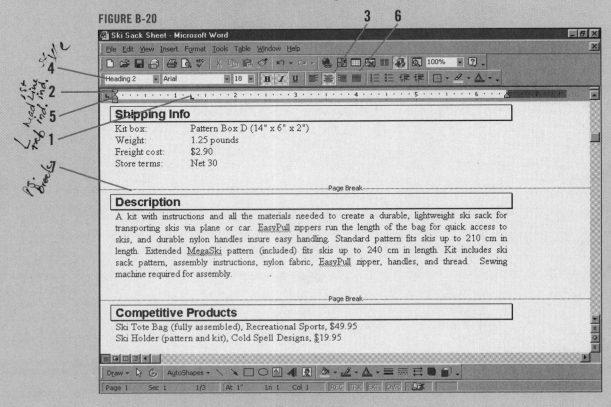

Match each toolbar button with the effect it creates.

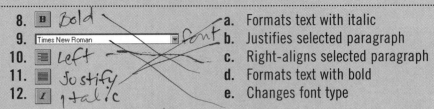

8. **B** *Bold*
9. Times New Roman *font*
10. *Left*
11. *Justify*
12. *I* *Italic*

a. Formats text with italic
b. Justifies selected paragraph
c. Right-aligns selected paragraph
d. Formats text with bold
e. Changes font type

Select the best answer from the list of choices.

13. What does Tr mean when it is listed next to a font in the Font Name list box?
   a. The font is a TrueType font.
   b. The font can be displayed only in Word.
   c. The font was designed by Technology Typeworks.
   d. The font works only with dot-matrix printers.

14. One point is equivalent to which of these measurements?
   a. 1 VGA screen pixel
   b. ⅟₇₂ of an inch
   c. 210 centimeters
   d. 1 ounce

15. If the alignment of text in a paragraph is justified, what is true about the text?
   a. It is aligned at the right margin.
   b. It is aligned at the left margin.
   c. It is aligned at the center of the page.
   d. It is aligned at both the right and left margins.

16. Which of these commands would you use to change paragraph spacing from single spacing to double spacing?
   a. The Double Spacing command on the View menu
   b. The Paragraph command on the Format menu
   c. The Page Setup command on the File menu
   d. The AutoFormat command on the Format menu

17. What are the default page margin settings in Word?
   a. ½" all around the document
   b. 1" all around the document
   c. 1.5" for the top and bottom margins, 2" for the left and right margins
   d. 1" for the top and bottom margins, 1.25" for the left and right margins

18. How do you insert a manual page break in a document?
   a. Click the Break command on the Insert menu.
   b. Click Format on the menu bar, then click New Page.
   c. Press [Ctrl][Shift].
   d. Double-click in the left margin.

19. How do you delete a manual page break?
   a. Double-click the page break.
   b. Click the left mouse button.
   c. Select the page break and press [Delete].
   d. Select the page break and press [Page Down].

20. How do the Find command and the Replace command differ?
   a. The Find command cannot be used to replace one word with another.
   b. The Find command works only with numbers.
   c. The Find command doesn't let you search for paragraph marks.
   d. The Find dialog box is bigger than the Replace dialog box.

Word 2000

▶ Skills Review

1. **Change font type and size.**
   a. Start Word, open the file WD B-2, then save it as "Ski Sack Update."
   b. Select the first three lines of the document.
   c. Click the Font Size list arrow on the Formatting toolbar, then click 14.
   d. Scroll until you see the lines "Outdoor Designs" and "Product Information Sheet UPDATE," then select them.
   e. Click the Font list arrow on the Formatting toolbar, then click Impact.
   f. Change the font size to 18.
   g. Save your changes to the document.

2. **Change font style.**
   a. Select the price "$22.75".
   b. Click the Underline button [U] on the Formatting toolbar.
   c. Underline the word "Orange" and the freight cost "$3.15."
   d. Select the lines "Outdoor Designs" and "Product Information Sheet UPDATE."
   e. Click the Bold button [B] on the Formatting toolbar.
   f. Press [Ctrl][I].
   g. Italicize the heading "About the Product."
   h. Save your changes.

3. **Change alignment.**
   a. Press [Ctrl][Home].
   b. Click in the first paragraph of the memo, which begins "The following is a new product information sheet...."
   c. Click Format on the menu bar, click Paragraph, then click the Indents and Spacing tab, if necessary.
   d. Click the Alignment list arrow, then click Justified.
   e. Click the Line spacing list arrow, then click Double.
   f. Click OK.
   g. Scroll down and select the lines "Outdoor Designs" and "Product Information Sheet UPDATE."
   h. Click the Align Right button on the Formatting toolbar.
   i. Save your changes.

4. **Change margin settings.**
   a. Click File on the menu bar, then click Page Setup.
   b. Click the Margins tab if necessary.
   c. Click the Top text box up arrow five times to change the Top margin to 1.5 inches.
   d. Double-click the Bottom text box, then type "1.5".
   e. Press [Tab], then type "1.75".
   f. Set the right margin to 1".
   g. Click OK.
   h. Switch to Page Layout view.
   i. Use the ruler to verify the new margin setting.
   j. Return to Normal view.
   k. Save your settings.

5. Use the ruler.

 a. Place the insertion point at the beginning of the first blank line after the Re: line, then press [Shift][Ctrl][End] to select all of the text from the insertion point to the end of the document.

 b. Click the 1.75" mark on the ruler.

 c. Select the five paragraphs (from "Producer name" through "August 2001") below the heading "About the Product."

 d. Click Format on the menu bar, then click Paragraph.

 e. Click the Left up arrow as needed to change the left indentation to .5", then click OK. The left indent marker on the ruler should now be on the ½" mark.

 f. Select the four paragraphs below the heading "Shipping Info."

 g. Position the mouse pointer on the Left Indent marker on the ruler, then drag it to the ½" mark on the ruler.

 h. Indent to ½" the paragraphs under the headings "Description," "Competitive Products," and "Kit Promotions," and under the paragraph that starts "Changes to the Cascade Ski Sack...."

 i. Click in the first paragraph below "Kit Promotions," then drag the Hanging Indent marker on the ruler to the 1.75" mark.

 j. Save your changes.

6. Apply and modify styles.

 a. Press [Ctrl][Home].

 b. Type "Memorandum", then press [Enter].

 c. Click in the paragraph you just typed, click the Style list arrow on the Formatting toolbar, then click Heading 1.

 d. Click Format on the menu bar, then click Style.

 e. Click Heading 1 in the Styles list, then click Modify.

 f. Click Format, then click Font.

 g. Click Courier New in the Font list (or a different one if that font is unavailable), click 22 in the Size list, then click OK.

 h. Click OK.

 i. Click Apply.

 j. Save your changes.

7. Insert manual page breaks.

 a. Move the insertion point before the heading "Outdoor Designs."

 b. Click Insert on the menu bar, click break, click the Page break option button, then click OK.

 c. Move the insertion point before the "Description" heading.

 d. Press [Ctrl][Enter].

 e. Click the Print Preview button on the Standard toolbar.

 f. Click the Multiple Pages button on the Print Preview toolbar, drag to select 1 x 3 pages, then release the mouse button.

 g. Click Close on the Print Preview toolbar.

 h. Make sure the mouse pointer is at the beginning of the line containing the "Description" heading, then press [Backspace] to delete the page break.

 i. Save your changes.

8. Replace text.

a. Press [Ctrl][Home].

b. Click Edit on the menu bar, then click Replace.

c. Type "95" in the Find what text box.

d. Type "59" in the Replace with text box.

e. Click the Find Next button.

f. Replace instances of 95 in the prices with 59.

g. Click OK to close the alert box, then click Close to close the Find and Replace dialog box to end the search.

h. Save your changes.

i. Preview the document.

j. Print your document and exit Word.

▶ Independent Challenges

1. Manuel Dominga, a sales representative at Wacky Words, asked you to format a letter and price sheet that he prepared for a customer. He used Wacky Words letterhead but didn't format anything else. If you can enhance the look of his materials, he's sure Samantha will put in a good-sized order for greeting cards.

To complete this independent challenge:

a. Open the file WD B-3, and save it as "Graduation Cards."

b. Scroll to the middle of page one, select "Wacky Words" in the second paragraph, and change it to 18-point Impact bold. Select the next four lines, change them to 14-point Impact italic and center them. Left-align the closing, signature, and title lines at the end of Manuel's letter.

c. Change the margin settings so all the margins of the document are 1.5."

d. Apply the Heading 3 style to the headings "Subject of Greeting Cards," "Available Series," and "Prices."

e. Separate the letter from the price sheet by inserting a manual page break at the line beginning "Wacky Words" after the letter.

f. Save your changes, preview, and then print the letter and price list.

2. Joel Rubin wants to create "Buy one dinner, get one free at The Steak Pit" certificates to donate to a local charity for its annual fund raiser. Last year, the group auctioned off 15 certificates and raised $1,100 from his donation alone. Joel has written the text of the certificate and asks you to format it.

To complete this independent challenge:

a. Open the file WD B-4, and save it as "Free Entree".

b. Change "The Steak Pit" to 48-point size, and change the two address lines to 36-point size. Change the rest of the text to 14-point Brush Script MT (or a different one if that font is unavailable) centered.

c. Underline the restaurant name in the first line of text. Make the words "free" and "complimentary" bold.

d. Indent the words "dessert" and "coffee or tea". Set a 1-inch left indent for the paragraphs containing the text "dessert" and "coffee or tea".

e. Change the top and bottom margins to 1.75" and the left and right margins to 1". Change the paper orientation to Landscape.

f. Use the Replace dialog box to change the instance of the word "Thursday" to "Friday."

g. Switch to Print Layout view.

h. Use the Spacing section in the Paragraph dialog box to add space before and after paragraphs until the main text is centered on the page. Use Print Preview to verify your changes.

i. Save your changes. Print your certificate, then close the document.

3. The Literary Loft wants to provide a new customer service—book reviews. The owner, Kristine, asks each employee to write a brief synopsis of two books they've read and include a recommendation so customers can tell if they might like them. She also wants each employee to use the Internet to look up two additional book reviews and print them.
To complete this independent challenge:

a. Start Word and open a new, blank document. Save the document as "Book Reviews".

b. Write a one-paragraph review for two books you've read and enjoyed. Write your recommendation in a second paragraph. Include each book's title on its own line before each review. Insert a manual page break before the second review.

c. Log on to the Internet, and use your browser to go to http://www.course.com. From there, click the link *Student Online Companions*, click the link for this textbook, then click the Word link for Unit B. Use the link there to find book reviews. After you find two that you want to print, select all the text, press [Ctrl][C] to copy it, switch to your Book Reviews Word document, position the insertion point in a new paragraph after your second review, then press [Ctrl][V] to paste the review into the Word document. Insert manual page breaks between each review.

d. Format the text so that the title of each review is in a different font and size from the rest of the text. Italicize each book title. Use styles to format each review and recommendation.

e. Save, preview, print, then close your review document.

4. Gerry Zell, the sales representative from Montana, calls and asks you to write a product description of the new pet collars being offered by Stuff for Pets and format it so he can send it out to his customers.
To complete this independent challenge:

a. Start Word and open a new, blank document. Save it as "Pet Collars".

b. Make up a name for the product and type it at the top of your document. Use any font you like. Center the text. Five lines below the product name, type the heading "Collar Description". On the next line, type a paragraph describing why these collars are better than any available on the market. Below that, list some benefits of using the collars.

c. Format the heading, paragraph, and list that you just typed. Use the Formatting toolbar, the Paragraph dialog box, and styles.

d. Italicize the product name every time it appears in your document.

e. Change line spacing for the entire document to double.

f. Change the name of your product. Replace each instance of the name using the Replace dialog box.

g. Preview your document. Make any formatting changes to improve your document's appearance and readability.

h. Save your changes.

i. Print and close the document.

Visual Workshop

Open the file WD B-5 and save it as "Product Sheet". Format the document so it appears as shown in Figure B-21. Don't worry if some lines wrap differently in your document than they do in Figure B-21. This can occur due to differences in monitors and in computer systems. When you have finished, print and close the document.

FIGURE B-21

Outdoor Designs
New Product Information Sheet

About the Product

Product name:	**Mountain Day Pack**
Product number:	**3350**
Price:	**$29.95**
Colors:	**Green, Red, Brown**
Available:	**October 2001**

Shipping Info

Kit box:	**Pattern Box D (14" x 6" x 2")**
Weight:	**2.25 pounds**
Freight cost:	**$3.00**
Store terms:	**Net 30**

Description
A kit with instructions and all the materials needed to create a durable, lightweight backpack for light hiking, skiing, or mountain biking. EasyPull zippers run the length of the bag for quick access to gear, and comfortable shoulder straps insure miles of trail comfort. Standard pattern can be tailored to men, women, and children. Kit includes backpack pattern, assembly instructions, nylon fabric, EasyPull zipper, shoulder straps, and thread. Sewing machine required for assembly.

Competitive Products
Back in the Saddle (mountain bike backpack), Team Encarta, Inc., $34.95
Wild Women Wear (pattern and kit), Cold Spell Designs, $19.95

Kit Promotions

Advertising:	*Profitable Craft Merchandising* (October), *Outside Magazine* (January)
Publicity:	Mailers to press list and consumer database
Prepacks:	Six for the price of five (wholesale) in November and December

Adding
Special Elements to a Document

► **Create a table**
► **Insert and delete columns and rows**
► **Use Table AutoFormat and adjust column widths**
► **Insert WordArt**
► **Add clip art**
► **Insert a footnote**
► **Use headers and footers**
► **Verify page layout**

You can add a variety of elements—including tables, graphics, footnotes, headers, and footers—to a document to make it more attractive and informative. ✐ Derek Hofbauer, marketing manager for Outdoor Designs, has asked you to finish a one-page promotional flyer he's been working on for the Kite Packs. You'll insert a table to organize the details on each kite pack, and you'll add WordArt and clip art to give the flyer visual appeal. You'll also document the information you use in the flyer by inserting a footnote, and you'll label the flyer as a first draft for Derek by using a header. Finally, you'll verify the flyer's layout and print a final copy for distribution.

Unit C

Word 2000

Creating a Table

Sometimes you might want part of your document to be organized into a table. For example, you might want rows of information to provide the names, prices, and colors of products within a report. You can insert a table using the Insert Table button on the Standard toolbar or the Insert Table command on the Table menu. When you first create a table, you specify the number of rows and columns you want in the table, but you can add and delete them as you modify the table. ✐ Derek gives you a file containing both the flyer's text and suggestions he typed. He suggests that you begin by inserting a table into the flyer to organize the information about all of the different Kite Packs.

Steps

1. **Start Word, open the file WD C-1 on your Project Disk, then save it as Kite Flyer on your Project Disk**
   The promotional flyer opens. To separate his notes to you from the flyer text, Derek enclosed them in double angle brackets, such as "<<Insert Clip Art>>."

2. **Make sure formatting marks are showing by clicking the Show/Hide ¶ button ¶ on the Standard toolbar once (twice if they were already showing)**

3. **Select the text <<Insert Table>> (but not the paragraph mark), then press [Delete]**
   This is where you will insert the table.

> **Trouble?**
> To use a button that is not visible, click the More Buttons button ⟫ on the right side of the appropriate toolbar, then click the button or list arrow you need. If it is still not visible, click Add or Remove buttons, click the desired button, click outside the list to close it, then click the button on the toolbar.

4. **Click the Insert Table button ▦ on the Standard toolbar**
   A grid opens next to the button, similar to Figure C-1.

5. **Click and drag to create a 7 × 6 table, as shown in Figure C-1**
   After you release the mouse button, a table with seven rows and six columns appears where you placed the insertion point. The intersection of each row and column is a **cell**. The insertion point appears in the first cell.

6. **Type Item Number, then press [Tab]**
   Pressing [Tab] moves the insertion point to the cell to the right of the current cell. Pressing [Enter] inserts a paragraph mark in the current cell, moving the insertion point down a line, but not to the next cell. The mark in each cell is the **end-of-cell mark**. Text you type is inserted to the left of the **end-of-cell mark**. The marks at the ends of the rows are the **end-of-row marks**.

> **QuickTip**
> You can also click the cell or use the arrow keys to move from cell to cell.

7. **Type the rest of the column headings, as shown in Figure C-2, pressing [Tab] after each heading to move to the next cell**
   After you type the last column heading, "Finished Size," pressing [Tab] moved the insertion point to the first cell in the second row.

> **Trouble?**
> If you pressed [Tab] after the last entry, a new row was added. Click the Undo button ↶ to delete the new row.

8. **Enter the rest of the information in the table shown in Figure C-2, but do not press [Tab] after the last entry**
   If each line in your cells does not end at exactly the same point as in the figure, don't worry. You will fix this later.

9. **Click the Save button ▦ on the Standard toolbar, then scroll through the entire document and read the rest of Derek's notes**

FIGURE C-1: Inserting a 7 × 6 table

Insert Table button

Click and drag to select 7 rows by 6 columns

Table will be inserted at location of insertion point

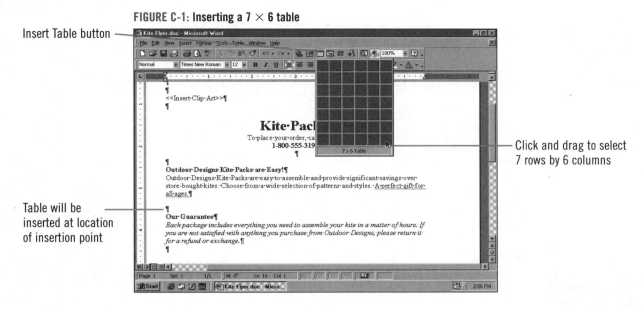

FIGURE C-2: Table to insert into kite flyer

Column

Column headings

End-of-cell mark

Row

End-of-row mark

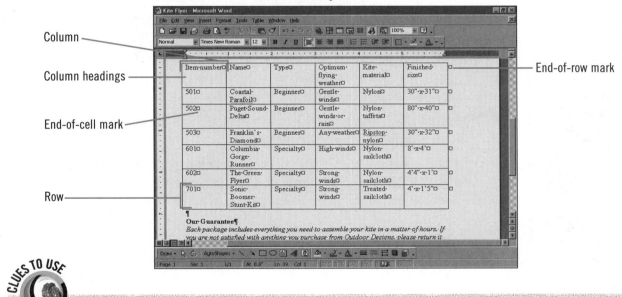

Creating multiple columns

Another way to organize text is to use **columns**, or vertical blocks of text. Multiple columns allow you to fit more words on a page while increasing the white space around the text. If you want to present all the information in your document in columns, you can click Format on the menu bar, then click Columns. The Columns dialog box opens, as shown in Figure C-3. Here you set the number of columns, the width of each column, and the space between columns. To apply the multiple columns format to the entire document, choose Whole document in the Apply to list box at the bottom of the dialog box. To apply the multiple columns to just part of the document, choose This point forward in the Apply to list box, then enter the desired text in the document. Then, to format the rest of the document as a single column, place the insertion point at the end of the multiple columns, open this dialog box again, choose one column, and again choose This point forward.

FIGURE C-3: Columns dialog box

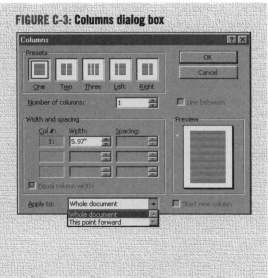

Inserting and Deleting Columns and Rows

After you create a table, you might need to add or delete rows or columns. When you insert a row using the Insert Rows button, the new row is inserted above the current row. When you insert a column using the Insert Columns button, the new column is inserted to the left of the current column. You can use the Insert command on the Table menu if you want your new column (or row) inserted to the right of (or below) the current column (or row). To delete a row or column, select it, click Table on the menu bar, click Delete, then click the name of the item you want to delete. You realize that you forgot to include the prices of the kites in the table. You decide to add a column to your table so you can include the kite prices.

Steps

1. **Scroll to the right, position the mouse pointer over the top of the column of end-of-row marks outside the table so that the pointer changes to ↓, then click**
   All of the end-of-row marks are selected as shown in Figure C-4. On the Standard toolbar, the Insert Table button changes to the Insert Columns button.

2. **Click**
   A new column is inserted as the last column in the table.

3. **Click in the first cell of the new column, type Price, then press [↓]**
   Pressing the arrow keys also moves the insertion point.

4. **Click View on the menu bar, click Zoom, double-click the number in the Percent text box, type 80, click OK, then scroll down so you can see the table again**
   Now you should be able to see the entire Price column.

5. **Enter the prices in the last column, as shown below**
   $22.95 $24.95 $19.95 $39.95 $29.95 $49.95

6. **Click in any cell in the row containing information about item number 502, click Table on the menu bar, point to Delete, then click Cells**
   The Delete Cells dialog box opens. Derek sent you e-mail telling you that item number 502, Puget Sound Delta, has been discontinued.

7. **Click the Delete entire row option button, then click OK**
   The entire row is deleted, and the rest of the rows move up to close up the space. See Figure C-5.

8. **Click the Save button on the Standard toolbar**

QuickTip

To insert a row above the current row, select the current row, then click the Insert Rows button on the Standard toolbar.

Trouble?

If the Price column still isn't completely visible on your screen, change the zoom by clicking the Zoom list arrow on the Standard toolbar, then clicking Page Width.

QuickTip

To delete an entire column or row quickly, select the entire row or column, click Table on the menu bar, point to Delete, then click Columns or Rows on the submenu.

FIGURE C-4: Inserting a new column

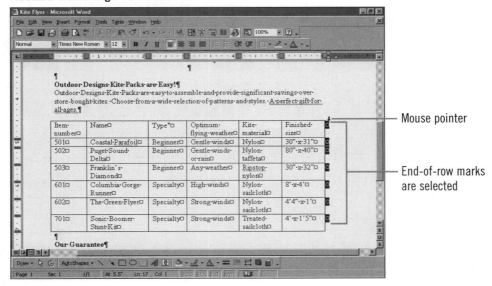

Mouse pointer

End-of-row marks are selected

FIGURE C-5: Table after row is deleted

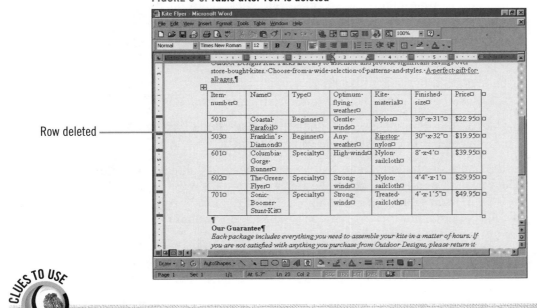

Row deleted

Placing borders around text

You can add borders around words, paragraphs, or entire pages to enhance a document. The border can be as plain as a single black line, or as elaborate as a customized picture repeated many times as in Figure C-6. The easiest way to add simple borders is to click the Border button list arrow ▦ ▾ on the Standard toolbar, then select the border style you want to use. You can add a line at the top, bottom, left, or right edges of the selected text, or outline the selected text with a border. To create more elaborate borders, click Format on the menu bar, click Borders and Shading to open the Borders and Shading dialog box, then click the Borders tab. To put a border around an entire page, click the Page Border tab.

FIGURE C-6: Using borders to enhance a document

Using Table AutoFormat and Adjusting Column Widths

After you create a table you can format it by adding borders, shading, and styles. You can also format the table quickly by using the Table AutoFormat command. Table AutoFormat provides 42 formats from which to choose. You can customize the way AutoFormat will format your table by selecting options in the Table AutoFormat dialog box. ◄━━━ Now that the information in your table is complete, you decide to format the table using Table AutoFormat.

1. **With the insertion point still in the table, click Table on the menu bar, then click Table AutoFormat**
   The Table AutoFormat dialog box opens, similar to Figure C-7. The Preview box displays a sample of the AutoFormat that is currently selected in the list.

2. **In the Formats list, click Classic 2**
   The Preview box changes to display the Classic 2 AutoFormat.

3. **In the Formats to apply section, click the Color check box to deselect it**
   This is the best setting for black and white printers.

4. **In the Apply special formats to section, click the First column check box to deselect it**
   The Classic 2 AutoFormat treats the first column differently from the body of the table because in many tables, the first column contains row headings. Your table contains data in the first column, however, so you don't want the first column to have special formatting. Compare your screen with Figure C-7.

5. **Click OK**
   The Table AutoFormat dialog box closes, and the table in your document is formatted with the selected AutoFormat.

6. **Position the mouse pointer between the "Finished size" column and the "Price" column so the pointer changes to ↔, then double-click**
   The width of the column to the left of the mouse pointer expands, so that any entry that occupied two lines now fits on one line.

7. **Double-click between the "Optimum flying weather" column and the "Kite material" column**
   You may have to double-click twice. The column width expands so that the column heading is two lines instead of three.

8. **Double-click between the "Name" and "Type" columns**

9. **Click and hold the mouse button between the "Item number" and "Name" columns so that a dotted line column divider appears, then drag the divider to the left approximately ¼" so that "Item number" is on two lines, then save your changes**
   Compare your screen with Figure C-8.

FIGURE C-7: Table AutoFormat dialog box

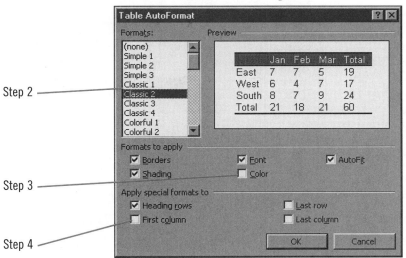

Step 2

Step 3

Step 4

FIGURE C-8: Table with columns resized

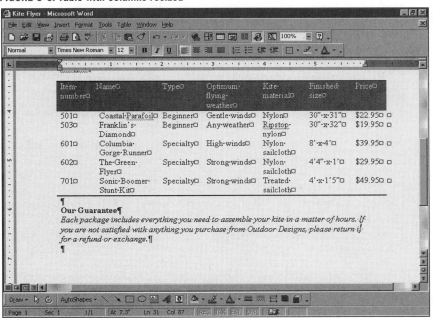

Using AutoFormat as you type

Some text is automatically formatted for you as you type. To see what changes will be made, click Tools on the menu bar, click AutoCorrect, then click the AutoFormat As You Type tab. See Figure C-9. You can turn off any or all of the options in this dialog box by deselecting the check boxes. To find out more about these options, click the Help button ? in the upper-right corner of the dialog box, and then click any option.

FIGURE C-9: AutoFormat As You Type tab in AutoCorrect dialog box

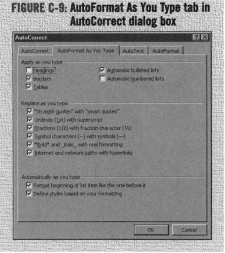

Word 2000

Inserting WordArt

You can insert several types of artistic elements into your documents. One type is **WordArt**, stylized text with sophisticated text formatting features. WordArt text is inserted into your document as an **object**, which means you can move and resize it as a single unit. You'll learn to use some of these features in this lesson; to learn about all the features of WordArt, consult Help. As Derek suggested, you'll use WordArt to add the name of the company to the kite flyer.

Steps

1. Select **<<Insert Company Name as WordArt>>** then press **[Delete]**

   Derek's suggestion disappears from the document, and the insertion point is on the blank line at the top of the flyer.

Trouble?

If the Drawing toolbar is not visible, click the Drawing button on the Standard toolbar.

2. Click the **Insert WordArt button** on the Drawing toolbar

   The WordArt Gallery dialog box opens, as shown in Figure C-10.

3. Click the **WordArt style** in the fourth row and the second column, then click **OK**

   The Edit WordArt Text dialog box opens. See Figure C-11. The text you type will replace the text "Your Text Here."

4. Type **Outdoor Designs**

5. Click the **Font list arrow**, scroll up, then click **Arial Rounded MT Bold**

   If you don't have this font, choose another one.

Trouble?

If the WordArt toolbar doesn't appear, click View on the menu bar, point to Toolbars, then click WordArt.

6. Click **OK**

   After a moment, the WordArt object appears in the document with selection handles around it, and the WordArt toolbar opens with options for modifying the WordArt object. **Selection handles** are small squares that appear when an object is selected and allow you to resize the object quickly.

QuickTip

To edit the WordArt object, double-click it.

7. Position the pointer over the WordArt object so that it changes to ‡, then drag the WordArt up and to the right so it is centered in the blank area at the top of the page

   Try to position the WordArt so there is at least ½" blank space at the top of the page. See Figure C-12.

QuickTip

To resize WordArt to exact specifications select the object, click Format on the menu bar, click WordArt, then click the Size tab.

8. Enlarge the WordArt by positioning the mouse pointer over the lower-left selection handle so it changes to ↙, then drag the handle to the left approximately ½"

9. Click anywhere in the document window to deselect the WordArt object, then save your changes

FIGURE C-10: WordArt Gallery

Step 3

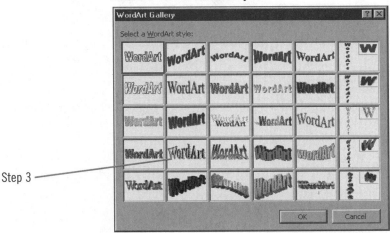

FIGURE C-11: Edit WordArt Text dialog box

Click to select a
different font

Text you type
replaces this text

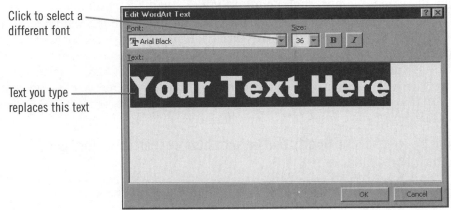

FIGURE C-12: WordArt in document

Selection
handles

WordArt
toolbar

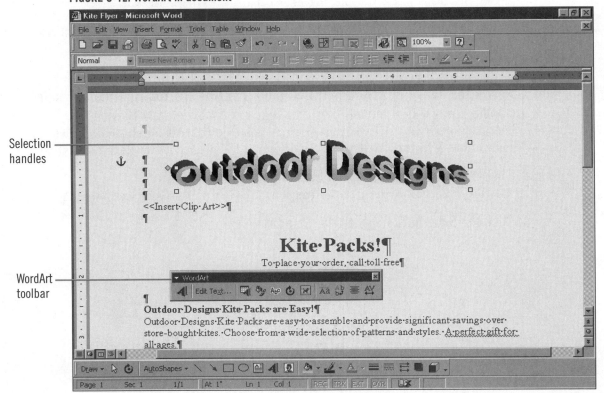

Adding Clip Art

Clip art, ready-to-use pictures, is another type of electronic art available in Word. The Clip Gallery is a small program that comes with Office and includes many groups of clip art in different shapes, sizes, and colors. You can purchase additional clip art images from the Web or computer stores and add them to the Clip Gallery. If you have Internet access, you can click the Clips Online button in the Insert Clip Art window to access a special Web site for Microsoft Office users and download additional clips. Derek suggested that you add clip art to the kite flyer to enhance its visual appeal.

Steps

1. Select the text **<<Insert Clip Art>>**, then press **[Delete]**

2. Click **Insert** on the menu bar, point to **Picture**, then click **Clip Art**

   The Insert ClipArt window opens with the Pictures tab in front; this window is actually part of the Clip Gallery program that starts when you click Clip Art. See Figure C-13. The Clip Gallery provides access to all the clip art on your hard disk and on the Office 2000 CD-ROM. Office 2000 comes with more than 3,500 clip art images. You may have additional images from other Microsoft programs or from additional clip art packages installed on your computer or purchased at computer stores. The pictures are organized by category. You can browse through each category or you can search for a specific image.

3. Scroll to and click the **Sports and Leisure button**, then scroll through the category to see the clips available

4. Click the **Back button** to return to the list of categories

5. Type **kite** in the Search for clips text box, then press **[Enter]**

   A Clips list displays all available images associated with the word "kite."

6. Click the image of a kite, click the **Insert Clip button** in the pop-up menu, then click the **Close button** to close the Insert ClipArt window

   The image appears in the document.

7. Resize the image by selecting it and then dragging the **top right corner selection handle** down and to the left until the image is approximately 1" wide

   The image is left-aligned (where the insertion point was). By default, clip images are formatted to be **inline with text**, so that they can be moved and aligned just like a text selection.

8. Click the **Center button** on the Formatting toolbar

   The clip art image is centered horizontally on the page. Compare your screen with Figure C-14.

9. Click the **Save button** on the Standard toolbar

FIGURE C-13: Microsoft Clip Gallery 5.0

Enter keyword to search for clips

Scroll through available categories

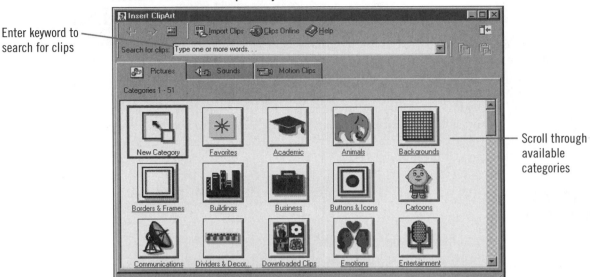

FIGURE C-14: Image centered on page

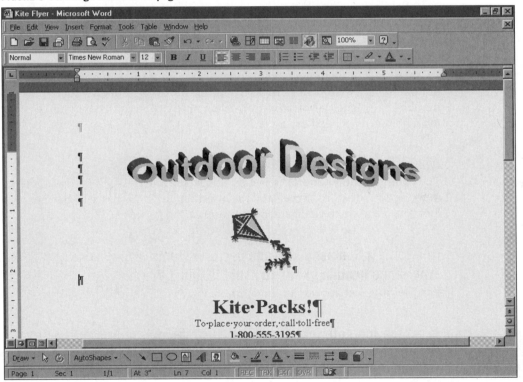

Inserting pictures, sounds, videos, and drawn objects

In addition to clip art, you can insert other types of objects in your document. To insert a picture, sound, or video from the Clip Gallery, follow the same procedure as for inserting clip art, but click the appropriate tab in the Clip Gallery instead. To insert an object from a file not in the Clip Gallery, click Insert on the menu bar, then click Object, or point to Picture and click From File. To draw an object to include in a document, use the buttons on the Drawing toolbar to draw shapes and lines and add color and texture to them.

Inserting a Footnote

You can easily add footnotes with the Footnote command on the Insert menu. **Footnotes** and **endnotes** contain two linked parts: the reference mark (usually a number or symbol) in a document and the corresponding note text. For a footnote, the corresponding text appears at the bottom of a page, while text for endnotes appears at the end of a document (used when you don't want to interrupt the flow of text). Footnotes are like other text so you can format their font and style in Page Layout view. Derek thinks some customers may not understand exactly the designations "Beginner" and "Specialty." He asks you to add a footnote to the table that clarifies the heading "Type."

Steps 1234

1. **Scroll down so you can see the table, then click directly after the word Type in the table**
   The insertion point should be just before the end-of-cell mark.

2. **Click Insert on the menu bar, then click Footnote**
   The Footnote and Endnote dialog box opens, similar to Figure C-15. Footnote is the default option, but you can also choose to enter an endnote.

3. **Click the Custom mark option button**
   The Custom mark option button is selected, and the insertion point moves to the text box on the right. In documents with more than one footnote, you can use the AutoNumber option to have Word automatically number the footnotes or endnotes and adjust the numbering whenever you insert or delete notes. You're inserting only one footnote in the flyer, however, so you'll use a mark.

4. **Type * and click OK**
   The Footnote and Endnote dialog box closes. The asterisk is inserted as a **footnote reference mark** next to the word "Type," and the insertion point moves to the bottom of the page in the footnote area, where you'll enter your footnote text.

5. **Type To fly a Specialty kite and perform stunts, you generally need at least some experience handling kites to avoid tangling the line.**
   The footnote text appears in the footnote area, with a small leading asterisk.

6. **Select the footnote text, then click the Italic button 𝐼 on the Formatting toolbar**
   The footnote style changes to italic. This will distinguish the footnote from the rest of the flyer and ensure that it doesn't distract the reader from the main text.

7. **Click the Font Size list arrow on the Formatting toolbar, click 8, then click anywhere in the document window to deselect the footnote text**
   The point size is reduced to 8 points, as shown in Figure C-16. The footnote text is displayed only in Print Layout view and in Print Preview, but you can click Footnotes on the View menu in any view to view and edit the footnote text.

8. **Click the Save button 🖫 on the Standard toolbar to save your changes**

FIGURE C-15: **Footnote and Endnote dialog box**

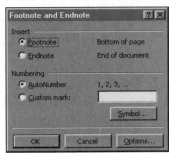

FIGURE C-16: **Completed footnote**

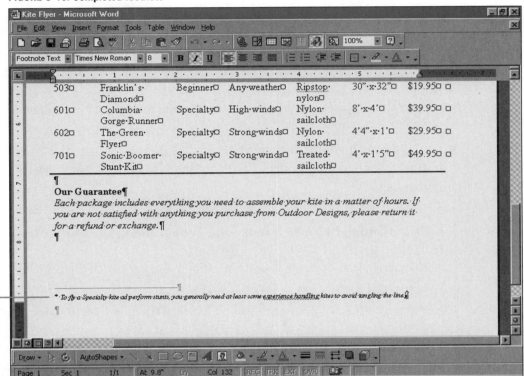

Footnote in —
8-point italic

Working with lengthy documents

In a lengthy document, it can be difficult for readers to find the information they need. You can make the document easier to navigate by inserting one or more reference tables: a table of contents, an index, a table of figures, or a table of authorities. You can insert a **table of contents** (a list of the headings in your document), an **index** (a list of key words and terms and their page location), a **table of figures** (a list of the figures in a document and their location), and a **table of authorities** (a list of references in a legal document, such as cases or statutes, and their page location). Word's Index and Tables command automates the creation and formatting of tables so they are updated whenever you make changes to the document. Depending on the type of table you insert, first

you might need to specify the headings or terms in your document that you want to include. Then click Insert on the menu bar, click Index and Tables, and then click the appropriate tab.

FIGURE C-17: **Index and Tables dialog box**

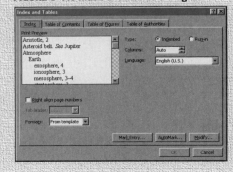

Word 2000

Using Headers and Footers

Word 2000

You might want to add certain text, such as page numbers, the print date, your name, or the file-name, to the top or the bottom of every page in a document. A **header** is text that appears just below the top margin of every page, and a **footer** appears just above the bottom margin of every page. ✎ Derek wants to review the flyer and provide feedback before you print the flyer, so you decide to add a header clarifying that this is a first draft.

Steps

Trouble?

If your WordArt object overlaps most of the Header area, click Close on the Header and Footer toolbar, move the WordArt object down, click Close on the WordArt toolbar if necessary, then repeat Step 1.

1. Click **View** on the menu bar, then click **Header and Footer**

   The insertion point moves to the header area at the top of the document, and the Header and Footer toolbar opens, as shown in Figure C-18. The text you enter in the Header area appears at the top of every page in a document. You can format header and footer text in the same way you format regular text.

2. Type **Outdoor Designs Confidential, Draft 1.0** in the header field, click the **Center button** 🔳 on the Formatting toolbar, then select the text and click the **Italic button** 𝐼

   The header text is centered at the top of the page and italicized.

3. Click the **Switch Between Header and Footer button** 🔳 on the Header and Footer toolbar

   The document scrolls down, and the insertion point appears in the Footer area.

4. Type **Printed on**, then press **[Spacebar]**

   Now you can insert the current date, so Derek will know when the information was last updated.

5. Click the **Insert Date button** 🔳 on the Header and Footer toolbar

   The current date appears in the footer. The date will be updated automatically each time you open the document.

Trouble?

If the Filename AutoText entry is not available, type "Kite Flyer".

6. Press **[Tab]** twice to move to the right margin, type **Filename:**, press **[Spacebar]**, click the **Insert AutoText button** on the Header and Footer toolbar, point to **Header/Footer**, then click **Filename**

   The filename appears in the footer. If you save the document under a new name, the footer will reflect the new filename.

7. Click **Close** on the Header and Footer toolbar

QuickTip

To edit a header or footer, you can click the Header and Footer command on the View menu and the header area will be displayed. In Print Layout view, you can simply double-click the header or footer area.

8. Scroll through the document and observe the header and footer

   The header and footer appear dimmed in the document. When you print the document, however, they will print normally.

9. Click the **Normal View button** 🔳 to the left of the horizontal scroll bar, then save your changes

   The header and footer are visible only in Print Layout view and Print Preview (but in all the views, you can display the header and footer areas by clicking Header and Footer on the View menu).

FIGURE C-18: Header area

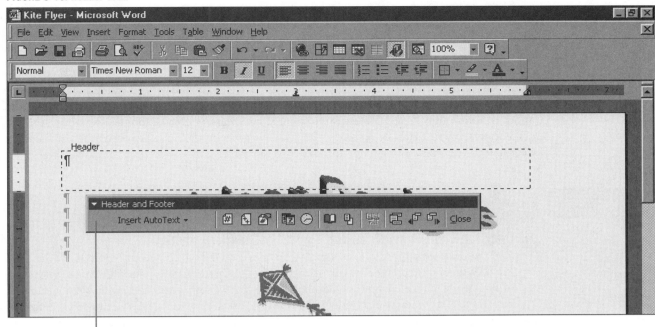

Header and Footer
toolbar

Working with headers and footers in a multi-page document

In a multi-page document, the first page often does not need a header or footer. For example, because the first page of a report might be a title page with your name, the date, and so on, you wouldn't want a header or footer containing this information. To eliminate the header and footer on the first page, click File on the menu bar, click Page Setup, then click the Layout tab. Click the Different first page check box to select it (see Figure C-19). If you want to add a different header or footer to the first page, click anywhere in the first page of the document, open the Header or Footer field, and type the new text. You can also create different headers or footers for odd- and even-numbered pages. For example, you might want the title and filename of a long, bound document to appear on all the odd-numbered pages, and the page number and date to appear on all the even-numbered pages. On the Layout tab in the Page Setup dialog box, click the Different Odd and Even check box to select it, then insert the appropriate text in the header or footer areas of any odd or even page.

FIGURE C-19: Page Setup dialog box

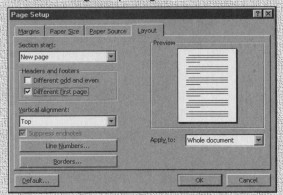

Word 2000

Verifying Page Layout

When you finish creating a document, it is wise to check page layout to make sure that everything is exactly where you want it and that the document looks good. WordArt, clip art, borders, and footnotes might take a few extra moments to print, so you want to make sure everything is correct before you print a final copy. ✎ You'll verify the page layout of the finished kite flyer before you print a final copy for Derek to review.

Steps 1234

1. **Click the Print Preview button** 🔍 **on the Standard toolbar**
   The Outdoor Designs kite flyer appears in Print Preview, as shown in Figure C-20. In Print Preview, the mouse pointer initially changes to 🔍. When you click with 🔍, the magnification of the view is increased, and the pointer changes to 🔍. After you click with 🔍, the pointer changes to 🔍; when you click with 🔍, the magnification is reduced. You can edit and format text and graphics in Print Preview by clicking the Magnifier button 🔍 on the Print Preview toolbar to change the mouse pointer to I.

QuickTip

If your document is only a few lines longer than one page, try clicking the Shrink to Fit button 📄. If the results are not what you expect, click Edit on the menu bar, then click Undo.

2. **Verify that the entire flyer fits on one page**
   You want the contents of the kite flyer to fit on one page. Check the vertical scroll bar. If the scroll box takes up the entire bar, then the document is exactly one page long. If everything doesn't fit on the number of pages you want, you can edit your document by resizing graphics or deleting unnecessary blank lines before you print. If the kite flyer fits on one page, skip to Step 4.

3. **If it is necessary to make changes, click the Magnifier button** 🔍 **on the Print Preview toolbar to change the mouse pointer to I, delete any extra blank lines in the kite flyer, resize the WordArt so it is slightly smaller, then click** 🔍 **again**
   Your document should now be on one page. If not, repeat Step 3 until it is.

4. **Verify that the margins are appropriate for the flyer**
   The kite flyer's margins look good. If the text looks out of proportion on the page, you might want to change the margin width. Changing these variables can also help fill up a short page or make room for extra text. To change document margins, use the Page Setup command on the File menu.

5. **Click the top of the table with** 🔍 **to verify that the footnote reference mark is in the "Type" heading in the table, then click with** 🔍 **to reduce magnification**

6. **Verify that footnotes and other items are correctly placed**
   The footnote should appear at the bottom of the flyer.

7. **Click the Print button** 🖨 **on the Print Preview toolbar**
   The final copy of the kite flyer is printed, as shown in Figure C-21.

8. **Click Close on the Print Preview toolbar**
   The flyer is finished.

9. **Click the Save button** 💾 **on the Standard toolbar, click File on the menu bar, then click Exit**
   The Kite Flyer document and the Word program close.

FIGURE C-20: **Final kite flyer in Print Preview**

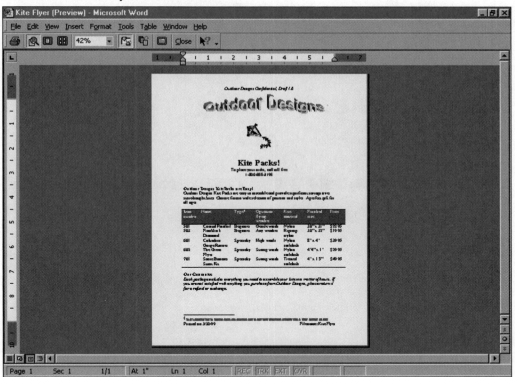

FIGURE C-21: **Printout of the Outdoor Designs kite flyer**

Kite Packs!

To place your order, call toll free
1-800-555-3195

Outdoor Designs Kite Packs are Easy!
Outdoor Designs Kite Packs are easy to assemble and provide significant savings over store-bought kites. Choose from a wide selection of patterns and styles. A perfect gift for all ages.

Item number	Name	Type*	Optimum flyin weather	Kite material	Finished size	Price
501	Coastal Parafoil	Beginner	Gentle winds	Nylon	30" x 31"	$22.95
503	Franklin's Diamond	Beginner	Any weather	Ripstop nylon	30" x 32"	$19.95
601	Columbia Gorge Runner	Specialty	High winds	Nylon sailcloth	8' x 4'	$39.95
602	The Green Flyer	Specialty	Strong winds	Nylon sailcloth	4'4" x 1'	$29.95
701	Sonic Boomer Stunt Kit	Specialty	Strong winds	Treated sailcloth	4' x 1'5"	$49.95

Our Guarantee
Each package includes everything you need to assemble your kite in a matter of hours. If you are not satisfied with anything you purchase from Outdoor Designs, please return it for a refund or exchange.

---

* *To fly a Specialty kite and perform stunts, you generally need at least some experience handling kites to avoid tangling the line.*

Word 2000

Practice

► Concepts Review

Label the Word window elements shown in Figure C-22.

FIGURE C-22

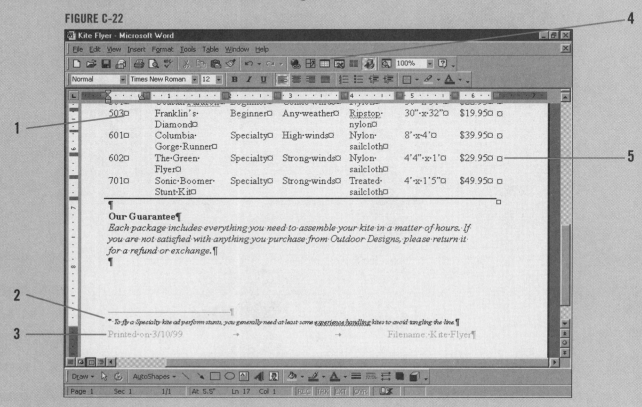

Match each toolbar button with its effect.

6.
7.
8.
9.
10.

a. Inserts a table
b. Inserts new WordArt
c. Inserts a new column in a table
d. Inserts a new row in a table
e. Inserts a border around text

Select the best answer from the list of choices.

11. In which view can you see footnote text without first clicking the View menu, then clicking Footnotes?
    a. Normal view
    b. Print Layout view
    c. Table view
    d. Web Layout view

12. Where does clip art appear in a document after you click the Insert Clip button in the Insert ClipArt window?
    a. At the top of the document
    b. At the bottom of the document
    c. At the location of the insertion point
    d. At the location of a footnote

13. Which command or button can you use to center a clip art image on the page?
    a. Center
    b. Distribute Horizontally
    c. Format Center
    d. Align Center

14. Which button would you click in the Footnote and Endnote dialog box to specify a custom footnote reference character?
    a. The Numbered option button
    b. The Special mark button
    c. The Custom mark option button
    d. The Insert option button

15. A header is text that appears:
    a. Just above the bottom margin of the page.
    b. Just above a table.
    c. Just below a clip art image.
    d. Just below the top margin of the page.

16. How do you center a footer on the page?
    a. Click the Center button on the Formatting toolbar.
    b. Double-click the right mouse button.
    c. Press [Ctrl][C].
    d. Click Format on the menu bar, then click Center Footer.

17. When you insert a column in a table using the Insert Columns button on the Standard toolbar, the new column appears
    a. To the left of the insertion point.
    b. To the right of the insertion point.
    c. As the last column in the table.
    d. Wherever you specify in the Insert Columns dialog box.

18. The Table AutoFormat command allows you to
    a. Design your own format for a table.
    b. Choose a predesigned format for a table.
    c. Modify the number of rows and columns in a table.
    d. Automatically change column widths.

▶ Skills Review

1. Create a table.
  a. Start Microsoft Word, open the file WD C-2, then save the file as "Kite Newsletter".
  b. Place the insertion point to the left of the paragraph mark below the paragraph that starts "The best kite flying winds…"
  c. Click the Insert Table button on the Standard toolbar.
  d. Click and drag to create a 5 x 3 table.
  e. Enter the data in Table C-1 into the table you created. Use [Tab], the arrow keys, and the mouse to place the insertion point in each cell.
  f. Click the Save button on the Standard toolbar to save your changes.

TABLE C-1

No. of Kites Ordered	Discount	Extra Line
1	10%	None
2-4	20%	500' of 30-lb. Line
5-7	30%	1000' of 30-lb. Line
8-10	40%	1500' of 30-lb. Line

2. Insert and delete columns and rows in a table.
  a. Click to the left of the end-of-row mark at the end of the last row.
  b. Press [tab] to insert a new row as the last row in the table.
  c. Insert the following information in the new row:
    11 or more
    50%
    1500' of 50-lb. Line
  d. Position the pointer over the top of the last column in the table (Extra Line) so the pointer changes to ↓, then click to select the whole column.
  e. Click the Insert Columns button on the Standard toolbar.
  f. Insert the information from Table C-2 into the new column.
  g. Save your changes.

3. Use Table AutoFormat and adjust column widths.
  a. With the insertion point still in the table, click Table on the menu bar, then click Table AutoFormat.
  b. Click the First column check box to deselect it.
  c. Click the Color check box to deselect it.
  d. Click Classic 4 in the Formats list.
  e. Click OK.

TABLE C-2

Shipping Available
2-day for additional cost
2-day for additional cost
2-day at no additional cost; Overnight for additional cost
2-day at no additional cost; Overnight for additional cost
Overnight at no additional cost

  f. Drag the first column divider approximately ½" to the left so the column is just wide enough for the "11 or more" entry, but the column heading "No. of Kites Ordered" remains on two lines.
  g. Double-click the second column-divider line.
  h. Double-click the third column-divider line so "Overnight for additional cost" appears on a second line and the last entry, in the Shipping column appears on one line. (You may have to double-click twice).
  i. Save your changes.

4. Insert WordArt.
  a. Place the insertion point in the blank line between "Outdoor Designs" and "Stock up on" at the top of the document.
  b. Click the Insert WordArt button on the Drawing toolbar.
  c. Select the WordArt style in the fourth row and the last column (this will insert a long vertical WordArt design), then click OK.

    d. Type "Go Fly a Kite Sale", then click OK.

    e. Click View on the menu bar, click Zoom, click the Whole page option button, then click OK.

    f. Drag the WordArt to the left margin, and drag it down to center it.

    g. Change the Zoom to Page width.

    h. Save your changes.

5. Insert clip art.

    a. Place the insertion point in the blank line between "Outdoor Designs" and "Stock up on" at the top of the document.

    b. Click Insert on the menu bar, point to Picture, then click Clip Art.

    c. Scroll down the category list and click the Nature category. (If this category isn't available, choose a different one.)

    d. Click an image of the sun. (If this image isn't available, choose a different one.)

    e. Click the Insert clip button, then close the Insert ClipArt window.

    f. Select the image if necessary, then drag the lower-right resize handle so the image is approximately 1" x 1". (Make sure the ruler is visible.)

    g. Save your changes.

6. Insert a footnote.

    a. Place the insertion point after the period at the end of the second sentence in the paragraph at the top of the document ("...for everyone in the family.").

    b. Click Insert on the menu bar, then click Footnote.

    c. Click the Custom mark option button, then type an asterisk (*) in the Custom mark text box

    d. Click OK.

    e. Type "Sale applies only to selected Kite Kits."

    f. Select the footnote text.

    g. Format the footnote as 8-point bold and italic.

    h. Place the insertion point after the name "Ben Franklin" in the paragraph below the heading "#503".

    i. Insert a footnote using two asterisks (**) as the Custom mark option.

    j. Type "Kite not endorsed by the Franklin family". and format the text as 8-point bold and italic.

    k. Save your changes.

7. Insert headers and footers.

    a. Click View on the menu bar, then click Header and Footer.

    b. Click the Switch Between Header and Footer button on the Header and Footer toolbar.

    c. Type the footer "Draft 1.0, updated on", then press [Spacebar].

    d. Click the Insert Date button on the Header and Footer toolbar.

    e. Press [Tab] twice, click Insert AutoText on the Header and Footer toolbar, point to Header/Footer, then click Last saved by. (If this AutoText entry is not available, choose a different AutoText entry from the list or type "Last name" followed by your name.)

    f. Close the Header and Footer toolbar.

8. Verify page layout.

    a. Click the Print Preview button on the Standard toolbar.

    b. Verify that the document fits on one page.

    c. If the document doesn't fit on one page, click the Magnifier button to change the pointer to I, then delete extra blank lines and resize the clip art until the document fits on one page.

d. Click the Magnifier button again to change the pointer to , then click at the bottom of the page.

e. Examine the footnotes to check your typing.

f. Click the Print button on the Print Preview toolbar.

g. Click Close on the Print Preview toolbar.

h. Save your changes.

i. Exit Word.

▶ Independent Challenges

1. Dianne Finn in the human relations department asked you to prepare a flyer for Wacky Words' annual Beach Bash on Saturday, June 12. The picnic will take place at Wildwood Park from 2 p.m. until dusk. The company will provide lobster and chicken dinners for adults, hot dogs and hamburgers for children, and build-your-own ice cream sundaes for all. Attendees can spend the day swimming, wind surfing, and playing volleyball. Other activities include a team sand castle building contest and a children's treasure hunt. The flyer should contain an RSVP section that asks for employee name, number of adults attending, and number of children attending.

To complete this independent challenge:

a. Prepare a one-page document based on the information supplied. Experiment with WordArt, and use the WordArt toolbar buttons to rotate text, create shaped text or sideways text, and adjust spacing between characters. Experiment with the Drawing toolbar buttons to add shading, shadows, or borders.

b. Use Print Preview as you work to produce an effective layout.

c. Save the file as "Beach Bash 2001".

d. Print a copy of your flyer.

2. Joel, the the owner of The Steak Pit, recently discovered that the other three steak restaurants in town charge much more for the same steak, potato, and garden salad than The Steak Pit does. Because Joel is going to have new menus printed for The Steak Pit, he wants to compare his prices with those of other local restaurants. He asks you to create a simple quick reference sheet that he can use to compare the information he has gathered. He asks you to put all the information in table format, with separate columns for the restaurant name, location, steak size, and price.

To complete this independent challenge:

a. Open the file WD C-3, and save it as "Restaurant Comparisons".

b. Double-click the WordArt at the top. Choose a new font. Click the WordArt Shape button on the WordArt toolbar, and choose a new shape.

c. Replace the text "<<Insert table>>" with a 4 x 4 table.

d. Enter the following information into the table, one row at a time:

For headings in row one, use: "Restaurant", "Location", "Steak Size", and "Price"

For row two, use: "Broderick's", "town square", "12 oz.", and "$17.99"

For row three, use: "The Grill", "mall", "8 oz.", and "$18.75"

For row four, use: "Hunter's", "outskirts of town", "10 oz.", and "$16.95"

e. Use the Table AutoFormat command to format the table appropriately.

Word 2000

f. Use the Table AutoFormat command to format the table appropriately.

g. Insert a footnote saying that Hunter's has been open only three months.

h. Log on to the Internet, and use your browser to go to http://www.course.com. From there, click the link Student Online Companions, click the link for this textbook, then click the Word link for Unit C. Use the links there to find restaurant reviews. Include two or three restaurants from these sites in your table.

i. Insert one or more clip art images above the table.

j. Add a footer that contains your name.

k. Save your changes.

l. Preview the document, then print a copy.

3. Kristine has just hired Josh Turney as the assistant for The Literary Loft. She asks you to prepare a flyer to announce his hiring and to welcome him to the job. Kristine wants the entire staff to gather at noon for a company lunch on his first day, February 3. The company will provide pizza, salad, and assorted beverages. She also plans to announce the employee-of-the-month award, which comes with a gift. The flyer should contain an RSVP section that asks for employee name, department, and funny gift suggestions.

To complete this independent challenge:

a. Open a new document, and save it as "New Hire".

b. Type appropriate text based on the information described above.

c. Use WordArt, clip art, and at least one footnote to communicate the necessary information.

d. Use Print Preview as you work to produce an effective and attractive layout and to keep the document one page long.

e. Save your changes, and print a copy of your flyer.

4. Orders have been slow for Nibblets, the gourmet rabbit food that Stuff for Pets sells. Lee Janson in the marketing department has decided to send out a promotional flyer to help spur orders. Lee wants to send the flyer to all retail pet shops that order from Stuff for Pets, so they can post them in their shops and convince more rabbit owners to switch to Nibblets. She started putting together the flyer as a two-column document, with WordArt and clip art. Now she decides the flyer would look better in a single column format. She asks you to format the document so that it is in one column, not two. She also wants you to add an appropriate clip art image and center it at the top of the page.

To complete this independent challenge:

a. Open WD C-4, and save it as "Nibblets".

b. Insert an appropriate clip art image at the end of the document. Resize the image to fill the bottom of the page.

c. Insert WordArt that says "Stuff for Pets" at the top of the document.

d. Insert the footnote "Based on an informal survey of rabbits" at the end of the paragraph that begins "Your rabbit will nibble away...." Use the number 1 as the reference mark.

e. Change the list above the text "If you answered yes..." to a table. *Hint*: Select the text, click the Convert command on the Table menu, click Text to Table, then click OK.

f. Change any text formatting you wish to make the document more interesting and readable.

g. Remove any unnecessary blank spaces so the document fits on one page, and examine the document in Print Preview to catch any layout problems.

h. Save your changes.

i. Preview your document, then print it.

► Visual Workshop

Create the document shown in Figure C-23, and save it as "Coffee." *Hint*: Increase the size of the left margin quite a bit to fit the WordArt, and use the Borders and Shading command to format the Daily Coffee Specials table.

FIGURE C-23

Daily Coffee Specials

Café Mocha with a Twist
A single shot of our rich, dark espresso mixed with just the right amount of imported Belgian chocolate powder and a touch of mint flavoring.

Tall Dark Cooler
A tall glass filled with iced Hawaiian Kona coffee, brewed to dark and rich tasting perfection.

Become a member of The Coffee Clubhouse for the price of a cup of coffee.[1]

Just fill out the "I'm a regular" card. Ask the person behind the coffeepot to stamp your card for each cup of coffee you buy here. When the card is full (10 stamps), you're a member. That's it. No membership dues or other fees.

Once you're a member, you'll receive a 15% discount on every purchase of one or more pounds of coffee beans.

Clubhouse Coffees[2]
Sumatra
French Roast
Mocha Java
Caramel Mocha
Special Blend
Espresso
And more

---

[1] Actually, ten cups of coffee.
[2] All coffees available in decaf also.

Unit A

Creating
and Enhancing a Worksheet with Excel 2000

Objectives

► **Navigate a workbook**
► **Enter numbers and labels**
► **Change column width and row height**
► **Use formulas**
► **Edit a worksheet**
► **Change alignment and number format**
► **Change font type and font style and add borders**
► **Preview and print a worksheet**

In this unit, you learn how to create and work with an Excel worksheet. A **worksheet** is an electronic spreadsheet consisting of rows and columns that is used for performing numeric calculations. You can use a worksheet for many purposes, such as performing data analysis, calculating a loan payment, or organizing and displaying your data in a chart. A **workbook** is the kind of file you create in Excel; it can contain one or more worksheets. To help the sales representatives track their product orders, Sue Ellen Monteiro, the sales manager for Outdoor Designs, asks you to build a worksheet to record orders as they arrive from the sales representatives. You will also enter the order information, modify the worksheet so it is easy to use, and print the final product for Sue Ellen's review.

Excel 2000

Navigating a Workbook

Many workbooks you create in Excel will use only one worksheet, with the other sheets remaining blank. You will recognize many of the toolbar buttons and menu commands because of the shared interface among the Office programs. Unlike a Word document, however, an Excel worksheet is divided into a grid of rows and columns. Figure A-1 identifies some important elements in the Excel workbook window. In order to start working on the product order worksheet, you need to start Excel, familiarize yourself with the workbook window, and save a blank workbook.

Steps

Trouble?

If this is the first time you are using Excel, click the Start using Microsoft Excel option button in the Welcome to Microsoft Excel dialog box, then close the Office Assistant.

1. Click **Start button** on the taskbar, point to **Programs**, then click **Microsoft Excel**

A blank workbook opens, as shown in Figure A-1. Excel contains elements that are found in every Microsoft Office program, including a menu bar, the Standard toolbar, the Formatting toolbar, a workspace (the workbook window), scroll bars, a status indicator, sizing buttons, a control menu box, and resizing buttons. The mouse pointer changes to a cross ✛ in the workbook window. A **cell** is the rectangular area formed where a row and a column intersect. When you open a new workbook, Excel selects the cell in the upper-left corner of the first worksheet, Sheet1. Referred to as "A1," this cell is where column A and row 1 intersect.

2. Click **View** on the menu bar, click **Toolbars**, click **Customize**, in the Customize dialog box, click the **Options tab** if necessary, click to deselect the **Standard and Formatting toolbars share one row checkbox** if necessary, click the **Reset My Usage data button**, click **Yes** in the message box, then click **Close**

QuickTip

You can get help in Excel by clicking the Office Assistant button ② on the Standard toolbar or by using the Help menu.

3. Click cell **B1**

This cell becomes selected. Table A-1 lists several methods for selecting worksheet cells with the mouse or keyboard. The **name box** shows the name of the currently selected cell, and the **formula bar** shows the contents of the cell (it is currently empty).

4. Press **[↓]**

Cell A2 is now the selected cell. You can also move to and select a cell by clicking it, using the arrow keys, or pressing [Tab] (to move one cell to the right) or [Shift]+[Tab] (to move one cell to the left), or by pressing [Enter] (to move one cell down).

5. Press **[→]** three times to move to cell **E2**

QuickTip

A blank worksheet contains 65,536 rows and 256 columns; however, it is unlikely you would ever fill an entire worksheet with data. Even when working on a large project, it is usually more convenient to use several worksheets within a workbook to organize your data.

6. Scroll down until you see row 65 and then click cell **H65**

To move among the sheets in a workbook, you click the sheet tab of the sheet you want to move to.

7. Click sheet tab **Sheet2**, as shown in Figure A-2

By default, a blank workbook contains three blank worksheets, but you can add or remove as many as you need, and you can rename and rearrange them.

8. Click the **Sheet1** sheet tab to return to this worksheet, then press **[Ctrl][Home]**

This keyboard shortcut returns you to cell A1.

9. Insert your Project Disk in the appropriate drive, click the **Save button** 🖫 on the Standard toolbar, then save the file as **Product Order 6-30** on your Project Disk

FIGURE A-1: Excel worksheet window with important elements labeled

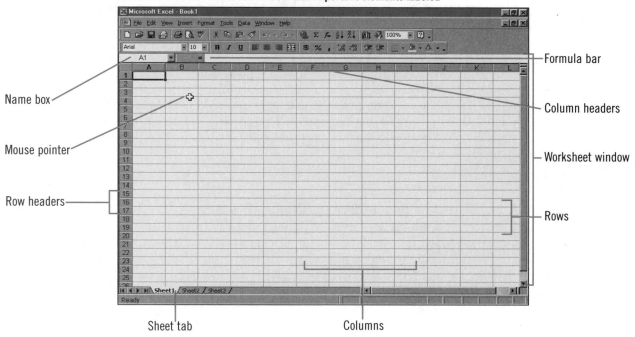

Name box

Mouse pointer

Row headers

Formula bar

Column headers

Worksheet window

Rows

Sheet tab

Columns

FIGURE A-2: Moving among worksheets in a workbook

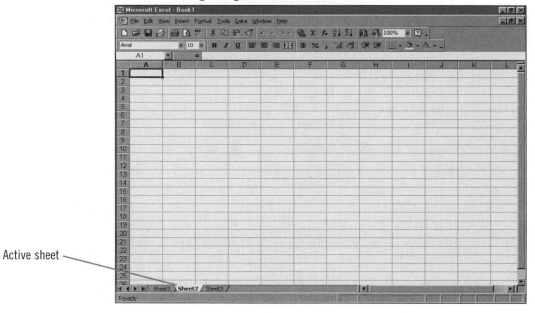

Active sheet

TABLE A-1: Methods for selecting worksheet cells

to select	with the mouse	with the keyboard
A cell	Click the cell	Use arrow keys
A row	Click the row number	Select a cell in the row, then press [Shift][Spacebar]
A column	Click the column letter	Select a cell in the column, then press [Ctrl][Spacebar]
A group of cells	Drag across the cells	Press [Shift], then use arrow keys
A worksheet	Click the box above row 1	Press [Ctrl][A]

Entering Numbers and Labels

Excel 2000

You enter numbers and labels into a worksheet by typing in cells and accepting your entry. You must select a cell before you can enter data in it. ✐ Practice entering numbers and labels into the worksheet by entering a product order from a sales representative. The completed product order serves as an internal tracking sheet that the Outdoor Designs accounting department will use to process the order.

Steps 1 2 3 4

1. **In cell A1 type Outdoor Designs Product Order**
   As you type, the text appears in cell A1 and in the formula bar, as shown in Figure A-3. The text you typed is a **label**, or a piece of text used for description, instead of a calculation. Labels can extend into neighboring cells that don't contain data, so the text "Outdoor Designs Product Order" extends into cells B1 and C1, but it is contained only in cell A1.

2. **Press [Enter]**
   Pressing [Enter] accepts your entry and moves you to the next cell in the column.

3. **Press [↓] to move to cell A3**
   Cell A3 is selected and "A3" appears in the name box, identifying your current location. You can use the arrow keys to accept an entry and move to the next cell in the direction of the arrow key. However, when you are entering data in multiple columns it is easier to press [Enter] after the last column because this moves to the first column, as you will see in Step 4.

4. **Type these four lines, remembering to press [Enter] after each line**
   Sales rep: Kimberly Ullom
   Store: Mountain Air, North Bend, WA
   Order date: June 30, 1999
   Terms: Payment 30 days after receipt (Net 30)

QuickTip
Pressing [Tab] is the same as pressing [→] in the worksheet. You might find that using [Tab] is more convenient for entering multiple columns of data.

5. **Press [Enter] to move to cell A8, then type the following text in columns A through D of rows 8 and 9, pressing [Tab] to move to the next cell in a row and pressing [Enter] at the end of each row**

Kit num	Kit name	Price	Quantity
#401	Cascade Ski Sack	19.95	5

   When you typed "19.95" in cell C9, the text in cell B9 was cut off. When text is wider than a cell, it spills into the adjacent cell unless that cell has data in it. You'll widen the necessary cells later.

6. **Beginning with cell A10, continue typing the following data in the worksheet; remember to press [Tab] to move one cell to the right and [Enter] to move to the next row**

#501	Coastal Parafoil Kite	22.95	1
#502	Puget Sound Delta Kite	24.95	2
#801	Olympic Rain Tent	79.95	2
#802	Tent Vestibule	19.95	1

   The text is entered in the worksheet, as shown in Figure A-4.

7. **Click the Save button 🖬 on the Standard toolbar**

FIGURE A-3: Worksheet text in Formula bar and in neighboring cells

Name box
displays name
of selected cell

Cell A1

Formula bar
displays contents
of selected cell

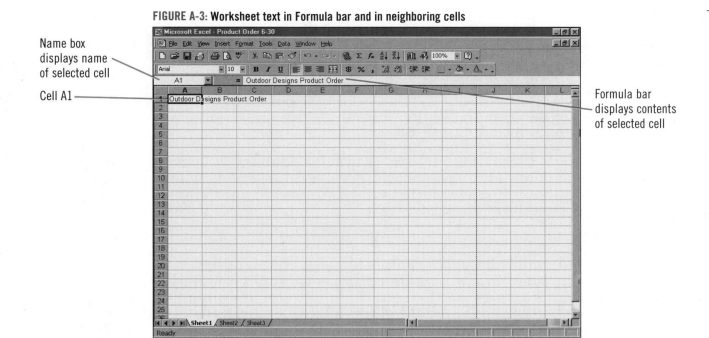

FIGURE A-4: Worksheet after entering product order data

Data that extends
beyond width of
column is hidden
because cells to the
right contain data;
you'll fix this later

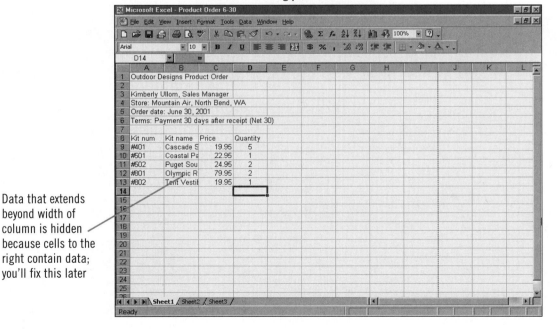

Excel 2000

Excel 2000

Changing Column Width and Row Height

You can adjust column widths and row heights by dragging the column or row borders with the mouse or by using the Format menu. You'll practice the first method next. You adjust the column width and row height in the Product Order 6-30 worksheet to make the information in the worksheet more readable.

Steps 123 4

1. Position the pointer on the column line between columns B and C in the column header area so the pointer changes to ↔, as shown in Figure A-5

QuickTip

You can also change column width and row height using the Format menu. To change the column width, click Width, then type the desired width (in number of characters) in the dialog box. To change the row height, click Height, then type the desired height (in points).

2. Double-click the **column line** to change the column width
   The width of Column B is automatically widened to fit the longest cell, using a feature called **AutoFit**.

3. Click the number **7** to the left of row 7 to select the row
   The row is selected.

4. Position the pointer on the row line between rows **7** and **8** in the row header area
   The pointer changes to ↕. Each row's height is automatically adjusted to be at least as large as the largest font in the row, so you need to change the row height only if you want to increase or decrease its size.

Trouble?

If you cannot resize the row height to exactly 21.00 points, make it as close to this measurement as possible.

5. Click the **row line** and slowly drag the pointer down until you see **Height: 21.00** in the ScreenTip box, as shown in Figure A-6, then release the mouse button
   The height of row 7 changes from 12 to 21 points.

FIGURE A-5: Changing the column width in the worksheet

Pointer on
column border

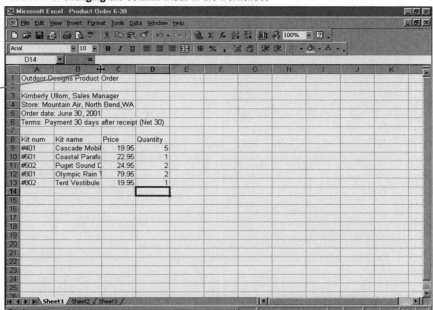

FIGURE A-6: Changing the row height in the worksheet

Current row
height in points
(and pixels)

Pointer on
row border

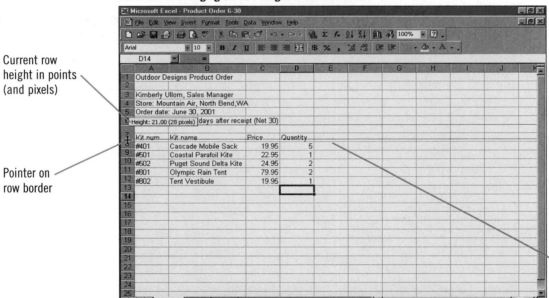

Outline indicates
new row size as you
drag the pointer

Using Formulas

To perform a calculation in the worksheet, you enter a formula in a cell. A **formula** is an equation that calculates a new value from existing values. Formulas can contain numbers, mathematical operators (+ for addition, − for minus, and so on), cell references (A1, E42), and **functions** (commonly used formulas that come preprogrammed with Excel). Table A-2 lists some mathematical operators you can use in a formula. Formulas can be copied and moved just like other data in a worksheet. It's a good idea to use cell references (such as A1 + B1) instead of actual values (such as 2 + 3) whenever possible in your formulas, so that Excel can update the results of a formula whenever the cell contents change or the formula moves. ✎ The product order worksheet should provide subtotals for each item ordered. You want to create a formula to calculate these subtotals.

Steps 1 2 3 4

1. Click cell **E8**, type **Subtotal**, then press [↓]

2. Type =
   The equal sign (=) indicates that you're about to enter a formula in cell E9. Everything you enter in a cell after the equal sign, including any numbers, mathematical operators, cell references, or functions, are included in the formula.

3. Press [←] twice to move to cell **C9**
   Cell C9, which appears as a **cell reference** in the formula, is selected, meaning that the number in cell C9 will be used when the formula is calculated. To help you keep track of the formula as you build it, the formula is displayed in both the formula bar and in cell E9.

4. Type * (an asterisk)
   When the formula is calculated, the asterisk will be used to multiply the number in cell C9 by the next cell reference you select.

5. Click cell **D9**
   You can also use the mouse to select cells for use in formulas. When the formula is calculated, the product price in cell C9 is multiplied by the quantity in cell D9.

6. Press **[Enter]**, then press [↑] to select cell **E9**
   The result of the formula (99.75) appears in cell E9. Notice that although the formula's result appears in cell E9, the original formula still appears in the formula bar.

7. Press [↓] , type **=C10*D10**, then press **[Enter]**
   You can type cell references as well as pressing the arrow keys or clicking to insert them.

8. Press [↑] to move to cell **E10**
   You can copy a formula from one cell into cells that appear below it or to its right by clicking and dragging the **Fill box** (the small black square in the lower corner of a selected cell) on the selected cell. When you move the pointer over a Fill box, the pointer changes to +, as shown in Figure A-7.

9. Click the **Fill box** for cell **E10**, and drag down to cell **E13** to copy the formula into cells **E11** through **E13**, release the mouse button, then click the **Save button** 🖫 on the Standard toolbar
   The subtotal formula is replicated in cells E10 through E13, and the subtotal for each product appears.

Trouble?

If you see your formula in cell E9 instead of the result, you forgot to type the equal sign, and the text is treated as a label. Select the cell, click the Equal button 🔲, then press [Enter].

QuickTip

If you want your worksheet to display formulas instead of their results in cells, click Tools on the menu bar, click Options, click the View tab, click the Formulas check box to select it, then click OK.

Equal sign indicates a formula

Results of this formula appear in cell E10

Fill pointer

TABLE A-2: **Useful mathematical operators (in order of evaluation)**

operator	description	example	result
( )	**Parentheses**	(3+6)*3	27
^	**Exponent**	10^2	100
*	**Multiplication**	7*5	35
/	**Division**	20/4	5
+	**Addition**	5+5	10
−	**Subtraction**	12−8	4

Calculating formulas in Excel

When you enter a formula that contains more than one mathematical operator, standard algebraic rules are followed to determine which calculation is performed first. First, the calculations within parentheses are evaluated. Then the rules dictate that exponential calculations be performed first, multiplication and division calculations second, and addition and subtraction calculations last. If there is more than one calculation in the same category, they are evaluated from left to right.

Excel 2000

Editing a Worksheet

You can edit cells in a worksheet in several ways. You can revise a single cell by clicking it and editing its contents in the formula bar. You can cut, copy, and paste blocks of cells using the Edit menu or the toolbar. You can also move cells using the drag and drop method. As in Word, you can use the Replace command to change one word to another automatically throughout the worksheet. ▰▰▰ Mountain Air increased its order for Coastal Parafoil kites and extended the payment grace period. You edit the product order worksheet to reflect these changes.

Steps

1. **Select cell D10 and type 3, then press [Enter]**
   The number in cell D10 changes from 1 to 3, and the formula in cell E10 is recalculated when you press [Enter], so the subtotal changes from 22.95 to 68.85.

2. **Click cell A6**
   The cell is selected, and the label "Terms: Payment 30 days after receipt (Net 30)" appears in the formula bar. If you began typing in a cell that contains data without first selecting any data, the complete contents of the cell are replaced by what you type.

   QuickTip

   The Find and Replace commands are available in Excel, just as they are in Word, by clicking Find or Replace on the Edit menu.

3. **Position the mouse over the formula bar, select the first 3 in the label, type 6, select the second 3 in the formula bar, then type 6**
   The number 3 is replaced when you type the new number, 6. When you select text, new text replaces selected text as you type. The formula bar now contains the label "Terms: Payment 60 days after receipt (Net 60)."

4. **Press [Enter] to confirm your formula bar changes**
   The updated label appears in the worksheet in cell A6.

   QuickTip

   If you realize that you made a mistake after pressing [Enter], click the Undo button on the Standard toolbar to return the cell contents to their original state.

5. **Select row 7 in the worksheet by clicking the number 7 to the left of row 7**
   When you insert a new row into the worksheet, it is inserted above the one that is selected.

6. **Click Insert on the menu bar, then click Rows**
   A new row is added to the worksheet, and the rows below it are renumbered. The new row has the formatting attributes of the row above the one that you select.

7. **Click row 3 to select it, position the pointer over the bottom of the row so it changes to ⇲, click row 3, drag it down until row 7 is selected, as shown in Figure A-8, then release the mouse button**
   The contents of row 3 move to row 7.

   QuickTip

   If you select a row or column and press [Delete], only the contents of the cells are deleted. You must click Delete on the Edit menu to delete the contents of the cells and the row or column.

8. **Click row 3 to select it, click Edit on the menu bar, then click Delete**
   This eliminates the empty row.

9. **Click the Save button 🖫 on the Standard toolbar**

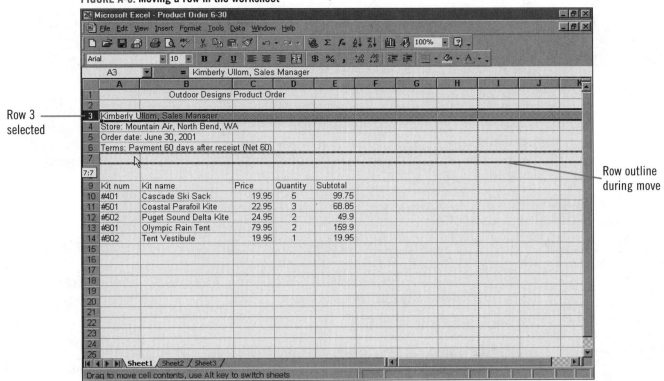

Row 3 selected

Row outline during move

Understanding relative and absolute cell references

By default, cell references in a worksheet are **relative**—that is, when you copy a formula, the cell references change to refer to cells relative to the new location. For example, a formula in cell D5 that reads "=B5*C5" changes to "=B6*C6" when you copy the formula down one row. This makes reusing formulas easy and convenient. However, there may be times when you want a cell reference to always refer to a specific cell, no matter where in the worksheet you copy the formula. For example, cell C5 might contain a value by which you want to multiply every cell in column B. In these situations, you use an **absolute** cell reference. To indicate an absolute cell reference, you type a dollar sign ($) before the part of the address you want to remain absolute. For example, if you want the entire cell address to be absolute, as in the example discussed here, you would type "C5" (you could also type "$C5" or "C$5" if you wanted only the row or column to remain absolute, but the rest of the cell reference to change according to the new location of the formula). Note that when you move a formula, the cell references remain absolute.

Excel 2000

Changing Alignment and Number Format

When you first enter data in a cell, labels are left-aligned and values are right-aligned by default, but you can change the alignment any time. You can also format numbers to appear in one of several standard formats, including currency, percent, and date. Changing alignment and number format can improve the look of your worksheet and make it easier to read. You use the formatting options to improve the appearance of the product order worksheet.

Trouble?

To use a button that is not visible, click the More Buttons button ➤ on the right side of the appropriate toolbar, then click the button you need. If it is still not visible, click Add or Remove buttons, click the desired button, click outside the list to close it, then click the button on the toolbar.

QuickTip

To deselect selected cells, click anywhere in the worksheet window.

QuickTip

You can press [F4] to repeat the last edit or formatting change you made.

1. Click row number **8** in the worksheet to select this row, then click the **Center button** ☰ on the Formatting toolbar
Each label in row 8 is centered in its cell. There are three ways to align cell data using the Formatting toolbar: right, center, or left.

2. Select cells **D9** through **D13**

3. Click **Format** on the menu bar, click **Cells**, then click the **Alignment tab**
You can use the Format Cells dialog box, shown in Figure A-9, to change a variety of cell attributes.

4. Click the **Horizontal list arrow**, click **Center**, then click **OK**
The contents of the five cells in the column are centered.

5. Select cells **A1** through **E1**
The cell containing the title "Outdoor Designs Product Order" and the four blank cells to the right of it are selected.

6. Click the **Merge and Center button** ☒ on the Formatting toolbar
The worksheet title is centered across the five selected cells. (Note that the cell reference of the title is still A1, however.)

7. Select cells **A9** through **A13**, then click ☰
The contents of the five cells are centered.

8. Select cells **C9** through **C13**, then click the **Currency Style button** ⑤ on the Formatting toolbar
The five cells in the Price column are formatted as currency (dollars and cents), as shown in Figure A-10.

9. Select cells **E9** through **E13**, click ⑤, then click the **Save button** 🖫 on the Standard toolbar
The five cells in the Subtotal column are formatted as currency and your changes are saved on disk.

FIGURE A-9: Format Cells dialog box

Changes how numbers are formatted

Changes cell alignment

Changes font type, style, size, and other font attributes changes

Protects worksheet so users cannot make changes

Adds patterns and shading

Adds and formats borders

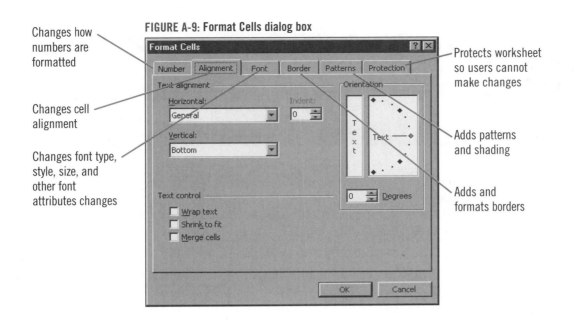

FIGURE A-10: Formatted information in the worksheet cells

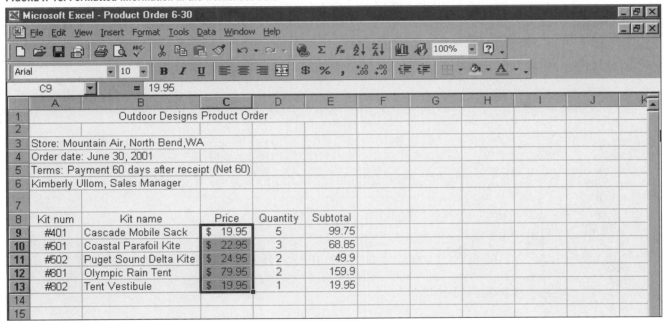

Changing the number format

You can format numbers in several ways. The Formatting toolbar has toolbar buttons for common number formats such as the Currency Style button $, the Percent Style button %, and the Comma Style button ,. Other useful number formats include Date, which lets you format a number using several date formats; Time, which formats numbers in various time formats; Fraction, which formats numbers as fractions; and Exponential, which formats numbers in scientific notation. To change the number format in cells, select the cell(s) to change, click the Cells command on the Format menu, then click the Number tab.

Changing Font Type and Font Style and Adding Borders

You can change the font type and font style of text in the Excel worksheet and add borders and shading to make important information stand out. The Border and Patterns tabs in the Format Cells dialog box help you take advantage of the unique rectangular design of worksheet cells to create impressive formatting effects. ✐ You change the border and patterns in the worksheet to enhance the product order worksheet.

Steps 1 2 3 4

1. Select cell **A1** and click the **Bold button** **B** and the **Italic button** **I** on the Formatting toolbar
   The title "Outdoor Designs Product Order" appears in bold italic style.

2. Click the **Font Size list arrow** on the Formatting toolbar, click **16**, click the **Font list arrow**, scroll down, then click **Times New Roman**
   The title text changes to 16-point Times New Roman font. Notice how the row height increases to accommodate the new font.

3. Select row **8** in the worksheet, then click **B**
   The font style of all the cells in the row changes to bold. Now you can add a border around the sales information in rows 3 through 6.

4. Select cell **A3**, click cell **A3** again and drag to cell **D6** to select all the cells in between, then release the mouse button
   The **range** of cells four cells wide and four cells long is selected. A range can also be referred to using a colon, such as "A3:D6" for the current selection.

5. Click **Format** on the menu bar, click **Cells**, then click the **Border tab**
   You can use the Border tab of the Format Cells dialog box to add or change borders, line styles, and color formatting options.

6. Click the **double line style** in the Style list box shown in Figure A-11 (the last item in the second column), click the **Outline button** in the Presets area, then click **OK**
   The Format Cells dialog box closes, and a double line border appears around the block of selected cells.

7. Select the range A8:E13 (a block of cells five cells wide and six cells long), click **Format** on the menu bar, click **Cells**, then click the **Border tab** if necessary

8. Click the **Outline** and the **Inside Preset buttons** in the Presets area, make sure that the last line style option in the first column is selected, click **OK**, then click anywhere outside of the selection to deselect the cells
   A single line border appears around each cell in the selection.

9. Click the **Save button** **🖫** on the Standard toolbar

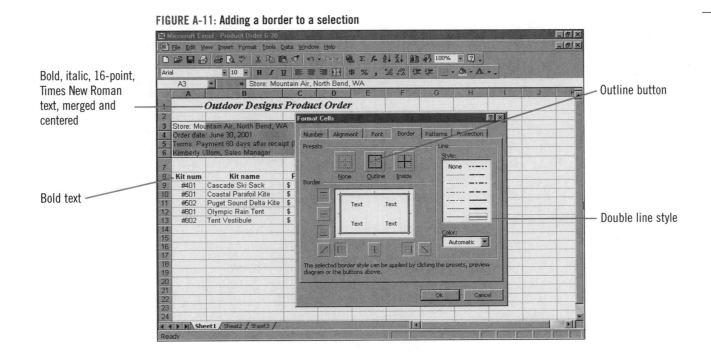

Bold, italic, 16-point, Times New Roman text, merged and centered

Bold text

Outline button

Double line style

 CLUES TO USE

Adding shading to cells

You can fill one or more worksheet cells with a shading pattern using the Patterns tab on the Format Cells dialog box. Shading formatting works like other types of formatting: first you select the cells you want to format, then you click the formatting options you want in the Patterns tab of the Format Cells dialog box. Select the shading color, then click the Pattern list arrow to apply different shading patterns to your selection. Figure A-12 shows the Shading tab and a range of cells formatted with yellow shading and a 12.5% gray pattern.

FIGURE A-12: Shading tab in the Format Cells dialog box

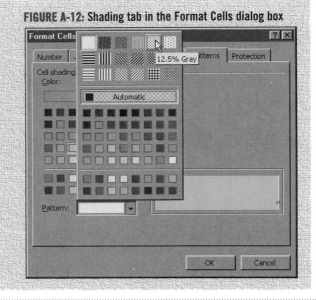

Excel 2000

Previewing and Printing a Worksheet

When you finish working with your worksheet and have saved your work, you are ready to print. It is important to save your work before printing so if you experience technical problems while printing, you do not lose your work. You can examine your document in Print Preview and verify the page layout with the zoom pointer. After you preview your document, you're ready to print a copy with the Print command. ✐ After you preview and print the product order worksheet, you save your changes again and exit Excel.

Steps 1 2 3 4

> **QuickTip**
> When you use color in your worksheets, the Print Preview window shows color only if you have a color printer. If you do not have a color printer, your document appears in black and white.

> **QuickTip**
> After zooming in on a part of a document, click anywhere in the document to return to a full page.

> **QuickTip**
> Use the Page Setup command on the File menu to change page margins, paper orientation, and other printing options.

1. Click **File** on the menu bar, then click **Print Preview**
The Print Preview window opens, and the Product Order 6–30 worksheet looks as it will on the printed page. Several command buttons that control the Print Preview window's operation appear across the top of the window.

2. Move the mouse pointer over the document page
The pointer changes to the **zoom pointer** 🔍, which you can use to examine parts of the document more closely.

3. Click the title of the worksheet with the zoom pointer
The worksheet enlarges to full size in the Print Preview window, as shown in Figure A-13.

4. Click **Close** on the Print Preview toolbar
The Print Preview window closes, and the product order worksheet reappears.

5. Click **File** on the menu bar, then click **Print**
The Print dialog box opens. You use this dialog box to specify the printer you want to use, the page range to print (the selected cells, the selected worksheet, or the whole workbook), the number of copies you want to print, and what to print. If you want to print one copy of the entire worksheet without changing any settings, click the **Print button** 🖨 on the Standard toolbar.

6. Verify that your printer is on and connected to your computer
If you have questions, ask your instructor or technical support person for help.

7. Click **OK**
The Print dialog box closes and the worksheet is printed.

8. Click the **Save button** 💾 on the Standard toolbar

9. Click the program window **Close button**
The Product Order 6-30 worksheet and the Excel program both close.

FIGURE A-13: Worksheet in Print Preview

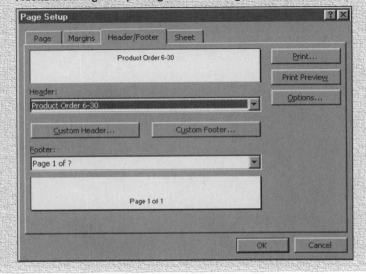

Print Preview toolbar

Outdoor Designs Product Order

Store: Mountain Air, North Bend,WA
Order date: June 30, 2001
Terms: Payment 60 days after receipt (Net 60)
Kimberly Ullom, Sales Manager

Kit num	Kit name	Price	Quantity	Subtotal
#401	Cascade Mobile Sack	$ 19.95	5	$ 99.75
#501	Coastal Parafoil Kite	$ 22.95	3	$ 68.85
#502	Puget Sound Delta Kite	$ 24.95	2	$ 49.90
#801	Olympic Rain Tent	$ 79.95	2	$ 159.90
#802	Tent Vestibule	$ 19.95	1	$ 19.95

Preview: Page 1 of 1

Adding headers and footers

Before you print your worksheet, you might want to add page numbers, the current date, or some other text to the top or bottom of each page. You can add this information to your worksheet using the Header and Footer command on the View menu. A standard header or footer in the worksheet is one line long and can contain standard or customized information. Figure A-14 shows a header that contains the filename and a footer that contains the page number and the total number of pages. You won't see headers and footers in the worksheet window, but you can examine them in Print Preview.

FIGURE A-14: Page Setup dialog box for creating headers and footers

Excel 2000

Practice

▶ Concepts Review

Label each worksheet element shown in Figure A-15.

FIGURE A-15

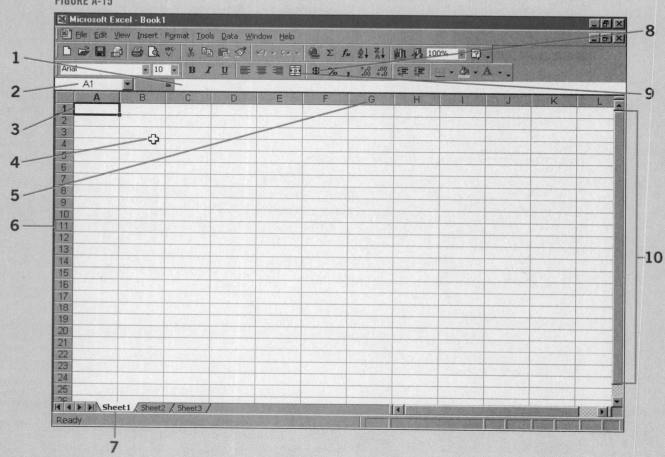

Match the mathematical operators with their uses in worksheet formulas.

11. ^   **a.** Multiplication
12. /   **b.** Division
13. *   **c.** Addition
14. −   **d.** Exponent
15. +   **e.** Subtraction

Select the best answer from the list of choices.

16. The name box shows the
    a. Currently selected cell.   **c.** Contents of the selected cell.
    b. Name of the worksheet in the workbook window.   **d.** Name of the open workbook.

17. Worksheet rows and columns intersect to form
   a. The toolbar.
   b. Cells.
   c. Paragraphs.
   d. Selected text.

18. The name of a cell in column B and row 2 is
   a. A1.
   b. 1A.
   c. B2.
   d. 2B.

19. To change the width of a column
   a. Click the Cells command on the Format menu.
   b. Double-click the column letter.
   c. Click the column border and drag it to a new location.
   d. Click the Width command on the Format menu.

20. How do you select an entire column in the worksheet?
   a. Press [Esc].
   b. Press [Shift][Spacebar].
   c. Click the row number to the left of the column.
   d. Click the column letter at the top of the column.

▶ Skills Review

1. Start Excel and identify the elements of the worksheet window.
   a. Click the Start button, point to Programs, then click Microsoft Excel.
   b. Identify the program window elements using Figure A-1 as a reference.
   c. Click cell H5.
   d. Scroll to and click cell Z100.
   e. Click sheet Sheet3.
   f. Click sheet Sheet1.
   g. Press [Ctrl][Home].

2. Enter numbers and labels.
   a. Type the following information (starting in cell A1), pressing [Enter] and [Tab] as indicated, to create an Outdoor Designs shipping ticket.
   Outdoor Designs Shipping Ticket [Enter]
   Ship to: [Enter]
   Pam's Kites [Enter]
   21 Vose Road [Enter]
   Edmonds, WA 98022 [Enter]
   Date: July 30, 2001 [Enter]

Kit num	[Tab]	Quantity	[Tab]	Kit name	[Tab]	Price	[Enter]
#401	[Tab]	2	[Tab]	Cascade Mobile Sack	[Tab]	19.95	[Enter]
#501	[Tab]	2	[Tab]	Coastal Parafoil Kite	[Tab]	22.95	[Enter]
#503	[Tab]	3	[Tab]	Franklin's Diamond	[Tab]	19.95	[Enter]
#701	[Tab]	2	[Tab]	Sonic Boomer Stunt Kite	[Tab]	49.95	[Enter]
#801	[Tab]	1	[Tab]	Olympic Rain Tent	[Tab]	79.95	[Enter]

   b. Save the workbook as "Shipping Ticket 7-30" on your Project Disk.

3. **Adjust column width and row height so all the information appears in the worksheet. Then add a new row and increase the space between the address and the data by increasing the height of the new row.**
   a. Select column C.
   b. Position the pointer on the column line between columns C and D.
   c. Double-click the column line.
   d. Select row 7.
   e. Click Insert on the menu bar, then click Rows.
   f. Position the pointer on the row line between rows 7 and 8.
   g. Drag the pointer down so the row is 27.00 points high, then release the mouse button.

4. **Enter a formula in cell E9 that calculates the value of the product price times the product quantity, then copy the formula in cells E10 through E13. Then enter a formula in cell B14 that calculates the total number of items shipped.**
   a. Click cell E8.
   b. Type "Item Total", then press [Enter].
   c. Type "=B9*D9" in cell E9, then press [Enter].
   d. Select cell E9.
   e. Use the Fill box to copy the formula from cell E9 into cells E10 through E13.
   f. Click cell A14, type "# Items", then press [Tab].
   g. In cell B14, type "=B9+B10+B11+B12+B13", then press [Enter].

5. **Practice editing the contents of cells in the formula bar and using the mouse to drag and drop text. What happens to the results of the formula in E9 when you edit the data?**
   a. Select cell D9.
   b. Click the formula bar.
   c. Change 19.95 in the formula bar to 20.95, then press [Enter].
   d. Select rows 9 and 10 (which contain information about items #401 and #501).
   e. Drag the selected rows to rows 15 and 16.
   f. Select rows 9 and 10 (which are now blank).
   g. Click Edit on the toolbar, then click Delete.

6. **Change cell alignment and number formats.**
   a. Select row 8.
   b. Click the Center button on the Formatting toolbar.
   c. Select cells A1 through E1.
   d. Click the Merge and Center button on the Formatting toolbar.
   e. Select the range A9:B13.
   f. Center-align the data in these cells using the Center button on the Formatting toolbar.
   g. Change the number format of the data in the Price and Item Total columns to currency using the Currency Style button on the Formatting toolbar.

7. **Change font type and style and add borders to worksheet data.**
   a. Select cell A1, then click the Underline button on the Formatting toolbar.
   b. Change the font type to Impact and the font size to 18 point.
   c. Select row 8, and change the font type for the column labels to Impact.

d. Select cell A2, then click the Italic button on the Formatting toolbar.

e. Select the range A3:B6.

f. Open the Format Cells dialog box, then click the Border tab.

g. Click the thickest line style (the sixth style in the second column), click the Outline button, then click OK.

h. Select range A8:E13, then open the Format Cells dialog box.

i. Use the Borders tab to add a black solid line (fifth row, second column) Outline border and a dotted line (second row, first column) Inside border. Make sure that you click the line style before clicking the Preset button.

j. With the range A8:E13 still selected, click the Bold button on the Formatting toolbar.

k. Double-click the divider between columns C and D to auto fit column C to accommodate the bold text.

l. Save your changes to the worksheet.

8. Add a footer, examine the worksheet in Print Preview, then print a final copy.

a. Click View on the menu bar, then click Header and Footer.

b. Click the Footer list arrow, click Page 1 of ?, then click OK.

c. Click the Print Preview button on the Standard toolbar.

d. Click the top of the worksheet once with the zoom pointer, and verify the contents.

e. Click in the document again to return to full page view, then click the worksheet footer. Verify that the footer is centered in the bottom margin and reads "Page 1 of 1."

f. Click the Close button on the Print Preview toolbar.

g. Save and print the worksheet, then exit Excel.

▶ Independent Challenges

1. At Wacky Words, you must provide the sales and marketing department with a monthly order summary. The summary includes the order number, account name, order date, order total, and payment. You also provide a monthly sales total and indicate what percentage of the year's sales to date the month's orders represent.

a. Open a new workbook, then enter the title "August Order Summary" in cell A1.

b. Enter the following information, starting in cell A3.

Order #	Account	Date	Total	Paid
600	Britts Books & Cards	8/5/01	1501	0
601	Songs and Such	8/10/01	950	950
602	Stationery Plus	8/7/01	2005	0
603	Cards-n-More	8/25/01	1261	0
604	Rita's Gift Shop	8/14/01	1800	1800
Monthly Total				
Percent of year to date			.09	

c. Widen or narrow each column as necessary so that the data in each column fits comfortably.

d. Drag rows 9 and 10, which contain the Monthly Total and Percent of year to date information, down to rows 10 and 11. Reduce the row height of row 9, which is now blank, to 6.00.

e. Enter a formula in cell D10 that adds the figures in the Total column. Then change the amount in cell D4 from 1501 to 1400.

f. Center the order numbers in cells A4 through A8.

g. Format the dates in the Date column so the years appear with four digits (for example, 8/7/01 becomes 08/07/2001). Format the numbers in D4 through E8 with commas and zero decimal places. Format cell D10 for Currency with no decimal places and cell D11 as Percent with no decimal places.

h. Center the title across columns A through E. Change the font to 18-point bold Arial Narrow. Center the column labels in row 3; make them bold, and change the font type to Arial Narrow. Change the labels in cells B10 and B11 to bold Arial Narrow as well.

i. Add a border line at the top and bottom of the column labels in cells A3 through E3. Choose the second line style in the second column, and change the line color to blue. Add the same type of line above cells A10 through E10 and below cells A11 through E11.

j. Save the workbook as "August Order Summary" on your Project Disk, preview it, then print it.

2. You compare sales for the menu items featured during the past month at The Steak Pit. The owner wants to determine how this has affected sales by comparing items sold and total sales to last month.

a. Start a new workbook. In cell A1, type "Featured Menu Items Comparison" as the worksheet title.

b. Enter the following information, starting in cell A3.

Featured Item	Price	May	May Sales	June	June Sales
12 oz. Sizzler	18	353		478	
Chicken Sizzler	15	321		398	
Roast Beef	20	349		403	
Filet	23	314		378	

c. Merge and center the text in cell A1 across columns A through E.

d. Adjust column widths so the data fits completely within the columns.

e. Add a formula to cell D4 that calculates the sales for May for the first item, 12 oz. Sizzler. (*Hint:* Multiply cell B4 by cell C4. Copy this formula down the column for the other items. Then repeat the process for cell F4, to calculate sales for each item in June as well.

f. Change the worksheet title's font to 18-point bold italic Times New Roman, and center it across columns A through F. Center the column labels in row 3, and make them 12-point bold Arial Black. Center the numbers in the May and June columns. Adjust the column widths as necessary.

g. Format the Price, May Sales, and June, and June Sales columns as currency with two decimal places. Then add solid light blue shading to the two Sales columns. Finally, add a colored border around the worksheet data (cells A3 through F7).

h. Save the workbook as "Items Comparison" on your Project Disk, preview it, then print it.

3. Stuff for Pets market research coordinator Rachel Palmer asked you to create a worksheet containing company sales figures for the last two quarters. Create a worksheet that presents the data for the third and fourth quarters attractively.

a. Start a new workbook. In cell A1, enter "Stuff for Pets" and, in cell A2 enter "First and Second Quarter 2001 Sales Data".

b. Enter the following information, starting in cell A4.

Region	1st Quarter	2nd Quarter
Northeast	80,000	85,000
South	62,000	60,000
Midwest	56,000	71,000
West	100,000	110,000
Totals		

c. Change the two rows of the worksheet title so that the first is 14-point bold Arial Black font and the second is 18-point bold Arial Narrow font. Then change the column labels in row 4 to bold Arial Narrow.

d. Widen row 3 to add more space between the title and the data.

e. Add formulas that calculate each quarter's totals. Format the quarterly data in cells B5 through C9 with commas and no decimal places. Adjust column widths if necessary.

f. Edit A5 so that it reads "East" instead of "Northeast".

g. Change the "Totals" label and numbers in row 9 to bold Arial Black font.

h. Add a colored border of your choice around the worksheet data, including the row and column labels (cells A4 through C9). Then add shading to the column labels in row 4 and the label and numbers in row 9.

i. Add a footer with "Confidential" on the left, the current date in the middle, and the page number on the right.

j. Save the workbook as "Quarterly Sales" on your Project Disk, preview it, then print it.

4. The president of the advertising agency you work for is leaving tomorrow for a whirlwind business trip to Chicago, Illinois, and Anchorage, Alaska. She has asked you to find out about local weather conditions. Use the World Wide Web to gather forecast information for these cities, then create an Excel worksheet to list the temperatures expected.

a. Open a new workbook, and save it as "Weather Data" on your Project Disk.

b. Log on to the Internet and use your browser to go to http://www.course.com. From there, click the Student Online Companions link, click the link for this textbook, then click the Excel link for Unit A.

c. Use the CNN Weather link to compile your data. Click the Weather link. Use the Zip Code list box on the Weather main page to gather data about the forecast for Chicago (use the Zip Code 60613) and Anchorage (use the Zip Code 99515). Record the highs and lows for the next four days. Log off the Internet and close your browser.

d. On Sheet1 of your Excel workbook, set up a table that shows the days of the week that are in the Chicago forecast across the top of the sheet, and use the rows to list the high temperature and low temperature for each day.

e. Include an average column that calculates the average high and the average low temperatures for the four-day period. (To determine an average, add all of the values, then divide by the number of values.)

f. Add a meaningful title to the top of each worksheet, and format them similarly.

g. On Sheet2 of your workbook, create a similar table for the Anchorage forecast. (*Hint:* use the Copy and Paste commands on the Edit menu to save some retyping on the second worksheet.)

h. Save your changes, preview both worksheets, then print them.

Excel 2000

Visual Workshop

Create the sales analysis shown in Figure A-16 using the commands and techniques you learned in this unit. Save the workbook as "Ticket Sales Analysis" on your Project Disk, preview it, then print a copy.

FIGURE A-16

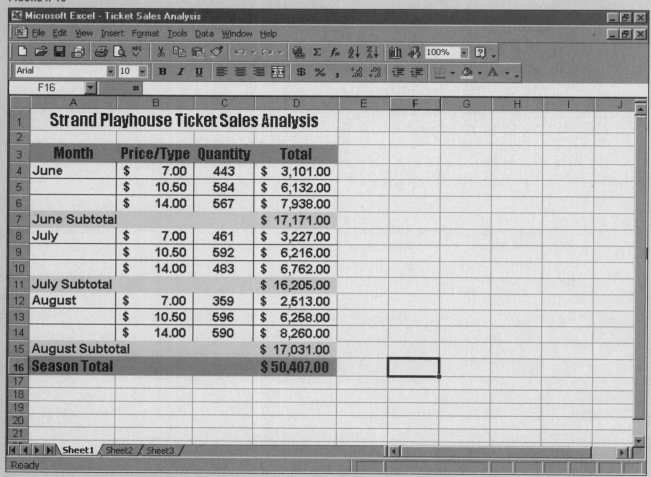

Working

with Excel Functions

Objectives

- ► **Understand functions**
- ► **Use the SUM function**
- ► **Use date and time functions**
- ► **Use statistical functions**
- ► **Use financial functions**
- ► **Use Goal Seek**
- ► **Sort rows**
- ► **Filter data and print**

In this unit you learn about **functions**, prewritten formulas that you can use instead of typing all the parts to a formula. When you use a function, usually all you have to do is enter the appropriate values or cell references. Excel comes with more than 200 functions, which you can use for simple calculations such as addition and averaging and for more complex calculations, such as calculating loan payments or finding the standard deviation of a selection of database entries. Derek Hofbauer, marketing manager for Outdoor Designs, has asked you to help him update the product order sheet. You'll use functions to finalize the worksheet so that it provides meaningful sales and account data for the marketing and accounting departments. When you finish, you'll print a copy of the document for the order processing department.

Unit B
Excel 2000

Understanding Functions

Each Excel function has a name that you usually see in all capital letters. The SUM function, for example, adds values, the ROUND function rounds a number to a specified number of digits, and so on. There are four parts to every function: an equal sign, the function name, a set of parentheses, and arguments separated by commas and enclosed in parentheses. **Arguments** are information a function needs to perform a task and can be values (such as 100 or .02) or cell references (such as B3 or A9:G16). Figure B-1 shows the anatomy of the Excel function named AVERAGE, which is used to calculate the average of a set of numbers contained in cells in a worksheet. The AVERAGE function accepts values from one or more cells, referred to as a **reference** or a **range reference**, as arguments. Derek asks you to open the Outdoor Designs product order worksheet and prepare to add functions to it that will help him evaluate product sales.

Steps

1. Start Excel

2. Insert your Project Disk in the appropriate drive, then click the **Open button** 📂 on the Standard toolbar

   The Open dialog box opens and lists the current folder's contents in the list box.

3. Open the worksheet **XL B-1** from your Project Disk, then save it as **Mountain Air Order** to your Project Disk

   The Outdoor Designs product order worksheet opens.

Trouble?

To use a button that is not visible, click the More Buttons button ⟩⟩ on the right side of the appropriate toolbar, then click the button you need. If it is still not visible, click Add or Remove buttons, click the desired button, click outside the list to close it, then click the button on the toolbar.

4. Click any cell, then click the **Paste Function button** 🔧 on the Standard toolbar

   The Paste Function dialog box opens. You can insert a function using the dialog box. You can also type the information that makes up a function directly in the formula bar, but you have to know the function name and the necessary arguments. In the next lesson, you will insert a function. For now, familiarize yourself with the variety of functions available. The Paste Function dialog box organizes functions into categories to make them easier to find. The categories are listed in the Function category list on the left side of the dialog box. Table B-1 describes some of the most commonly used categories. You are now ready to enhance your worksheet with functions. You will add totals to row 14 for the Quantity and Subtotal columns using the SUM function. In rows 16 through 22, you will add functions to calculate the current date, payment due date, average price per item in the order, and payment due if Outdoor Designs has extended credit to a store.

5. Click **Statistical** in the Function category list

   The Function name list on the right shows all the functions in the currently selected category, the Statistical category. See Figure B-2.

6. Click **AVERAGE** in the Function name list

   The area at the bottom of the dialog box displays the name of the currently selected function, its arguments, and a brief description of the function's purpose.

7. Click **All** in the Function category list, then scroll through the list of function names

   The ALL category lists all functions available in Excel, regardless of category.

8. Click **Cancel**

FIGURE B-1: Anatomy of the AVERAGE function

Numeric arguments (values or cell references) that you want to average

=AVERAGE (number1, number2, ...)

Commas separate arguments

Function name

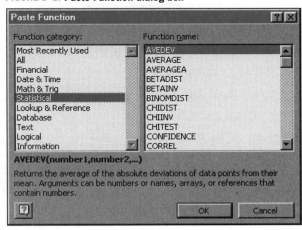

FIGURE B-2: Paste Function dialog box

TABLE B-1: Categories of some common worksheet functions

category	used for
Date & Time	Calculations involving dates and times
Financial	Loan payments, appreciation, and depreciation
Information	Determining the type of data stored within a cell
Logical	Calculations that produce the result TRUE or FALSE
Lookup & Reference	Finding values in lists or tables or finding references for cells
Math & Trig	Simple and complex mathematical calculations
Statistical	Average, sum, variance, and standard deviation calculations
Text	Comparing, converting, and reformatting text strings in cells

Planning to use functions

Using functions in a worksheet requires that you plan in advance because many arguments used in functions come from worksheet cells. Because you can include worksheet ranges as arguments, you should organize your rows and columns when building a worksheet so you can select and include them in functions. Before you start creating formulas from scratch, you need to determine what results you want from your worksheet data and examine the list of Excel functions in the Help system to see if any functions are available for your calculations. Many Excel functions also can be used in Access.

Using the SUM Function

The most frequently used worksheet function, **SUM**, totals all numbers and cell references included as function arguments. Table B-2 lists other commonly used mathematical functions. To use the SUM function in a formula, click the AutoSum button on the Standard toolbar, then edit the function arguments in the formula bar. You can also click the Paste Function button on the Standard toolbar to insert any Excel function, including the SUM function, into your worksheets. ✎ The product order worksheet would not be complete without the total dollar amount and the total number of items to be shipped. Use the SUM function to total the Quantity and Subtotal columns.

Steps

1. Click cell **C14**, click the **Align Right button** on the Formatting toolbar, click the **Bold button** on the Formatting toolbar, type **Totals**, then press **[Tab]**
   The label "Totals" is entered in cell C14 with the specified formatting.

2. Click the **Paste Function button** on the Standard toolbar
   The Paste Function dialog box opens.

3. Click the **Math & Trig Function category**, then scroll down the Function name list and click **SUM**
   The description changes to show you the format for the SUM function and its description.

4. Click **OK**
   The Paste Function dialog box closes, and the SUM dialog box opens, as shown in Figure B-3. The arguments (D9:D13) are already entered in the Number1 text box.

5. Make sure the Number1 range reference is **D9:D13**, then click **OK**
   You can use a colon to indicate a range of values, or a **range reference**. The formula calculates the sum of cells D9 through D13 and displays the result, 13, in cell D14. (If your range reference is not D9:D13, click in the Number1 text box, delete the current value, then type the correct references.)

QuickTip

You can change the suggested range reference by typing or selecting a new range reference in the cell or in the formula bar.

6. Click cell **E14**, then click the **AutoSum button** on the Standard toolbar
   AutoSum is a quicker method for calculating sums in consecutive cells. The cells in the range E9:E13 (see Figure B-4) are selected in the worksheet and appear in the cell and in the formula bar.

7. Press **[Enter]** to complete the formula
   The formula calculates and displays the result, $398.35, in cell E14. Notice that the currency style was applied to cell E14 to match the style in the SUM range reference.

8. Click cell **D14**, then click the **Center button** on the Formatting toolbar

9. Click the **Save button** on the Standard toolbar

FIGURE B-3: Using the SUM function to calculate a column total

Range reference

SUM dialog box

Formula result

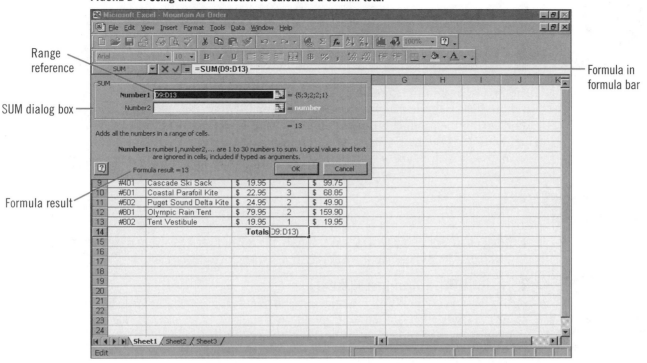

Formula in formula bar

FIGURE B-4: Using the AutoSum button to calculate a column total

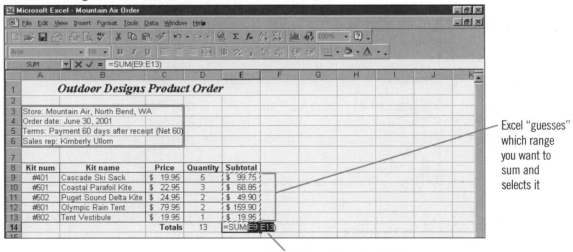

Excel "guesses" which range you want to sum and selects it

Formula in cell (result will appear here when you press [Enter])

TABLE B-2: Commonly used mathematical functions

function	description
AVERAGE(argument)	Calculates the average value of the arguments
COUNT(argument)	Calculates the number of values in the argument list
MAX(argument)	Calculates the largest value in the argument list
MIN(argument)	Calculates the smallest value in the argument list
SUM(argument)	Calculates the sum of the arguments

Using Date and Time Functions

The Excel date and time functions let you display the current date and time in your worksheet and can help you calculate the time between important events. ✐ Derek asks you to add a formula to the product order worksheet that calculates payment due dates for the store placing the order. Use the NOW function to enter the current date in the worksheet, and use the Format Cells dialog box to format the date's style. Then enter a formula that uses the current date to calculate when a payment is due.

Steps 1 2 3 4

1. **If necessary, scroll down to see cell A16, click cell A16, type Ship date:, then press [Tab]**
   The label "Ship date:" appears in cell A16, and cell B16 is selected.

QuickTip

Function names are not case sensitive. When typing function names, you can use uppercase or lowercase letters.

2. **Type =NOW( ), then press [Enter]**
   You have typed the NOW function in cell B16 instead of using the Paste Function dialog box. You did not enter any arguments within the parentheses because this function does not require any. The results of this function, the current date and time, appear in the cell.

3. **Select cell B16, click Format on the menu bar, then click Cells**
   The Number tab in the Format Cells dialog box opens, as shown in Figure B-5. You can change the way the date and time are displayed by using the Number tab in the Format Cells dialog box.

4. **Click the Date category, click March 14, 2001 in the Type list to display dates in that format, then click OK**
   The Format Cells dialog box closes, and today's date appears in cell B16, with the month spelled out, followed by the day and year.

5. **Click cell A17, type Pmt due:, then press [Tab]**
   The label "Pmt due:" is entered in cell A17, and cell B17 is selected. In this cell, you'll enter a formula that calculates the day when full payment is due from the store, assuming a 60-day payment grace period.

6. **Type =, press ↑ to select cell B16, type +60, then press [Enter]**
   The payment due date appears in cell B17, as shown in Figure B-6. The payment due date is calculated by adding 60 days (net 60) to the current date. The number of days in each month is considered in the calculation.

7. **Click the Save button 🖫 on the Standard toolbar**
   Your additions to the worksheet are saved.

FIGURE B-5: Changing the date format

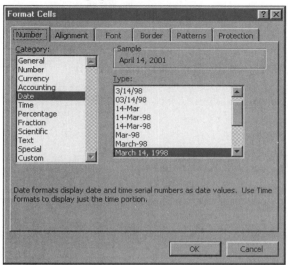

FIGURE B-6: Product order worksheet after date calculations

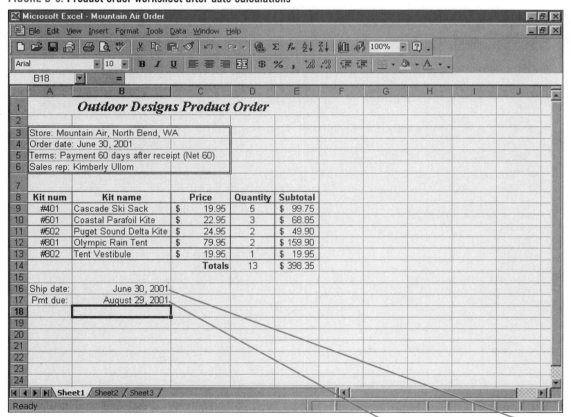

Result of formula =B16+60
(your date may differ)

Result of NOW function
(your date may differ)

How dates are calculated using serial numbers

When you enter a date in a worksheet cell, the date appears in a familiar format (such as August 11, 2001) but it is really stored as a serial number that represents the number of days since January 1, 1900. Dates are stored as serial numbers so they can be used in calculations. For example, in this lesson you added 60 days to the current date. To Excel, the formula in cell B17 in Figure B-4 is really =36995+60.

Using Statistical Functions

Excel's statistical functions let you assemble, classify, and tabulate numeric data in your worksheet. ✏️ Derek wants to know the average amount for each item in the product order.

Steps 1 2 3 4

1. Click cell **A19**, type **Avg order:**, then press **[Tab]**

   The label "Avg order:" is entered in cell A19, and cell B19 is selected.

2. Click the **Paste Function button** 🔧 on the Standard toolbar

   The Paste Function dialog box opens.

3. Click the **Statistical Function category**, click the **AVERAGE function name**, then click **OK**

   The Paste Function dialog box closes, and the AVERAGE dialog box opens.

4. Click the **Reduce button** 📷 in the Number1 text box, as shown in Figure B-7

   The dialog box changes size and moves out of the way. Now you can use the pointer to select the range on which to calculate an average.

QuickTip

You can include one function as an argument in another function if its result is compatible. For example, the formula =SUM(5,SQRT(9)) adds the number 5 to the square root (SQRT) of 9 and displays the result (8).

5. Select the range **E9:E13** (the Subtotal column), press **[Enter]**, then click **OK**

   The range E9:E13 is an argument in the AVERAGE function in the formula bar. The result, $79.67, is displayed in cell B19, as shown in Figure B-8.

6. Click the **Save button** 💾 on the Standard toolbar

FIGURE B-7: Reducing the size of the AVERAGE dialog box

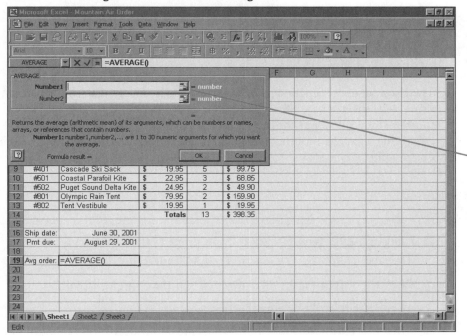

Reduce button
(click to reduce
dialog box, then
click to select
desired cell or
drag to select
desired range)

FIGURE B-8: Product order worksheet with AVERAGE function

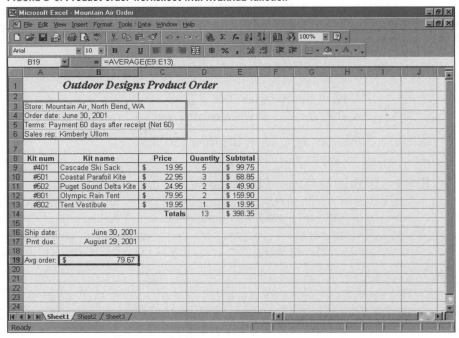

Mathematical functions

Another useful category of functions that produce numbers as results is the mathematical functions. These functions perform many mathematical and trigonometric calculations found on a standard scientific calculator, including ABS (absolute value), COS (cosine), LOG (logarithm), and SQRT (square root). Most mathematical functions take a single number as an argument and produce a single number as a result. For more information about using the mathematical functions, search for "mathematical functions" in Help.

Unit B
Excel 2000

Using Financial Functions

The Excel financial functions help you calculate loan payments, appreciation, and depreciation using worksheet data. ✎——— Outdoor Designs extends credit to approved wholesale customers who want to pay for their purchases over a 12-month period. Use the PMT function to determine what the monthly payment would be if the Mountain Air store chose to finance its outstanding balance.

Steps 1 2 3 4

1. **Click cell A20, type 12 pmts:, then press [Tab]**
   The label "12 pmts:" is entered in cell A20, and cell B20 is selected.

2. **Click the Paste Function button 📌 on the Standard toolbar**
   The Paste Function dialog box opens.

3. **Click the Financial function category, scroll down the Function name list, click the PMT function name, then click OK**
   The Insert Function dialog box closes, and the PMT dialog box opens. The PMT function determines the periodic payment for a loan based on the interest rate charged, the payment term (number of payments), and the principal loan amount. As with all functions, you can specify the function arguments as numbers or cell references. The arguments are Rate (the interest rate), Nper (the number of payments), and Pv (present value of the loan, or the principal).

4. **Type 10%/12 in the Rate text box**
   The rate is 10%, and the rate is calculated over a 12-month period.

5. **Press [Tab], then type 12 in the Nper text box**
   There are 12 payments in the loan term.

6. **Press [Tab], then type -E14 in the Pv text box**
   You can enter a cell reference or an amount in the Pv text box. The PMT dialog box is shown in Figure B-9. Pv represents the amount of the loan at the beginning of the loan period. Money that is paid out, such as a loan payment, is represented by a negative number, represented by a minus sign (–). Money that you receive, such as a deposit, is represented as a positive number.

Trouble?

If your result is a negative number, you did not enter the Pv amount as a negative value. Click cell B20, then edit the formula in the formula bar so it is =PMT(10%/12,12,-E14).

7. **Click OK**
   The result, $35.02, appears in cell B20, as shown in Figure B-10. Mountain Air will pay this amount monthly for 12 months if it chooses to finance its purchase.

8. **Click the Save button 💾 on the Standard toolbar**

FIGURE B-9: Completed PMT dialog box

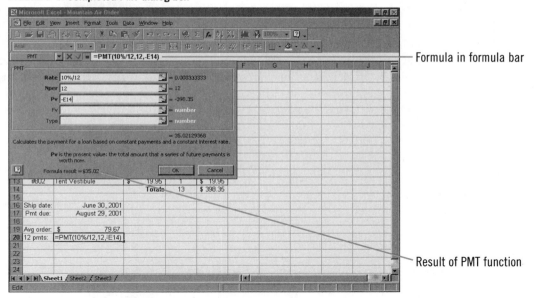

Formula in formula bar

Result of PMT function

FIGURE B-10: Product order worksheet with PMT function

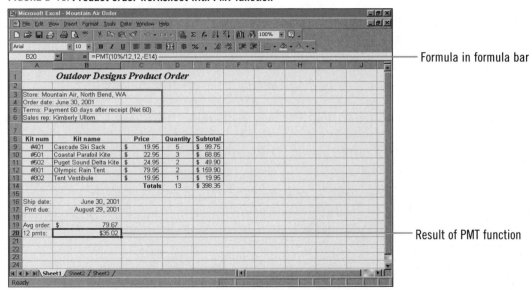

Formula in formula bar

Result of PMT function

Using Excel templates

Excel includes preformatted templates for common office forms, such as an expense statement, an invoice, and a purchase order. You can use these templates by clicking New on the File menu, then clicking the Spreadsheet Solutions tab. Figure B-11 shows a Purchase Order template that you can use to quickly create a purchase order. The purchase order contains formulas and functions to compute totals and other calculations. You can use the template as is, or change it using the same techniques you would use for a worksheet you created yourself.

FIGURE B-11: Purchase Order template

Using Goal Seek

Excel has tools that let you manipulate a worksheet to test conditions for different results. The Excel Goal Seek command automates the trial-and-error process of changing the value in one cell to produce a desired value (result) in another cell. You specify the results you want and Excel changes the input values in the formula. ✍ After calculating the total cost of the Mountain Air order, your client indicates that she can spend up to $200 on Coastal Parafoil kites. Use the Excel Goal Seek command to find out how many kites she can order.

Steps 1 2 3 4

1. **Click cell E10**
   You will seek a goal in cell E10. This is the cell containing the amount that Mountain Air can spend on Coastal Parafoil Kites.

2. **Click Tools on the menu bar, then click Goal Seek**
   The Goal Seek dialog box opens, as shown in Figure B-12. The Set cell is cell E10, the cell that you clicked before opening the Goal Seek dialog box.

   > **Trouble?**
   >
   > If the Goal Seek dialog box covers your worksheet data, click the title bar and drag it out of the way.

3. **Click in the To value text box, then type 200**
   This is the amount that Mountain Air can spend on Coastal Parafoil Kites.

4. **Click in the By changing cell text box, then click cell D10 in the worksheet**
   Now your Goal Seek parameters are set. Goal Seek is different from **what-if analysis**, which is used to find the output based on data you provide—for example, the total price of five parafoil kites if they cost $22.95 each. Goal Seek lets you determine the output and find out what input is required, as you do next.

5. **Click OK in the Goal Seek dialog box, then click OK in the Goal Seek Status dialog box to close it after finding a solution**
   The solution appears in cell D10 as shown in Figure B-13. The target cell—cell E10—shows the target value of 200.

   > **Trouble?**
   >
   > Goal Seek finds the exact value based on the requested result and on the cell you've changed. So you may often need to round the number up or down for practical purposes.

6. **Click cell D10, type 8, then press [Enter]**
   The value in cell E10 changes to show the cost for eight kites, a whole number, and the value in cell E10 changes to $183.60.

7. **Click the Save button 🖫 on the Standard toolbar**

FIGURE B-12: Using the Goal Seek command

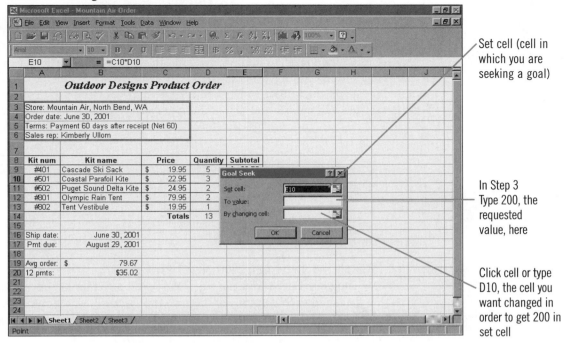

Set cell (cell in which you are seeking a goal)

In Step 3 Type 200, the requested value, here

Click cell or type D10, the cell you want changed in order to get 200 in set cell

FIGURE B-13: Goal Seek command results

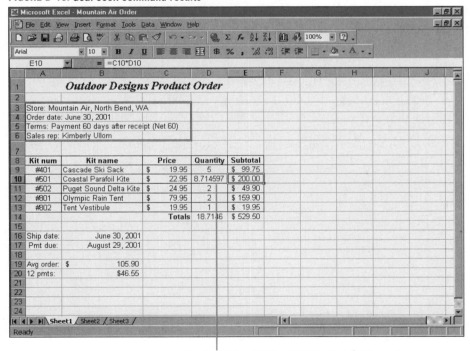

Number of Coastal Parafoil kites that $200 can buy

CLUES TO USE

Using Solver to solve complex problems

Solver is an Excel add-in program that you can install on your computer to solve complex problems. Solver automatically calculates a maximum or a minimum value of a cell by changing the values in other cells in the worksheet using a formula that you specify. You can use Solver by clicking Solver on the Tools menu. If Solver does not appear in the Tools menu, install it by inserting your Microsoft Office 2000 CD, clicking theTools menu, clicking Add-ins, clicking the Solver Add-in checkbox to select it, clicking OK, then clicking Yes.

Unit B

Excel 2000

Sorting Rows

In Excel there are many sort commands that allow you to sort rows in the worksheet by comparing values in one or more columns. You can sort rows alphabetically or numerically, and in ascending or descending order. ✐ You added all of the information that Derek requested to the product order worksheet. Use the Sort command to organize the information so the lowest-priced item is listed first and the highest-priced item is listed last.

Steps 1 2 3 4

1. Select rows **9** through **13**

QuickTip

If your selection includes headers (text that identifies the values in the columns), then click the Header row option button in the Sort dialog box so the headers will not be sorted.

2. Click **Data** on the menu bar, then click **Sort**

   The Sort dialog box opens. You can sort based on three columns in case some cells contain the same data, and each column can be sorted in ascending or descending order. The Sort list arrow indicates that the values in Column A will be sorted in ascending order.

3. Click the **No header row option button**, if necessary, to select it

   You did not select the headers in the table.

4. Click the **Sort by list arrow**, then click **Column C**

   You indicated you want to use Column C (Price) as your primary sort criterion, as shown in Figure B-14.

QuickTip

You can sort the rows in your worksheet any number of times, depending on the order in which you want your information presented. To undo the results of a sort immediately after performing it, click the Undo button on the Standard toolbar.

5. Click **OK** to sort the rows

   The Sort dialog box closes, and the rows appear in the specified sort order, as shown in Figure B-15.

6. Click the **Save button** 🖫 on the Standard toolbar

FIGURE B-14: Sort dialog box

FIGURE B-15: Order information sorted by kit price (column C)

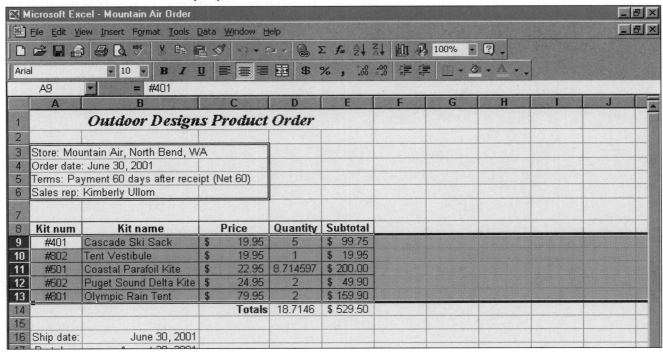

Sorting by more than one column

If more than one row contains the same value in the column you are sorting by, the sort results in a "tie." For example, if you sort a list of customers by last name, you might have a list that shows several customers with the same last name. In this case you would sort first by last name, then by first name. You can sort up to three columns this way.

Filtering Data and Printing

Excel 2000

When your worksheet contains a large amount of data, you might need to filter the data to display only the data you need. You can apply a filter to only one worksheet column at a time by specifying the value that you want to see. A filter is different from a sort. A sort lists all of your data in a specified order, but a **filter** displays only the data you want to see. Derek wants you to filter the data so he can see only order lines that contain a kit price of $19.95. Then he asks you to print the worksheet.

Steps

1. Click cell **A8**

2. Click **Data** on the menu bar, point to **Filter**, then click **AutoFilter**
   List arrows appear in the column headings in row 8, as shown in Figure B-16. You can click any list arrow to display the list of available filters for that column. Excel creates filters for each of the values in the column, plus default filters to select all values, custom values, or the top 10 values. You can also customize a filter to find values using comparison operators and specific values.

3. Click the **Price list arrow**, then click **$19.95**
   Only the rows that contain a value of $19.95 in the price column appear, as shown in Figure B-17.

4. Click the **Print button** on the Standard toolbar
   Turn on your printer first, if necessary. After a few moments the worksheet emerges from your printer ready for Derek to review.

5. Click the **Price list arrow** again, then click **(All)** to display all worksheet data

6. Click **Data** on the menu bar, point to **Filter**, then click **AutoFilter** to turn it off
   Now all of your worksheet data appears.

7. Click the **Save button** on the Standard toolbar
   Your changes are saved.

8. Click the **Close button** to close Excel
   The Sales Analysis workbook and Excel both close.

WORKING WITH EXCEL FUNCTIONS

FIGURE B-16: Worksheet with filter list arrows

Filter list arrows

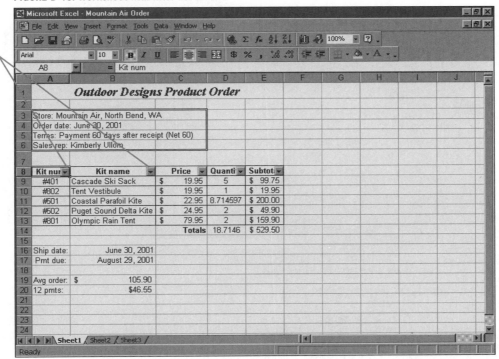

FIGURE B-17: Worksheet after applying filter

Filtered data

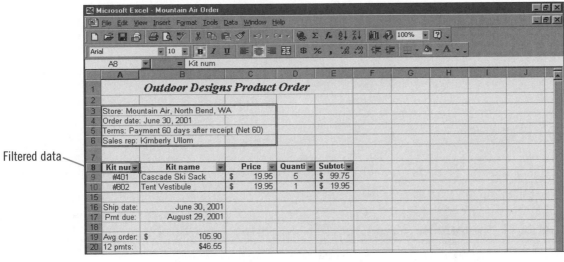

Customizing a filter

You can use any of the predefined filters to filter your worksheet data, but sometimes you might need to show filters that require calculations, such as customer records with a balance that is greater than the credit limit. To do this, click the (Custom…) option in the filter list, then use the Custom AutoFilter dialog box to enter your filter information. Click the list arrow to see the available choices. You can filter using comparison operations (greater than, equal to, etc.) against another value. Look up the word "filters" in Help to learn more about using custom filters.

Practice

▶ Concepts Review

Label each of the elements of the Excel worksheet window shown in Figure B-18.

FIGURE B-18

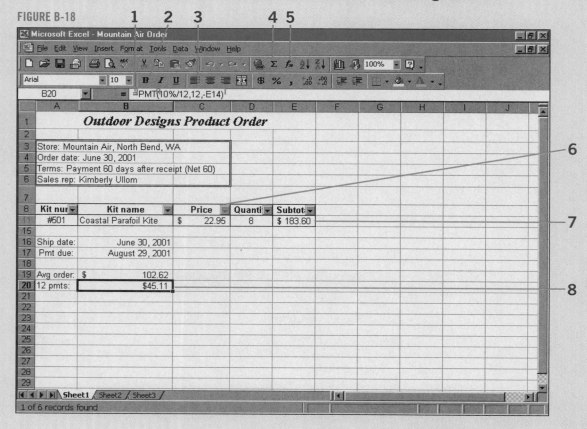

Match components of the formula =SUM(5,SQRT(9)) with their descriptions.

9. SUM
10. 5
11. SQRT(9)
12. =
13. ,

a. Symbol used to separate arguments in functions
b. Function name
c. Function used as an argument in a function
d. Number used as an argument in a function
e. Symbol that indicates that the following text is a formula

Select the best answer from the list of choices.

14. **Which answer best describes a function argument?**
    a. A number, cell reference, or expression that a function uses to perform a calculation
    b. The result of a function calculation
    c. The abbreviated name of the function
    d. The parentheses following the function name in the formula bar

15. **Which answer best describes statistical functions?**
    a. Functions used for loan payments, appreciation, and depreciation calculations
    b. Functions used for average, sum, variance, and standard deviation calculations
    c. Functions used for mathematical and trigonometric calculations
    d. Functions involving date and time calculations

16. **Which toolbar button opens the Paste Function dialog box?**
    a. [icon]
    b. [Σ icon]
    c. [fx icon]
    d. [A↓ icon]

17. **What answer does Excel calculate for the formula =AVERAGE(5,3,1)?**
    a. 3
    b. 9
    c. 10
    d. 15

18. **What type of argument do you use with the NOW( ) function?**
    a. number1, number2, ...
    b. A cell reference
    c. A cell range
    d. The NOW( ) function doesn't have any arguments.

19. **What does E9:E12 represent in the formula =SUM(E9:E12)?**
    a. A range of three cells
    b. A range of four cells
    c. Two cell references
    d. The average of cells E9 and E12

20. **How would Excel evaluate the formula =SUM(2,SQRT(16))?**
    a. 2
    b. 4
    c. 6
    d. 8

Excel 2000

21. What command would you use to find out how many items you can purchase with $100?
   a. Goal Seek
   b. Solver
   c. What-if
   d. Trial and error

 # Skills Review

1. Start Excel, and open the file XL B-2.
   a. Start Excel.
   b. Open the file XL B-2 on your Project Disk.
   c. Save the file as "August Sales" on your Project Disk.

2. Use the SUM function to total the Amount column and calculate the monthly total.
   a. Click cell D15.
   b. Click the AutoSum button on the Standard toolbar.
   c. Change the range reference to cells D5:D13, then press [Enter].
   d. Click the Save button on the Standard toolbar to save your changes.

3. Look at the Order Date entries, then calculate the payment date considering a 45-day payment grace period.
   a. Click cell F5, enter the formula =E5+45, then press [Enter].
   b. Click cell F5, then use the Fill handle to copy the formula into cells F6:F13.
   c. Select the range E5:F13.
   d. Click Format on the menu bar, click Cells, then click the Number tab, if necessary.
   e. Change the date format to display dates in the format Day-Month-Year, then click OK.

4. Use the AVG function to determine the average order amount for the month.
   a. Scroll down until you see cell D17.
   b. Click cell D17.
   c. Click the Paste Function button on the Standard toolbar.
   d. Click the Statistical Function category.
   e. Double-click the AVERAGE function name.
   f. Enter cells D5:D13 as the Number1 range, then click OK.
   g. Click the Save button on the Standard toolbar to save your changes.

5. Use the PMT function to determine monthly payments for the orders, using a 9% annual interest rate and a 12-month term.
   a. Click cell G5.
   b. Click the Paste Function button on the Standard toolbar.
   c. Click the Financial Function category.
   d. Double-click the PMT function name.
   e. Enter 9%/12 as the rate, 12 as the term (Nper), cell −D5 (you are specifying this cell reference as negative so that the result of the function will be positive) as the principal amount (Pv), then click OK.
   f. Use the Fill handle to copy the formula into cells G6:G13.

6. **Use the Goal Seek command to find out how much more Mountain Air should order to hit the target sales amount of $20,000 for the month.**
   a. Select cell D15.
   b. Click Tools on the menu bar, then click Goal Seek.
   c. Enter 20000 in the To value text box.
   d. Enter D6 in the By changing cell text box, then click OK.
   e. Click OK again to close the Goal Seek Status dialog box.

7. **Use the Sort command to sort the sales information by region and then by amount.**
   a. Select rows 4 through 13.
   b. Click Data on the menu bar, then click Sort.
   c. Make sure the Header row option button is selected. Notice that when this option is selected, the Sort by list displays column headings from the worksheet rather than column letters.
   d. Click the Sort by list arrow, then click Region.
   e. Click the Then by list arrow, then click Amount.
   f. Click OK.
   g. Verify the sorting order in rows 5 through 13. (The worksheet should be sorted by region first, and then the amounts should be sorted within each region.)

8. **Use a filter to display orders over $1,000.**
   a. Click cell A4.
   b. Click Data on the menu bar, point to Filter, then click AutoFilter.
   c. Click the Amount list arrow.
   d. Click the (Custom…) option in the list.
   e. Click the Amount list arrow, then click is greater than.
   f. Press [Tab], then type 1000.
   g. Click OK.
   h. Click the Print button to print a copy of the filtered worksheet. Click the Amount list arrow then click (All) to restore the worksheet.
   i. Click Data on the menu bar, point to Filter, then click AutoFilter to turn off the filter.
   j. Save your changes, then exit Excel.

► Independent Challenges

1. The Wacky Words card company is thinking about raising the prices of its cards and wants to know how this change will affect its bottom line. The sales director thinks the price of cards should jump from $1.50 to $2.25 but estimates that orders will drop by 15% as buyers adjust to the new pricing. Create a worksheet that demonstrates the effect of the proposed pricing change on gross income.

To complete this independent challenge:

a. Open a new worksheet and save it as "Card Price Hike" on your Project Disk. Enter the label "Price Increase Analysis" in cell A1.
b. In cells A3, B3, and C3, create the column labels "Cards Produced", "Price", and "Sales". Widen column A so the labels fit comfortably.
c. In rows 4 and 5, enter card quantities of 5000 and 10000, each at a price of $1.50. Insert formulas in cells C4 and C5 that compute estimated sales at existing prices.

d. In rows 6 and 7, enter quantities of 4250 and 8500 (85% of the existing levels), priced at $2.25. Insert formulas in cells C6 and C7 that compute estimated sales at the new levels.

e. Format cells B4 through C7 as currency with two decimal places. Widen the columns if necessary.

f. Use the Goal Seek command in cell C5 to determine how many cards must be produced at $1.50 each to match the highest amount of sales in the worksheet.

g. Save your changes, print the Card Price Hike worksheet, then close the file.

2. The veterinary clinic you work for, Palmer's Pet Hospital, decided to sell a small collection of pet products and supplies. Your boss asked you to prepare an invoice based on the information given below.

To complete this independent challenge:

a. Click File on the menu bar, then click New. Click the Spreadsheet Solutions tab, then double-click the Invoice icon. (*Hint:* If a dialog box opens, click Enable Macros to continue. You may need to insert your Microsoft Office 2000 CD into the appropriate drive, and follow the prompts to install the template.)

b. Close the Invoice toolbar, if necessary, by clicking the Close Window button on the Invoice toolbar.

c. Click the Customize button in the upper-right corner of the invoice, then replace the text in each field of the Type Company Information Here box with the following values:
Palmer's Pet Hospital
32 North Street
West Springs, CO 80502
303-555-3433 (Telephone)
303-555-3434 (FAX)

d. Click the Invoice sheet tab to return to the invoice.

e. Save the invoice as "Pet Supply Invoice" on your Project Disk. (In the Template File - Save As dialog box that opens, click the Continue without Updating option button, then proceed with the save.)

f. Add prices to the invoice using the following information:

Quantity	Description	Unit Price
10	Nylon Dog Bone	$7.95
15	Dog Dish	$19.95
12	Pet Blanket	$24.95
1	Cat Collar	$9.95
2	Fish Food	$6.95
10	Cat Toys (misc.)	$6.95
15	Dog Leash	$12.95

g. Enter your name, address, and phone number in the Customer part of the invoice.

h. Save your changes, print the worksheet, then close the file.

3. A local art gallery that uses travel guides from Outdoor Designs is marketing guided outdoor adventures—including helicopter skiing, orienteering, hang gliding, ballooning, trail riding, and backpacking. Outdoor Designs assigned you the task of reviewing last year's trip data to determine the most popular trips, how long it takes to save for trips, and other variables.

To complete this independent challenge:

a. Open the file XL B-3 on your Project Disk. This file contains the data on the number of trips sold for each sport by month for 2000. Save the file as "Art Trips 2001" on your Project Disk.

b. Use statistical functions to analyze the data. Use the SUM function to find the total number of trips taken each month. Enter these totals in cells B11:M11. Also use the SUM function to enter a grand total in cell N11.

c. Use the MAX function to identify the most popular trip, based on the totals in cells B14:B19. Enter the label "Most Popular" in cell A21 and the function in cell B21. Enter the title of the most popular trip in cell C21.

d. Use financial functions for estimating costs. Use the NPER function to find how long it will take to save $1,950 for a balloon vacation in France if you save $150 per month in a savings account that earns 4½% interest compounded monthly. Enter the label "Save $150/month for" in cell A22 and the function in cell B22. (Use the Help system to learn about the NPER function. The Rate is 4.5%, the payment is how much you want to save each month (entered as a negative number, because it's cash going out), the present value is zero, and the future value is the amount you want to save.) Format cell B22 using the accounting format, with one decimal place, and no symbol in the cell.

e. Add the word "months" in cell C22.

f. Use the PMT function to find the monthly payment if you borrowed the $1,950 at a 10% annual rate with 12 months to repay. Enter the label "Monthly Payment" in cell A23 and the function in cell B23.

g. Save your changes, print the worksheet in the Landscape orientation, then close the file.

4. Your grandmother just gave you $5,000 and you decide to invest it in the stock market. The World Wide Web has many sites that make it easy to find information about the current prices of stocks. Before investing your money, you decide to investigate the purchase of three stocks: Exxon, 3M, and Chevron. You can use the Web to find this information.
To complete this independent challenge:

1. Open a new workbook and save it as "Stock Workbook" on your Project Disk.
2. Log on to the Internet and use your browser to go to http://www.course.com. From there, click the Student Online Companions link, then click the link for this book, then click the Excel link for Unit B.
3. Use the New York Stock Exchange link to find the NYSE abbreviations for your three stocks. The official company names are Exxon Corporation, Minnesota Mining and Manufacturing Company, and Chevron Corporation. Look on the Listed Companies page, and write down the abbreviations for each company.
4. Return to the Excel Unit B page, then click the NASDAQ link to go to the NASDAQ home page. Use the Quotes link to find quote information for each of the stocks that you plan to purchase. Find all three quotes at once, then print the page.
5. Log off the Internet, and close your browser.
6. Enter the following labels in row 2, starting in cell B2: "Today's High", "Today's Low", "Last Sale", "Previous Close", and "Net Change".
7. Enter the following labels in column A, starting in cell A3: "Exxon", "3M", and "Chevron".
8. Enter the values into the appropriate cells using the information you printed from the NASDAQ site.
9. Format the cells that contain dollar values to appear as currency with four decimal places.
10. Enter the label "Investment" in cell G2 and the label "Shares" in cell H2. You will spend $1,000 for Exxon stock, $2,000 for 3M stock, and $2,000 for Chevron stock. Enter these values into the Investment column, then add formulas to the Shares column to show the number of shares you can purchase based on the last sale price.
11. Use the Goal Seek command in cells H3:H5 to find out how much it would cost to buy 20 shares each of Exxon and 3M, and 30 shares of Chevron. The change value is the investment amount. Add a total in cell G6 to show the new investment amount, then add a total in cell H6 to calculate the total number of shares.
12. Save your changes, preview the worksheet, then print it.

Excel 2000

▶ Visual Workshop

Create the worksheet shown in Figure B-19 using commands and techniques you learned in this unit. Save the worksheet as "Playhouse Analysis" on your Project Disk.

FIGURE B-19

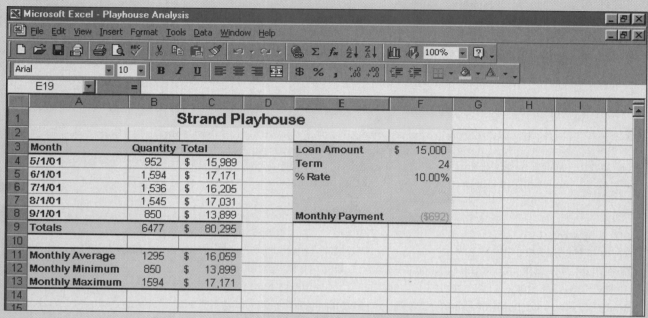

Creating

Excel Charts

Objectives

- ► **Plan a chart**
- ► **Create a chart**
- ► **Move and resize a chart and chart objects**
- ► **Change the chart type**
- ► **Add axis labels and gridlines**
- ► **Change fonts and colors**
- ► **Enhance a chart**
- ► **Preview and print a chart**

In this unit you learn how to create and work with charts. A **chart** is a visual representation of worksheet data. For example, a chart can present the number of kite kits sold in a month or the amount of water consumed each summer in a format that is easy to understand and remember. In this unit you will create a chart for Derek Hofbauer, marketing manager for Outdoor Designs, to show the regional sales figures graphically for the first and second quarters of 2001. You'll also customize the chart, then print a final copy of the chart, which Derek can distribute to the sales and marketing group.

Excel 2000

Planning a Chart

Before you create a chart, you need to do some general planning, deciding what data you want to display, what kind of chart you want to use, and so on. Table C-1 describes the most popular use for each chart type. The steps in this lesson show the kinds of questions you need to ask as you plan to create the Outdoor Designs regional sales chart for Derek, as well as when you plan future chart projects.

Details

Plan your presentation
What data are you including in the worksheet? How will the data fit in the report or memo you're creating? What data would you like to highlight with a chart? For example, the sales and marketing group will use the chart that you create for Derek to evaluate how business is growing and to determine which regions need special attention.

Determine the chart type
Consider the chart types shown in Figure C-1 and described in Table C-2. What chart type will best represent the data you want to include? Do you want to show one category of data or make comparisons between two categories? Several chart types are appropriate for the regional sales figures; however, Derek's preference for column charts might influence your final decision.

> **QuickTip**
>
> In addition to the chart types shown in Figure C-1, Excel provides 3-D versions of the area, bar, line, and pie charts, and similar variations for the other chart types.

Design the worksheet so Excel will create the chart you want
Group your data into logical rows and columns. As you'll learn in the next lesson, Excel uses the worksheet row and column labels to create labels and other identifiers for the chart. Review the chart terms and descriptions shown in Table C-1 to make sure that you understand them before moving on to the next lesson. The worksheet data from Derek is likely to be designed appropriately because he uses many of his own worksheets for charts.

Now you're ready to choose the chart type you want, create the chart, and edit it.

You'll start Excel and create your first chart in the next lesson.

TABLE C-1: Chart terms

term	definition
Gridlines	Horizontal and vertical lines connecting to the X-axis and Y-axis
Labels	Text describing data in the chart
Legend	Box explaining what labels, colors, and patterns in the chart represent
X-axis	Horizontal line in a chart containing a series of related values from the worksheet
Y-axis	Vertical line in a chart containing a series of related values from the worksheet

FIGURE C-1: **Common Excel chart types**

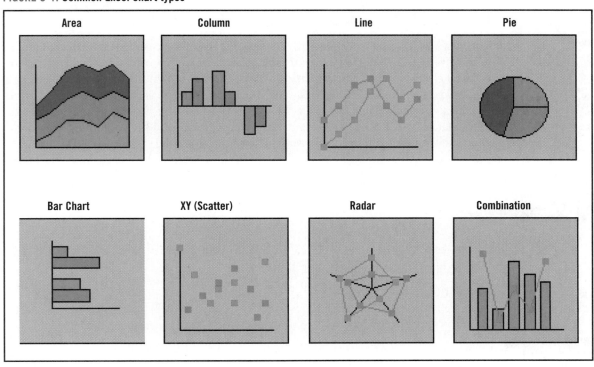

TABLE C-2: **Commonly used chart types and descriptions**

chart type	description	sample
Area	Shows relative importance of values over a period of time	
Bar	Compares values across categories	
Column	Compares values across categories	
Line	Shows trends by category over time	
Pie	Describes the relationship of parts to the whole	
Radar	Shows changes in data or data frequency relative to a center point	
XY (Scatter)	Shows the relationship between two kinds of related data	

Creating a Chart

Excel 2000

Creating an Excel chart is simple. You open a worksheet file, select the cells that contain the data you want to display in a chart, then use the Chart Wizard to create and format the chart. After creating a chart, if the worksheet data on which the chart is based changes, the chart automatically displays the new values. ▰▰▰ The worksheet you will use to create the Outdoor Designs sales chart contains sales figures for the past two quarters for the four sales territories in the United States: North, South, East, and West. Derek provided a file containing the sales data, so you have everything you need to create the chart he requested.

Steps 1234

1. **Start Excel, open the workbook XL C-1 on your Project Disk, then save the workbook as Sales Chart on your Project Disk**

2. **Select cells A5 through C9**
   The cell range A5:C9 is selected in the worksheet and will be used to create the chart. Notice that you selected the row and column labels, but not the column totals.

3. **Click the Chart Wizard button 📊 on the Standard toolbar**
   The first dialog box of the Chart Wizard opens, as shown in Figure C-1. You use the Chart Wizard to choose the type of chart you want to create, to select the data range (if you did not select it first), and to add a title, border, or gridlines to the chart.

   > **Trouble?**
   > To use a button that is not visible, click the More Buttons button ⏵⏵ on the right side of the appropriate toolbar, then click the button you need. If it is still not visible, click Add or Remove buttons, click the desired button, click outside the list to close it, then click the button on the toolbar. If the Office Assistant opens, close it.

4. **Click Next to accept the default Column chart**
   The second dialog box lets you choose the data to chart and whether the data will appear in rows or columns in the worksheet. You selected the correct data before clicking the Chart Wizard button, so the data range is correct. You accept the default setting that selects the columns as the data source.

5. **Click Next**
   In the third Chart Wizard dialog box, you see a sample of your chart with the default settings. You can change the chart title, the way data appears in the chart, and other formatting options in this dialog box. Notice that the region names from the worksheet are on the chart's X-axis and that the sales amounts from the worksheet are on the chart's Y-axis. Sales data is graphically displayed in the chart; the blue and purple bars correspond to the first quarter and second quarter, respectively.

   > **Trouble?**
   > If you don't see the Chart title text box, click the Titles tab.

6. **Type Regional Sales 2001 in the Chart title text box**
   The title appears in the sample chart box, as shown in Figure C-3.

7. **Click Next**
   In the final Chart Wizard dialog box you assign the location for the chart. You can place it as an object in the current worksheet or in another worksheet in the workbook.

   > **QuickTip**
   > To move a chart to another sheet in a workbook, click the chart to select it, click the Cut button ✂, click the destination sheet tab, then click the Paste button 📋.

8. **Click Finish, then click the Save button 💾 on the Standard toolbar**
   Charts are saved as a part of the workbook file. The column chart appears in the current worksheet, as shown in Figure C-4. The chart is selected, as indicated by the selection handles around the chart. The Chart toolbar usually appears when a chart is selected, as it is now. Your Chart toolbar might appear in a different position from what is shown in Figure C-4; it might be docked or floating in the window, or it might not appear at all.

FIGURE C-2: Using the Chart Wizard to create a chart

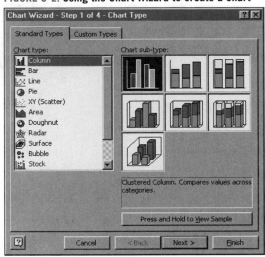

FIGURE C-3: Adding a title to a chart

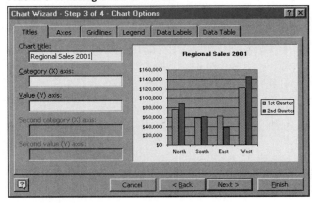

FIGURE C-4: Completed chart in the worksheet

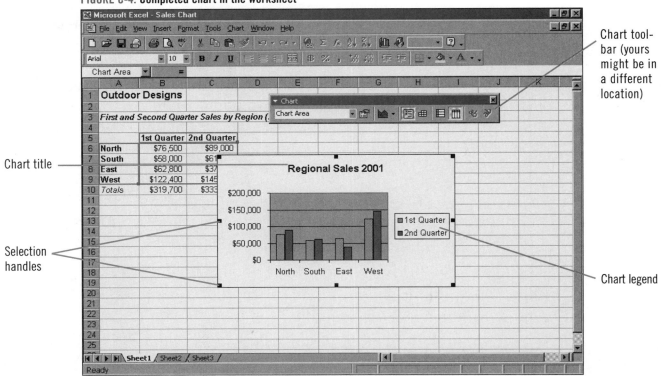

Chart title

Selection handles

Chart tool-bar (yours might be in a different location)

Chart legend

Moving and Resizing a Chart and Chart Objects

You can move, resize, copy, and paste charts in a worksheet just like objects in other Office programs. Each chart has several components (or objects) that you can modify independently of the rest of the chart. To move an object, select it first, then use the selection handles and the pointer to change its size or click and drag it to a new location. ▰▰▰▰ Derek wants the chart to appear below the worksheet data. He also wants you to change the location of the legend.

Steps

Trouble?

If you select the chart and the Chart toolbar does not appear, click View on the menu bar, point to Toolbars, then click Chart.

1. If the chart is not selected, click anywhere inside the chart to select it

2. If the Chart toolbar is below the chart, drag the Chart toolbar title bar up to move the toolbar so it's above the chart

3. Move the pointer into the chart so the ScreenTip "Chart Area" appears, then click and drag the entire chart down so that the top left corner of the chart is aligned with the top left corner of cell **A12**, then release the mouse button
   You moved the chart so the worksheet data is visible.

4. Scroll down the worksheet so you can see cell **H28**

QuickTip

If you make a mistake when moving or resizing a chart, click the Undo button 🔙 on the Standard toolbar, then try again.

5. Position the pointer over the lower-right selection handle so it changes to ⬊, then click and drag the selection handle down so the chart's lower-right edge is aligned with the lower-right edge of cell **H28**, then release the mouse button
   The chart enlarges to the new dimensions. Figure C-5 shows the chart while you are resizing it. If you drag a corner selection handle, you increase or decrease a chart size proportionally. To increase or decrease only the height or width of a chart, drag one of the side selection handles.

6. Scroll the worksheet up so you can see the chart legend and title, click the **legend** to select it, then drag it up to the position shown in Figure C-6
   The legend moves to its new location. Figure C-6 shows the legend while you are moving it.

QuickTip

To delete a chart or chart object, select it, then press [Delete].

7. Click outside the chart area in the worksheet to deselect the legend and the chart

8. Click the **Save button** 💾 on the Standard toolbar

FIGURE C-5: Resizing a chart

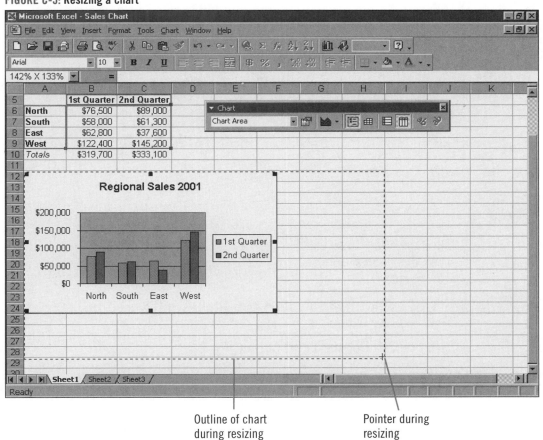

Outline of chart during resizing

Pointer during resizing

FIGURE C-6: Moving the legend

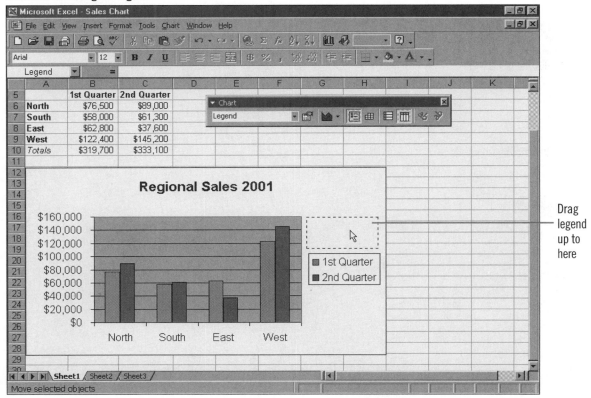

Drag legend up to here

Changing the Chart Type

The Chart toolbar includes buttons to change the chart type. In addition, you can display each chart type in one of several ways, depending on how you want to present the information. Table C-3 describes the different toolbar buttons on the Chart toolbar. ✐ You decide to experiment with some different chart types to add flair to your presentation.

Steps

1. Click the chart to select it

The Chart toolbar appears, and selection handles appear around the chart to indicate that it is selected.

QuickTip

You can position the pointer on a button to display the ScreenTip that identifies it.

2. Click the **Chart Type list arrow** on the Chart toolbar

The chart type buttons appear, as shown in Figure C-7.

3. Click the **3-D Column Chart button**

The chart type changes to a 3-D column chart, as shown in Figure C-8. The first and second quarter sales figures appear as separate bars, so you can compare each quarter's results as well as the overall results. This chart emphasizes that each region experienced growth in sales except the East region, whose sales declined by approximately 40%. The sales and marketing group will probably find this trend very interesting. You're not sure if this is what you want, so you decide to look at the 3-D pie chart.

4. Click on the Chart toolbar, then click the **3-D Pie Chart button**

The chart changes to a 3-D pie chart. This doesn't display your data clearly, as shown in Figure C-8.

QuickTip

The Chart Type button changes to display the last chart type you selected.

5. Click , then click to return to the column chart

6. Click the **Save button** on the Standard toolbar

TABLE C-3: Chart toolbar buttons

icon	button name	description
	Format	Changes the properties of the currently selected chart object
	Chart Type	Changes the chart type
	Legend	Displays or hides the chart legend
	Data Table	Changes to chart data as values or as a chart
	By Row	Changes the chart to display worksheet data by rows
	By Column	Changes the chart to display worksheet data by columns
	Angle Text Downward	Changes selected text to appear downward and diagonally
	Angle Text Upward	Changes selected text to appear upward and diagonally

FIGURE C-7: **Chart type buttons**

3-D Column Chart button

3-D Pie Chart button

FIGURE C-8: **3-D Column chart of the worksheet data**

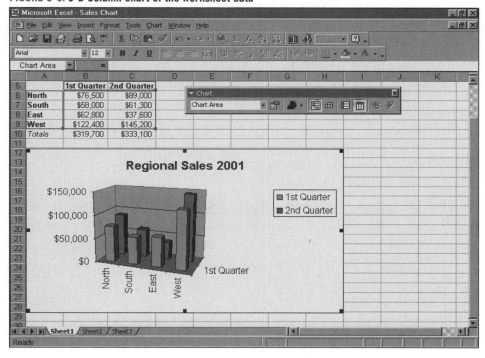

FIGURE C-9: **3-D Pie chart of the worksheet data**

This chart type shows only one data series

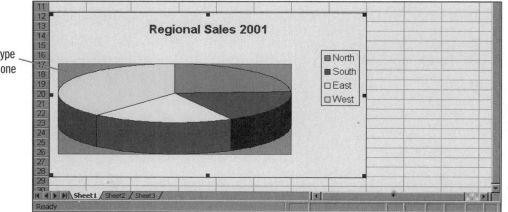

Adding Axis Labels and Gridlines

Now that you have created a chart in the worksheet, you can customize it in a variety of ways. You can add axis labels to clarify the chart data. You can format each axis, add gridlines, change the placement of the chart legend, control label placement, and so on. ➤ To clarify data in the regional sales chart, Derek asks you to add labels to the axes and add gridlines to the x-axis so the data is easier to read. These changes will also match the standard chart style used at Outdoor Designs.

Steps

1. Click **Chart** on the menu bar, then click **Chart Options**
   The Chart Options dialog box opens and displays tabs for changing the attributes of the title, axes, gridlines, legend, data labels, and data table.

2. Click the **Titles tab** in the Chart Options dialog box if necessary
   The Titles tab lets you change the chart title and add labels for the chart axes.

3. Type **Region** in the Category (X) axis text box, press **[Tab]** to move the insertion point to the Value (Y) axis text box, type **Amount**, then click **OK**
   The new labels for the X- and Y-axes appear on the chart, as shown in Figure C-10.

4. Click **Chart** on the menu bar, click **Chart Options**, click the **Gridlines tab**, click the **Major gridlines check box** for the Category (X) axis, then click **OK**
   Your chart now has gridlines for each axis. The Y-axis already has gridlines by default for this chart type.

5. Deselect the chart by clicking anywhere outside the chart, then scroll down the worksheet if necessary to see the entire chart
   The data in the chart is easy to read. See Figure C-11. You will enhance the appearance of the chart in the next lesson.

6. Click the **Save button** 🖫 on the Standard toolbar

FIGURE C-10: Adding labels to the chart axes

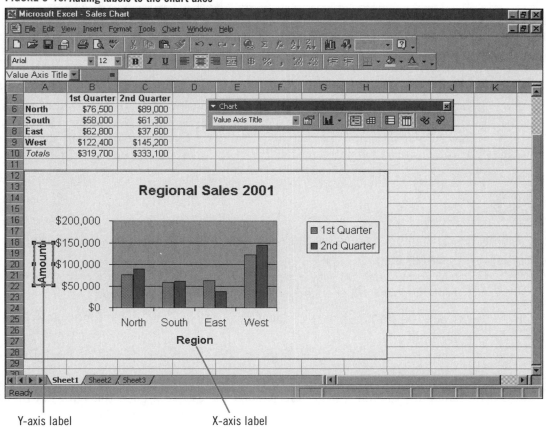

Y-axis label   X-axis label

FIGURE C-11: Chart with major axis gridlines added

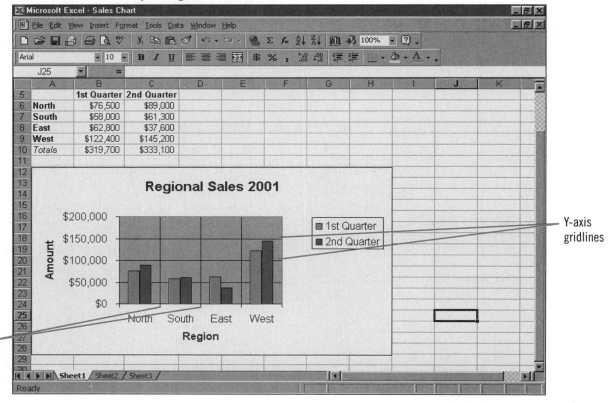

X-axis gridlines   Y-axis gridlines

Excel 2000

Changing Fonts and Colors

You can also customize the font and style of chart text and the color and pattern of bars in the chart. Such customization makes your charts readable, effective, and adapted to your specific needs. ✏ Outdoor Designs traditionally uses Times New Roman for the axis labels. Change the fonts used in the chart, then change the chart bar colors to blue and yellow to match the colors in next month's campaign.

QuickTip

You can also select any Y-axis label, then click the Format Axis button 📷 on the Chart Toolbar to open the Format Axis dialog box. This button name changes depending on what is selected in the chart.

QuickTip

Click the Font Size list arrow on the Formatting toolbar to change the font size.

1. **Right-click any label on the Y-axis (such as "50,000"), then click Format Axis on the shortcut menu**
   The Format Axis dialog box opens. You can use this dialog box to change the patterns, scale, font, number style, or alignment of the Y-axis labels.

2. **Click the Font tab, scroll down the Font list and click Times New Roman, then click OK**
   The Format Axis dialog box closes, and the sales chart appears. The Y-axis labels change to Times New Roman font.

3. **Click one of the X-axis labels (such as "North"), click the Font list arrow on the Formatting toolbar, then click Times New Roman in the list**
   You can also use the Formatting toolbar to change labels. The X-axis labels change to Times New Roman font.

4. **Double-click one of the 1st Quarter (blue) bars in the chart**
   The Patterns tab of the Format Data Series dialog box opens, as shown in Figure C-12. You can change the colors and patterns of the columns in your chart.

5. **Click the bright blue box (the last box in the last row) in the Area color palette, then click OK**
   The 1st Quarter bars and the 1st Quarter legend box change to bright blue.

6. **Double-click one of the 2nd Quarter (purple) bars in the chart, click the bright yellow box (the third box in the last row), then click OK**
   The 2nd Quarter bars and the 2nd Quarter legend box change to bright yellow.

7. **Click anywhere outside of the chart to deselect it, then click the Save button 💾 on the Standard toolbar**
   Figure C-13 shows the completed chart. Notice that the Chart toolbar closes when the chart is not selected.

FIGURE C-12: Format Data Series dialog box

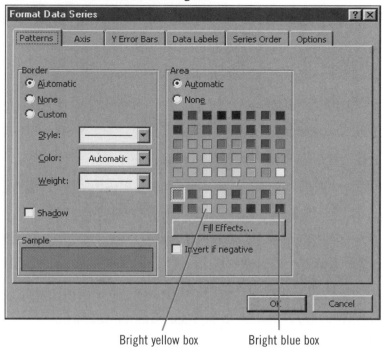

Bright yellow box   Bright blue box

FIGURE C-13: Chart with new labels and colors

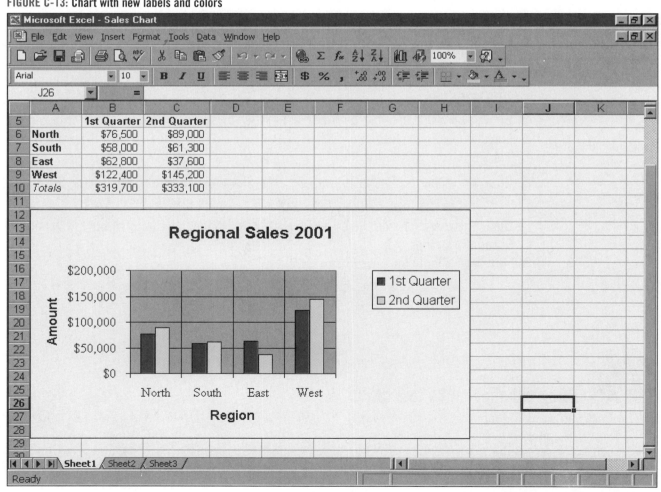

Enhancing a Chart

There are many ways to change the appearance of a chart to increase its visual appeal and effectiveness. ✐━━ Derek asks you to change the chart background and put the title in a shadow box to make the chart look more professional.

Steps 1 2 3 4

1. **Right-click anywhere in the chart area, click Format Chart Area on the shortcut menu, then click the Patterns tab, if necessary**
   The Format Chart Area dialog box opens. You can use this dialog box to change the chart background.

2. **Click the Fill Effects button, then click the Texture tab**
   The Texture tab of the Fill Effects dialog box lets you change the background to include interesting textures.

3. **Click the Parchment box (the third box in the first row), click OK to close the Fill Effects dialog box, then click OK to close the Format Chart Area dialog box**
   The chart area appears with the new background, as shown in Figure C-14.

Trouble?

If the Chart toolbar covers the chart title, click the toolbar and drag it out of the way.

4. **Click the chart title to select it, then click the Format Chart Title button 🖼 on the Chart toolbar**
   The Format Chart Title dialog box opens. You can use this dialog box to change the appearance of the title.

5. **Click the Font tab, click the Color list arrow, click the Blue box (the first box in the last row), then click OK**
   The title changes to dark yellow.

6. **Click 🖼, click the Patterns tab, click the Shadow check box, then click OK**
   The title appears with a white background and a shadow around the box.

7. **Click anywhere outside the chart to deselect it, then click the Save button 🖫 on the Standard toolbar**
   Your chart should look like Figure C-15.

CLUES TO USE

Adding enhancements to a chart

You can change the chart appearance in many ways to make your chart more interesting and visually appealing. Make sure that you don't overdo it: a chart with too many colors or too many visual effects distracts your audience from the information you are trying to present. Make sure you use complementary colors. Remember, your primary goal when using charts is to communicate worksheet information effectively.

FIGURE C-14: Chart with parchment background

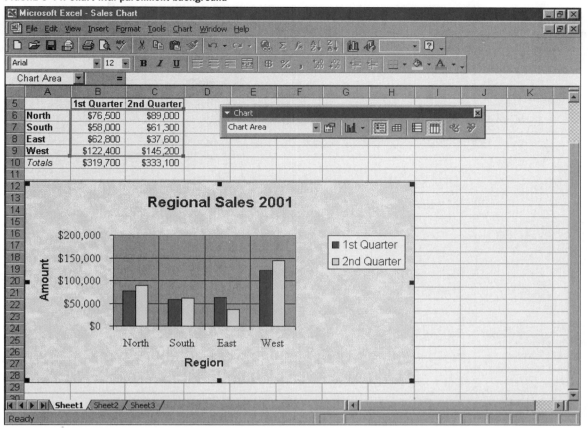

FIGURE C-15: Completed chart with new title style

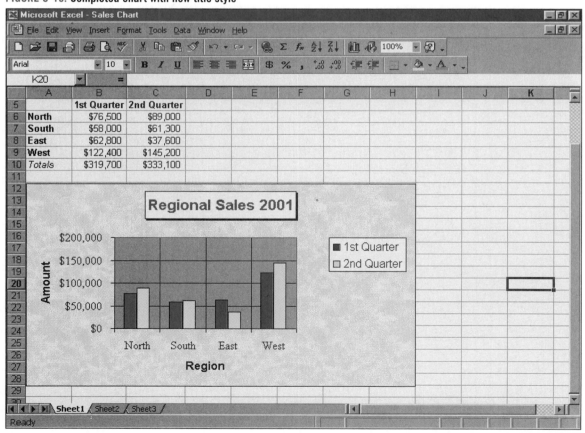

Previewing and Printing a Chart

There are two ways to print a chart—by itself or with the worksheet data on which it is based. To preview or print only the chart, click the Print Preview or Print button with the chart selected. To preview or print the chart with the worksheet, deselect the chart, then click the Print Preview or Print button. If you have a color printer attached to your system, your print preview will show any colors that are used in the chart. If you have a black and white printer, any chart colors will appear as grayscale, or as shades of gray. ✎━━━ Derek is happy with your chart. He wants you to add a footer with the word "Confidential," today's date, and the page number to the bottom of the page before printing it. He asks you to preview the worksheet with the chart, then print a copy for distribution to the sales and marketing group.

Steps

1. Make sure the chart is not selected, then click the **Print Preview button** 🔍 on the Standard toolbar
   The worksheet appears in the Print Preview window.

> **Trouble?**
>
> If your worksheet appears in landscape orientation instead of portrait orientation, click Page Setup, click the Page tab, click the Portrait option button, then click OK.

2. Click the **Setup button** on the Print Preview toolbar, then click the **Header/Footer tab** in the Page Setup dialog box

3. Click the **Footer list arrow**, then click the **Confidential, <date>, Page 1** option in the list (or a similar option if this one is not available)
   You can add a variety of preformatted headers and footers to your worksheet to identify the date, filename, author, or page number of your workbook. Excel personalizes some of the information in the preformatted headers and footers based on the registered user information entered when Excel is installed, so your choices may vary. You can customize the header or footer with your own information by clicking one of the Custom buttons.

> **Trouble?**
>
> If you have a black and white printer, your preview chart will appear as grayscale, even though you formatted the chart using color.

4. Click **OK**
   The worksheet appears in Print Preview as it will appear on the page when printed. See Figure C-16.

5. Use the **Zoom pointer** 🔍 to click the chart
   Make sure the chart is correct, as shown in Figure C-17.

6. Click the **Print button** on the Print Preview toolbar, then click **OK**
   The page is printed.

7. Click the **Save button** 💾 on the Standard toolbar

8. Click the program window **Close button** to close Excel
   The workbook and Excel close.

FIGURE C-16: Print Preview of worksheet

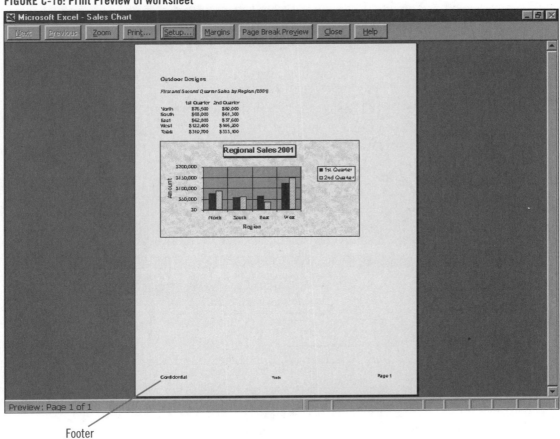

Footer

FIGURE C-17: Zooming the chart in Print Preview

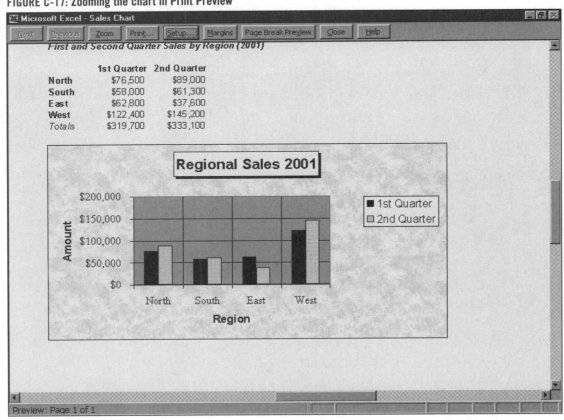

Practice

► Concepts Review

Label each element of the chart window shown in Figure C-18.

FIGURE C-18

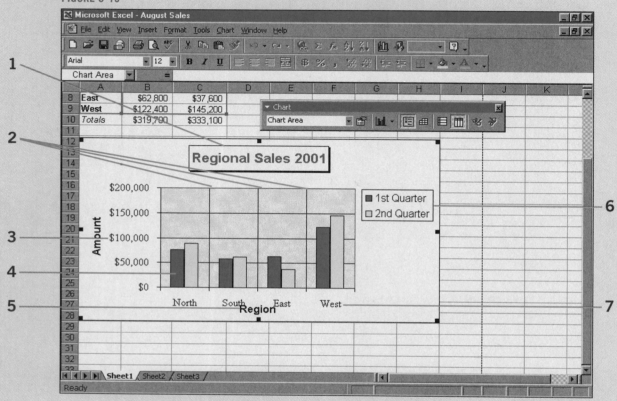

Match each chart button on the toolbar with the chart type it creates.

8. 🖼
9. 🗡
10. 📊
11. 📈
12. 📉
13. 📄
14. ⭐
15. 📊
16. 🥧

a. 3-D Pie Chart button
b. 3-D Line Chart button
c. 3-D Bar Chart button
d. 3-D Area Chart button
e. Radar Chart button
f. Column Chart button
g. Pie Chart button
h. Line Chart button
i. Bar Chart button

Select the best answer from the choices listed.

17. Which definition best describes the X-axis in an Excel chart?
   a. The vertical line that contains a series of related worksheet values
   b. The horizontal line that contains a series of related worksheet values
   c. A box that explains what the labels, colors, and patterns in the chart represent
   d. Horizontal and vertical lines that connect to the X-axis and Y-axis

18. Which toolbar button do you click to create a new chart in a worksheet?
   a.
   b.
   c.
   d.

19. Which type of chart displays line and bar graphs in the same chart?
   a. Bar
   b. Line/bar
   c. Combination
   d. Area

20. For which task do you use selection handles?
   a. Resizing an object
   b. Moving an object
   c. Changing the color of an object
   d. Changing what is selected

21. What is the function of the button?
   a. Changing the way data appears in a chart
   b. Hiding or displaying the legend
   c. Changing the chart to display worksheet data by columns
   d. Changing the chart to display worksheet data by rows

22. What button do you click to change the texture of the chart background?
   a. Fill Background
   b. Fill Chart Area
   c. Fill Effects
   d. Fill Chart

23. What is a good rule of thumb when formatting a chart?
   a. Use as many colors as possible.
   b. Make sure your chart communicates your worksheet data effectively.
   c. Use colors that are not complementary for readability.
   d. Use as many elements as possible.

Excel 2000

▶ Skills Review

1. **Open the file XL C-2 on your Student Disk, and create a chart of the trip information it contains.**
   a. Start Excel, and open the file XL C-2 on your Project Disk.
   b. Save the workbook as "Adventure Chart" on your Project Disk.
   c. Select cells A4 through C10, then click the Chart Wizard button on the Standard toolbar.
   d. Click the Bar Chart type, then click Next.
   e. Click Next again.
   f. Click the Titles tab.
   g. Click in the Chart title text box, type "Total Trips", then click Next.
   h. Click Finish to create the chart. The chart will look small and unfinished; you fix that in the steps below.

2. **Move and resize the chart and chart objects.**
   a. Drag the chart so that the upper-left corner of the chart is aligned with the upper-left corner of cell A12.
   b. Use the lower-right corner selection handle to drag the lower-right corner of the chart to align with the lower-right corner of cell G28.
   c. Click and drag the legend to the lower-right corner of the chart area.

3. **Experiment with different chart types.**
   a. Display the Chart toolbar if necessary, click the Chart Type list arrow, then click the Pie Chart button.
   b. Click the Chart Type list arrow, then click the Line Chart button. (Use the ScreenTips to identify each chart button if necessary.)
   c. Click the Chart Type list arrow, then click the 3-D Bar Chart button.
   d. Click the Chart Type list arrow, then click the Bar Chart button.

4. **Add axis labels and gridlines to the bar chart.**
   a. Right-click any label on the X-axis, then click Format Axis on the shortcut menu.
   b. Click the Font tab in the Format Axis dialog box.
   c. Scroll down the Font list, then click Book Antiqua.
   d. Click OK.
   e. Click any label on the Y-axis, click the Font list arrow on the Formatting toolbar, then scroll down the list and click Book Antiqua.
   f. Click the Font Size list arrow on the Formatting toolbar, then click 10.
   g. Click Chart on the menu bar, then click Chart Options.
   h. Click the Gridlines tab, then click the Major gridlines check box for the Value (Y) axis to clear it, click the Minor gridlines check boxes for both axes to select them, then click OK.
   i. Click the Save button to save your changes.

5. Change the chart fonts and the chart colors.

    a. Click the chart title, then click the Format Chart Title button on the Chart toolbar.

    b. Click the Font tab if necessary.

    c. Scroll down the Font list, then click Times New Roman.

    d. Click the Color list arrow, click the Sea Green box (the fourth box in the third row), then click OK.

    e. Double-click one of the Totals '01 bars in the chart.

    f. Change the color to Dark Green (the seventh box in the last row), then click OK.

    g. Double-click one of the Projected '02 bars in the chart.

    h. Change the color to Light Green (the fourth box in the fifth row), then click OK.

    i. Click the Save button to save your changes.

6. Enhance the chart by adding a background and title effects.

    a. Right-click the chart area, then click Format Chart Area on the shortcut menu.

    b. Click the Patterns tab if necessary.

    c. Click the Fill Effects button, then click the Texture tab.

    d. Click the Newsprint box (the first box in the first row), click OK, then click OK again.

    e. Click the title, then click the Format Chart Title button on the Chart toolbar.

    f. Click the Shadow check box.

    g. Click OK.

    h. Click the Save button to save your changes.

7. Preview and print the chart.

    a. With the chart selected, click the Print Preview button on the Standard toolbar.

    b. Click the Setup button on the Print Preview toolbar.

    c. Click the Footer list arrow.

    d. Click the option that adds your name, the page number, and today's date.

    e. Click OK.

    f. Use the Zoom pointer to make sure that your chart and footer are correct on the page.

    g. Click the Print button, then click OK to print the chart.

    h. Click the Save button to save your workbook.

    i. Close the file, and exit Excel.

▶ Independent Challenges

1. The Wacky Words Card Company is evaluating last year's Christmas card sales and is hoping to spot important selling trends. Use the XL C-3 workbook on your Project Disk to create a line chart that graphically depicts Christmas card sales from October through January. Experiment with line chart variations to create a chart that looks ready for distribution.

To complete this independent challenge:

a. Open the file XL C-3 on your Project Disk, then save it as "Card Chart" on your Project Disk.

b. Create a line chart of the data from October through January, excluding the column totals, and using an appropriate chart title.

c. Move the chart down in the worksheet, then enlarge it.

d. Experiment with three different chart types. Which types did you try? Would they be appropriate or inappropriate for card sales data? Why?

e. Change back to the Line Chart type.

f. Add major gridlines for both axes, then add the title "Month" to the X-axis and "# Sold" to the Y-axis.

g. Change the font size of the labels for the values on the X- and Y-axes to 11-point.

h. Change the chart area background to a solid color of your choice.

i. Save your changes, preview the chart, print it, then close the file.

2. Palmer's Pet Hospital is evaluating its January business. Ellen Smith, the office manager, wants to know what percentage of time employees spend treating each type of animal. This information will be useful when it's time to hire additional staff. Use the XL C-4 workbook on your Project Disk to create a pie chart that shows what percentage of visits each animal type accounts for in January. Also use the chart to settle a bet you have with Ellen that pigs accounted for more than 10% of the total January business.

To complete this independent challenge:

a. Open the file XL C-4 on your Project Disk, then save it as "Animal Chart" on your Project Disk.

b. Create a 3-D Pie Chart of the data with the title "Treatment by Animal Type".

c. Move the chart down in the worksheet, then enlarge it.

d. Use the Data Labels tab of the Chart Options dialog box to add labels to each slice of the pie. After you close the Chart Options dialog box, click and drag individual data labels as necessary so the chart is easy to read.

e. Separate the Pigs pie slice from the pie chart. (*Hint:* You will need to click the Pigs pie slice to select it, then drag it up and away from the pie to "explode" it.)

f. Who wins the bet?

g. Save your changes, preview the worksheet with the chart, print it, then close the file.

3. The local art gallery is conducting research to determine how many people viewed a recent art exhibit. They want you to create an area chart that depicts the number of people who attended over a six-month period and includes a breakdown of men, women, and children under age 10 who attended. The attendance data is stored in the XL C-5 worksheet; you just need to create the chart.

To complete this independent challenge:

a. Open the file XL C-5 on your Project Disk, then save it as "Attendance Chart" on your Project Disk.

b. Create a stacked area chart of the data with the title "Gallery Attendance". (*Hint*: Click the Chart sub-types and look in the description below the sub-types for the name "Stacked Area" to find this chart.) How does this chart type meet the art gallery's needs?

c. Move the chart down in the worksheet, then enlarge it.

d. Change the title font to 20-point Arial Black.

e. Add labels to the X- and Y-axes of "Month" and "Total", respectively.

f. Change the font size of the value labels on the X- and Y-axes to 12-point.

g. Change the chart background to an attractive texture.

h. Change the color of the chart title, then add a shadow box.

i. Add a header to the chart (*not* the worksheet) that includes the filename, centered on the page. (*Hint*: Use the Custom Header button.)

j. Save your changes, preview the chart, print the chart, then close the file.

4. When a movie is released, the studio pays close attention to its weekend gross amount as compared to its total gross. Sometimes the ratio of weekend gross to total gross indicates whether the movie is still popular. Use the World Wide Web to find information for last weekend's top grossing films. Then create an Excel chart to show the relationship between the weekend gross and the total gross of the top three film's revenues.

To complete this independent challenge:

a. Open a new workbook, and save it as "Movie Chart" on your Project Disk.

b. Log on to the Internet, and use your browser to go to http://www.course.com. From there, click the Student Online Companions link, click the link for this book, then click the Excel link for Unit C.

c. Use the The Box Office link to find a list of the top ten grossing movies for last weekend. Make sure you see the figures for last weekend, then print the page.

d. Log off the Internet, and close your browser.

e. Enter the movie name, weekend gross, and total gross for each movie listed.

f. Create a chart for the three top grossing films. Choose an appropriate chart type for displaying the weekend gross versus the total gross.

g. Add an appropriate title and axis titles to the chart. Format the labels so they are easy to read.

h. Format the chart using the commands and techniques you learned in this unit.

i. Save your changes, preview the worksheet with the chart, print the worksheet, then close the file.

Excel 2000

▶ Visual Workshop

Create the chart shown in Figure C-19 using the commands and techniques you learned in this unit. Approximate numbers as best as you can using the chart shown. Save the workbook as "Sales Rep Chart" on your Project Disk. Save your changes, preview the chart, print it, then close the file.

FIGURE C-19

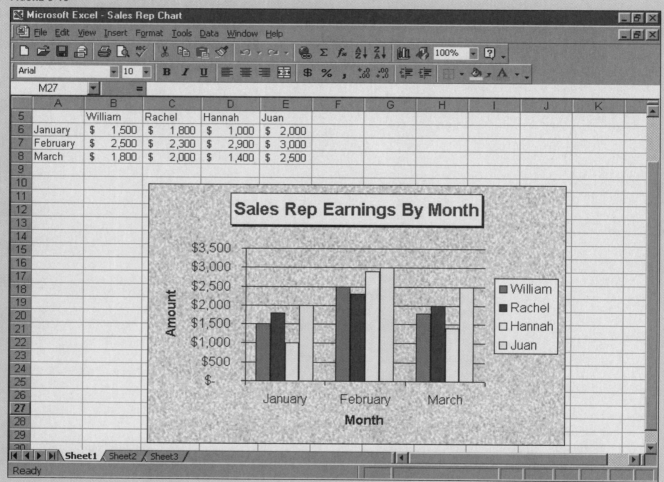

Building
a Database with Access 2000

Objectives

- ► Plan a database
- ► Start Access 2000
- ► Create a database
- ► Modify a table
- ► Build a data entry form
- ► Enter data into a database
- ► Add and edit records in a database
- ► Print a database and exit Access

In this unit you learn about Microsoft Access 2000, the database program in Microsoft Office. A **database** is a collection of information organized in tables and stored electronically in a file. A database can contain information of any kind, from sales and financial records about your business, to lists of school friends and associates, and even the compact discs in your music collection. In this unit you'll help Elizabeth Fried, the database administrator for Outdoor Designs, use Access to create a database to help Outdoor Designs keep track of customers. After you create the database, you will create a data entry form and practice entering, editing, and manipulating data in it. You will then print the database and exit Access.

Access 2000

Planning a Database

Before you create a new database, you should plan it. Consider what type of information the database will contain and how you need to work with that information. A well-designed database saves you time and effort in the future and requires less maintenance. ✏ Elizabeth has assigned you the task of keeping track of each Outdoor Designs customer by creating a database with the customer's company name and contact information. You will use the following guidelines to define your database.

Details

Determine the purpose of the database
You need to create a database to store information about each Outdoor Designs customer. Each customer's information will be stored in a record. A **record** contains all information pertaining to a person, business product or other entity. A record consists of **fields**, specific categories of information such as name, address, and phone number. A collection of related records is called a **table**. A database created with Access is called a **relational database**, a collection of one or more related tables, forms, and other objects that can share information. Figure A-1 shows an example of a relational database.

Determine potential uses for the database
You will use this database to locate and update information on a customer or group of customers, perform sales comparisons, and produce various reports. A **report** is a summary of database information specifically designed for printing.

Collect the information needed to produce the results you want
Talk to all possible database users to gather additional ideas that might enhance the design. At this time, all your customer data is on index cards. Current customer information cards, like the one shown in Figure A-2, provide the information Outdoor Designs wants to store in the database.

Choose the right fields for your database tables
This is an important task. Fields affect how data is entered into the database, as well as how it sorts, searches, and reports on the database later. Determine a unique field for each category of information. Access ensures that each record is unique by providing a **primary key field** for each table. A primary key field might be a Social Security number or customer ID number. It's usually good to create specific fields, including enough fields so that you can break out important information, but not so many that using the forms becomes a burden. For example, using separate fields for city, state, and zip code elements is usually better than combining them in a single field because you can later search for records for a particular city, state, or zip code. Because Access is a relational database program, you can share information among tables, which means you don't have to enter repetitive information, such as a customer's address, more than once in the database and run the risk of introducing errors.

Sketch the form's structure, including each field's format
A **form** is where the database fields are displayed one record at a time so you can enter the information as if you were filling in a paper form. The cards are a good basis for the form you will create. Using all the information on the original customer information cards, you plan your form and the fields it will contain, as shown in Figure A-3.

FIGURE A-1: **Structure of a relational database**

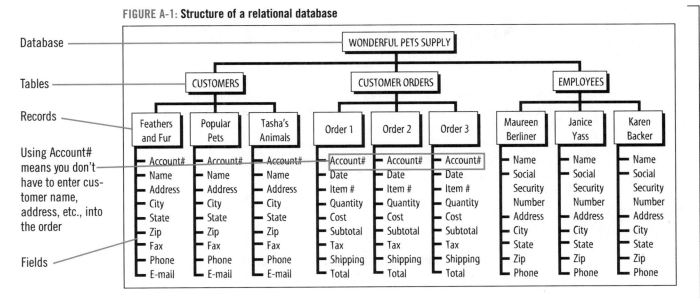

Database — WONDERFUL PETS SUPPLY

Tables — CUSTOMERS | CUSTOMER ORDERS | EMPLOYEES

Records — Feathers and Fur | Popular Pets | Tasha's Animals | Order 1 | Order 2 | Order 3 | Maureen Berliner | Janice Yass | Karen Backer

Using Account# means you don't have to enter customer name, address, etc., into the order

Fields —

Feathers and Fur	Popular Pets	Tasha's Animals	Order 1	Order 2	Order 3	Maureen Berliner	Janice Yass	Karen Backer
Account#	Account#	Account#	Account#	Account#	Account#	Name	Name	Name
Name	Name	Name	Date	Date	Date	Social Security Number	Social Security Number	Social Security Number
Address	Address	Address	Item #	Item #	Item #	Address	Address	Address
City	City	City	Quantity	Quantity	Quantity	City	City	City
State	State	State	Cost	Cost	Cost	State	State	State
Zip	Zip	Zip	Subtotal	Subtotal	Subtotal	Zip	Zip	Zip
Fax	Fax	Fax	Tax	Tax	Tax	Phone	Phone	Phone
Phone	Phone	Phone	Shipping	Shipping	Shipping			
E-mail	E-mail	E-mail	Total	Total	Total			

FIGURE A-2: **Original customer information card**

Outdoor Designs
Customer Information Card

Company Name and Address: Cambridge Kite Supplies
                             1437 Main Street
                             Cambridge, MA 02142

Name: Jennifer Keller
Phone: 617-555-2323
Fax: 555-2424
Email: JenKeller@kites.com

First purchase: 1/9/94

Active: yes

FIGURE A-3: **Planned form and fields**

ID _____   Customer Since

Company _____   Active [____]

First Name _____

Last Name _____

Address _____

City _____

State _____

Zip _____

Phone _____

Fax _____

E-mail _____

Access 2000

Starting Access 2000

There are several ways to start Access: You can choose the New Office Document command on the Start menu; you can point to Programs on the Start menu, then click Microsoft Access; or, if you want to work with an existing file you can choose the Open Office Document command on the Start menu or point to Documents on the Start menu and then choose the file you want. If you need assistance starting Access, ask your instructor or technical support person for help. The Access window contains many elements that help you enter and manipulate the information in your database. Some of these elements are common to all Windows programs. ✐ You need to start Access so you can begin to learn how to use it.

Steps 1 2 3 4

1. Click the Start button on the taskbar, then point to Programs

Microsoft Access is located in the Programs group located in the Start menu.

2. Click Microsoft Access

Access starts and displays the Access window. A dialog box opens, as shown in Figure A-4, asking you if you want to open a new or existing database.

3. Click the Blank Access Database option button, then click OK

The dialog box closes, and the File New Database dialog box opens.

4. Make sure the Save in box displays the drive and folder for your Project Files, type Outdoor Designs in the File name text box, then click Create

The dialog box closes, and the Outdoor Designs database window opens. See Figure A-5. Here you specify the object you want to create and the way in which you want to create it. Tables, queries, forms, reports, macros, and modules are objects in Access; you will learn how to create and work with these objects as you learn more about Access. When you click a button in the Objects list on the left, the choices for creating it are displayed in the right pane. You have three choices for creating a table: creating it in Design view lets you create and organize the fields before you begin entering data; if you prefer to start with a sample table and modify it for your purposes, you can use a wizard; creating the table by entering data allows you to begin typing data in a blank table and specify the fields and field properties as you work.

5. Double-click Create table in Design view

The new table opens in Design view, as shown in Figure A-6. Here you create the fields you want in your database and determine the order in which they should appear in the data form.

6. Click the Maximize button if the table window does not fill the screen

Refer to Figure A-6. The title bar displays the filename of the object you are creating (currently "Table 1") and the type of object you are creating. The menu bar contains the commands used in Access. These commands change depending on the specific Access window that is open. The Table Design toolbar contains buttons for the tasks you need to perform. This toolbar also changes depending on the Access window that is open. The Status bar displays important messages as you work with Access. The Field Properties pane provides information about the currently selected field. (Your table doesn't have any fields yet; you'll create them in the next lesson.)

Trouble?

If this is the first time you are using Access, click the Start using Microsoft Access option button in the Welcome to Microsoft Access dialog box, then close the Office Assistant.

QuickTip

Remember that you can always get online help by clicking the Microsoft Access Help button 🔲 on the toolbar.

FIGURE A-4: Microsoft Access Startup dialog box

FIGURE A-5: Outdoor Designs

Objects list ——

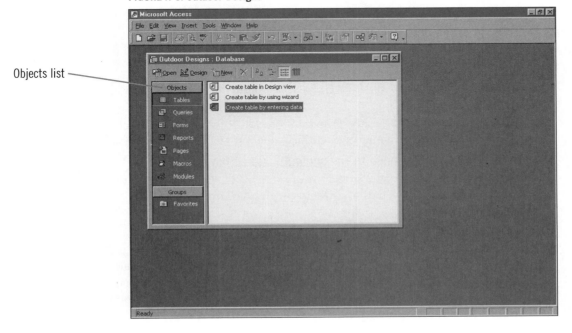

FIGURE A-6: Outdoor Designs database table window

Title bar ——
Table Design toolbar ——

Field Properties pane ——

Status bar ——

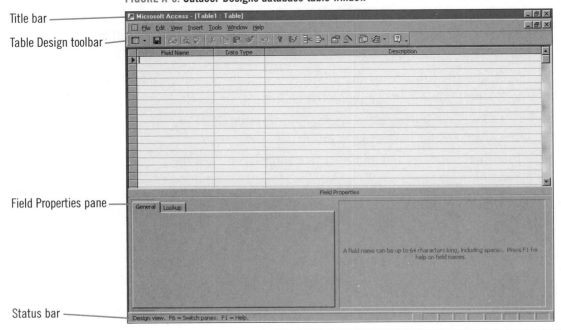

Access 2000

Creating a Database

To create the database table, you need to specify a name for each field and its data type (you can also enter a description, but it's not necessary). You also need to specify the primary sort key. The order in which you enter fields in Design view determines the structure of the database table and the layout of the **data form**, an electronic form that you can use to enter data. You can modify the table structure at any time. ✐ You are ready to design the customers table in the database. Based on your planning, you know this table will contain 14 fields.

QuickTip

Field names can contain up to 64 characters, including letters, numbers, spaces, and some special characters.

1. **Click in the first Field Name cell if necessary, type Customer ID, then press [Tab]**
   Customer ID is entered as the first field in the table, and the insertion point moves to the Data Type column, where you specify the field's **data type**, which determines what type of data the user will be able to type in the field and how it will be formatted.

2. **Click the Data Type list arrow, then click AutoNumber**
   The AutoNumber data type assigns a unique sequential number to each record in the database as it is entered.

3. **Click the Primary Key button 🔑 on the toolbar to format this field as the primary key field**
   This is a good field to use as the primary key field because the AutoNumber data type guarantees that each record is uniquely identified even if some fields contain identical information.

4. **Press [Tab] twice to move to the second Field Name cell**
   Navigating in Design view is similar to working in Excel: you can click the cell you want to move to, you can press [Tab] to move to the next cell or [Shift][Tab] to move to the previous cell, or you can use the arrow keys.

5. **Type Company, then press [Tab]**
   The default data type, Text, appears in the Data Type column, as shown in Figure A-7. If you don't specify a field type, the Text data type is assigned. This data type lets you enter text (such as names), numbers that don't require calculations (such as phone numbers), or combinations of text and numbers (such as street addresses). The Field Properties pane shows the default information for this field. For example, the Field Size is 50 characters (which you can increase up to 255 characters) and the user is not required to enter a value for this field. See Table A-1 for descriptions of common data types.

6. **Click in the third Field Name cell, type First Name, press [Tab] three times to accept the Text data type and move to the fourth Field Name cell, type Last Name, then press [Tab] three times**

7. **Complete the table using Figure A-8 as a guide, pressing [Tab] as needed to move to the next cell; when you reach the last entry, press [Tab]**

8. **Click the Save button 💾 on the toolbar to save this table**
   The Save As dialog box opens, as shown in Figure A-9.

9. **Type Customers as the name for this table, then click OK**
   The table is saved as part of the Outdoor Designs Customers database.

FIGURE A-7: **Creating a table in Design view**

Primary key
field indicator

First field name

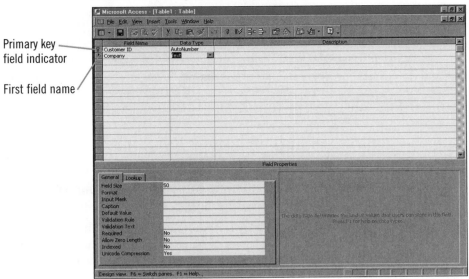

FIGURE A-8: **Completed Customers table structure**

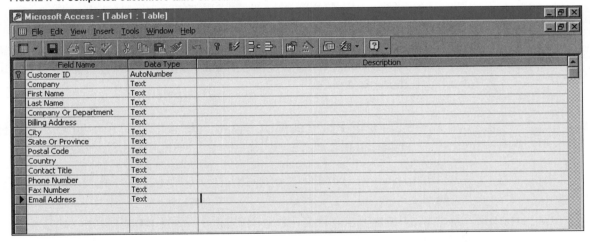

FIGURE A-9: **Save As dialog box**

TABLE A-1: **Common field data types**

data type	description
Text	Text, numbers that don't require calculations, or a combination of text and numbers
Memo	Lengthy text (which can also contain numbers that don't require calculations)
Number	Numeric data to be used in calculations
Date/Time	Date and time values
Currency	Currency values and numeric data used in calculations
Yes/No	Fields that can contain only one of two values
AutoNumber	Unique sequential number that Access assigns to each new record; can't be edited

Unit **A**

Access 2000

Modifying a Table

The structure of a table can be modified in Design view. You can add and delete fields, change data types, add **field descriptions** to help document the database by explaining the contents of a field, and change field properties. **Field properties** determine how field data is stored, handled, and displayed. ✎ Elizabeth is pleased with the table, but she wants you to delete three fields, add two new fields, then change the field properties for four existing fields.

Steps 1 2 3 4

1. Click the **Company Or Department field row selector**, as shown in Figure A-10, right-click the **selected row**, click **Delete Rows**, click the **Country field row selector**, right-click the **selected row**, click **Delete Rows**, click the **Contact Title row selector**, right-click the **selected row**, then click **Delete Rows**
   When you delete a field, you lose all the data that is stored in that field. You have not entered any data in the database, so you can delete fields without losing any data.

> **QuickTip**
> Each data type begins with a unique letter so you can type the first letter of a data type to enter it in the database instead of using the Data Type list arrow.

2. Scroll down and click in the **first blank field name cell**, type **Customer Since**, press **[Tab]**, click the **Data Type list arrow**, click **Date/Time**, press **[Tab]**, type **Date of first sale**, press **[Enter]**
   You will use this field to track how long a customer has been with Outdoor Designs based on the date of their first purchase.

3. Type **Active** in the next field name cell, press **[Tab]**, click the **Data Type list arrow**, click **Yes/No**, press **[Tab]**, then type **Yes if less than six months since last purchase; No if more than six months**
   You will use this field to track whether a customer is active.

4. Click in the **State Or Province field name cell**, delete **Or Province**, press **[F6]** to move to the Field Properties panel, then type **2** in the **Field Size text box**
   See Figure A-11. The Field Properties panel changes, depending on which field is currently selected. Different data types have different field properties. You want the database to record the states by their two-letter abbreviations.

5. Click in the **Postal Code field name cell**, click in **the Input Mask text box**, click the **Input Mask Wizard button** ⊞ to the right of the text box, click **Yes** to save the table before proceeding, click **Zip Code** in the Input Mask list, then click **Finish**
   An **input mask** determines the formatting for a field to ensure that users input data correctly. This input mask formats the field for a hyphenated nine-digit zip code to make sure users type a complete zip code, including the four-digit extension, when entering data.

6. Click in the **Phone Number field name cell**, click in the **Input Mask text box**, click ⊞, click **Yes** to save the table, click **Phone Number** in the Input Mask list, then click **Finish**; repeat this step using the phone number input mask for the **Fax Number field name cell**
   Now both cells are formatted with an input mask to ensure that users type a complete phone number, including the area code, when they input data.

7. Click the **Datasheet View button** ▦ on the Table Design toolbar, click **Yes** to save your changes, then maximize the Outdoor Designs Customers datasheet window if necessary
   Your screen should look like Figure A-12. The datasheet consists of a grid of rows and columns. As you complete each row of data, a new row appears. You can scroll to the right to see all the fields in the table.

8. Click the **Datasheet Window Close button**

FIGURE A-10: Selecting a row to delete

Current field indicator

Field row selectors

Company or Department field is selected

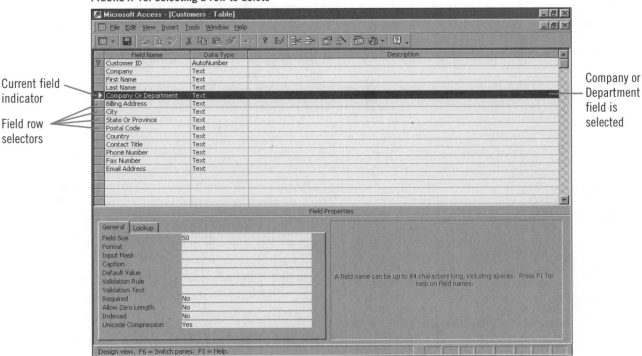

FIGURE A-11: Changing a field property

Field name changed

New fields added

Field descriptions help document a database

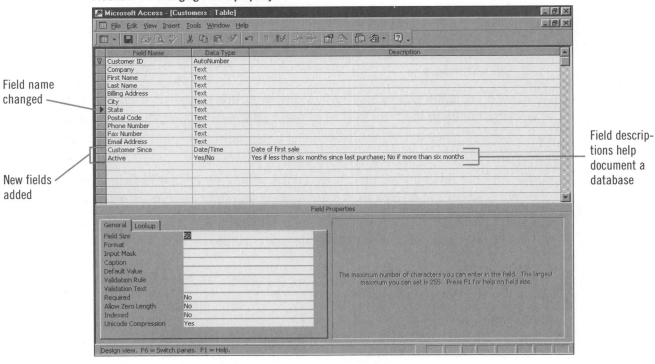

FIGURE A-12: Modified table in Datasheet view

First record is blank except for Customer ID field, which is completed automatically using AutoNumber

Access 2000

Building a Data Entry Form

You can enter database information directly into the rows and columns in Datasheet view. However, working in Form view makes entering database information easier. To facilitate the often repetitive process of entering data, a **form** displays the fields for one record at a time, with fields arranged and formatted as you wish. You can build a form using the Form Wizard to step you through the process, you can use a wizard to create a predesigned form in a specified layout (such as columnar format), or you can design the form yourself in Design view. 🖋️ Your colleagues will need to enter data for hundreds of customers to complete the Outdoor Designs database. To make this process easier, you decide to build an Outdoor Designs form using the Form Wizard.

1. Click the **Forms button** in the Objects list, then double-click **Create form by using wizard**
   The Form Wizard dialog box opens, as shown in Figure A-13. Here you choose the database table on which the form is based and select the fields to include in the form.

2. Click the **Tables/Queries list arrow**, then click **Table:Customers** if necessary

3. Click the **Select All Fields button** `>>`
   The fields move into the Selected Fields list box. Because this form will be used to enter all the data into the Customers table, you want to use all the available fields.

4. Click `Next >` to continue through the Form Wizard

5. Click `Next >` to accept the default layout for a Columnar Form

6. Click **Standard** in the Style list box if necessary, then click `Next >`

7. Type **Customer Data Entry Form** in the What title do you want for your form text box, click the **Open the form to view or enter information option button** if necessary, click `Finish`, then maximize the Customer Data Entry Form Form view window if necessary
   Review all the features of the Form shown in Figure A-14.

8. Click the **Design View button** 🖼️ on the Form View toolbar to switch to Design view
   Your screen should look like Figure A-15. In this view, you can see how the form is constructed, and make any modifications.

9. Click the **Save button** 🖼️ on the Standard toolbar
   Your changes are saved.

Working in Datasheet view

When you click the Datasheet View button on the toolbar, the database appears in its original datasheet format. In this format, you can compare different database records for overall consistency, quickly search for individual records, and easily edit existing records. You can also add new records anywhere in the database by using the Insert Record command or the Insert Record button. To widen a column of cells so that you can read a field's entire contents, click the column selector of the column you want to adjust, click Format on the menu bar, click Column Width, then click Best Fit.

FIGURE A-13: Form Wizard dialog box

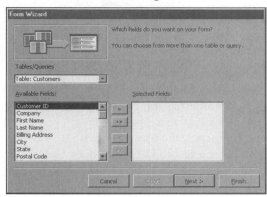

FIGURE A-14: Customer Data Entry Form in Form view

Current field indicator

Field names

Click the record navigation buttons to move from record to record

Form name

Field value box

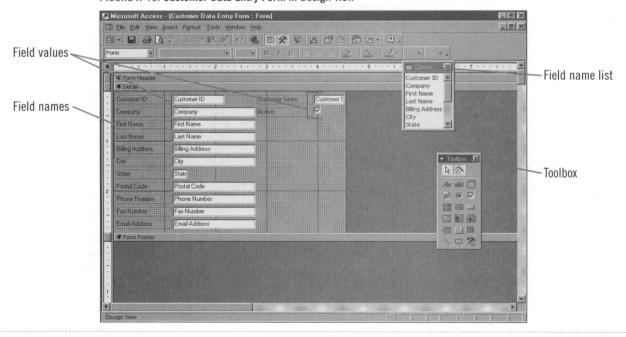

FIGURE A-15: Customer Data Entry Form in Design view

Field values

Field names

Field name list

Toolbox

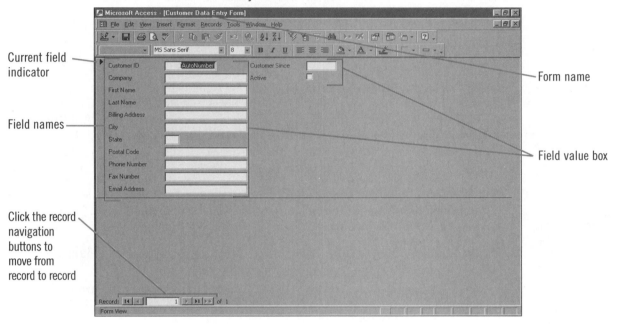

Access 2000

Entering Data Into a Database

To enter information in a database field, you select the record and the field, then type the appropriate data. The field properties sometimes limit what you can enter in a field to help with accuracy and integrity in your database. For example, if you typed "Mass" in the state field, which you formatted as two characters, the form would only accept the first two letters, "Ma." ◢▬▬ To test the form, you enter a record in the Outdoor Designs database for the company Cambridge Kite Supplies in Form view.

Steps 1 2 3 4

1. Click the **Field list button** 🔲 on the Form Design toolbar to close this window, then click the **Toolbox button** 🛠 to close the Toolbox

2. Click the **Form View button** 🔲 on the Form Design toolbar
   The data entry portion of the Customer ID field is highlighted. This part of the field is called the **field value**. The first part of the field (the words "Customer ID") is called the **field name**. The Customer ID field is the primary key field for this database. It is an **AutoNumber field**, a unique number that is assigned to each record in sequence, so you do not have to enter anything in it. Pressing the [Tab] key confirms your entry and moves you to the next field. See Table A-2 for keyboard shortcuts for working with database fields in a form.

> **QuickTip**
>
> You can determine the sequence, whether random or incremental, of numbers in an AutoNumber field by changing the field property for that field.

3. Press [**Tab**], then type **Cambridge Kite Supplies** in the Company field
   Cambridge Kite Supplies appears in the Company field, the number "1" is assigned as the Customer ID for the record, and the insertion point is in the next field.

4. Type **Jennifer**, press [**Tab**], type **Heller**, press [**Tab**], type **1437 Main Street**, press [**Tab**], type **Cambridge**, press [**Tab**], type **MA**, then press [**Tab**]
   The contact name, street address, city, and state are entered in the appropriate fields. See Figure A-16.

5. Type **021421225**, press [**Tab**], type **6175552323**, press [**Tab**], type **6175552424**, press [**Tab**], then press [**Tab**]
   The input masks you created when modifying the field properties determine the format for data entry for the Postal Code field in the xxxxx-xxxx format, and the Phone Number fields in the (area) xxx-xxxx format.

6. Type **94/1/9**, then press [**Tab**]
   Access converted the entry to 1/9/94 because you set the field properties for this field to accept only valid dates. If you had entered an invalid date, you would have received a warning box.

7. Click the **Active check box**
   A check mark appears in the box. The Yes/No field can be displayed as either a checkbox or a yes/no field, depending on the field property. The first record is complete, as shown in Figure A-17.

8. Click the **Customer Data Entry Form Close Window button**
   Data edited in forms is automatically saved, so you can close the form without saving first. The Customer Data Entry Form appears as an object on the Forms tab in the Outdoor Designs database window.

FIGURE A-16: **Entering the first record**

Indicates editing current record

This field value determined based on AutoNumber field

Record number indicates this is the first record in database

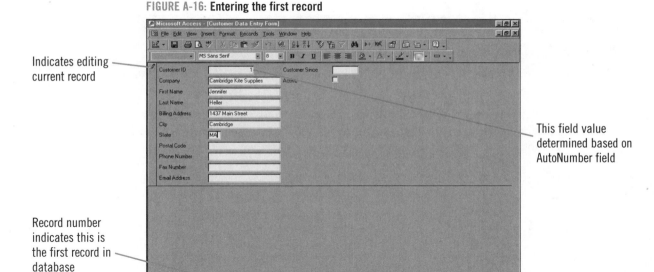

FIGURE A-17: **Completed record**

Checkmark indicates yes

Selected field

Field name description appears on status bar to help user input data

Input masks control formatting

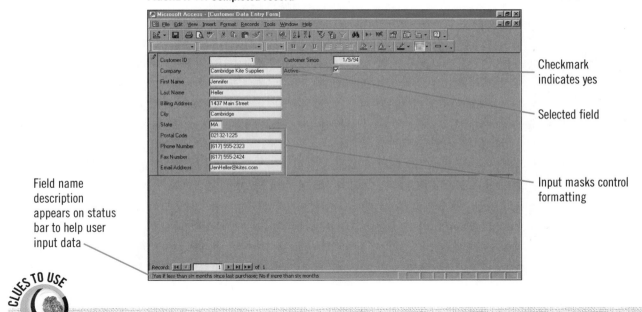

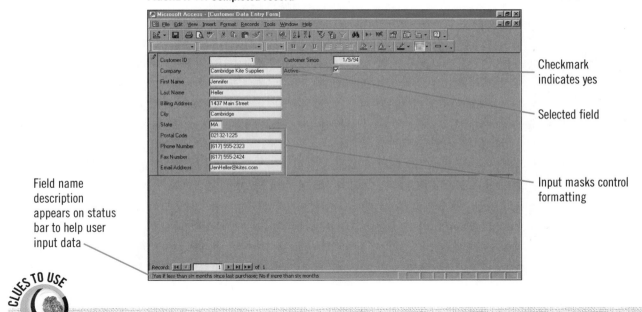

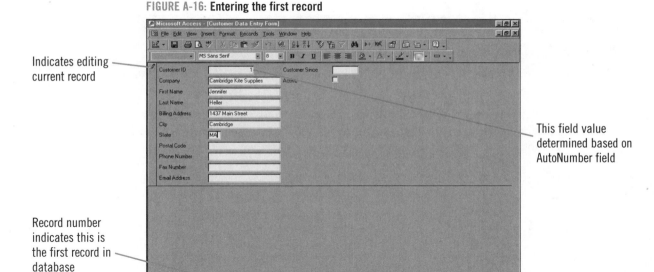

CLUES TO USE

Changing tab order

When you set up a form, the order in which you advance when you press [Tab] to enter data into the form is determined by the order of the fields in the table that the form is based on. If you want to change this for any reason, open the form in Design View, then click View on the menu bar to open the Tab Order dialog box. Drag the field selectors to reorder the listed fields, then click OK.

TABLE A-2: **Keyboard shortcuts for working with database fields in a form**

key	function
[Tab]	Moves to the next field in the database
[Shift][Tab]	Moves to the previous field in the database
[F2]	Selects the entry in the selected field in the form
[Delete]	Deletes the contents of the selected field

Adding and Editing Records in a Database

You can add records to a database using either a form or the table's Datasheet. Almost inevitably the data you enter in a database needs correcting or revising. Fortunately, you can replace the information stored in a field by highlighting the field, typing the new entry, and pressing [Enter] or using the standard cut, copy, and paste commands. When your database contains more than one record, you can scroll through the database using the record navigation buttons located just above the status bar. ✐ You add more clients to the Outdoor Designs database and make minor edits.

Steps

1. **Click the Tables button** in the Objects list, click **Customers** if necessary, then click **Open**
   See Figure A-18. You see that the record for Cambridge Kite Supplies is entered in the database.

2. **Click the New Record button** ▸* on the Table Datasheet toolbar
   The current record indicator moves to the blank record below the row for the Cambridge Kite Supplies record. The AutoNumber field is highlighted, and Record 2 appears in the record number indicator above the status bar.

   > **QuickTip**
   >
   > The New Record button is located on the Datasheet toolbar and on the record navigation buttons. You can also click Insert on the menu bar, then click New Record or, when the insertion point is in the field of the last record, you can press [Tab] to create a new record.

3. **Press [Tab]**, then enter the following customer data as the second record **Mountain Air [Tab] Maureen [Tab] Koh [Tab] 9 Poplar Street [Tab] North Bend [Tab] WA [Tab] 980457998 [Tab] 2065551541 [Tab] 2068881532 [Tab] amber@air.com [Tab] 8/1/87 [Tab]**, then click the **Active check box**
   Your new record is complete.

4. **Press [Tab]** to add a new record, then type the following customer data as the third record: **[Tab] Ken's Outdoor Gear [Tab] Ken [Tab] Smith [Tab] 4545 Overlook Ave. SE [Tab] Olympia [Tab] WA [Tab] 985032227 [Tab] 2064912222 [Tab] 2064912255 [Tab] ksmith@outdoor.com [Tab] 8/1/92**, then press **[Tab]**

   > **QuickTip**
   >
   > You can also edit a field value on the form by selecting the field and pressing [F2].

5. **Click the Customers Table Close Window button**, click the **Forms button** in the Objects list, click **Customer Data Entry Form**, click **Open**, then click the **Last Record navigation button** ▸|
   Your screen displays the last record you entered into the database in Form view, as shown in Figure A-19.

6. **Click the Previous Record navigation button** ◂, view Record 2 in the database, then click ◂ to view the customer record for Cambridge Kite Supplies

7. **Click the Company field**, double-click **Supplies**, type **Factory**, then press **[Enter]**
   Cambridge Kite Supplies has changed its name to "Cambridge Kite Factory." The revised business name is entered.

8. **Click the Next Record navigation button** ▸ twice to display Ken's Outdoor Gear, click **Fax Number** to select **(206) 491-2255** then press **[Delete]**
   Ken's Outdoor Gear has disconnected its separate fax line. Access deletes the old fax number from the record.

9. **Click Phone Number** to select **206-491-2222**, click the **Copy button** 🗎 on the Form View toolbar, click the **Fax Number field name**, click the **Paste button** 🗎, then save your changes
   The phone number is pasted in the Fax Number field, as shown in Figure A-20.

FIGURE A-18: Customers table with first record

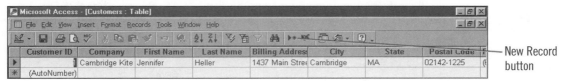

New Record button

FIGURE A-19: Last record in Form view

Third record is the last record

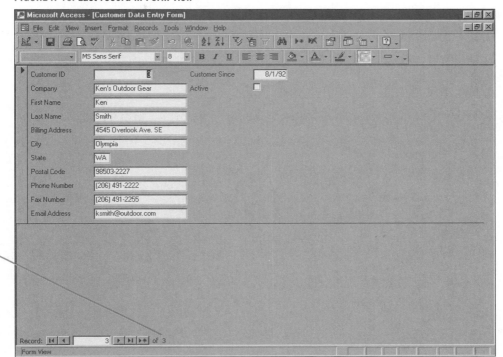

FIGURE A-20: Record for Ken's Outdoor Gear after editing in Form view

Fax number copied from phone number field

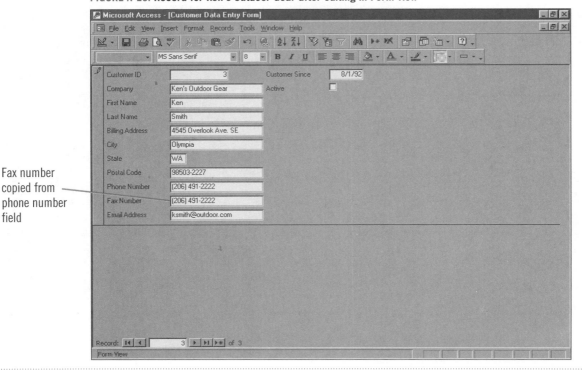

Access 2000

Printing a Database and Exiting Access

Entire databases are rarely printed because they usually contain hundreds or even thousands of records; printing them all can be very time-consuming and impractical. However, printing one or more records for quick reference or mailing information is often useful. ✐ You decide to print the records in the Customer Data Entry Form to review your work with Elizabeth before you continue entering the remaining customers in the database.

Steps 1 2 3 4

Trouble?

If the three records don't fit on one page, make sure you are using one-inch margins and Portrait Orientation.

1. Click the **Print Preview button** 🔍 on the Form View toolbar

The Print Preview window opens, as shown in Figure A-21. By default Access prints as many records as will fit per page. It turns out that all three records fit nicely on one page.

2. Click the **Zoom button** 🔍 on the Print Preview toolbar

The page enlarges to fill the Print Preview window so you can get a better look at what will be printed.

3. Verify that your printer is on and properly connected to your computer

If you have any questions, ask your instructor or technical support person for help.

QuickTip

You can print the entire database, but not individual pages or records, from Print Preview. The Print command on the File menu lets you select specific pages for printing.

4. Click the **Print button** 🖶 on the Print Preview toolbar

The page with the three records is printed.

5. Click **Close** on the Print Preview toolbar

You return to Form view.

6. Click the **Save button** 💾 on the Form View toolbar

It is good practice to always save any changes you make during a working session before you exit Access.

7. Click **File** on the menu bar

The File menu in Form view has a Close command that closes the current form but keeps the current database and Access running; see Figure A-22. If you open the File menu in the Database window, the Close command closes the current database but keeps Access running.

8. Click **Exit**

The Outdoor Design database file closes, and Access closes.

FIGURE A-21: Print Preview window

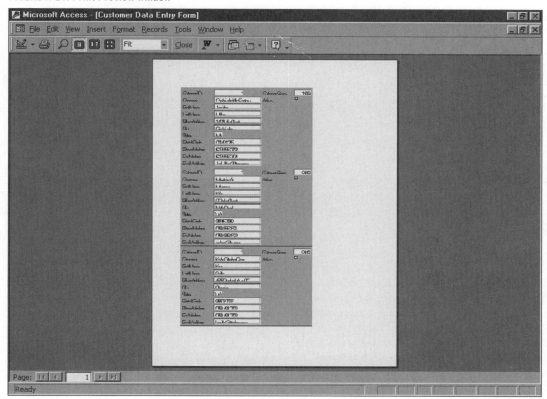

FIGURE A-22: File menu in Form view

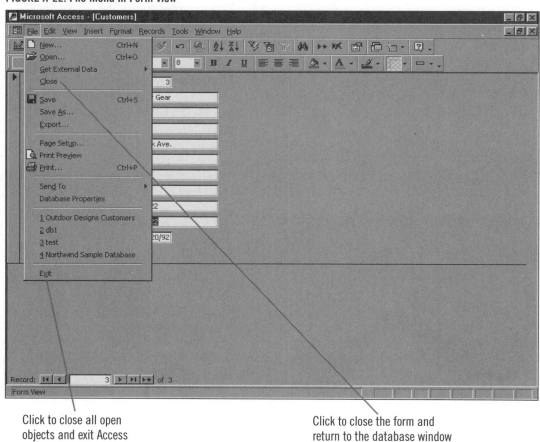

Click to close all open
objects and exit Access

Click to close the form and
return to the database window

Practice

▶ Concepts Review

Label each of the elements of the Access window shown in Figure A-23.

FIGURE A-23

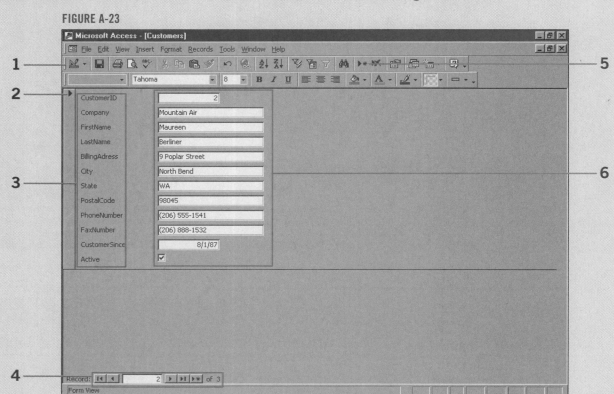

Match each of the terms with the statement that describes its function.

7. record
8. field
9. table
10. form
11. key field

a. is used to enter data in the database
b. makes sure each record is unique
c. is all the information about one person, business, product, or other entity
d. a grid of fields and records
e. is a category of information

Select the best answer from the list of choices.

12. A database
   a. Is an organized collection of information
   b. Is stored electronically
   c. Can contain information of any kind
   d. All of the above

13. **Datasheet view displays the records in a format resembling**
    a. A word processing document
    b. A spreadsheet
    c. A form filled out on paper
    d. A Fax cover sheet
14. **Form view displays the records in a format resembling**
    a. A word processing document
    b. A spreadsheet
    c. A form filled out on paper
    d. A Fax cover sheet
15. **If you want to use the keyboard to move between fields on a database form, you use**
    a. [Tab]
    b. [Enter]
    c. [Esc]
    d. [F1]
16. **If you wanted to select the contents of a field, you would press**
    a. [Tab]
    b. [F1]
    c. [F2]
    d. [Esc]
17. **To add a new record to the database, you would**
    a. Press [Tab] when the last field in the last record is highlighted in Datasheet view
    b. Click the New Record button on the toolbar
    c. Choose the New Record command on the Insert menu
    d. All of the above
18. **An input mask ensures that**
    a. Users input data in the correct format
    b. Users input correct data
    c. Users can hide selected information
    d. Important fields are hidden from view
19. **Fields deleted from a database**
    a. Can be restored with the Undo command
    b. Are removed from every record in the database
    c. Remove only recently entered data
    d. Are placed in a separate cache file
20. **When there is more than one record in the database, you can move to other records using the**
    a. Record navigation buttons
    b. Scroll bars
    c. [Enter] key
    d. All of the above
21. **You can add records or edit records in**
    a. Form view
    b. Datasheet view
    c. Record Wizard
    d. Answers a and b

▶ Skills Review

1. **Plan a database.**
   a. Think about what type of database would be used for inventory.
   b. Sketch a list of fields and what they might contain.
   c. Create a sketch of a form listing all the fields.
2. **Start Access.**
   a. Click Start on the menu bar.
   b. Start Access.
   c. Create a new blank database.
   d. Name the database Edalia Camping Supply Inventory.
3. **Create a database.**
   a. Click New to create a new table.
   b. Click Create table in Design View to create the table, then click OK.
   c. Type "Department", press [Tab], press [Tab] to accept the text Data Type, then press [Tab] to move to the next field row.

Access 2000

d. Type "Item", press [Tab], press [Tab] to accept the text Data Type, then press [Tab] to move to the next field row.

e. Continue to name the fields with the data types listed below:

Type "Color", Data Type is Text.

Type "Size", Data Type is Text.

Type "Description", Data Type is Text.

Type "Cost", Data Type is Currency.

Type "Season", Data Type is Date/Time.

f. Save the table as "Edalia Inventory table", clicking No in the Message box that suggests defining a primary key.

g. Click the Datasheet View button to display the database fields in Datasheet view.

4. **Modify the table.**

a. Add a new field called "On-Hand" with the Data Type Text.

b. Delete the Season field.

c. Change the Field Size field property for the Size field to 10.

d. Save the changes to the table.

e. Close the table.

5. **Build a data entry form.**

a. Click the Forms button in the Objects list of the Database window.

b. Use the Form Wizard to create a data entry form from the Edalia Inventory table.

c. Select all the fields, pick the Columnar layout, use the Expedition style, name the form Edalia Outdoor Supply Data Entry Form, then select the option to open the form in Form view.

6. **Enter data into the database.**

a. Maximize the form in the window.

b. Type "Camping", press [Tab], type "Tent", press [Tab], type "blue", press [Tab], type "11 x 14", press [Tab], type "dome", press [Tab], type "259.00", press [Tab], type "7".

c. Press [Enter] to insert a new record.

d. Type "Clothing", press [Tab], type "Shirt", press [Tab], type "green", press [Tab], type "L", press [Tab], type "pull-over", press [Tab], type "9.99", press [Tab], type "30".

e. Click the New Record button to insert a new record.

f. Type "Camping", press [Tab], type "Stove", press [Tab], type "green", press [Tab], type "2-burner", press [Tab], type "propane", press [Tab], type "29.99", press [Tab], type "15".

g. Insert a new record.

h. Type "Shoes", press [Tab], type "Hiking Boots", press [Tab], type "brown", press [Tab], type "7", press [Tab], type "high-top", press [Tab], type "39.99", press [Tab], type "4".

i. Insert a new record.

j. Type "Clothing", press [Tab], type "Shirt", press [Tab], type "maroon", press [Tab], type "L", press [Tab], type "pull-over", press [Tab], type "19.99", press [Tab], type "24", press [Tab].

k. Type "Camping", press [Tab], type "sleeping bag", press [Tab], type "red", press [Tab], type "single", press [Tab], type "light weight", press [Tab], type "19.99", press [Tab], type "20".

l. Insert a new record.

m. Type "Shoes", press [Tab], type "Running", press [Tab], type "white", press [Tab], type "9", press [Tab], type "full-support", press [Tab], type "19.99", press [Tab], type "15".

n. Insert a new record.

o. Type "Boats", press [Tab], type "canoe", press [Tab], type "green", press [Tab], type "15-foot", press [Tab], type "2-person", press [Tab], type "109.99", press [Tab], type "3".

p. Insert a new record.

q. Type "Accessories", press [Tab], type "knife", press [Tab], type "red", press [Tab], type "20", press [Tab], type "Swiss Army", press [Tab], type "29.99", press [Tab], type "40", press [Tab].

r. Click the Save button to save your changes to the file.

7. Edit records in the database.

a. Be sure you are in Form view.

b. Use the Record Navigation buttons to move to the first record.

c. Select the Cost field.

d. Type "299.99".

e. Press [Tab].

f. Move to the last record.

g. Select the Size field.

h. Press the [Delete] key.

i. Type "25-feature".

j. Click the Save button to save changes to the file.

8. Print the database and exit Access.

a. Click the Print Preview button.

b. Verify that your fields and records look correct on the page.

c. Use Zoom as needed to review the pages.

d. Verify that the printer is on and properly connected.

e. Click the Print button.

f. Click File on the menu bar.

g. Click the Close command to close the form, clicking Yes to save changes when prompted.

h. Click File on the menu bar, then click Exit.

► Independent Challenges

1. In order to analyze pet sales at Stuff for Pets, you decide to create a database of animals that have been for sale in the store this year. You will need to include information on each animal so you can look at sales trends for the store. To complete this independent challenge:

a. Create a new blank database, save the database as "Pets" on your Project Disk and create a new table in Design view with the following fields and data types.

Field Name	Data Type	Field Name	Data Type
Type	Text	DOB	Date/Time
Breed	Text	Cost	Currency
Gender	Text	Retail	Currency

b. Save the table as "Animals"; you do not need to set a primary key.

c. Add the following records to the database using Datasheet view.

Type	Breed	Gender	DOB	Cost	Retail
Dog	Poodle	F	3/7/95	125.00	499.99
Dog	Collie	M	4/1/95	110.00	459.99
Cat	Persian	F	2/3/95	120.00	299.99
Dog	Yorkie	M	3/1/95	100.00	359.99
Bird	Parrot	M	5/15/94	150.00	659.99

d. Print the database and exit Access.

2. As part of a long-term marketing strategy at Stuff for Pets, you create the database of customers who have purchased animals at the store. You will use the database to notify customers of information of interest to them.

To complete this independent challenge:

a. Start Access.

b. Create a new blank database named "Pets Marketing" and create a new table in Design view with the following fields and data types.

Field Name	Data Type	Field Name	Data Type
Type	Text	City	Text
Breed	Text	State	Text
First	Text	Zip	Text
Last	Text	Follow up?	Yes/No
Address	Text		

c. Modify the table by inserting a new field before the Type field that is named "Customer ID" and has the AutoNumber data type. Make this new field the primary key field.

d. Save the table as "Customers".

e. Add the following records to the database using Datasheet view.

Type	Breed	First	Last	Address	City	State	Zip	Follow-up
Dog	Yorkie	Carolyn	Sariyan	987 Lincoln Ave.	Seattle	WA	98701	yes
Dog	Poodle	Mary	Miller	717 Adams Ave.	Bellingham	WA	98551	no
Cat	Calico	Jerry	Smith	789 Old Mill Ln.	Snohomish	WA	98456	yes
Turtle	Box	Steven	Reynolds	654 Riverview Rd.	Seattle	WA	98765	no
Dog	Mixed	Linda	James	345 Augusta Rd.	Seattle	WA	98765	yes

f. Change the record for Linda James to Lynda James.

g. Print the database and exit Access.

3. As human resources manager for Washington County, you are responsible for tracking all employee records. You decide to create an electronic database of all full-time and part-time employees. This database will help you create reports for the managers and county commissioners.

To complete this independent challenge:

a. Start Access.

b. Create a new blank database named "County Employees" and create a new table in Design view with the following fields and data types.

Field Name	Data Type	Field Name	Data Type
Employee Number	AutoNumber	Salary	Currency
First Name	Text	Gender	Text
Middle	Text	Status	Yes/No
Last Name	Text	Dept	Text
Hire Date	Date/Time		

c. Save the tables as "Employees" and set the Employee Number field as the primary key.

d. Use the Form Wizard to create a form based on the County Employees table and using all the fields, the Columnar layout, the Standard style, and the name "Employee Data Entry Form."

e. Add the following records to the database using Form view.

First Name	Middle	Last Name	Hire Date	Salary	Gender	Status	Dept
Mary	S.	Walker	10/1/89	28,000.00	F	Yes	PW
Lisa	W.	Quinones	5/7/92	30,000.00	M	No	Safety
Sherry	M.	Kim	6/4/85	32,000.00	F	Yes	Safety
Susan	E.	Boyd	9/9/99	15,000.00	F	No	PW
James	W.	Johnson	5/10/99	17,500.00	M	Yes	Legal

f. Print the table from Datasheet view and Exit Access.

4. As manager of the Quick Stop Video Store, you create the electronic database of movies that are for sale in the store. You will use this database to track video sales for the store.

To complete this independent challenge:

a. Log on to the Internet, and use your browser to go to http://www.course.com. From there, click Student Online Companions, click the link for the book you are using, then click the Access link for Unit A.

b. Use either link to find information on current video releases, and print out the pages that give you the latest data.

c. Start Access, create a new database named "Video Store Database," and then create a new table in Design view with the following fields and data types.

Field Name	Data Type	Field Name	Data Type
Category	Text	Cost	Currency
Movie Name	Text	Sold	Number
Release Date	Date/Time	In Stock	Yes/No
Rating	Text		

d. Create a data entry form using the Form Wizard. You determine the layout, style, and the name of the form.

e. Add the following older videos as records to the database using Form view.

Category	Movie Name	Release Date	Rating	Cost	Sold	In Stock
Adventure	Speed	10/1/94	R	10.99	123	yes
Children's	Splash	3/6/89	G	15.99	150	yes
Comedy	Tommy Boy	10/15/95	PG-13	12.99	70	no
Comedy	Casper	11/1/95	PG	12.99	45	yes
Children's	Pocahontas	1/1/96	G	24.99	400	yes

f. Add the records for the current videos that you found on your search. Make up any of the information that you couldn't find on your Internet search.

g. Print the database from Form view and exit Access.

Access 2000

▶ **Visual Workshop**

Create the database form shown below. First, use the Table Wizard to create the Recipes table, clicking the Personal option button in the Table Wizard dialog box. Then, when you create the form based on the Recipes table, use the Form Wizard, and choose the Columnar layout and the International Style.

FIGURE A-24

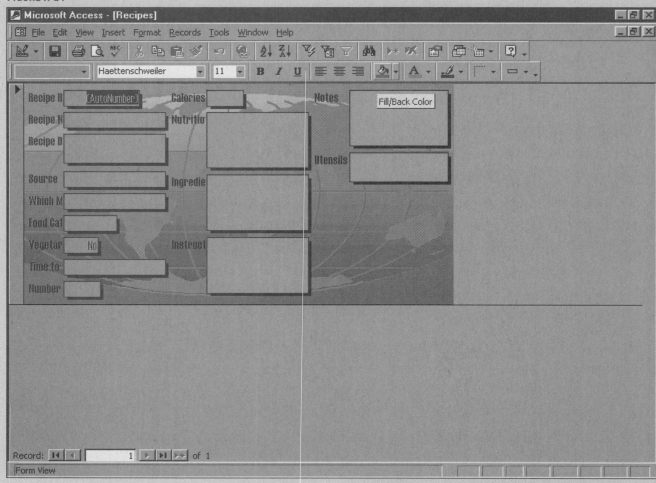

Enhancing
a Database

- ► **Open an existing database**
- ► **Modify a form's layout**
- ► **Change fonts and styles on a form**
- ► **Add clip art to a form**
- ► **Filter a database**
- ► **Sort database records**
- ► **Create a query**
- ► **Protect a database**

Now that you know how to create a database, you are ready to add more data to it and work with the data to get information. In this unit, you learn how to open an existing database, and how to enhance a database form by using fonts, styles, and clip art. You learn how to search for information in a database with filters, by sorting, and by creating queries. You will also learn how to protect a database so that it cannot be modified without your permission. ✐ Elizabeth Fried, the database administrator for Outdoor Designs, has put you in charge of customizing the Outdoor Designs database so that Sue Ellen Monteiro, the sales manager, can use it to track sales. You need to work with the database you created to answer some simple questions, improve the appearance of the data entry form, and add new fields to help employees who use it regularly. You also want to protect the database from unauthorized use.

Opening an Existing Database

Opening an existing database in Access is a little different than opening an existing file in Word or Excel. When you first start Access, you are asked whether you want to create a new database (either a blank one that you create from scratch or one created by a wizard) or open an existing database. To open an existing database, you can select it from a list if it was opened recently, or you can locate the drive and folder containing the database you want. If your computer is set up to display file extensions, you will notice that Access files have an .mdb extension. You have been working on the Outdoor Designs database. You need to open the database and the form that Elizabeth wants you to modify.

QuickTip

Be sure that you have a backup copy of your project files on a separate disk.

1. Start Access, then put your Project Disk in the appropriate drive

2. Click the **Open an existing file option button** in the Microsoft Access dialog box, click **More Files**, then click **OK**
   The Open dialog box opens.

3. Click the **Look in list arrow**, then click the drive that contains your Project Disk
   The names of files and folders on your Project Disk appear in the Open dialog box.

QuickTip

Although you cannot save an Access database with a new name, you can save individual database objects, such as forms and tables, under new names using the Save As dialog box.

4. Click **Outdoor Designs Sales Reps**, then click **Open**
   The dialog box closes. After a moment the Outdoor Designs Sales Reps database window opens, as shown in Figure B-1.

5. Click the **Tables button** in the Objects list, click **Open**, then maximize the **Customers : Table window**
   There are 10 records in the Customers table in this database file, as shown in Figure B-2.

6. Click the **Design View button** on the Table Datasheet toolbar
   There are 10 fields in this table. The CUSTOMERID is the primary key field in this table.

7. Click the **Customers Table Close Window button**, click the **Forms button** in the Objects list, then click **Open**
   The Customers form is a very basic form, as shown in Figure B-3. You will enhance it in the next lesson.

8. Click the **Customers Form Close Window button**

Opening more than one database file at a time

Unlike in many programs, in Access you can open only one database file at a time. In programs such as Microsoft Word or Excel, you can switch between one or more open files through the buttons on the taskbar or through the Window menu on the menu bar. To work with more than one database at a time, you need to start Access again for each database you want to open. However, because Access is a relational database, you should design your database with all the tables, forms, and so on, that you'll need so you don't have to work with more than one database file at the same time.

FIGURE B-1: Database window

FIGURE B-2: Customers: Table window

Records and fields in Customers database table

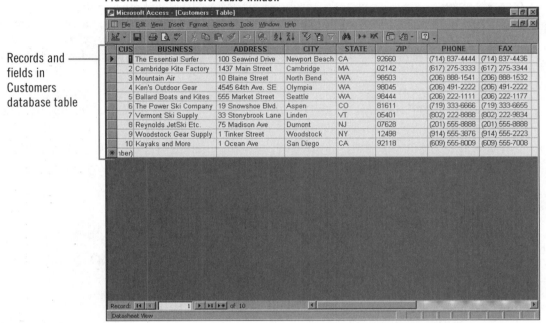

FIGURE B-3: Customers form

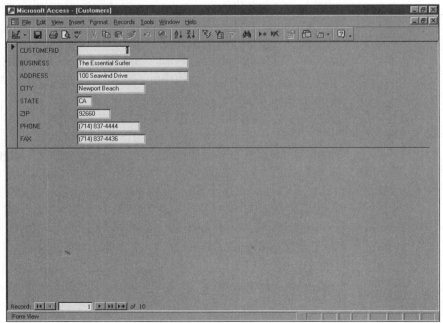

Access 2000

Modifying a Form's Layout

Once you create a form, you can modify it to meet your data entry or display needs. You can move, add, or delete the fields in a form using Design view. You can add fields to a form using the **field list**, a list you can open using the View menu or the Field List button on the Form Design toolbar. A field is called a **control**. A control consists of the identifying **field label** and the data it contains, which is in the **field value text box**. The three types of controls are: bound, unbound, and calculated control. A **bound control** has a table or query as its information source. An **unbound control**, such as a label or graphic image, is created in the form or has its data source outside the database. A **calculated control** uses an expression as its data source, which may include a bound control. You can open the **property sheet** (a window containing the formatting, data-related, and other settings for an object) for one or more objects and make formatting changes by entering information in the appropriate text box on the Format tab. You want to be able to add the sales data as well as the Outdoor Designs sales representative information to the form, so you will add the Sales field and Rep field to the customer form, then rearrange the fields on the form.

Steps

1. Click the **Forms** button in the Objects list and click **Customers** if necessary, click **Design**, then maximize the form window

2. Place the pointer on the right edge of the form, then when it changes to ↔, drag to the **6" mark** on the horizontal ruler, as shown in Figure B-4
   This widens the form to make room for the new fields.

QuickTip

A scroll bar appears if the Field List window is not maximized. You can resize it to display all the fields or scroll to find the fields you want.

3. Click the **Field List button** 🔲 on the Form Design toolbar
   The field list opens.

4. Scroll if necessary and click **REP** in the field list, then drag the **REP field** to the intersection of the **4" mark** on the horizontal ruler and the **1" mark** on the vertical ruler, as shown in Figure B-5
   By dragging the field name from the field list, you add the bound and unbound controls for the REP field to the form.

QuickTip

The Properties, Field List, and Toolbox buttons work as toggles to open and close the property sheets, field list and Toolbox, respectively.

5. Click **SALES** in the Field List window, drag the **SALES field** just below the REP field to the intersection of the **4" mark** on the horizontal ruler and the **1½" mark** on the vertical ruler, then click 🔲 to close the field list

6. Click the **CUSTOMERID field value text box** to select the bound and unbound controls, place the pointer on the **right edge of the field value text box**, then when the pointer changes to ✋, drag the **CUSTOMERID field** so the right edge of the control is at the **5" mark** on the horizontal ruler
   The form looks better with the CUSTOMERID field in this corner of the form.

QuickTip

To select more than one field at a time, press and hold [Shift] as you click each field.

7. Press and hold [Shift], click the **REP field value text box**, click the **SALES field value text box**, release [Shift], click **Format** on the menu bar, point to **Align**, then click **Right**
   This right-aligns the CUSTOMERID, SALES, and REP fields with respect to each other.

8. Double-click the **CUSTOMERID field label** to open the CUSTOMERID property sheet, double-click **CUSTOMERID** in the Caption text box, type **Customer ID Number**, click the **Properties button** 🔲 on the Form Design toolbar to close the property sheet, then drag the **left sizing handle** if necessary to enlarge the field label
   The modified form is shown in Figure B-6.

9. Click the **Form View button** 🔲 on the Form Design toolbar, then save your changes
   The form displays Record number 1, the record for the Essential Surfer, in Form view.

FIGURE B-4: Widening the form

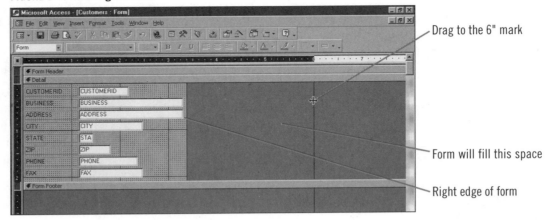

Drag to the 6" mark

Form will fill this space

Right edge of form

FIGURE B-5: Dragging a field from the field list

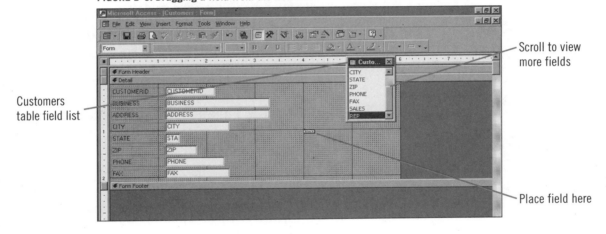

Scroll to view more fields

Customers table field list

Place field here

FIGURE B-6: Modified form in Design view

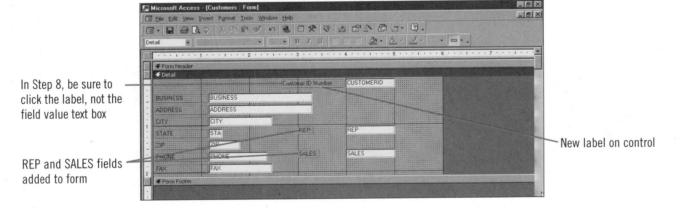

In Step 8, be sure to click the label, not the field value text box

REP and SALES fields added to form

New label on control

Parts of the form

A form is divided into three sections: Form Header, Detail, and Form Footer. Each section is identified by a **bar** which contains the section name and an arrow pointing to the section. The **Form Header** appears at the top of each form and can contain additional information, such as a company title or logo. The **Detail section** displays the field labels and data for each record. The **Form Footer** appears at the bottom of each form and can contain totals, instructions, or command buttons. You can resize a section by dragging the top edge of the section's bar up or down.

Changing Fonts and Styles on a Form

You can enhance a database form by changing the font type and style of labels and field values, adding borders and shading, and adding labels. The Formatting (Form/Report) toolbar contains buttons for many common formatting changes, such as changing a label's border, font style, font size, color, and special effects. Those formatting options not available on the toolbar must be changed through the control's property sheet. ✎ To make this form simple to use as well as attractive for the sales representatives, you decide to change font size and color of the field labels, and to add a label to identify the form.

Steps

1. Click the **Design View button** 🗏 on the Form View toolbar

> **QuickTip**
> Click the field value text box to select the label and the bound control; click the label to select only the unbound control.

2. Click the **Customer ID Number field label**, click the **Font/Fore Color button list arrow** 🅰▾ on the Formatting toolbar to open the Font/Fore color palette, then click the **blue color box** (sixth box, second row)
   The Customer ID Number label appears in blue.

3. Click the **BUSINESS field value text box**, press and hold **[Shift]**, click the **ADDRESS field value text box**, click the **CITY field value text box**, click the **STATE field value text box**, click the **ZIP field value text box**, click the **PHONE field value text box**, click the **FAX field value text box**, release **[Shift]**, click 🅰▾, click the **Red color box** (first box, third row), click the **Font Size list arrow**, then click **12**

4. Leaving all the fields selected, place the pointer on the **BUSINESS field value text box top center resizing handle** until the pointer changes to ↕, then drag up ¼" using the vertical ruler as a guide
   All the fields are resized at once, and your screen should look similar to Figure B-7.

5. Click the **SALES field value text box**, click the **Line/Border Width button list arrow** ▭▾ on the Formatting toolbar, click **Line Width 2** ▭, click the **Special Effect button list arrow** ▭▾ on the Formatting toolbar, then click the **Shadowed button** ▭

6. Place the pointer on the top edge of the **Detail** bar until the pointer changes to ✢, then drag down to the ½" mark on the vertical ruler
   The Form Header section opens so that you can add additional information to the form.

7. Click the **Toolbox button** 🛠 on the Form Design toolbar to open the Control Toolbox if necessary, click the **Label button** 🗛 on the Toolbox, click the **Label Pointer** ⁺A in the top left corner of the Form Header section, then drag ⁺A down to the bottom of the Form section and over to the 5" mark on the horizontal ruler, release the mouse button, then type **Outdoor Designs Customer Entry Form** in the label
   See Figure B-8.

> **QuickTip**
> Since red is the last color you used, the Font/Fore Color button is set to red.

8. Click to select the **Outdoor Designs Customer Entry Form label control**, click 🅰▾, click the **Font Size list arrow**, click **18**, then click the **Center button** ▤
   The label is formatted to be red, 18-point, center-aligned text.

9. Click the **Form View button** 🗗 on the Form Design toolbar
   Your screen should look like Figure B-9.

FIGURE B-7: Form with color changes and resized fields

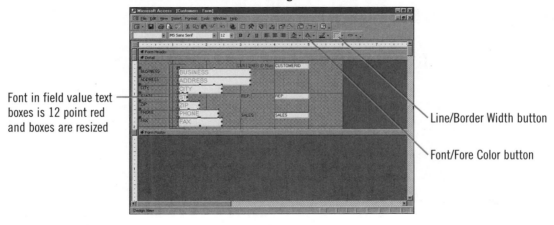

Font in field value text boxes is 12 point red and boxes are resized

Line/Border Width button

Font/Fore Color button

FIGURE B-8: Label added to the form header

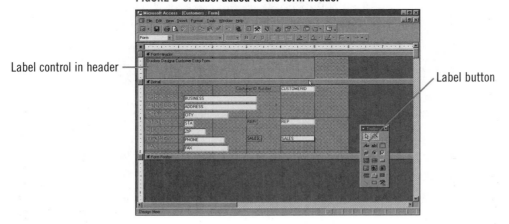

Label control in header

Label button

FIGURE B-9: Modified Customer Entry Form in Form view

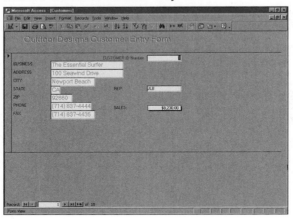

CLUES TO USE

Formatting controls using the property sheet

Modifying the property sheet is a very good way to create a uniform style using advanced formatting options in a form. Click the Properties button in Design view to open the property sheet window. You can open the property sheet for one or more controls. The Format tab includes formatting options for back style, back color, special effects, border widths, styles, colors, font color, name, size, weight, italic, underline, and text alignment. Each section of the form also has a property sheet with appropriate formatting options to help design your form.

Access 2000

Adding Clip Art to a Form

Adding clip art to your data entry form can enhance and personalize the form. You can add a company logo, an illustration, or any piece of clip art that comes with Office or any other program on your computer that includes graphics. ➤ You decide to add an autumn leaves clip art to the Outdoor Designs database form to give the database an outdoor theme. You want to add the image to the bottom of the Detail section. First you need to resize the Detail section to accommodate the clip art.

1. Click the **Design View button** 🔲 on the Form view toolbar
   The form appears in Design view.

QuickTip

If the Toolbox is covering any critical parts of the form, drag it out of the way.

2. Place ✛ on the bottom edge of the Detail section, then drag ✛ down approximately ½"

3. Click the **Image button** 🔲 on the Toolbox, then click the **Image pointer** ⁺🔲 just below the FAX number label control
   The Insert Picture dialog box opens, so that you can locate and insert the image file you want.

Trouble?

If you don't see the image in the preview pane, click the Preview button 🔲.

4. Click the **Look in list arrow**, locate and double-click **Program Files**, double-click **Common Files**, double-click **MicrosoftShared**, double-click **Clipart**, double-click **themes1**, double-click **lines**, then click **Bd14594_**
   See Figure B-10. If you cannot locate the Clipart folder, ask your instructor or technical support person for assistance. This step assumes Access is installed as part of a typical Microsoft Office installation on drive C:.

5. Click **OK**
   The image is inserted in the form.

6. Click the **Form View button** 🔲 on the Form Design toolbar
   Your screen looks like Figure B-11.

7. Click the **Save button** 🔲 on the Standard toolbar, click **File** on the menu bar, then click **Close**

FIGURE B-10: Insert Picture dialog box

Image is located in this folder →

Image will be → inserted here

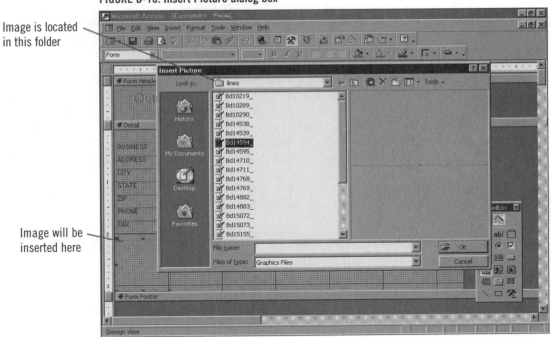

FIGURE B-11: Form with clip art in Form view

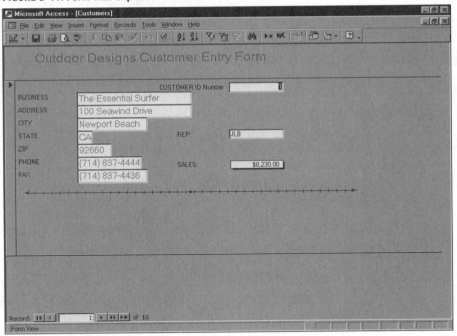

CLUES TO USE

Working with clip art

You can drag the Image pointer to create the exact size of the frame when inserting a clip art image in a form, or let the size of the frame be determined by the image. Clip art images can be selected, moved, copied, pasted, and deleted like any other element of the database form. You can use menu commands or the toolbar buttons to perform these basic operations.

You can resize a clip art object by clicking it and dragging it to the right or left edge of the clip art frame with the sizing pointers. Double-clicking a clip art image in Design View opens the property sheet, where you can modify alignment, tiling, and other formatting properties of the image by clicking the Format tab.

Filtering a Database

A **filter** organizes the records in a database to display only those records that meet certain criteria. **Criteria** are conditions or qualifications that must be met for a record to be chosen. There are four methods you can use to filter records: Filter By Selection, Filter By Form, Filter For Input, and Advanced Filter/Sort. A filter cannot be saved as an object, but you can print the results of a filter or save a filter as a **query**. Also when you save a table or form, the filter is saved, so you can reapply the filter the next time you open the table or form. ✐ Sue Ellen has asked you to determine which California-based companies purchased at least $5,000 worth of Outdoor Designs products; you decide to build a filter to display records that meet this criteria.

Steps 1234

1. Click the **Tables button** in the Objects list, click the **Customers** table if necessary, then click **Open**
   The Customers table opens in Datasheet view.

> **QuickTip**
> Double-click a field name in the field list to move it to the first available column in the filter grid.

2. Click **Records** on the menu bar, point to **Filter**, click **Advanced Filter/Sort**, then click the **Clear Grid button** ☒ on the Filter/Sort toolbar to clear the grid of any preexisting criteria
   The CustomersFilter1: Filter window opens, as shown in Figure B-12. The Customers Table field list is open in the top pane. You specify the criteria in the filter design grid by dragging fields from the field list to the design grid in the lower pane. The Filter/Sort toolbar provides shortcuts to common filtering commands.

> **QuickTip**
> The Find command on the Edit menu searches for a specific item in the database.

3. Scroll to and click the **SALES field** in the field list, drag the **SALES field** to the first field cell column in the filter design grid, click the **SALES field Criteria cell**, type **>5000**, as shown in Figure B-13, click the **Apply Filter button** ▽ on the Filter/Sort toolbar, then scroll to the right as needed
   The records for the three businesses with sales greater than $5,000 appear in the window in Datasheet view, as shown in Figure B-14. You can use the Filter dialog box to conduct a search based on more than one criterion by linking the criterion with the And or Or conjunctions. You use the And conjunction when you want both comparisons to be true in the filter, and the Or conjunction when either criterion can be true.

> **QuickTip**
> You can also use the taskbar to switch to a different open object in Access.

4. Click **Window** on the menu bar, then click **CutomersFilter1:Filter** to switch back to the Filter window

5. Scroll to and click the **STATE field** in the field list window, drag the **STATE field** to the second field cell column in the filter design grid, type **CA** in the State Criteria cell, then press **[Enter]**
   Quotation marks are added around the entry to distinguish this text from values.

6. Click ▽ on the Filter/Sort toolbar; then drag the horizontal scroll box to adjust your view if necessary
   The Essential Surfer, with purchases of $8,230, is the only record matching the filter.

> **QuickTip**
> To reapply the filter, click Records on the menu bar, then click Apply Filter/Sort.

7. Click the **Remove Filter button** ▽ on the Table Datasheet toolbar
   All the records appear.

8. Click the **Customers Table Close Window button**, then click **Yes** to save the filter along with the table

FIGURE B-12: Filter window

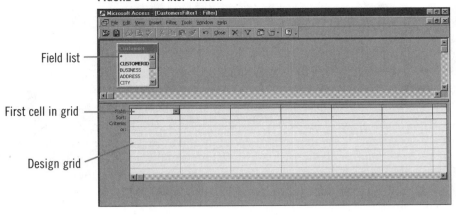

Field list

First cell in grid

Design grid

FIGURE B-13: Filter grid with criteria specified

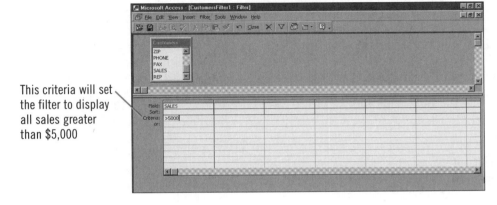

This criteria will set
the filter to display
all sales greater
than $5,000

FIGURE B-14: Filtered table

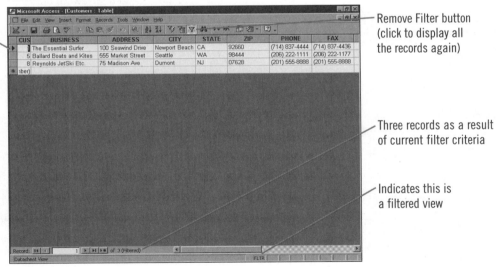

Only records meeting
the filter criteria are
displayed in table;
others are temporarily
hidden

Remove Filter button
(click to display all
the records again)

Three records as a result
of current filter criteria

Indicates this is
a filtered view

Filtering by selection

Filter By Selection, Filter By Form, and Filter For Input are the easiest ways to filter records. Use Filter By Selection if you can easily find one occurrence of the value in a field you want the filtered records to contain. Click the value, and then click the Filter By Selection button on the toolbar. How you select the value determines which records the filter returns. If you place the insertion point in the field or select the contents of the field, the filter returns all the records with that exact data in the field.

Sorting Database Records

You can rearrange, or **sort**, the records in your database in alphabetical or numerical order. When you sort your database, you need to specify the primary field for the sort. For example, in a customer database you could sort records by the Business, Zip, or Sales field. You also must specify whether to sort the database in ascending order (alphabetically from A to Z or numerically from 0–9) or descending order (alphabetically from Z to A or numerically from 9–0). You want to sort the database alphabetically by company name to match other records in the Outdoor Designs office.

Steps

1. Click the **Customers** table if necessary, then click **Open**

2. Click in any record in the **BUSINESS field** on the datasheet

   The insertion point is placed in the BUSINESS field. You can sort on a field either by selecting the entire column or by simply clicking any record in the field. You see that the datasheet is currently sorted in ascending order by Customer ID, as shown in Figure B-15.

3. Click the **Sort Ascending button** on the Table Datasheet toolbar

   The records are sorted in alphabetical order by business name, as shown in Figure B-16.

4. Scroll to the right if necessary, click the **SALES field**, then click the **Sort Descending button** on the Table Datasheet toolbar

   The records are now sorted in descending order by sales amounts as shown in Figure B-17. You see that Reynolds JetSki has had the highest sales this year with $8900 in sales.

5. Click **File** on the menu bar, click **Close**, then click **No** to close without saving your changes

> **QuickTip**
>
> You can sort on more than one field (for example, primarily by city and then within city by zip code) by clicking Records on the menu bar, pointing to Filter, clicking Advanced Filter/Sort on the submenu, then dragging the fields by which you want to sort to the field columns in the filter design grid and setting sort criteria in the Sort cells.

FIGURE B-15: Datasheet sorted in ascending order by Customer ID

Sort Ascending button

Sort Descending button

Datasheet records sorted in ascending order by CUSTOMERID field

Because insertion point is in a BUSINESS field, records will be sorted by BUSINESS

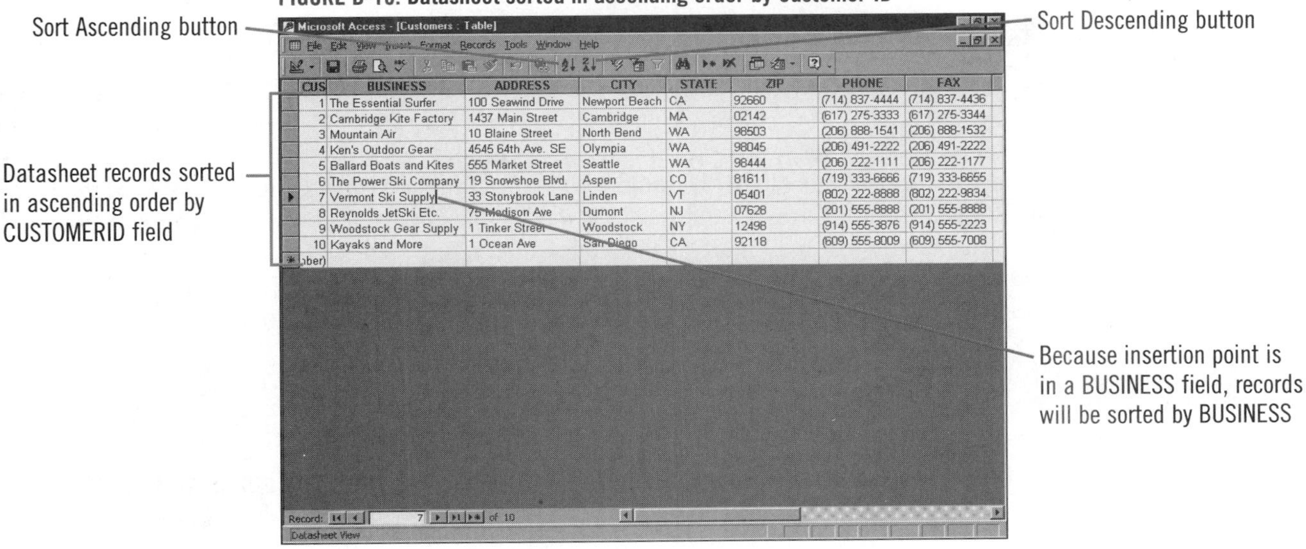

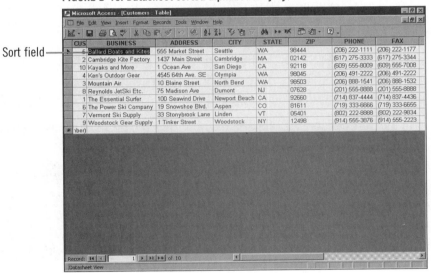

FIGURE B-16: Datasheet sorted alphabetically by business name

Sort field

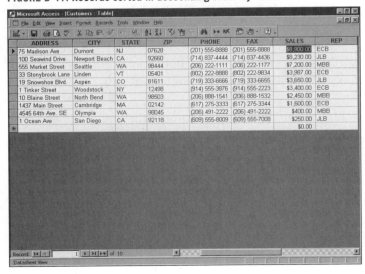

FIGURE B-17: Records sorted in descending order by sales

Access 2000

Creating a Query

A **query** is a set of criteria you specify to retrieve certain data from a database. Unlike a filter, it can be saved as an object; therefore, you can use a query to pull together information from several tables. Another feature that makes queries more powerful than filters is that you can set a query to display only the fields you have specified, unlike a filter, which shows all of the table's fields. Records resulting from a query look like a table but are merely a view based on the query. The most commonly used query is the **select query**, in which records are collected and viewed, and can be modified later. ✒️ You want to design one query to create a list of customers and additional queries to identify the sales representative who is assigned to each customer.

Steps 1234

1. **Click the Queries button in the Objects list, click New, click Design View, then click OK**
   The Show Table dialog box opens in the Select Query window, as shown in Figure B-18.

2. **Click Add, click Close, then maximize the Query1: Select Query window**
   The Query design grid looks similar to the Filter/Sort design grid. You add the fields you want to display in the query results by dragging them from the field list, then you specify the criteria and a sort order for each field in the design grid area.

3. **Click the BUSINESS field in the field list, drag the BUSINESS field to the first Field cell column in the Query design grid, click the REP field in the field list, then drag the REP field to the second field cell column in the Query design grid**

4. **Click the Sort cell in the BUSINESS column, click the Sort list arrow, then click Ascending**
   This sorts the query in ascending order by business name.

5. **Click the Datasheet View button 📰 on the Query Design toolbar**
   The results of this simple query appear, as shown in Figure B-19.

QuickTip

Fields will appear in the order you place them in the design grid. You can insert new fields between existing ones and move fields by dragging the columns.

6. **Click the Design View button 📐 on the Query Datasheet toolbar, click the Criteria cell in the REP column, type ECB, then press [Enter]**
   You have created a query to show only those customers who are assigned to Emily Brown, Rep ECB. See Figure B-20.

7. **Click 📰, view the results, click the Save button 💾, type Emily's Customers in the Query name Save As text box, then click OK**

QuickTip

You can print the results of a query at any time by clicking the Print button on the toolbar.

8. **Click 📐, double-click ECB in the criteria cell for the REP field, type MBB, click 📰, view the results, click File on the menu bar, click Save As, type Michael's Customers in the Save Query, Emily's Customers To: text box, click OK, click 📐, double-click MBB in the criteria cell for the REP field, type JLB, click 📰, view the results, use the Save As command to save the results as Jennifer's Customers, then click OK**
   Now you have created a query for each sales representative by simply modifying the criteria in the REP column and saving each query with a new name.

9. **Click File on the menu bar, then click Close**
   The three queries are saved as objects in the database file. If records are added to the database, you can open these queries to see the updated information for each sales representative.

FIGURE B-18: Select Query window

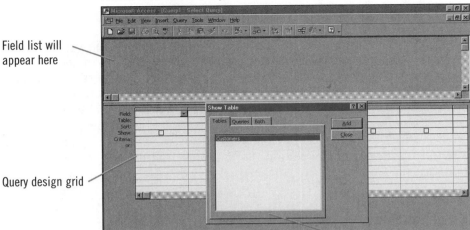

Field list will appear here

Query design grid

Show Table dialog box lists all tables in database that can be added to the query

FIGURE B-19: Query results

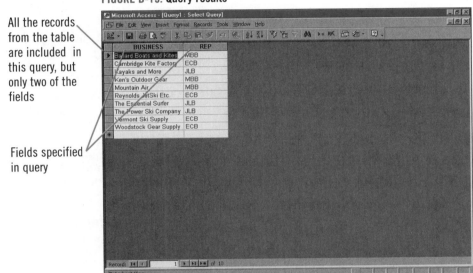

All the records from the table are included in this query, but only two of the fields

Fields specified in query

BUSINESS	REP
Ballard Boats and Kites	MBB
Cambridge Kite Factory	ECB
Kayaks and More	JLB
Ken's Outdoor Gear	MBB
Mountain Air	MBB
Reynolds JetSki Etc.	ECB
The Essential Surfer	JLB
The Power Ski Company	JLB
Vermont Ski Supply	ECB
Woodstock Gear Supply	ECB

FIGURE B-20: Query design grid with criteria

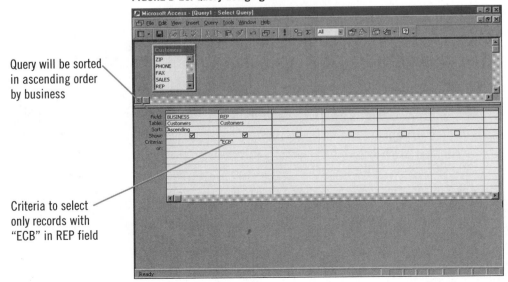

Query will be sorted in ascending order by business

Criteria to select only records with "ECB" in REP field

Protecting a Database

You can protect a database from unauthorized viewing or modification by setting a password and by encrypting the database file. Setting a **password** means that to open the database file users must enter the correct characters in a dialog box. **Encrypting** further protects a database by compacting and scrambling the database file if it is opened by a utility program or other program in an attempt to bypass the password. **Decrypting** a database reverses the encryption process. To create a password protected database, you must open it in **exclusive mode**, which means that no other users (on a network, for example) have access to it while it's open. Because this database contains sensitive data, Elizabeth wants you to password protect and encrypt the database.

Steps

1. Click **File** on the menu bar, click **Close**, click **File** on the menu bar, click **Open**, click the **Look in list arrow**, click the drive and folder location of your Project Files, click **Outdoor Designs Sales Reps**, click the **Open list arrow**, then click **Open Exclusive**
   The Outdoor Designs database opens and, because you have exclusive rights to it, you are able to set a database password.

2. Click **Tools** on the menu bar, point to **Security**, then click **Set Database Password**
   The Set Database Password dialog box opens, as shown in Figure B-21, where you can enter and verify a password.

3. Type **IOWAstate**, press **[Tab]**, type **IOWAstate** again, then click **OK**
   Passwords are case-sensitive, so you must pay attention to capitalization when you enter and verify the password.

4. Click **File** on the menu bar, then click **Close**
   You can't encrypt or decrypt a database when it is open. In a **multi-user environment**, which permits more than one person to modify the same set of data at the same time, all users need to close the database before it can be encrypted.

5. Click **Tools** on the menu bar, point to **Security**, then click **Encrypt/Decrypt Database**
   The Encrypt/Decrypt Database dialog box opens, as shown in Figure B-22, displaying the database files on your Project Disk.

6. Click **Outdoor Designs Sales Reps**, then click **OK**
   Because a password is required to get back into the database, the Password Required dialog box opens.

7. Type **IOWAstate**, then press **[Enter]**
   The Encrypt Database As dialog box opens, prompting you to enter a new filename for the encrypted database. If you specify the name of the database file that you chose to encrypt, the original file is automatically replaced with the encrypted version. If an error occurs, the original file isn't deleted.

8. Click **Outdoor Designs Sales Reps** in the File list box, click **Save**, then click **Yes** when prompted to replace the existing file
   The database has been given a password and has also been encrypted. To decrypt the file, you would click Tools on the menu bar, point to Security, then click Encrypt/Decrypt.

9. Click **File** on the menu bar, then click **Exit**

FIGURE B-21: **Set Database Password dialog box**

FIGURE B-22: **Encrypt/Decrypt Database window**

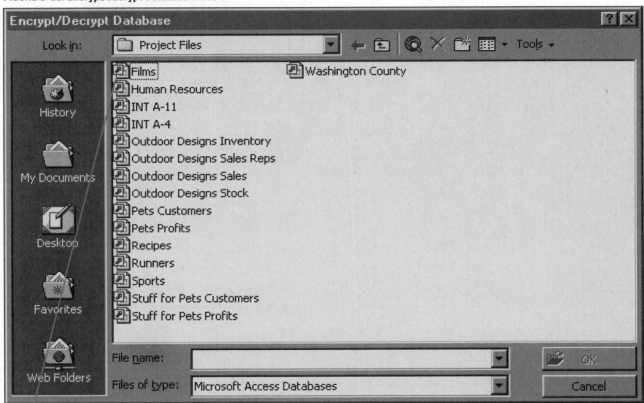

List of database files

Access 2000

Practice

► Concepts Review

Label each of the elements of the Access window shown in Figure B-23.

FIGURE B-23

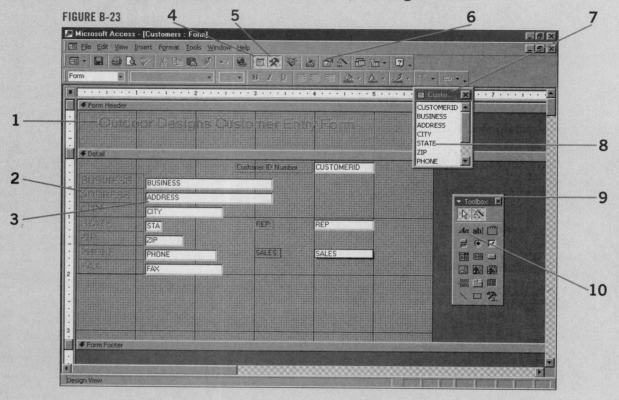

Match each of the buttons with its description.

11. Apply Filter
12. Sort Ascending
13. Sort Descending
14. Query Design view
15. Query Datasheet view
16. Clear Grid
17. Field List

a.
b.
c.
d.
e.
f.
g.

Select the best answer from the list of choices.

18. **To delete, copy, or move clip art on a form, you must first**
    a. Drag it
    b. Select it
    c. Paste it
    d. View it

19. **You can sort a database in**
    a. Ascending order
    b. Descending order
    c. Alphabetical or numerical order
    d. All of the above

20. **In order to be able to set a password you must**
    a. Have a special code
    b. Open the database in Exclusive Mode
    c. Close all open applications
    d. Encrypt the database

21. **If a database has a state field, the best way to get a quick view of all customers who live in California is to**
    a. Use a filter
    b. Sort the database by state
    c. Create a form with the state field
    d. Search for California in the state field

22. **Which of the following can be added to enhance a form?**
    a. Labels
    b. Clip art
    c. Color
    d. All of the above

23. **Which of the following *cannot* be saved as an object in a database?**
    a. Queries
    b. Forms
    c. Tables
    d. Records

24. **All of the following are true about a simple query, *except* that it**
    a. Automatically shows all the fields in the resulting datasheet
    b. Is based on specified criteria
    c. Can be sorted
    d. Can be saved as an object

▶ Skills Review

1. Open an existing database
   a. Start Access.
   b. Locate the files on your Project Disk.
   c. Open the Outdoor Designs Inventory database file on your Project Disk.

2. Modify a form layout
   a. Open the form Inventory Form in Design view. Maximize the window if necessary.
   b. Widen the Inventory form to 6".
   c. Use the field list to add the REORDER DATE field to the form; position the field to the right of the ITEM NUMBER field.
   d. Move the ON-HAND field to below the REORDER DATE field.
   e. Use the Shift key to select the REORDER DATE field and the ON-HAND field, then right-align these fields.
   f. Add a label to the Form Header that says "Outdoor Designs Inventory".
   g. Format the label in 24-point red so the text fills the header across the top of the form and is centered.

3. Change fonts and styles on a form
   a. Change the font color of the REORDER DATE field label to purple.
   b. Change the font size of the ON-HAND field value text box to 12-point, and resize the field.

4. Add clip art to a form
   a. Click the Image button on the toolbox.
   b. Drag an image frame between 3"–5" on the horizontal ruler and between 1" and 3" on the vertical ruler below the On Hand field.
   c. Insert the Bd85219 image from the cagcat50 folder in the Clipart folder. If this clipart file is not available, choose a different image.
   d. Click the Properties button to open the property sheet for the image, click the Format tab, click the Size Mode text box, then click Zoom.
   e. Close the property sheet.
   f. View, save, and close the form.

5. Filter a database
   a. Open the Inventory table in Datasheet view.
   b. Click Records on the menu bar, point to Filter, click Advanced Filter/Sort, then clear the grid of any preexisting criteria.
   c. Create a filter to find all items that cost more than $25.00 using the criteria >25.00.
   d. Apply the filter and view the results.
   e. Clear the filter grid by clicking Records on the menu bar and clicking Remove Filter/Sort, then create a new filter that finds all items of which there are fewer than 15 on hand (*Hint*: use the less than sign (<) in the filter grid).
   f. Apply the filter and view the results.
   g. Click Records on the menu bar, then click Remove Filter/Sort.

6. Sort database records
   a. Click any record in the Cost field in the datasheet.
   b. Sort the database by Cost in ascending order.

c. Print the results.

d. Sort the database by Department in ascending order.

e. Sort the database by Reorder Date in descending order.

f. Close the table datasheet without saving the changes.

7. Create a simple query

a. Click the Queries button in the Objects list.

b. Create a new query in Design view.

c. Add the Inventory table to the Query design grid, then close the Show Table dialog box.

d. Add the Item, Item Number, and Cost fields, in that order, to the Query design grid.

e. Sort the query by Cost in ascending order.

f. View the query results.

g. Save the query as "Costs in Ascending Order."

h. Add the Department field to the Query design grid.

i. Add a criterion to display only those items in the Camping department.

j. View the results in Datasheet view.

k. Save the query as "Camping Department Costs."

8. Protect a database

a. Close the current database.

b. Open the Outdoor Designs Inventory database in Exclusive Mode.

c. Open the Set Database Password dialog box and set the password to "Rocco."

d. Verify the password.

e. Encrypt the database, then save it using the same filename.

f. Close the database.

g. Exit Access.

► Independent Challenges

1. In preparation for a Stuff for Pets marketing meeting, you need to create lists that tell the marketing manager how sales of each animal are doing. You also need to enhance the Animals form, which is currently very difficult to use.

To complete this independent challenge:

a. Start Access, and open the file Stuff for Pets Profits on your Project Disk.

b. Open the Animals form.

c. Enhance the form. Use the field list to add any fields you think may help employees to enter data into the database.

d. Change the font styles, colors, and layout of the form.

e. Add a label to the header with the company name.

f. Add a relevant piece of clip art to the form.

g. Close the form.

h. Open the Animals table.

i. Sort the database in descending order on the Retail field.

j. Use a filter to find all the records for dogs.

k. Use a filter to find all the animals that cost more than $100.00.

l. Protect the database from changes. Set the password to "Tasha".

m. Save and print the database, then exit Access.

2. Stuff for Pets recently purchased a large quantity of dog beds. The store is also over-stocked on a book about Persian cats. You decide to use the customer database to create a form to help you enter data. You also want to use this database to help you find out who is purchasing which items.

To complete this independent challenge:

a. Open the file Stuff for Pets Customers on your Project Disk.

b. Use a filter to locate customers who have purchased a dog.

c. Create a new form in Design view using the Customer Sales table.

d. Use fonts and colors on the form.

e. Add clip art to the form, and create a label in the form header (*Hint:* Click View on the menu bar, then click Form Header/Footer).

f. Save the form as "Sales."

g. Sort the database in ascending order by last name, and print the results.

h. Use a filter to locate customers who have purchased a Persian cat.

i. Create a query to find all customers who have purchased a dog.

j. Save the query on your Project Disk as "Dog Customers."

k. Save your changes, and exit Access.

3. As human resources manager for Washington County, you are creating a database form for your assistant to use. You decide to include a pop-up note as a way to include instructions on the form.

To complete this independent challenge:

a. Open the file Washington County on your Student Disk.

b. Open the Employee Data Entry form.

c. Enhance the form so it is easy to use.

d. Add clip art to the form, selecting an appropriate image from the Clipart folder.

e. Use the Label button in the Toolbox to insert the label "More Information" in the Detail section of the form.

f. Type the note "Use the following abbreviations: PW for Public Works, Safety for Public Safety, Legal for County Courts." as a label below the More Information label.

g. Print the form.

h. Save the file.

i. This is a sensitive file; protect the database using the password "SEATTLE".

j. Close the database, and exit Access.

4. You want to develop a database that tracks some of your favorite films. The Internet has many Web pages that offer synopses of films available on video.

To complete this independent challenge:

a. Log on to the Internet, and use your browser to go to http://www.course.com. From there, click Student Online Companions, then click the link for the book you are using, then click the Access link for Unit B.

b. Search the database for information on five of your favorite recently released films. Print the results of your search.

c. Search the database for information on five of your favorite films that were released at least 10 years ago. Print the results of your search.

d. Start Access, and open the database file Films on your Project Disk.

e. Modify the existing table to include any new fields you might need to store the information you found on your Internet search.

f. Add a Yes/No field for whether you would see the film again.

g. Create a form to enter the data. Use Design view to create the form.

h. Enter the data for the 10 films you found on your Internet search.

i. Filter the database to see all the films you would see again.

j. Sort the database in alphabetical order by title. Print the datasheet.

k. Print the form for five of the records you entered.

l. Close the database, and exit Access.

Access 2000

► Visual Workshop

Open the database Sports on your Project Disk. Modify the RUNNERS form so that it looks like the form shown in Figure B-24. Save the form as Runners to your Project Disk and print it when you are finished.

FIGURE B-24

Creating
Database Reports

Objectives

- ► **Create a report**
- ► **Modify a report**
- ► **Create a report from a query**
- ► **Add summary information to a report**
- ► **Add an expression to a report**
- ► **View a report in Print Preview**
- ► **Add clip art to a report**
- ► **Create mailing labels**

In this unit you organize the fields of a database into reports. A **report** is a summary of database information designed specifically for printing. A report can include one or more database fields, summary information, clip art, and descriptive labels. You create reports from tables or queries in the database. You can also save a form as a report. ◢ Elizabeth Fried, the database administrator for Outdoor Designs, has asked you to help her create a series of reports containing summary information from the Outdoor Designs customer database. She wants you to create the reports, add statistical data, and print copies for distribution to the Outdoor Designs sales representatives.

Creating a Report

When a database grows large, spotting statistical trends in the data can be difficult. For example, if a sales database contains hundreds of records, it's hard to determine the amount of an average sale, or the total sales. With Access, this problem is solved by letting you create summary reports of your database. You can create new reports in Design view or with the help of the Report Wizard. Reports are divided into sections, which are explained in Table C-1. Each report is stored in your database file as an object so you can print it or refer to it later. ✐ Elizabeth asks you to create a new report that lists all of the customer information contained in the Customers table within the Outdoor Designs database, organized by sales representative.

Steps 1 2 3 4

1. Start Access, and open the file **Outdoor Designs Sales** on your Student Disk

2. In the Outdoor Designs Sales: Database window, click the **Reports** button in the Objects list, then click **New**
   The options in the New Report dialog box are very similar to those you choose from when creating a new form. In Design View you can manually add controls (objects which display or label data or perform an action such as a calculation) to the report. You can use one of the two AutoReports to create a report based on the chosen object with predefined settings. You can use one of the three wizards to create a report, a chart, or a set of labels.

3. Click **Report Wizard** in the New Report dialog box, click the **Choose the table or query where the object's data comes from list arrow**, click **Customers**, then click **OK**
   The Customers table has the fields needed for this report, as shown in Figure C-1.

4. Click the **Select All Fields button** >> , then click Next >
   The next dialog box determines how the records are grouped. Grouping organizes a report by field or values in a field so that you can spot trends or find important information more easily.

5. Click **REP**, click the **Select Field button** > , notice that the REP field appears in blue text above the remaining fields in the list, then click Next >
   The next dialog box determines how the records within the detail section of the report will be sorted.

6. Click the first **Sort list arrow**, click **BUSINESS**, then click Next >
   This sorts the records in ascending alphabetical order by the name of the business.

7. Verify that the **Stepped Layout option button**, the **Portrait Orientation option button**, and the **Adjust the field width so all fields fit on a page check box** are all selected, click Next > , click the **Corporate style**, click Next > , type **Outdoor Designs Customers Report** as the report title, click Finish , then maximize the report window
   The report is shown in Print Preview in Figure C-2. In Print Preview you can't make any changes to the report, but you can see exactly how your report will be printed. You see that the report needs some work; you will make modifications in the next lesson.

8. Click **File** on the menu bar, then click **Close**
   The Outdoor Designs Customers Report is saved as an object in the Outdoor Designs Sales database.

FIGURE C-1: Report Wizard dialog box

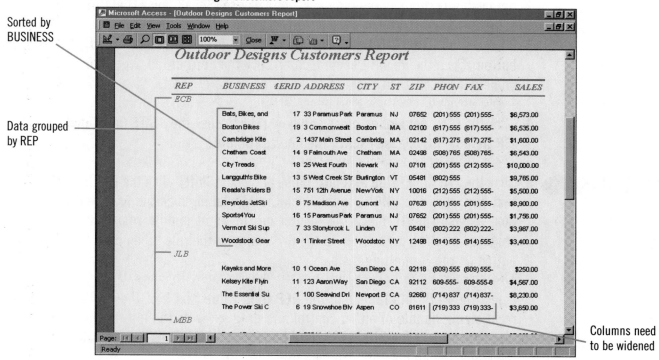

Report will be based on Customers table

Fields available in Customers table

Click to add all fields to report

FIGURE C-2: Outdoor Designs Customers report

Sorted by BUSINESS

Data grouped by REP

Columns need to be widened

TABLE C-1: Report sections

section	description
Report header	Appears only at the top of the first page of the report and usually contains the report name or company logo
Page header	Appears at the top of every page (but below the report header on the first page); can contain field labels as well as graphic elements
Group header	Appears at the beginning of a group of records ("Group" is replaced by the field name)
Detail	Appears once for every record in the underlying datasheet and usually contains bound controls
Group footer	Appears at the end of each group of records ("Group" is replaced by the field name)
Page footer	Appears at the bottom of each page and usually contains the current date and page number
Report footer	Appears at the end of the last page of the report, just above the page footer

Modifying a Report

In Design view, you can modify a report's alignment and placement of the bound and unbound controls, add labels and art to enhance the presentation, and format labels and data in different fonts, styles, special effects, and colors. ◆━━ You want to improve the appearance and readability of the Outdoor Designs Customers Report. You want to delete the Sales information, which is not relevent to this report, to make room for the PHONE and FAX fields, change the CUSTOMERID label to ID, delete the CITY, STATE, and ZIP labels from the header, resize several controls, center the field labels, and add color to the report.

Steps

Trouble?

If the Customers field list and the Toolbox are in the way, close them by clicking the Close button in the title bar of each.

1. Click **Outdoor Designs Customers Report** in the Outdoor Designs Sales: Database window, then click **Design**
   The report opens in Design view, as shown in Figure C-3.

2. Click the **SALES field label** in the Page Header, press and hold [Shift], click the **SALES field value text box** in the Detail section, release [Shift], press [Delete]
   The Sales label and text box are deleted.

3. Click the **CUSTOMERID field label** in the Page Header section, click the **Properties button** 📇 on the Report Design toolbar, click the **Format tab**, type **ID** in the Caption property text box, then click 📇 to close the property sheet
   The Customer ID label now reads simply "ID".

4. Click the **CITY field label**, press and hold [Shift], click the **STATE field label**, click the **ZIP field label**, release [Shift], then press [Delete]
   These labels aren't necessary since they all fit under the label "Address".

Trouble?

You may have to scroll the window and move the fields around a bit to get them positioned properly.

5. Click the **ZIP field value text box**, press and hold [Shift], click the **PHONE field value text box**, click the **PHONE label**, click the **FAX label**, click the **FAX field value text box**, release [Shift], place the pointer on the **right middle resize handle of any selected control**, drag ◆━━▶ to the 6 ½" mark on the ruler, then click the **Align Left** button on the Formatting toolbar
   The three text boxes and one label are resized to accommodate the data.

6. Select the **REP field label** and the **REP field value text box**, then click the **middle right sizing handle** of either control and drag ◆━━▶ to the left (to the ½" mark on the ruler); select the **BUSINESS field label** and the **BUSINESS field value text box**, then click the middle left sizing handle and drag ◆━━▶ to the ½" mark on the ruler; then select all four controls and click the **Align Left button** 📄. Now there is more room to display the business names and the new alignment will make the information easier to read.

7. Place the pointer in the left margin of the Detail section, when the pointer changes to ➡, click to select all the **field value text boxes**, click the **Font/Fore Color button list arrow** 🄰▾ on the Report Design toolbar, then click the **Red color box**
   The data will stand out more in red on the report.

8. Click the **Print Preview button** 🔍 on the Report Design toolbar, then click the **Zoom List arrow**, then click **Fit**
   Compare your report to Figure C-4.

9. Click the **Print button** 🖶 on the Print Preview toolbar, then close Print Preview and close the report, saving changes when prompted

FIGURE C-3: Report in Design view

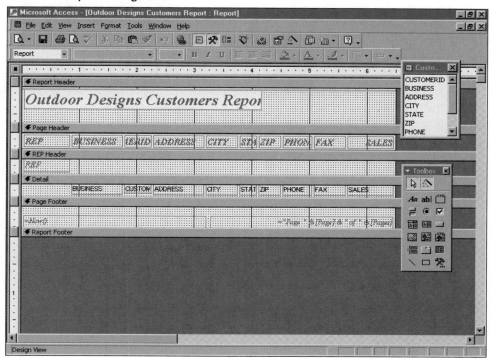

FIGURE C-4: Modified report

Report in
Fit view

Field labels
are centered

Field value text
is formatted
in red

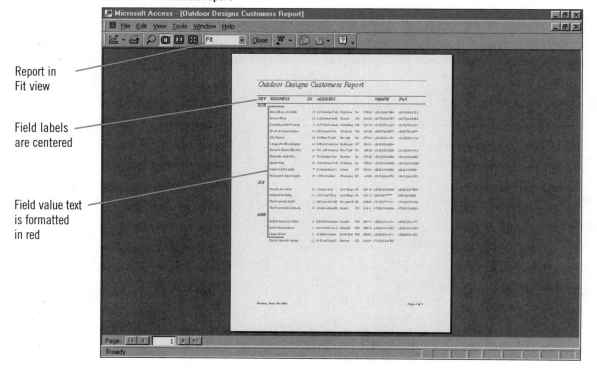

Creating a Report from a Query

Queries answer questions about the data in the database. Although you can simply print query results, the results are usually easier to read when formatted attractively in a report based on a query. ✒ Elizabeth created a Customers query that identifies the sales representative assigned to each customer and also displays the total sales made to each customer. She needs you to create two reports based on that query for the sales manager. The first report must show all customers whose sales totaled more than $5,000, and the second report is for all customers whose sales totaled more $1,000. First you modify the query, then you create the report.

Steps

1. In the Outdoor Designs Sales: Database window, click the **Queries button** in the Objects list, click **Customers Query**, click **Design**, scroll to the **SALES field**, click the **SALES field Criteria cell**, type **>5000**, click the **Datasheet View button** 🏢 on the Query Design toolbar, view the nine records in the query results, click the **Customers Query Close Window button**, then click **Yes** to save the changes
   Now the query shows only customers whose orders total more than $5000.

2. In the Outdoor Designs Sales: Database window, click the **Reports button** in the Objects list, click **New**, click **Report Wizard** in the New Report dialog box, click the **Choose the table or query where the object's data comes from list arrow**, click **Customers Query**, then click **OK**

3. Click **BUSINESS**, click the **Select Field button** ⊳, click **STATE**, click ⊳, click **SALES**, click ⊳, click **REP**, click ⊳, then click Next >
   Now, instead of showing all the fields contained in the query, the report will show just the business name, state, sales, and the sales representative fields.

4. Click **REP**, click ⊳, then click Next >
   This groups the records by sales rep.

5. Click the first **Sort list arrow**, click **BUSINESS**, then click Next >
   This sorts the records in ascending alphabetical order by the name of the business.

6. Click the **Block Layout option button**, verify that the **Portrait Orientation option button** is selected, click Next >, click the **Casual style**, click Next >, type **Customers by Rep Query Report** as the report title, click Finish, maximize the report window if necessary, then scroll to see the SALES column if necessary
   Compare your screen to Figure C-5.

7. Click **File** on the menu bar, click **Close** to close the report, click the **Queries button** in the Objects list, click **Customers Query**, click **Design**, scroll to the **Sales field**, double-click **5000** in the Sales field Criteria cell, type **1000**, click the **Customers Query Close Window button**, click **Yes** to save the changes, click the **Reports button** in the Objects list, click the **Customers by Rep Query Report**, click **Preview**, then scroll to see the Sales figures
   The report now includes all customers whose sales totaled more than $1,000. Because the report is based on the Customers query, it always shows the results of the last version of the query. See Figure C-6.

8. Click the **Print button** 🖨 on the Print Preview toolbar to print the report, then click **Close**
   If you wanted to run and print a report that showed customers whose sales totalled more than $5000, you would query, change the criteria, and then run the report again.

FIGURE C-5: Customers by Rep report for sales greater than $5,000

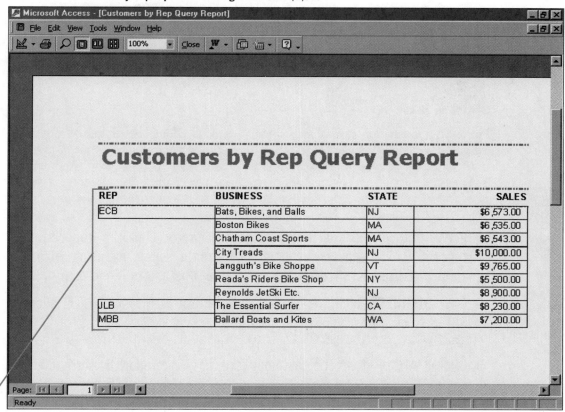

Records grouped by REP
and sorted by BUSINESS

FIGURE C-6: Customers by Rep report for sales greater than $1,000

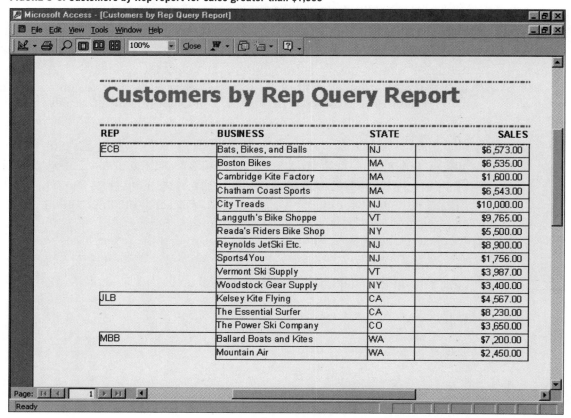

Adding Summary Information to a Report

Summary information in a report displays statistics about one or more fields in a database. Summaries can include statistics on the sum, average, minimum, or maximum value in any numeric field. Table C-2 lists common summary calculations available for your database reports. As part of an ongoing effort to target new markets for Outdoor Designs, you help Elizabeth prepare a report that shows statistics for sales by state using the Customers table.

1. In the Outdoor Designs Sales: Database window, click the **Reports button** in the Objects list if necessary, double-click **Create report by using wizard**, click the **Tables/Queries list arrow**, then click **Table: Customers** if necessary

2. Click **BUSINESS**, click the **Select Field button** `>`, click **STATE**, click `>`, click **SALES**, click `>`, click **REP**, click `>`, then click `Next >`
   The BUSINESS, STATE, SALES, and REP fields will be used in the report.

3. Click **STATE** to group the customer records in the report by state, click `>`, then click `Next >`
   In addition to sorting, you can choose summary options in this wizard dialog box.

4. Click **Summary Options**
   The Summary Options dialog box opens, as shown in Figure C-7. Of the fields you selected for this report, summary options are available only for the SALES field because this is the only field containing numeric values.

5. Click the **Sum check box**, click the **Avg check box**, click the **Min check box**, click the **Max check box**, click the **Calculate percent of total for sums check box**, click the **Detail and Summary option button**, then click **OK**
   This specifies that you want to see the total sales, the average sales, the minimum sales, and the maximum sales for each state, and that you want to see the details (sales for each account) in addition to the summary information (calculated for each state).

6. Click the first **Sort list arrow**, click **BUSINESS**, click `Next >`, click the **Block option button**, verify that the **Portrait option button** is selected, click `Next >`, click the **Compact style**, click `Next >`, type **Sales by State Report** as the report title, click `Finish`, then scroll through the report until you reach the information for California and Colorado
   Your screen should look like Figure C-8. You see that the report needs some formatting work. You will work on enhancing and polishing this report in the next lesson.

7. Click **File** on the menu bar, then click **Close**

FIGURE C-7: Summary Options dialog box

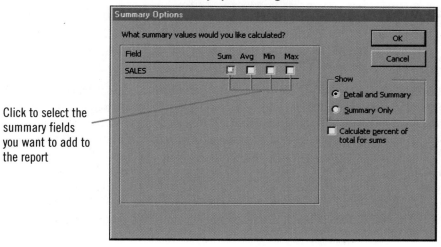

Click to select the summary fields you want to add to the report

FIGURE C-8: Sales by State report

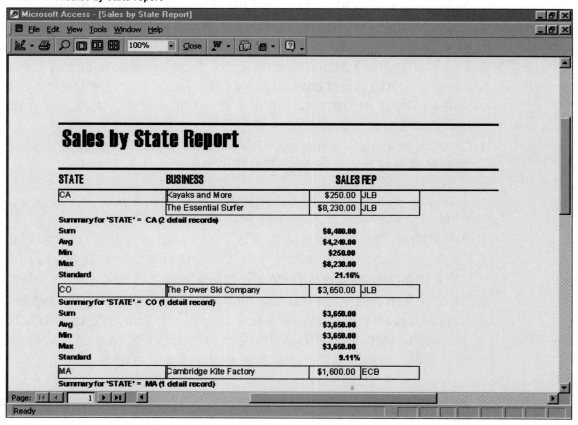

TABLE: C-2: Common summary calculations available in database reports

summary	statistic	calculates
SUM	Sum	Total of all values in the field
AVG	Average	Average of all values in the field
COUNT	Count	Number of records in the database
MIN	Minimum	Smallest value in the field
MAX	Maximum	Largest value in the field

Adding an Expression to a Report

You can include calculated expressions in a report. **Expressions** are calculated fields that provide additional data. They can include field names, calculations you type, and built-in functions. To ensure database integrity, you should use fields from the report's source when creating expressions, results rather than adding a new field. That way, the expressions' results will be updated to reflect the most current data in the database every time the data changes. You want to include commission data in the Sales by State Report. The Customers table does not contain a commissions field, so you decide to add an expression which calculates this information. You want the information (which is calculated as 15% of sales) to appear in the STATE footer section of the report with the rest of the statistics. You also have to format the report for printing.

Steps

1. Verify that the Reports button is selected in the Outdoor Designs Sales: Database window, click **Sales by State Report** in the Reports list, then click **Design**

2. Place the pointer on the top of the **Page footer bar**, then when the pointer changes to ⌖, drag the divider down ½" on the vertical ruler

QuickTip

Text box labels are numbered by the sequence in which they are added to a form or report. The number of the text box label on your report will vary from the one shown here.

3. Click the **Toolbox button** ⚒ on the Report Design toolbar to display the Toolbox if necessary, click the **Text box button** abl on the Toolbox, click the **Text box pointer** ⁺abl at the 1" mark on the horizontal ruler below the summary statistics in the STATE footer section, as shown in Figure C-9

4. Click the **Properties button** 🗂, click the **Data tab** on the property sheet, click the **Control Source text box**, type **=[SALES]*0.15**, then press **[Enter]**

   You have changed the control's properties to include the expression to calculate commissions by multiplying the value in the SALES field in the Customers table by 15%. As shown in Figure C-10, =[SALES]*0.15 is entered in the control.

5. Click the new **text box label** in the STATE footer section, click the **Format tab** on the property sheet, type **Commissions** in the Caption text box, click 🗂, position the pointer on the **Commissions label right middle resize handle**, then drag ⬌ to the 1" mark

6. Click the **Sum field value text box**, press and hold [Shift], click the **Avg field value text box**, click the **Min field value text box**, click the **Max field value text box**, click the **Sum for percent field value text box**, release [Shift], position the pointer on any **right middle resize handle**, then drag ⬌ to the 5" mark

QuickTip

Currency formatting is displayed only in Print Preview.

7. Press and hold [Shift], click the **=[Sales]*0.15** text box, release [Shift], click 🗂, click the **Format tab**, click the **Format list arrow**, scroll down, click **Currency**, as shown in Figure C-11, then click 🗂

8. Click the **REP field label** in the Page Header section, press and hold [Shift], click the **REP field value text box**, release [Shift], then when the pointer changes to ✋ drag the **REP field** so the left edge is at the 5" mark

   The REP field label and text box are now left-aligned at the 5" mark.

9. Save your changes to the report

FIGURE C-9: Text box control in State header

Toolbox button

In Step 3,
click here

Properties button

Text box button

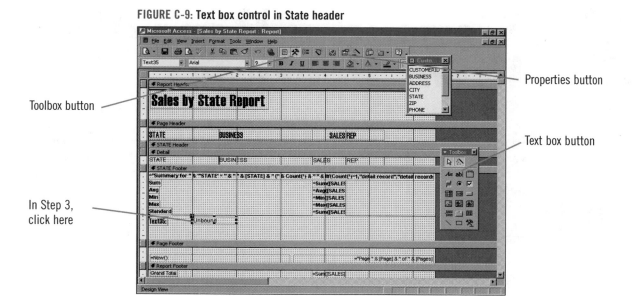

FIGURE C-10: Expression in control

Control Source
text box

Property sheet

Label for new
control (your label
number will vary)

Expression entered
in new control

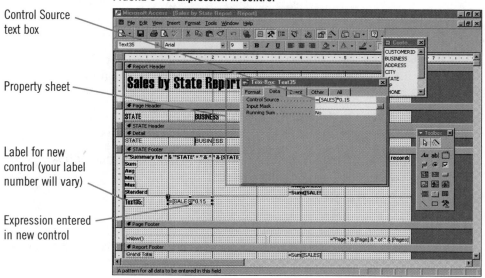

FIGURE C-11: Sales by State Report in Design view

Property sheet for
all currently
selected fields

All six text boxes
will be formatted
as currency

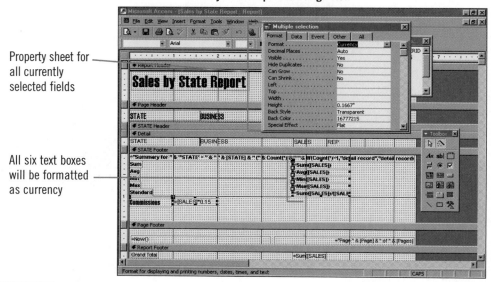

Access 2000

Viewing a Report in Print Preview

To view a report as it will be printed, you need to use Print Preview. Print Preview displays the report with the title, headings, records, and summary information you specified. Examining the report in Print Preview is an important step because you can catch any formatting problems before you print. Print Preview has many options that are worth exploring. 🖋 To verify that it is attractive and easy to understand, you want to preview the Sales by State report before printing it for your colleagues.

Steps

1. Click the **Print Preview button** 🔍 on the Report Design toolbar
   The Print Preview window opens.

2. Click the **Zoom button** 🔍 on the Print Preview toolbar
   The zoom level changes to Fit and the pointer changes to the magnification pointer, as shown in Figure C-12. You can zoom in on any section of the report to get a good look at the details. You can also use the page navigation buttons to view each page of the report

3. Point to the lower half of the screen, then click 🔍
   You see the information for the state of Massachusetts enlarged on the screen. Sometimes reports have more than one page.

4. Click the **Two Pages button** 🔲 on the Print Preview toolbar
   Both pages of this report appear on the screen, as shown in Figure C-13.

5. Click the **Zoom list arrow** on the Print Preview toolbar, then click **50%**
   You see both pages in 50% view on the screen.

6. Click the **Print button** 🖨 on the Print Preview toolbar

7. Click **File** on the menu bar, then click **Close**
   The Print Preview window closes and you return to the Reports tab in the database window.

> **QuickTip**
> If your report has several pages, you can click the Multiple Pages button 🔲, then click the number of pages you want to view.

FIGURE C-12: Zooming in on a section

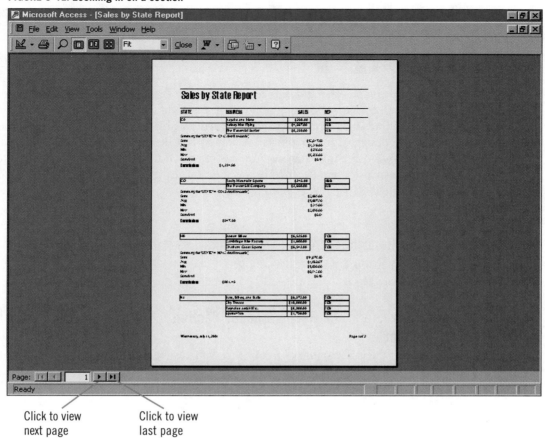

Click to view
next page

Click to view
last page

FIGURE C-13: Viewing two pages of the report

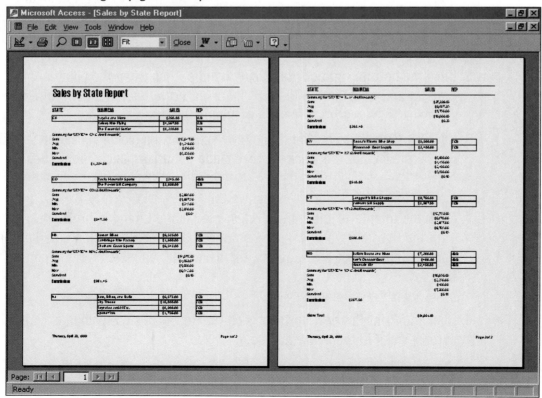

Adding Clip Art to a Report

You can add clip art and other graphics to a report or a form. Graphics enhance any printed report. If you have a color printer, colorful graphic images can add visual interest to what otherwise might be a dull page of facts and figures. A report printed on a black and white printer is enhanced with a monochrome design. Company logos, as well as any design elements, can identify a report as belonging to your company. ✐ You decide to add a cheerful image to brighten up the Outdoor Designs Customers Report. You decide to place an image of a sun in the Report header so it will be printed on the first page of the report.

Steps 1 2 3 4

1. **Click the Reports button** in the Objects list if necessary, click **Outdoor Designs Customers Report**, then click **Design**
   The Outdoor Designs Customers Report opens in Design view.

2. **Click anywhere in the Report Header Section**, click **Insert** on the menu bar, then click **Object**
   The Insert Object dialog box opens. Here you can add an object of any type listed in the Object Type list to the report.

3. **Verify that the Create New option button** is selected, click **Microsoft Clip Gallery** in the Object Type list, then click **OK**
   The Microsoft Clip Gallery opens.

Trouble?
If the Sun Picture shown in Figure C-14 is not available, choose another suitable image.

4. **Type Sun** in the Search for clips text box, press **[Enter]**, scroll through the clip art that matches this keyword description, click the **Sun picture** shown in Figure C-14, then click the **Insert clip button** 📷
   The clip is inserted and aligned at the top left corner of the Page header section. The image is too large and obscures the report title.

QuickTip
If you want a graphic to appear on each page of the report insert it into the page header section.

5. **Click the bottom right corner sizing handle**, then when the pointer changes to ↘, drag up and to the left to the 1 ½" mark on the vertical and horizontal rulers
   The image is resized, but it is too large to fit in the frame.

6. **Click the Properties button** 📷 on the Report Design toolbar, click the **Size Mode text box** on the Format tab, click the **Size Mode list arrow**, click **Zoom**, then click 📷
   Now that you have changed the clip art properties, the image fits nicely in the frame, but it still obscures the report title.

7. **Click the middle of the image**; when the pointer changes to 🖐, drag to the right until the right edge of the image is aligned at the **6 ⅜" mark** on the horizontal ruler and the top edge of the image is just below the top edge of the Report Header section
   Compare your screen to Figure C-15.

8. **Click the Print Preview button** 🔍 on the Report Design toolbar, click the **Zoom list arrow**, click **Fit**, then view the report

9. **Click the Print button** 🖨 on the Print Preview toolbar, click **File** on the menu bar, click **Close**, then click **Yes** to save your changes

FIGURE C-14: Searching for clipart in the Microsoft Clip Gallery

Type one or more words to describe the clip you are looking for here

Choose this clip

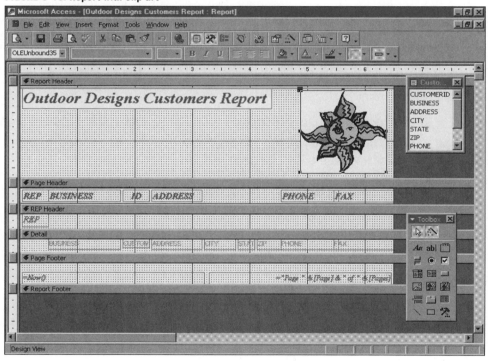

FIGURE C-15: Report with clip art

Inserting Pictures

You can insert pictures other than clip art, such as company logos, scanned art, or other image files, in reports and forms. In order to insert a picture, you first insert an image control in the document, then you insert the picture file. Click the Image button [icon] on the Toolbox, click the [icon] in the section where you want to insert the picture, drag to create a placeholder for the picture, then release the mouse button. The Insert Picture dialog box opens. Locate the file you want to insert, then click OK. The image is inserted in the placeholder you drew. You can change the image properties using the Properties window, and can move and resize the image just as you do other objects in the Report or Form design window.

Unit C

Access 2000

Creating Mailing Labels

Reports don't have to be printed on sheets of paper. You may want to use the data in the database to create other forms of printed output, such as labels or envelopes. With Access, there is a Label Wizard to help you create a label containing data from any fields in the database. You can create labels based on queries or filters to generate a report for specific needs, such as a mailing to all clients in New Jersey or all employees in the legal department. ✎ Elizabeth asked you to create mailing labels for a big promotional mailing that is going to all Outdoor Designs customers announcing the product lines. You decide to use the Label Wizard to create labels for all Outdoor Designs customers based on the Customers table.

Steps

1. In the Outdoor Designs Sales: Database window, click the **Reports button** in the Objects list if necessary, then click **New**
The New Report dialog box opens.

> **QuickTip**
> The labels are organized in numerical order.

2. Click **Label Wizard**, click the **Choose the Table or query where the object's data comes from list arrow**, click **Customers**, then click **OK**
In the first dialog box of this wizard, there is a list of predefined formats for labels made by several manufacturers from which you can choose.

3. Click the **Filter by manufacturer list arrow**, click **Avery**, click the **English Unit of Measure option button**, click **5160**, then click **Next >**
This form has three labels that are each 1" × 2⅝" across a sheet. In the next dialog box you can change font, font size, and other text attributes.

4. Click the **Font name list arrow**, click **Comic Sans MS**, click the **Font Weight list arrow**, click **Normal**, then click **Next >**
In the next dialog box, you choose which fields you want to include on each label, as well as their placement. You select each field from the Available fields list in the order in which you want them on the label. Any spaces, punctuation, or hard returns have to be entered using the keyboard.

> **QuickTip**
> Double-click the field name in the Available fields list to move it to the Prototype label text box.

5. Click **BUSINESS**, click the **Select Field button** **>**, press **[Enter]**, click **ADDRESS**, click **>**, press **[Enter]**, click **CITY**, click **>**, type **, (a comma)**, press the **[Spacebar]**, click **STATE**, click **>**, press the **[Spacebar]**, click **ZIP**, then click **>**
Your screen should look like Figure C-16.

6. Click **Next >**
In the next dialog box, you need to decide how the records should be sorted when they are printed.

7. Scroll to and click **REP**, click **>**, click **BUSINESS**, click **>**, click **Next >**, click **Finish** to accept the default report name, then maximize the report window
The labels appear in Print Preview as shown in Figure C-17. If you have a sheet of Avery 5160 labels, you can put it in your printer and print this report, or you can print the labels on an 8½ × 11" sheet of paper to see what they would look like.

8. Click the **Print button** 🖨 on the Print Preview toolbar
Review the printout. You are pleased with the labels so you close the database and exit Access.

9. Click **File** on the menu bar, then click **Exit**

FIGURE C-16: Label Wizard dialog box

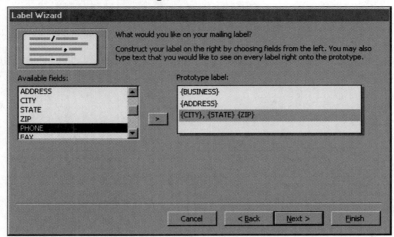

FIGURE C-17: Completed labels in Print Preview

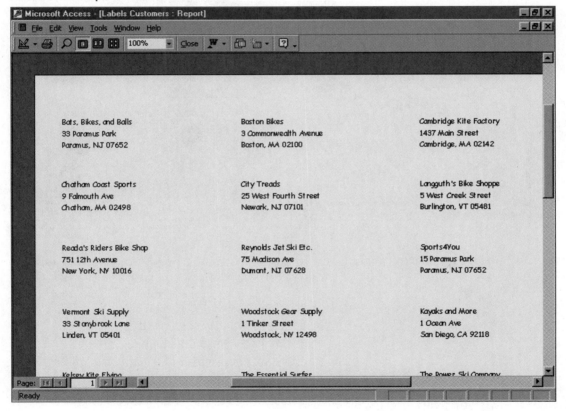

Modifying labels in Design view

Because labels are a kind of report, you can modify them in Design view, just as you do other kinds of reports. Experiment with adding images and color to create interesting, eye-catching labels. Note, however, that the wizard sets the important label parameters for printing, so do not change the size if you want to print on preprinted label forms.

Practice

► Concepts Review

Label each of the elements of the Access window shown in Figure C-18.

FIGURE C-18

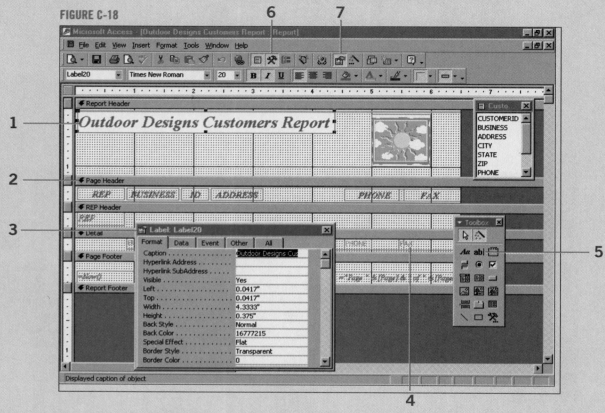

Match the statistical calculations available in the Summary Options dialog box with their descriptions.

8. Sum
9. Average
10. Count
11. Minimum
12. Maximum

a. Largest value in the field
b. Total of all values in the field
c. Smallest value in the field
d. Number of records in the database
e. Average of all values in the field

Select the best answer from the list of choices.

13. A report is a summary of database information specifically designed for
    a. Searching
    b. Sorting
    c. Examining in Form view
    d. Printing

14. **Which of these elements cannot be included in a database report?**
    a. Fields
    b. Statistics
    c. Clip art
    d. Forms

15. **Which of the following calculations is not available in a Summary report?**
    a. Minimum value
    b. Net present value
    c. Maximum value
    d. Average

16. **When you are finished defining the report using the Report Wizard, the report is displayed in**
    a. Print Preview
    b. The Database window
    c. Form view
    d. Datasheet view

17. **Access includes each of the following sections in the report design *except*:**
    a. Title
    b. Headings
    c. Footer
    d. Details

18. **If you want to see an entire report page in Print Preview, select a _____ zoom level**
    a. Fit
    b. 125%
    c. 50%
    d. Page

19. **Reports *cannot* be**
    a. Sorted on up to four fields.
    b. Based on a query.
    c. Based on a form.
    d. Based on a table.

20. **If you want to show data in a report that meets a certain value, you could use a**
    a. Query
    b. Variance
    c. Summary
    d. Standard Deviation

21. **To view the actual report on the screen, you would use**
    a. Form view
    b. Print Preview
    c. List view
    d. Report view

22. **When working in report Design view, you can**
    a. Change fonts.
    b. Align titles.
    c. Insert images.
    d. All of the above.
23. **To create a report, you can use**
    a. The Report Wizard.
    b. The Label Wizard.
    c. Design view.
    d. All of the above.

 # Skills Review

1. **Create a report**
    a. Start Access, and open the file Outdoor Designs Stock on your Project Disk.
    b. Use the Report Wizard to create a new report.
    c. Base the report on the Inventory table.
    d. Select all the fields.
    e. Group the report by DEPARTMENT.
    f. Sort in descending order by Cost (*Hint*: click the Ascending Sort button on the Wizard dialog box to switch to a descending sort order).
    g. Select the Stepped Layout and the Bold style.
    h. Title the report "Inventory Report".
    i. View the report in Print Preview.
2. **Modify a report**
    a. View the Inventory Report in Design view.
    b. Delete the Description field and field label.
    c. Use the property sheet to change the ITEM NUMBER label to "ITEM NO." and the "REORDER DATE" label to "REORDER."
    d. Change the color of the field value text boxes to purple (first box in the fourth row) except the Department field.
    e. Change the font size of all the field labels to 8 points except the Department field.
    f. Resize the Report title label text box so the text is not cut off.
    g. Move, resize, and horizontally align the controls as necessary so that all information fits attractively on the report.
    h. Save and close the report.
3. **Create a report from a query**
    a. Create a new report using the Report Wizard.
    b. Base the report on the Inventory Query.
    c. Select all the fields, group by DEPARTMENT, sort in ascending order by ITEM NUMBER, use the Block layout, use the Soft Gray style, and title the report "Inventory Query Report."
    d. View the results in Print Preview.
    e. Close the report.
    f. Open the Inventory Query.
    g. Modify the query to select only those items that meet the criterion "green" in the color field.
    h. Save the query changes.
    i. Open the Inventory Query Report in Print Preview.
    j. Switch to Design view and resize, move, rename, and re-align field labels and field value text boxes as necessary so all the information is displayed clearly. Switch between Design view and Print Preview as necessary until you are satisfied with the result.

    k. Print the report.

    l. Close the report.

4. Add summary information

    a. Create a new report using the Report Wizard based on the Inventory table.

    b. Select all the fields, then group by DEPARTMENT.

    c. Open the Summary Options dialog box, click to select all the checkboxes for the COST field, and click to select the Sum check box for the ON-HAND field.

    d. Sort in ascending order by ITEM NUMBER, use the Block layout, use the Formal style, and title the report "Inventory Statistics Report."

    e. Preview the report.

    f. Use Design view to format the field labels in the Page Header section as red, Arial, 8-point.

    g. Format the statistics field values in the Department Footer section as Currency.

    h. Preview and then print the report.

    i. Save your changes.

    j. Close the report.

5. Add an expression to a report

    a. Open the Inventory Statistics Report in Design View.

    b. Drag the top of the Detail bar down ½" to make room in the Inventory Query Report.

    c. Use the Toolbox to add a Text box control to the Department Header section.

    d. Change the TEXT 24 label to "TAX." (Your text label number may vary.)

    e. You want to know the tax that you will pay by department. The formula is COST multiplied by 7%. Open the property sheet for the new control, then click the Data tab. Type the expression =[COST]*.07 in the Control Source text box. Do not close the property sheet.

    f. Click the Format tab, click the Format list arrow, then click Currency. Close the property sheet.

6. View a report in Print Preview

    a. View the Inventory Query Report in Print Preview.

    b. Use the Magnifier to zoom in on the top section of the report if necessary.

    c. Close the report, saving any changes.

7. Add clip art

    a. Open the Inventory Query Report in Design view.

    b. Click anywhere in the Detail section.

    c. Click Insert on the menu bar, click Object, in the Insert Object dialog box click Microsoft Clip Gallery, then click OK.

    d. In the Microsoft Clip Gallery, enter "border" in the Search for Clips text box.

    e. Scroll through the available borders, find one that is appropriate for this report, click the clip, then click the Insert Clip button.

    f. Resize the border so it stretches across the width of the report.

    g. Drag the top of the Page Footer section bar up to eliminate extra space in the Detail section.

    h. Use the Image property sheet to set the Size Mode to Zoom.

    i. Preview the report.

    j. Print the report.

    k. Close the report and save.

8. Create labels

    a. Start the Label Wizard.

    b. Base the labels on the Inventory table.

    c. Click the Filter by Manufacturer list arrow, click Avery, click the English option button, then scroll to and click Avery USA ReadyIndex (2" × 3").

d. Change the font to Footlight MT Light 12-point or a font of your choice.

e. Set up the label as shown in Figure C-19.

FIGURE C-19

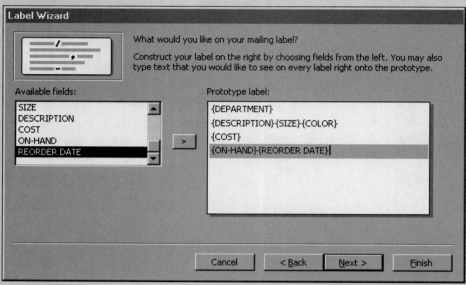

f. Sort by Department.

g. Accept the default label title.

h. Preview, then print the labels.

i. Save the labels as Inventory Labels, then close the report.

j. Exit Access.

▶ Independent Challenges

1. The president of Stuff for Pets, Donna Rand, has asked you to run and print three reports based on data in the Pets Profits database. She is trying to expand the business and needs to see what inventory is in stock, her cost basis, and how the business has been performing in each product area.

To complete this independent challenge:

a. Start Access, and open the file Pets Profits on your Project Disk.

b. Use the Report Wizard to create a report based on the Animals table.

c. Include all the fields, group by Category, sort by Breed, and choose an appropriate layout and style.

d. Modify the report so you can see all the fields clearly. Delete the TIME field from the Page Header and Detail section.

e. Use color to enhance the display of the data.

f. Create a text box in the Detail section and label it PROFIT. Enter the expression =[RETAIL]–[COST]. Delete the unbound text label and add a new label to the Page Header PROFIT.

g. Preview and print the report, then save and close the report.

h. Create a report from the Animals query for all dogs (You'll need to modify the Animals query first to include a filter that filters out records that do not meet the criteria "dog" in the CATEGORY field. Include only the BREED, DOB, COST, and RETAIL fields.

i. Preview and print the report, then save and close it.

j. Modify the Animals query by changing the filter criteria to cat. Then close the query and create a report for all cats using the query you just modified. Include the CATEGORY, GENDER, BREED, DOB, COST and RETAIL fields.

k. Preview the new data and print the report. Save and close the report.

l. Close the database, and exit Access.

2. Stuff for Pets is planning a campaign to target good customers. You need to create several reports to present to the sales force to help their effort to generate new business.

To complete this independent challenge:

a. Start Access, and open the file Pets Customers on your Project Disk.

b. View the Customers Sales Query Report in Print Preview.

c. Modify the Customers Sales Query to select only customers who purchased dogs, then save and close the query.

d. Reopen the Customers Sales Query Report in Design view. Insert a clip art image into the Report Header. Move, resize, and change the clip's properties to format it attractively in the report.

e. Preview and print the report.

f. Modify the Customers Sales Query to select only customers who purchased cats.

g. Open the Customer Sales Query Report and Insert an image into the Report Header.

h. Preview and print the report.

i. Create a mailing label for all customers based on the Customers Sales table. Use Avery label 5160, and include the customer's first and last name, address, city, state, and zip code on the label, inserting spaces and punctuation where appropriate.

j. Preview and print the report. Close the database, and exit Access.

3. As director of the Human Resources department, you need to provide the department heads with information about the staff. You create a series of reports to fill this need.

To complete this independent challenge:

a. Start Access, and open the file Human Resources on your Student Disk.

b. Use the Report Wizard to design a report based on all the fields in the Employees table.

c. Group the report by DEPT, and sort in ascending order by Last Name.

d. Include summary information on salary that includes the minimum and the maximum fields, in both detail and summary form.

e. Choose an appropriate layout, title, and style for the report.

f. Modify the report so that all fields are visible. Delete and change labels as needed.

g. Insert a clip art image into the Report Header of the report. Move, resize, and change the clip's properties to format it attractively in the report.

h. Use color to enhance the report.

i. Preview the report. Print the report. Close the database, and exit Access.

4. The World Wide Web has many sites for finding recipes and information on nutrition and food. Imagine that you are going to start your own restaurant. Search the Web for interesting recipes and food ideas. Create a database of your favorite ideas, and create reports based on your research.

To complete this independent challenge:

a. Log on to the Internet, and use your browser to go to http://www.course.com. From there, click Student Online Companions, click the link for this book, then click the Access link for Unit C.

b. Find recipes and food ideas that interest you, and save or print the pages with the best ideas.

c. Start Access, and open the database Recipes.

d. Open the Recipes table, and modify the fields as needed for the data you found.

e. Enter at least 10 records.

f. Create three different reports based on your data. One report must be based on a query.

g. Be sure to include clip art in your report. You can use an image from any source.

h. Preview and print the reports. Save your work. Close the database, and exit Access.

Access 2000

► Visual Workshop

Open the database Runners on your Project Disk. Create the report shown in Figure C-20 based on the Runners table.

FIGURE C-20

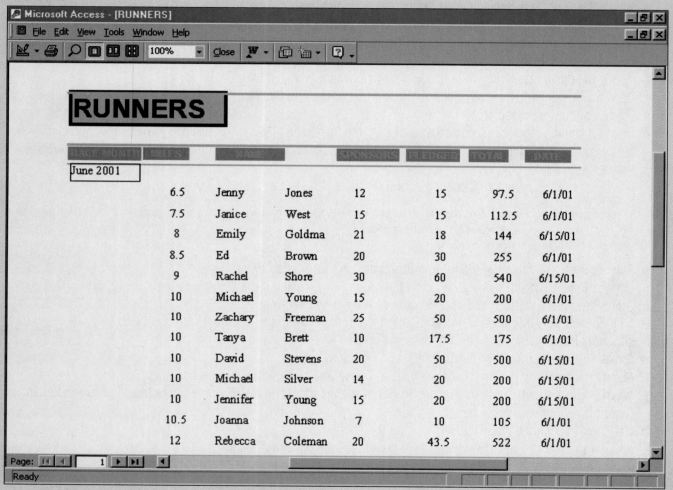

Creating
and Modifying a Presentation

Objectives

- ► **Create a presentation**
- ► **Navigate a presentation**
- ► **Enter text in Outline view**
- ► **Enter text in Slide view**
- ► **Format text**
- ► **Use the Drawing toolbar**
- ► **Add text boxes**
- ► **Check spelling and preview the presentation**

Microsoft PowerPoint is a **presentation graphics** program, a program that makes it easy to create on-screen slide shows, overheads, 35mm slides, and other commonly used business presentation materials. It takes just minutes to turn basic information about a company, product, or other topic into a professional-quality presentation, complete with speaker's notes for you and handouts for your audience. Kimberly Ullom, a sales representative at Outdoor Designs, is preparing for a tour of her retail accounts, where she will present the fall product line. She asks you to prepare a PowerPoint presentation that she can use on these sales calls.

Creating a Presentation

To create an effective presentation, you need to decide what information you want to convey and how you want to convey it. There are several presentation options with PowerPoint, including **on-screen presentations**, where you run a slide show from your computer; 35mm slides, requiring you to take PowerPoint slide files to a film-processing service for conversion; black-and-white or color overheads, which you can print directly on transparencies; and supporting materials, including speaker's notes, audience handouts, and presentation outlines, which are usually printed on paper. The purpose of Kimberly's presentation is to present the new fall product line to retailers. She will be making one-on-one presentations at the headquarters of each retail account, usually in the buyer's office or a small conference room. You decide to create both an on-screen slide show so she can run the presentation on her laptop computer, and speakers notes she can refer to if necessary.

Steps

1. Start **PowerPoint**

   The PowerPoint dialog box is displayed, as shown in Figure A-1. In this dialog box, you can choose to start a new presentation by using the AutoContent Wizard, a PowerPoint template, or a blank presentation. Or, you can open an existing presentation, either by clicking one of the presentations in the list of recently opened files or by locating the file in the Open dialog box.

2. Make sure the **AutoContent Wizard option button** is selected, then click **OK**

   The AutoContent Wizard opens, as shown in Figure A-2. This method offers a quick and easy way to create a presentation. The chart along the left side of the dialog box shows that you complete three simple steps to create the basic presentation: choose a presentation type, a presentation style, and presentation options. Once you have completed the steps in the Wizard, you replace prompt text with the text of your presentation.

3. Click **Next**

   In this dialog box, you can choose from a variety of presentation types. By default, the General button is selected, showing the most common presentation types. To see a different category, you click a different button.

4. Click the **Sales/Marketing button**, click **Product/Services Overview**, then click **Next**

   In the Presentation style dialog box, you specify how the presentation will be **output**, or produced, so that PowerPoint can format it correctly.

5. Click the **On-screen presentation option button** if necessary, then click **Next**

   In the Presentation options dialog box, you specify a name for the presentation and any additional information you want to appear on the slides.

6. Click in the **Presentation title text box** and type **Fall Product Highlights**, then click the **Date last updated checkbox** and the **slide number** checkbox to deselect them

   Compare your screen with Figure A-3.

7. Click **Finish**

8. Click the **Save button** 🖫 on the Standard toolbar, display the drive and folder containing your Project Files, then save the presentation as **Outdoor Designs Sales Presentation**

FIGURE A-1: Starting a new presentation

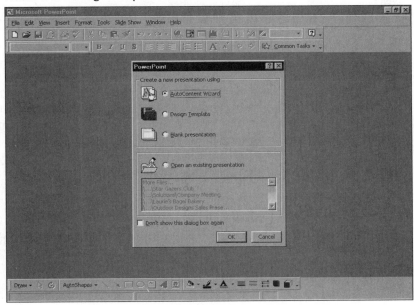

FIGURE A-2: AutoContent Wizard dialog box

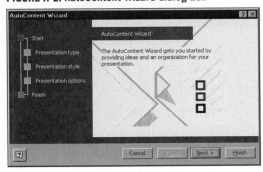

FIGURE A-3: Presentation options dialog box

These buttons
should be deselected

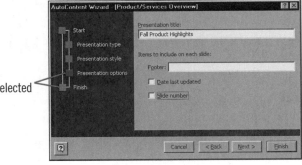

Navigating a Presentation

The PowerPoint program window shares many common features, such as the menu bar and toolbars, with other Office programs. Because a PowerPoint presentation can take many forms, such as an onscreen presentation, printed slides, or transparencies, and may contain additional materials such as speakers notes and audience handouts, you can work in a variety of views: Outline view, Slide view, Slide Sorter view, Notes Page view, Slide Show, and Normal view. ▶ Before customizing the presentation the AutoContent wizard created, you decide to review its contents and familiarize yourself with the PowerPoint program window.

Steps

QuickTip

Normal view, the default PowerPoint view, displays the presentation in three panes, or scrollable windows, so that you can work with several aspects of a presentation at once. In the Outline pane you can work with the text of the presentation. In the Slide pane you can work with all slide elements, including the graphics, and see them exactly as they will appear in an onscreen presentation or a printout, and in the Notes pane you can add speakers notes to remind you of key points.

1. Click **View** on the menu bar, point to **Toolbars**, click **Customize**, click the **Options tab** if necessary, click to deselect the **Standard and Formatting toolbars share one row checkbox** if necessary, click the **Reset my usage data button**, click **Yes** in the message box, then click **Close**

   Now there is room to display more buttons on each toolbar. Figure A-4 identifies many of the important elements in the PowerPoint program window.

2. In the Outline pane, drag the **scroll box** in the vertical scroll bar down slowly

   The AutoContent wizard created a presentation with seven slides. In the Outline pane, you can see only the text of each slide, with slide titles and bullet text indicated in outline levels, but with no indications of graphics or slide formats. In the Slide pane, you can see the slide that is selected in the Outline pane, complete with background and the formatting of the slide elements (such as the title, the bullet point, and the fonts and font sizes).

3. In the Outline pane, click anywhere in the slide title **Availablity** to the right of slide icon 7

   Notice that the Slide pane now displays slide 7. When you change to a different slide in one pane, the other panes reflect the move. The status bar displays "Outline" because you are currently working in the Outline pane.

4. In the Slide pane, click the **Previous Slide button** 🔼 in the vertical scroll bar

   The Slide pane now displays slide 6, titled "Pricing," and the status bar displays "Slide 6 of 7," indicating that you are working in the Slide pane and the 6th slide is active. When you work in the Notes pane, the status bar displays "Notes Page."

5. In the Outline pane, select the word **available** in the bullet text in slide 6, then press **[Delete]**

   The deletion is reflected in both the Outline pane and in the Slide pane, as shown in Figure A-5.

6. In the Slide pane, drag the **scroll box** in the vertical scroll bar up slowly until the ScreenTip reads "Slide: 3 of 7 Features & Benefits," then release the **mouse button**

   In the Slide pane, the ScreenTips display both the slide number and the slide title, so it's easy to navigate to the slide you want.

7. Click in the Notes pane, then type **Kite kits aren't just for kids. Our marketing research shows that sales to adults in the 40-65 age range have increased 38% in the past year.**

   This text does not display in the Outline or Slide pane because it does not appear on the slide itself, only on the speakers notes.

8. Click anywhere in the **Outline pane**, then press **[Ctrl][Home]**

   This keyboard shortcut takes you to slide 1.

FIGURE A-4: PowerPoint Program window

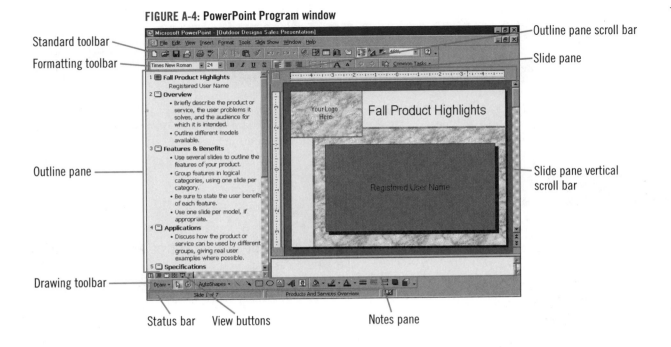

Standard toolbar
Formatting toolbar
Outline pane
Drawing toolbar
Status bar   View buttons
Outline pane scroll bar
Slide pane
Slide pane vertical scroll bar
Notes pane

FIGURE A-5: Navigating through a presentation

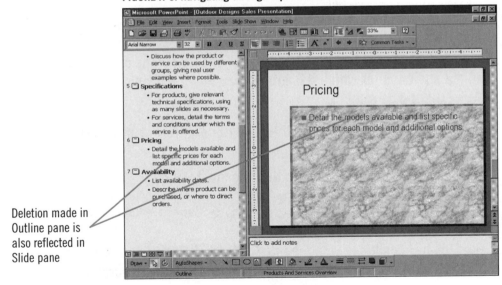

Deletion made in Outline pane is also reflected in Slide pane

PowerPoint 2000

CLUES TO USE

Working with PowerPoint views

When working in PowerPoint, you can quickly switch from view to view using the View menu or the View buttons to the left of the horizontal scroll bar. **Outline view** displays the text of the entire presentation in outline format, similar to a word processor, and is ideal when you are writing or editing content. **Slide view** displays one slide at a time as it will appear when it is output, including the layout, formatting, and any graphics. **Slide Sorter view** is useful for organizing slides and planning transitions. **Slide Show** runs the onscreen presentation. **Notes Page** view (available only on the View menu) lets you add speakers notes to your presentation, which you can then print with or without the accompanying slides. Because Normal view combines the Outline, Slide, and Notes Page views and lets you adjust the size of each pane to suit your needs, you may find this the most convenient view for most of your work.

Entering Text in Outline View

Outline view displays the text of a presentation in outline format, making it easy to enter text and organize the flow of information. ✍ You are ready to customize the content provided by the AutoContent Wizard to match your presentation goals.

Steps

1. In the Outline pane, as shown in Figure A-6, select the first line of text below the heading "Fall Product Highlights," press **[Delete]**, then type **Kimberly Ullom**
   Because Kimberly will be making the sales presentation, you want her name to appear on the first slide of the presentation. Notice that when you make the change in the Outline pane, the text in the Slide pane changes as well.

2. Click the **Outline View button** 🔲 to the left of the horizontal scroll bar in the Outline pane, as shown in Figure A-6, click **View** on the menu bar, point to **Toolbars**, then, if necessary to display the Outlining toolbar, click **Outlining**
   Take a moment to familiarize yourself with Outline view, using Figure A-7 as a reference. This view contains a large Outline pane, with a view of the document text in outline format, as well as a miniature view of the current slide and a small Notes pane. The Outlining toolbar makes it easy to work with levels of text in the outline.

3. Select the text **Briefly describe the product or service, the user problems it solves, and the audience for which it is intended.** under the heading "Overview" in Slide 2

4. Type **Exciting New Products**

5. Select the second line of bulleted text, **Outline different products available.** and type **Exciting New Product Line**

6. Press **[Enter]**, then type **Fantastic New Discount Policy**
   To create a new bullet, you simply press [Enter], as you would in a Word document. The current outline level is automatically assigned to a new line of text and the current slide layout is assigned when a new slide is added.

7. Select the text beginning with the title **Features & Benefits** and ending with the last bullet text of the last slide (**Describe where product can be purchased, or where to direct orders**), press **[Delete]**, then click **Yes** to confirm the deletion
   The slides you deleted do not match your plans for this presentation.

8. Press **[Enter]**, click the **Promote button** 🔲 on the Outlining toolbar, then type **New Products for Fall**
   Creating new slides in Outline view is easy. You press [Enter] to start a new line of text, and use the buttons on the Formatting toolbar to **promote** text, moving it up one outline level, or **demote** it, moving it down one level. The highest level you can promote a line of text to is the slide title. There are several subordinate levels available. PowerPoint formats the text as title text and assigns a number and slide layout to the slide, as shown in Figure A-7.

9. Press **[Enter]**, click the **Demote button** 🔲 on the Outlining toolbar, type **NightSky 3000 Tent**, press **[Enter]**, type **North by North Beach Kite Kit**, then save your changes

Trouble?
If you deleted the paragraph return between the first and second bullet point, simply press [Enter] after typing the text.

FIGURE A-6: Outline view

Selected text

Outline view button

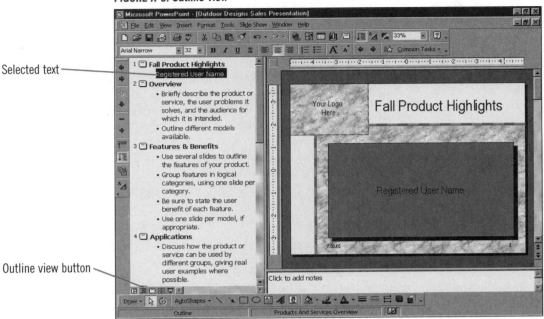

FIGURE A-7: Demoting a line of text

Promote button (active when selected text is not already at highest level)

Demote button

Outlining toolbar

Some Outlining buttons are also available on Formatting toolbar

Text is promoted to a slide title for a new Slide 3, formatted like the previous slide

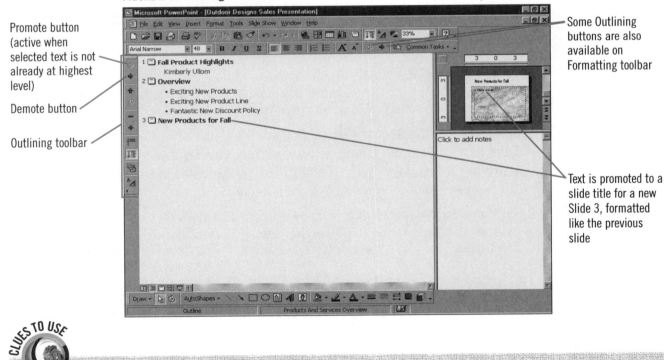

CLUES TO USE

Working with text in Outline view

You work with text in Outline view just as you do with an outline in a word processor such as Microsoft Word. An Outlining toolbar, which appears along the left edge of the screen, provides shortcuts to common outlining actions such as promoting or demoting text, viewing selected levels of the outline, and moving text around. For example, the Collapse button ⊟ displays only the titles of the selected slide or slides so you can view them without being distracted by the slide text. The Move Up button ⬆ moves the selected text above the previous line. To change the layout of a slide while in Outline view, click anywhere in the slide text, click Common Tasks on the Formatting toolbar, then click Slide Layout. A dialog box opens to let you choose a different layout.

Entering Text in Slide View

Slide view lets you see exactly how a slide will appear as you enter and edit text, graphics, and other elements. It also provides a reduced view of the Outline pane, which you can hide or enlarge if you wish, and a bar for opening the Notes pane if necessary. This view is best for working with the appearance of a slide, but you can also use it to enter and edit text. On a slide, each graphic or line of text is an **object**, which can be moved, resized or edited. To edit the text within a text object, click the object, then move the insertion point to the appropriate location. You decide to use Slide view to enter text for three more slides.

Steps

1. **Click the Slide view button 🔲 to the left of the horizontal scroll bar**
   The current slide appears in Slide view, as shown in Figure A-8.

2. **Click Common Tasks on the Formatting toolbar, then click New Slide**
   You want to create a new slide to contain information about the new product line. The New Slide dialog box opens, as shown in Figure A-9. In this dialog box, you specify an AutoLayout for the new slide you want to create. An **AutoLayout** contains formatting and **placeholders** for text and graphics. The preview box shows the name of the currently selected AutoLayout.

3. **Click the first box in the bottom row** (Text & ClipArt), **then click OK**
   You decide to use this AutoLayout for the food kits product line. This AutoLayout contains placeholders for a title, a bulleted list, and a piece of clip art.

4. **Click the title placeholder, which is labeled "Click to add title"**
   A **selection box** appears around the placeholder, indicating that you can enter or edit text at the insertion point, use the sizing boxes to resize the placeholder, or drag any edge to move it.

5. **Type Back Country Gourmet Kits, click in the bulleted list placeholder, type Dehydrated Food Kits for Gourmet Campers, press [Enter], type Lightweight, press [Enter], type Nutritious & Delicious!, press [Enter], then type Available in September**
   You will insert clip art for this slide in the next unit.

QuickTip
You can also use the Insert menu or the New Slide button 🔲 on the Standard toolbar to insert a new slide.

6. **Create and enter text for two more slides based on the information below:**

Use this AutoLayout:	In Title Placeholder type:	In Bulleted List Placeholder type:
Bulleted List	Improved Discount Policy	• 60% discount for orders over $1000
		• 62% discount for orders over $2000
		• 64% discount for orders over $3000
Bulleted List	Thanks for a Great Year So Far!	• Sales are up 58%!
		• 78 new retail partners!
		• Let's keep the business booming!

QuickTip
To move to a different slide in Slide view or the Slide pane, you can use the arrows and scroll box on the vertical scroll bar, click the Next Slide and Previous Slide buttons at the bottom of the scroll bar, click the desired slide icon in the Outline pane, or press the [PgUp] and [PgDn] keys on the keyboard.

7. **Drag the scroll box on the vertical scroll bar up to the top of the scroll bar to move to Slide 1**

8. **Click after the text "Kimberly Ullom," press [Enter], type Outdoor Designs, then save your changes**
   Compare your screen with Figure A-10.

FIGURE A-8: Slide view

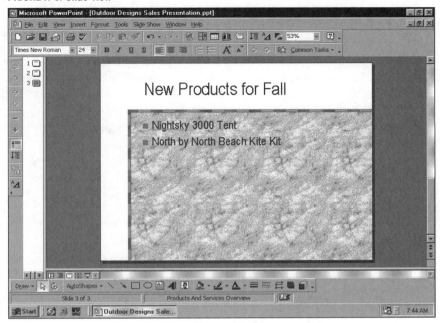

FIGURE A-9: New Slide dialog box

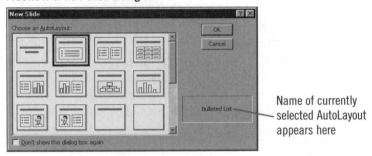

Name of currently
selected AutoLayout
appears here

FIGURE A-10: Edited slide

Icons for new slides

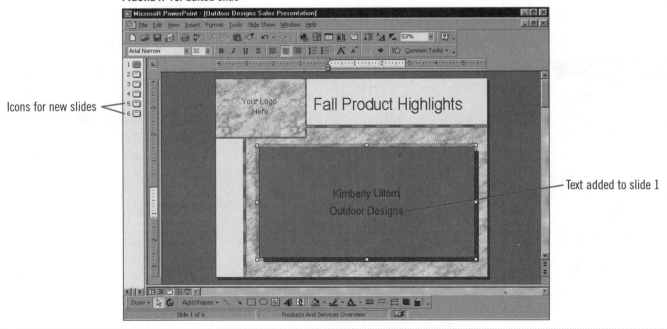

Text added to slide 1

PowerPoint 2000

PowerPoint 2000

Formatting Text

You can format text in a presentation to make certain messages stand out. In a bulleted list, for example, you might want to distinguish one point by changing its color or selecting a different font type. You can format selected text or turn on formatting options before typing new text. As with entering and editing text, you can format text in Outline view or Slide view. ✒ You want to format some of the text in Kimberly's sales presentation to highlight important information, such as her name, the company name, and the agenda for the presentation. You should still be in Slide view, with the first slide active.

Steps

1. **Press [Shift], then click in the main text box**
   This keyboard shortcut selects all the text in the text box. The Font Size list box shows that the current font size is 32 points.

2. **Click the Font Size list arrow on the Formatting toolbar, then scroll to and click 48**

QuickTip

To access more formatting options using the Font dialog box, click Format on the menu bar, then click Font.

3. **Select the text Outdoor Designs, then click the Increase Font Size button A on the Formatting toolbar twice**
   The size of the selected text changes to 60 points. See Table A-1 for a description of the buttons on the Formatting toolbar.

4. **Click Format on the menu bar, click Font, in the Font dialog box click the Color list arrow, click More Colors, then click the Standard tab if necessary**
   The Colors dialog box contains a large palette of colors from which to choose. Below the color palette is a black and white palette, which is useful when you are preparing a presentation that will be printed on a black and white printer.

5. **Click the shade of green shown in Figure A-11, click OK, click OK to close the Font dialog box, then click outside the text to deselect it**
   The new color reflects the active, natural image of Outdoor Designs.

6. **Select the text Kimberly Ullom, click the Font Color list arrow A ▾ on the Drawing toolbar, then click the shade of white (the first box in the second row)**

7. **Click the Next slide button ▼ at the bottom of the vertical scroll bar**

Trouble?

If you click ≣ too many times, simply click ≣ to reduce spacing.

8. **Press [Shift], click anywhere in the bulleted text, click the Bold button B on the Formatting toolbar, then click the Shadow button S on the Formatting toolbar**

9. **Click Format on the menu bar, click Line Spacing, click the Line spacing text box to select the text, type 1.5, click OK, then click outside the bullet text to deselect it**
   The bold and shadow attributes and the increased line spacing help each point stand out, as shown in Figure A-12.

FIGURE A-11: Changing font color

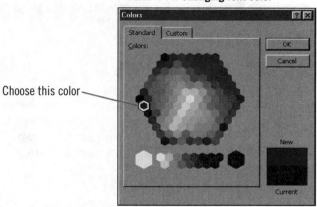

Choose this color

FIGURE A-12: Formatted text

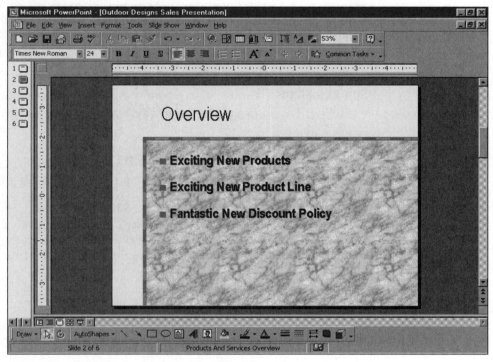

TABLE A-1: Formatting toolbar buttons

toolbar button	description	toolbar button	description
B	Turns on bold formatting	☰	Formats text in bullets
I	Turns on italic formatting	A	Increases font size
U	Turns on underlining	A	Decreases font size
S	Turns on text shadow formatting	←	Promotes text one level
☰	Turns on left alignment	→	Demotes text one level
☰	Turns on center alignment	⭐	Opens a palette of animation effects
☰	Turns on right alignment	Common Tasks ▼	Opens the Common Tasks menu
☰	Formats text in numbered bullets		

Using the Drawing Toolbar

The Drawing toolbar contains drawing tools that let you enhance your presentations with shapes, lines and simple pictures. Like text boxes and graphics, the shapes and lines you create are objects that can be moved, resized, and formatted. The AutoShape button opens a list of several custom shape categories to speed up your drawing tasks. You decide to add graphics—a sun and a moon—to two slides in Kimberly's presentation.

Steps

1. Click the **Previous Slide button** on the vertical scroll bar
   The first slide in the presentation contains a placeholder box for inserting a company logo.

2. Click **AutoShapes** on the Drawing toolbar, then click **Basic Shapes**
   The Basic Shapes palette opens, as shown in Figure A-13. Refer to the figure for guidance in locating the shape and drawing it on the slide.

3. Click the **Sun AutoShape**, then when the pointer changes to + click above and to the right of the **Your Logo Here placeholder text**, then drag down and to the bottom left corner of the logo box

4. Make sure the Sun shape is selected, click the **Fill Color list arrow**, click **More Fill Colors**, then click the **Custom tab** in the Colors dialog box if necessary

5. Click the **yellow color** and drag the **slider** up, as shown in Figure A-14, then click **OK**
   The color of the new AutoShape brightens up. In the Colors dialog box, you can choose a custom color by clicking anywhere in the palette or entering values in the text boxes below it, and adjust the luminosity of the selected color by dragging the slider to achieve the effect you want.

6. Press **[PgDn]** twice to move to the third slide
   This slide contains two bullet points.

7. Click **AutoShapes**, click **Basic Shapes**, click the **Moon shape**, press and hold **[Shift]**, click to the right of the bulleted text and drag down to the bottom right corner to draw a moon, release the mouse button and [Shift], click the **Fill Color list arrow**, then click the **white box**
   Pressing and holding [Shift] while you draw or resize a shape maintains its original proportions. See Table A-2 to learn more about working with objects.

8. Click **Draw** on the Drawing toolbar, click **Rotate or Flip**, click **Flip Horizontal**, then click away from the shape to deselect it
   The moon looks better facing this new direction.

9. Click on the Drawing toolbar, click the **Moon shape**, click the **Shadow button**, click the **second box in the second row** of the Shadow palette, click away from the shape, then save your changes
   Compare your screen with Figure A-15.

FIGURE A-13: Drawing with an AutoShape

In Step 4, click here to begin drawing

In Step 4, release mouse button to finish drawing here

Sun AutoShape

FIGURE A-14: Custom tab of the Colors dialog box

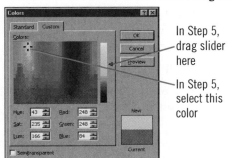

In Step 5, drag slider here

In Step 5, select this color

FIGURE A-15: Formatted AutoShape

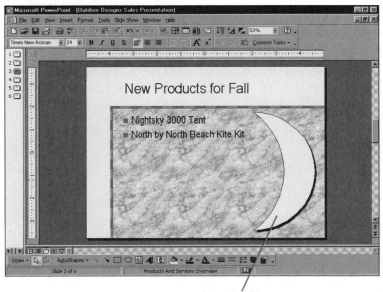

Moon AutoShape, with new fill color and drop shadow

TABLE A-2: Working with Objects

if you want to	do this
Select an object	Click the Selection button 🔲 on the Drawing toolbar, then click the object you want to select
Move an object	Select the object, then click in the middle of the object and drag in the desired direction
Resize an object	Select the object, then drag a corner sizing handle in the desired direction. Press [Shift] while dragging to maintain the object's proportions
Delete an object	Select the object, then press [Delete]
Draw a proportional object	Press [Shift] while drawing a circle or square to make it proportional from the edge of the object; Press [Ctrl] to make it proportional from the center of the object

PowerPoint 2000

Adding Text Boxes

You can use the Drawing toolbar to add text boxes to a slide. **Text boxes** are similar to text place-holders but allow more flexibility in terms of the shape and format of the text. You can create text boxes where text does not automatically wrap to the next line. These are useful for labels and brief messages. By layering text boxes over existing shapes, you can bring important messages to life. ▰▰▰ Kimberly asks you to add a last-minute addition to the discount policy: All orders posted by August 15 receive free shipping. You decide to use a text box and an AutoShape on the "Improved Discount Policy" slide to make the new information stand out.

Steps

1. Click the **Next Slide button** on the vertical scroll bar twice to move to the fifth slide
   Under the last bullet on the slide titled "Improved Discount Policy", there is room to insert a graphic to contain the new discount information.

2. Click **AutoShapes**, click **Stars and Banners**, click the **second shape (Explosion 2)**, click in the **upper left corner of the blank area below the bulleted list**, then click and drag to the **bottom right corner of the main text area**
   An Explosion shape is inserted and filled with the default color. If necessary, move or resize your shape so it matches Figure A-16.

QuickTip

You can also add text to a shape by right-clicking in the shape where you want to begin typing. Press [Enter] when you want the text to wrap to a new line.

3. Click the **Text Box button** 🔳 on the Drawing toolbar, click in the **upper left corner** of the Explosion shape, then when the cursor changes to ╋, click and drag down and to the right to draw a rectangle that fits within the edges of the Explosion shape

4. Type **Free Shipping**, press **[Enter]** if you have not reached the end of the text box, type **til August 15!**, then click outside the text label
   As in other programs, the AutoCorrect feature corrects apparent errors as you type. AutoCorrect automatically capitalizes the first letter of the word "til" after you pressed [Spacebar] if it begins a new line.

QuickTip

When you create a text box, you do not need to click in the box before entering text. Once you release the mouse button after drawing the box, simply begin typing.

5. Click to select the text box, select the two lines of text, press **[Ctrl][B]**, click the **Font Type list box** on the Formatting toolbar and click **Arial Narrow**, click the **Font Size list box** and click **28**, then click outside the text
   This formatting makes the text easier to read. You format text in a text box just as you do in other slide text: by selecting it, then using the Format menu, the Formatting toolbar, or a keyboard shortcut. Text you type wraps automatically to maintain the width of the text box.

6. Select the **text box**, select the two lines, click the **Center button** 🔳 on the Formatting toolbar, then click away from the text

QuickTip

Remember that you can select any object by clicking the Selection tool on the Drawing toolbar, then clicking the object you want to select.

7. Select the **Explosion shape**, click the **Fill Color button list arrow** 🔳 on the Drawing toolbar, then click the yellow color (the first box in the second row)
   Because you used this custom color elsewhere in the presentation, it now appears on the standard fill palette. The slide is complete. Compare your screen with Figure A-17.

8. Save your changes

FIGURE A-16: Explosion 2 star AutoShape

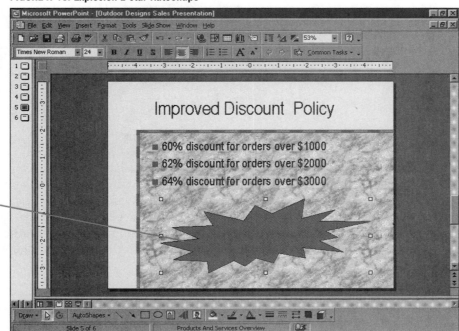

In Step 2, place and size the explosion AutoShape so it is similar to this one

FIGURE A-17: Completed text box stacked on explosion shape

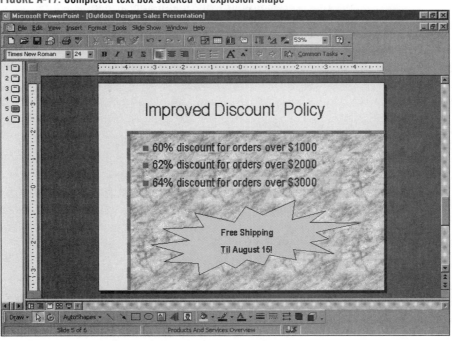

Working with stacked objects

Inserting one object on top of another object is called **stacking** the objects. The last object you insert is on top, or in the front, of the stack. You can change the stacking order by right-clicking an object, clicking Order on the submenu, then clicking an option to send the object closer to the back or closer to the front of the stacking order. Click Bring to Front or Send to Back to move the object to the very front or back of a stack of objects. Click Bring Forward or Send Backward to move the object only one layer in either direction.

Checking Spelling and Previewing the Presentation

PowerPoint contains tools for ensuring that your presentation is free of errors before you run it in front of an audience. The AutoCorrect feature corrects common spelling and typing errors as you work. The Spelling Checker underlines additional misspellings as you type, and you can run the Spell Checking feature to find and correct these additional errors all at once. You can preview your work in Slide Sorter view to check the flow of information and the overall design, then run the presentation in Slide Show view to see the slides full-screen. ◀━━ You're almost ready to show Kimberly the first draft of the sales presentation. First, you want to run the Spelling Checker. Then you want to review your work in Slide Sorter view to decide whether the flow of information is logical.

Steps 1 2 3 4

1. Press **[Ctrl][Home]** to move to the beginning of the presentation

2. Click **Tools** on the menu bar, then click **Spelling**
   The spelling check begins. The Spelling dialog box opens when it finds a word it doesn't recognize. As shown in Figure A-18, the first word it finds is "Nightsky". (If you made typing errors before this point, another word might appear here.)

3. Click **Ignore All**
   Although the Spelling Checker doesn't recognize this word, you know it is spelled as the manufacturer intended. The spelling check continues. The next misspelled word is "Til". The suggested correction, "Till", is selected in the Change to text box.

4. Scroll through the list of suggestions to find the word "Until"
   This word does not appear in the list.

5. Type **Until**, then click **Change**
   The spell check continues.

6. If necessary, respond to any additional prompts in the Spelling dialog box, then click **OK** when you get the message that the spelling check is complete

7. Click the **Slide Sorter View button** ▦ to the left of the horizontal scroll bar
   The presentation is displayed in **Slide Sorter view**, which shows all the slides in the presentation in miniature and allows you to move them easily.

8. Click **slide 5** to select it if necessary, then drag it on top of **slide 6**
   The "Improved Discount Policy" slide becomes slide 6, changing places with the "Thanks for a great year so far!" slide, as shown in Figure A-19. It makes more sense to discuss the new discount policy after thanking buyers for a great year.

9. Click **slide 1**, click the **Slide Show View button** ▭ to the left of the horizontal scroll bar, press **[Spacebar]** to move through each slide in order, then save and close the presentation

FIGURE A-18: Spelling dialog box

FIGURE A-19: Slide Sorter view

Currently selected slide

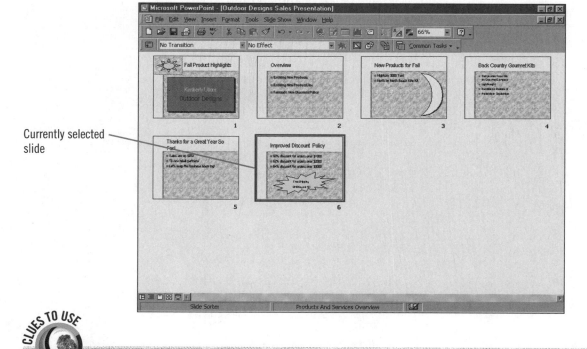

CLUES TO USE

Working with the Spelling Checker

The Spelling Checker feature works by finding words within the main text of a presentation that are not contained in PowerPoint's dictionary files, and suggesting alternative spellings. You should also review the text of a presentation to find any grammatical or word usage errors (such as "it's" instead of "its"). In the Spelling dialog box, you can leave the word as it is by clicking Ignore or Ignore All (to ignore all instances of this word in the presentation), change the spelling to the highlighted suggestion by clicking Change or Change All (to change all instances of this word to the suggested alternative), choose a different spelling in the Suggestions list by clicking it, enter your own correction in the Change to text box, add the word to your custom dictionary file so that PowerPoint never flags it again, or stop checking spelling by clicking Close.

Practice

► Concepts Review

Label each of the PowerPoint elements shown in Figure A-20.

FIGURE A-20

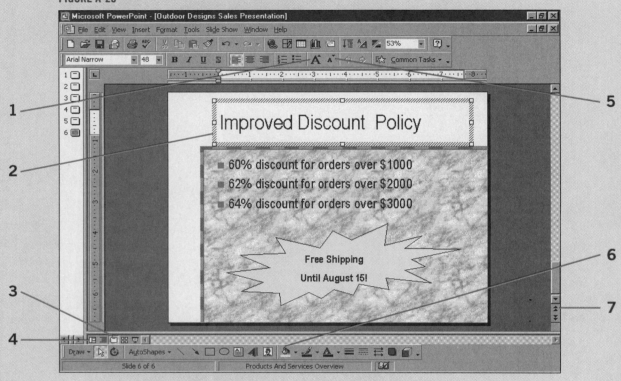

Match each of the following views with the activity for which it is most useful.

8. Outline view   a. Running the slide full-screen, one slide at a time
9. Normal view   b. Working with Presentation content, individual slides, and speakers notes all at once
10. Slide Sorter view   c. Working with slide text
11. Slide Show view   d. Rearranging the order of slides

Select the best answer from the list of choices.

12. **A presentation graphics program is primarily used to**
    a. Create presentation materials such as slides and transparencies.
    b. Create clip art.
    c. Run videos on personal computers.
    d. Compose lectures.

13. **A PowerPoint presentation may include**
    a. 35mm slides.
    b. Speaker's notes.
    c. Handouts.
    d. All of the above.

14. **An on-screen presentation involves**
    a. Demonstrating the use of a computer program using a laptop computer.
    b. Running a PowerPoint slide show from a computer.
    c. Opening Word files and scrolling through them with a client or customer.
    d. Processing PowerPoint slides into 35mm color slides.

15. **Which of the following is *not* a valid way to start creating a PowerPoint presentation?**
    a. Use the AutoContent Wizard
    b. Use a Presentation Design template
    c. Use the Blank Presentation Design template
    d. Use Slide Sorter view

16. **The Common Tasks button is located on the**
    a. Standard toolbar
    b. Formatting toolbar
    c. Outline pane
    d. Menu bar

17. **When you click the A button on the Formatting toolbar, it**
    a. Promotes the current line of text to the next level.
    b. Decreases the current font size.
    c. Increases the current font size.
    d. Changes the current font color.

18. **You can use the AutoShapes button to**
    a. Import clip art.
    b. Draw freestyle designs.
    c. Fill shapes with color.
    d. Change slide shapes.

PowerPoint 2000

19. **Which view button do you click to switch to Slide view?**
    a.
    b. ⊞
    c. 🖵
    d. None of the above

▶ Skills Review

1. **Create a presentation.**
    a. Identify three goals for a new presentation: make an informational presentation to the Outdoor Designs staff regarding company performance; inform employees about the status of sales and marketing goals; and recognize outstanding individuals.
    b. Start PowerPoint.
    c. Start a new presentation using the AutoContent Wizard.
    d. In the Presentation style dialog box of the AutoContent Wizard, select the Company Meeting presentation type in the Corporate category. If prompted to install this template, insert your Office 2000 CD and click Yes.
    e. In the Presentation dialog box, choose the On-Screen presentation type.
    f. In the Presentation Options dialog box, do not type a title or deselect any check boxes.
    g. After completing the wizard, save the presentation as "Fall Company Meeting".

2. **Navigate a presentation.**
    a. In the Outline pane, drag the scroll box in the vertical scroll bar down slowly, pausing to read the content of the entire presentation.
    b. Click anywhere in the text of the slide 13.
    c. In the Slide pane, click the previous slide button on the vertical scroll bar to move to Slide 12.
    d. In the Outline pane, scroll to and click in the bullet or title text of Slide 7 to move to that slide.
    e. In the Slide pane, drag the vertical scroll box down until the ScreenTip reads "Slide: 9 of 13 Revenue and Profit."
    f. Click in the Notes pane and type "Outdoor Designs has increased its market share by 10% in the past year."
    g. Click anywhere in the Outline pane, then press [Ctrl][Home] to move to the beginning of the first slide.
    h. Save your changes.

3. **Enter text in Outline view.**
    a. Switch to Outline view. Display the Outlining toolbar in necessary.
    b. Click after the title "Agenda" in the second slide, then press [Enter].
    c. Click the Demote button on the Outlining toolbar.
    d. Enter the following text in bulleted list format: Review Key Objectives; Review Our Progress; Discuss Top Issues; Explain Goals for Next Period; Summary.
    e. Select all the slide text from slide 5 through slide 11, then delete it.
    f. Save your changes.

4. **Enter text in Slide view.**
    a. Switch to Slide view.
    b. Use the Previous slide button to move to slide 4.
    c. Click the Common Tasks button on the Formatting toolbar, then click New Slide.
    d. In the New Slide dialog box, choose the layout containing two bulleted lists, then click OK.
    e. Click in the title placeholder of the new slide, and type "Shining Stars".

f. Click the left placeholder text labeled "Click to add text", and type "Frasier Cary".

g. Click the right placeholder text labeled "Click to add text", and type "Kimberly Ullom".

5. Format text.

a. Change the font size of the names "Frasier Cary" and "Kimberly Ullom" to 36 points.

b. Select the text "Frasier Cary," then use the Color list box in the Font dialog box to change the font color to the shade of dark green that follows the Accent and Followed Hyperlink Scheme color.

c. Move to the previous slide, titled "How Did We Do?," then use [Shift] to select all of the main text.

d. Format the selection in bold and italic.

e. Select the word "Brief", then use the Color list box in the Font dialog box to change the font color to the shade of tan that follows the Accent and Hyperlink Scheme color.

f. Save your changes.

6. Use the Drawing toolbar.

a. Move to slide 5, titled "Shining Stars."

b. Use the Stars and Banners AutoShapes menu on the Drawing toolbar to draw one vertical scroll banner approximately 1" long under Frasier's name and another, slightly shorter vertical scroll banner under Kimberly's name. Each banner should span the width of the name above it.

c. Use the Rotate or Flip command on the Draw menu to horizontally flip the banner under Kimberly's name.

d. Select the banner under Frasier's name, and use the Line Color button on the Drawing toolbar to change the line color to the shade of dark green that follows the Accent and Followed Hyperlink Scheme color.

e. Save your changes.

7. Add text objects.

a. Click the Text box tool on the Drawing toolbar, then click and drag to create a text box in the banner under Frasier's name that extends almost to the edges of the banner.

b. Enter the text "Marketing initiatives have paid off!" in the text box. (*Hint*: You may need to increase the size of the banner.)

c. Create another text box in the second banner that reads "Top Sales Representative!"

d. Select each text box, and center-align it.

e. Save your changes.

8. Check spelling and preview the presentation.

a. Run the Spelling Checker, and correct any spelling errors in the presentation.

b. Change to Slide Sorter view, and view the slides.

c. Change the order of the third and fourth slides.

d. Change to Slide Show view.

e. Press [Spacebar] to progress through each slide title, bullet point, and slide.

f. When you return to Slide Sorter view, close the presentation, saving changes when prompted.

PowerPoint 2000

▶ Independent Challenges

1. The Wacky Words Card Company is looking for ways to explore new greeting card markets and distribute their cards through more retail channels. You've been assigned the task of creating a presentation that introduces potential customers to Wacky Words. You've heard of Dale Carnegie, author of *How to Win Friends and Influence People*, so you decide to use a template designed by the Dale Carnegie Institute to create your presentation.

To complete this independent challenge:

a. Start PowerPoint or, if PowerPoint is currently running, open the New dialog box.

b. Click the Presentations tab, then scroll down to the bottom of the list and click the template titled "Selling Your Ideas." View the Preview, then click OK.

c. Switch to Slide Show view, and view the slide show.

d. Save the presentation as "Wacky Words Introduction."

e. Switch to Normal view if necessary, move to the first slide in the presentation, then modify text throughout the presentation to achieve your goal of presenting the Wacky Words company to prospective new customers in the best possible light. Follow the Wacky words philosophy that greeting cards enhance the quality of life of those who give and receive them. Use testimonials from happy customers and any tools to prove that Wacky Words cards are a valuable resource that no retailer should be without.

f. Delete any slides that do not meet your needs, and add new slides as necessary.

g. Use drawing shapes and formatting to enhance your message as appropriate.

h. When you are finished, check the spelling in the presentation, preview your work in Slide Sorter view, and adjust the placement of individual slides if necessary.

i. Run the Slide show in Slide Show view.

j. Save your changes, and close the presentation.

2. The Microsoft Web site offers several tools for becoming a more effective PowerPoint user. The Product PowerPoint Web site contains several resources for learning more about PowerPoint, communicating with other PowerPoint users, and downloading additional materials related to PowerPoint. Explore the Product PowerPoint Web site now, and visit a newsgroup to find out how other users are using PowerPoint in the workplace. (Note that you need to have a newsreader, such as Microsoft Outlook Newsreader, installed on your system in order to complete this project.)

a. Start PowerPoint if necessary.

b. If necessary, connect to the Internet.

c. Click Help on the menu bar, then click Office on the Web.

d. On the Product PowerPoint Web site, click the Assistance link to move to the Assistance page.

e. On the Assistance page, click the PowerPoint Newsgroups link.

f. On the PowerPoint Newsgroups page, click the Miscellaneous Office questions link.

g. In the microsoft.public.office.misc newsgroup, click message headers that interest you, read their contents, and reply to messages if you have additional information to add.

h. If you wish, post your own question or comment about PowerPoint.

i. When you are finished, exit your newsreader program. If prompted, do not subscribe to the microsoft.public.office.misc newsgroup.

j. Disconnect from the Internet if necessary, then close PowerPoint.

3. Stuff For Pets is preparing to expand by opening a new store on the south side of town. In order to finance the opening of the store, investor support is needed. Six individuals who invested in the first Stuff for Pets Store are pleased with its success, and the store owner has organized a meeting with them to propose the expansion. You have been asked to create a marketing plan that will inspire investors to commit funds so the new store can open quickly.

The new store will feature the most extensive line of tropical fish and supplies in the state. The south side location is considered somewhat remote, but this side of town is growing rapidly. You want to establish the new store before a national chain comes in with the same idea. Sales for the original Stuff for Pets have been growing at a rate of over 15% each year. It is your belief that establishing another store will increase the visibility of the first store, increasing sales by over 20%. You expect sales at the new store to reach $100,000 in the first year, though profits will be low due to start-up costs.

To complete this independent challenge:

a. Start PowerPoint if necessary.

b. Use the AutoContent Wizard to create a Marketing Plan. The presentation will be presented using a slide projector, so plan to output PowerPoint slides and take them to a film processor to be developed into 35mm slides.

c. Save the presentation as "Stuff for Pets Expansion."

d. Customize the content, formatting, and other elements to create an effective, inspiring marketing plan.

e. Check the spelling of the presentation before viewing it in Slide Show view.

f. When you are satisfied with the presentation, close it, saving your changes.

4. Office Assistant can extend your knowledge of PowerPoint by answering specific questions. As you continue working in PowerPoint, you may want to create presentations that are more interactive, especially for clients and co-workers with whom you communicate over the Internet. Find out how you can use the Internet to produce and enhance your PowerPoint presentations.

To complete this independent challenge:

a. Start PowerPoint if it is not currently open.

b. Open Office Assistant by clicking Help on the menu bar, then clicking Show the Office Assistant.

c. Type "Create online presentations."

d. Explore the topics Office Assistant provides, clicking links to read related text and topics.

e. Print at least two topics concerning publishing a presentation on the Web and collaborating with others on a presentation.

f. When you are finished, close Office Assistant.

▶ Visual Workshop

Create the slide shown in Figure A-21 using the skills you have learned in this unit. The Presentation template is available in the Presentations tab of the New dialog box. (*Hint*: The bagel graphic was created using three tools on the Drawing toolbar, including the More Colors option of the Fill Colors tool. The second bagel was copied from the first.) When you have finished, save the presentation as "Laurie's Bagel Bakery", then print the slide using the Print button on the Standard toolbar.

FIGURE A-21

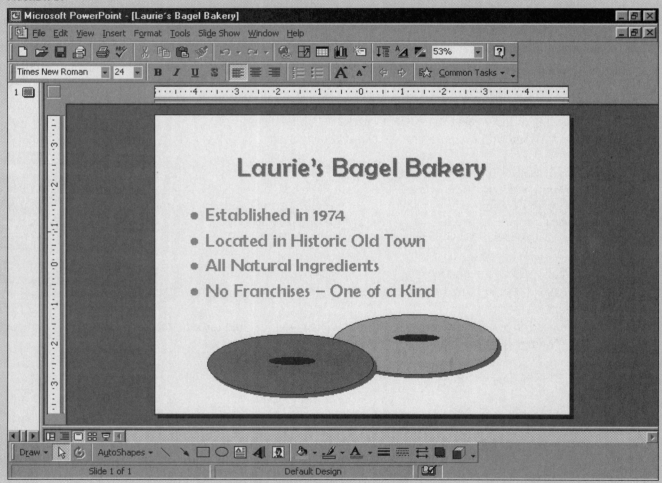

Polishing
and Running a Presentation

Objectives

- ► Change the color scheme of an existing presentation
- ► Use clip art
- ► Work with pictures
- ► Run an online slide show
- ► Set preset timing and transitions
- ► Set animation effects
- ► Create speaker's notes and printed materials

You can enhance a PowerPoint presentation by changing colors, adding graphics, and customizing other visual elements. If you plan to run your presentation on a PC, you can use PowerPoint controls to advance through the presentation at your own pace. If you prefer, you can set the timing of the slides to advance automatically, and use special effects to add impact. ✎ Kimberly Ullom, sales representative for Outdoor Designs, is pleased with the progress of her sales presentation. She suggests that you modify the colors of the slide show to suit the fall theme and add a graphic to highlight a new product. She plans to run the slide show automatically, so you'll need to set timing and effects. Finally, she asks you to add some notes to help her remember key points.

PowerPoint 2000

Changing the Color Scheme of an Existing Presentation

Each PowerPoint presentation template contains a preset **color scheme**, a set of eight coordinated colors for each element in a presentation, including the slide background, title text, and fills and shadows. Every slide or element you create is automatically formatted with these colors so the entire presentation looks professional. You can choose a different color scheme or modify aspects of it to customize your presentation. ✎▬▬ You decide to change the color scheme of the sales presentation to include a fall color.

QuickTip
If PowerPoint is already running, click File on the menu bar, then click Open.

1. Start PowerPoint, in the startup dialog box click the **Open an existing presentation option button**, then click **OK**
   The Open dialog box appears. The preview box displays the first slide in the selected presentation.

2. Click the **Look in list arrow**, locate and click the drive that contains your Project files, click **PPT B-1**, then click **Open**

3. Click **File** on the menu bar, click **Save As**, make sure the Save in list box displays the drive containing your Project Files and the filename in the File name text box is selected, type **Fall Sales Presentation**, then click **Save**
   The color scheme of this presentation currently includes a white background color.

QuickTip
If necessary, maximize the PowerPoint program and presentation windows.

4. Scroll through the presentation in the slide pane

5. Click **Format** on the menu bar, then click **Slide Color Scheme**
   In the Color Scheme dialog box, you can change the entire color scheme of a presentation by choosing one of the schemes listed on the Standard tab, or change selected color scheme elements by using the Custom tab.

6. Click the **Custom tab**
   As shown in Figure B-1, this tab lists the eight elements whose colors you can change in a PowerPoint presentation: Background, Text and lines, Shadows, Title text, Fills, Accent, Accent and hyperlink, and Accent and followed hyperlink. The last two options apply only to Web site presentations. The preview box shows the current selected colors for the elements in the current presentation, so you can easily make color choices using the dialog box.

7. Click the **Background color box** as shown in Figure B-1, then click **Change Color**
   In the Background Color dialog box, you can choose one of the colors on the Standard tab, or specify a custom color on the Custom tab.

8. Click the **Standard tab** if necessary, click the **shade** shown in Figure B-2, then click **OK**

QuickTip
Clicking Apply instead of Apply to All would apply the changes only to the current slide or to slides selected in Slide Sorter view.

9. In the Color Scheme dialog box, double-click the **Title text color box**, in the Title Text Color dialog box click the **Standard tab** if necessary, click the **shade of white** in the color palette, click **OK**, click **Apply to All**, then save your changes
   This command applies your color scheme changes to the entire presentation so the color of the title text on all the slides changes to white, which contrasts nicely with the new background color.

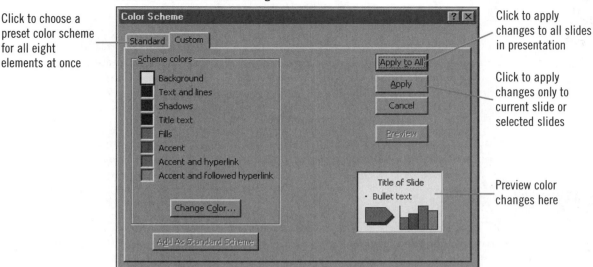

FIGURE B-1: Color Scheme dialog box

Click to choose a preset color scheme for all eight elements at once

Click to apply changes to all slides in presentation

Click to apply changes only to current slide or selected slides

Preview color changes here

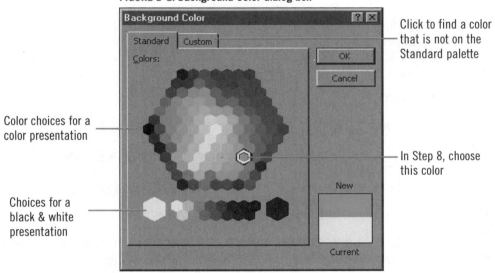

FIGURE B-2: Background Color dialog box

Click to find a color that is not on the Standard palette

Color choices for a color presentation

In Step 8, choose this color

Choices for a black & white presentation

CLUES TO USE

Designing your presentation

When changing the visual elements of your presentation, remember some basic design principles:

- Use colors that contrast and complement each other within a slide and within the whole presentation. The color combinations provided in a design template provide a solid base to work from. Changing more than two or three colors throughout a presentation can weaken the unified, professional look of the finished product.
- If you plan to present on a PC or are using color slides, you can use rich, dark colors for backgrounds and lighter colors for text; if you plan to use transparencies or black and white printouts of your slides, light background and dark text colors

are more effective. The Standard tab of the Color dialog box offers color schemes suitable for both these situations.

- Make choices that support the desired tone of your presentation. A wild combination of colors might be fun to create but detract from your message.
- Edit text as necessary to keep your messages short and simple.
- Use clip art and other pictures that convey information clearly and simply. Complex illustrations or detailed images that are difficult to recognize when shrunk to a small size that will fit on a slide can confuse rather than enlighten.

Using Clip Art

PowerPoint 2000

Graphics files you can use copyright-free, for any purpose, are known as **clip art**. You can insert a clip image anywhere in a PowerPoint slide (some slide layouts contain a clip art placeholder which can be helpful when planning a slide layout). Hundreds of clip images are available on the Microsoft Office CD-ROM, and many of these are installed with PowerPoint. To make it easy to organize and find clip art on your system, on the Office CD-ROM, or on another disk, use the Microsoft Clip Gallery. Kimberly wants to illustrate the food kits from Back Country Gourmet, but the manufacturer did not provide a picture of the new product. You decide to find a piece of clip art to convey the high quality and sophistication of these ready-to-travel meals.

Steps

QuickTip

To insert clip art on a slide that does not have a clip art placeholder, click Insert on the menu bar, point to Picture, then click Insert Clip Art. If you want to insert a picture that is not in the Clip Art gallery, click Insert on the menu bar, point to Picture, click From File, locate the file in the Insert Picture dialog box, then click Insert.

Trouble?

If the clip shown in Figure B-4 does not appear on your screen, click Keep Looking at the bottom of the clips list. If you locate the image but a message box opens requesting that you insert the source CD, insert the appropriate Office 2000 CD and click Try again. This image is also available on your Project Disk. To use it, click Insert on the menu bar, point to Picture, click From File, locate your Project Files, then double-click the Food Platter file.

1. Move to and select **Slide 4**, then double-click the **Double click to add clip art** clip art placeholder
   The Microsoft Clip Gallery, as shown in Figure B-3, displays all clip art currently installed on your system and lets you organize these clips or import others. To browse through the gallery, click a category in the category list, then scroll through the available choices. To search for a clip that is filed under a specific keyword or keywords, type the word or words in the Search for clips text box, then press [Enter]. You can click the Clips Online button to search for more clips on the Web. You can also click the Import Clips button to import clip art from the Office CD-ROM or from another location, such as a disk, to the Clip Gallery.

2. Scroll through the list of categories

3. Click **Food & Dining** in the Categories list

4. Scroll to the clip, as shown in Figure B-4, right-click the **clip**, then in the shortcut menu click **Insert**
   The clip image is inserted in the slide in place of the placeholder.

5. Click the **Close button** in the Insert ClipArt window.

6. Point to the **center of the picture**, then click and drag to the lower-right corner of the slide, as shown in Figure B-5, to move the clip art

7. Compare your screen with Figure B-5 to decide whether you need to resize your image, then if necessary, click the **upper-left corner sizing handle** of the image and drag up and to the left to resize the image
   Your screen should match the screen shown in Figure B-5.

8. Save your changes

Inserting other types of pictures

In addition to inserting clip art, you can insert almost any kind of graphic file in a PowerPoint presentation. These are identified as **pictures** in PowerPoint and may include a scanned photograph, a piece of line art created in a drawing program, or a graphic file such as a JPEG, GIF, or TIF file. To insert a picture, click Insert on the menu bar, point to Picture, and then click From File. Use pictures to customize a presentation by adding your company logo, the picture of a featured product, or other specific visual reference to selected slides.

FIGURE B-3: Microsoft Clip Gallery dialog box

Search for a specific type of clip by typing keyword here, then pressing [Enter]

Categories list

Scroll to see more categories

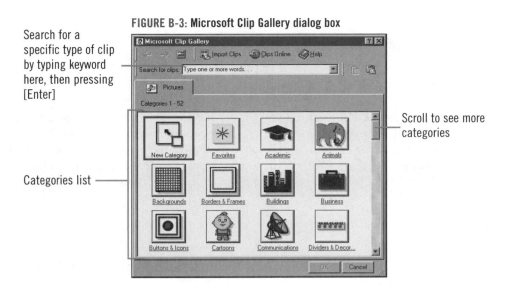

FIGURE B-4: Browsing for a clip

Choose this clip

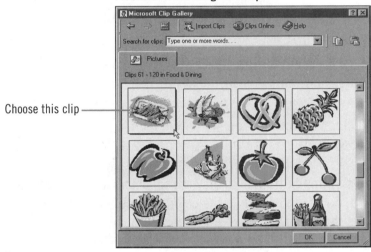

FIGURE B-5: Moving the image

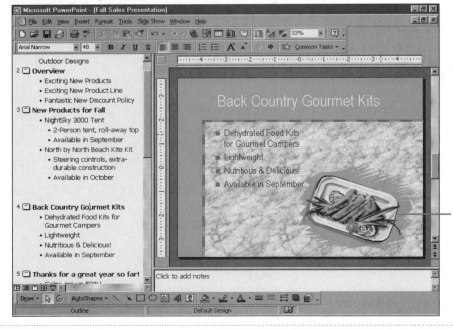

Picture should be this size in this location

Working with Pictures

You can change the formatting and properties of pictures in PowerPoint to suit the needs of your presentation. In addition to simply moving and resizing an image, you can change **image properties,** such as brightness and contrast, change the colors, and even crop an image to use only part of it. ✐ You decide to change the picture on the Back Country Gourmet Kits slide to better coordinate it with your presentation's color scheme.

Steps

Trouble?

If the Picture toolbar is not open on your screen, click View on the menu bar, point to Toolbars, then click Picture.

1. Click the **picture** to select it if necessary, then click the **Image Control button** 🖼 on the Picture toolbar
   A list of image control options opens. See Table B-1 for a list of the Picture toolbar buttons.

2. Click **Black & White**, review the change, click 🖼 again, then click **Automatic** to return to the default colors

3. Click the **More Contrast button** 🔲 on the Picture toolbar three times, then click the **More Brightness button** ☀ once
   Note the increase in contrast and brightness as you click.

4. Click the **Recolor Picture button** 🖼 on the Picture toolbar
   The Recolor Picture dialog box opens, as shown in Figure B-6. In this dialog box, you can change the background colors and fill colors in a picture.

5. Click the **Fills option button** to display the fill colors, click the **check box** next to the shade of pink **color box**, which is the color of the plate, then click the **color box list arrow** next to that color
   A color palette opens. In the top row are colors that match the current color scheme of the presentation. In the bottom row are custom colors.

6. Click the **green box**, click **OK**, then click outside the picture to deselect it
   The color of the plate changes to green. It looks slightly brighter than it did in the dialog box because of the previous formatting changes you made to the picture.

7. Click the **picture** to select it, then click the **Format Picture button** 🖼 on the Picture toolbar
   In the Format Picture dialog box, you can make all of the changes available on the Picture toolbar, such as cropping, changing fill and line colors, and changing image control, plus many more, and you can make some changes with a greater degree of control. For example, when cropping, you can enter the exact amount you want to trim from the picture.

QuickTip

When you print a slide that contains a transparent color, the color appears solid.

8. Click the **Colors and Lines tab**, in the Fill area click the **Color list box**, click the **white box** in the top row, click the **Semitransparent check box** to select it, click **OK**, then click anywhere outside the picture to deselect it
   The semitransparent fill makes the picture stand out more distinctly from the rest of the slide. Compare your screen with Figure B-7.

9. Save your changes to the presentation

FIGURE B-6: Recolor Picture dialog box

Click a check box to change the accompanying color, then click the New list box to the right to choose a color

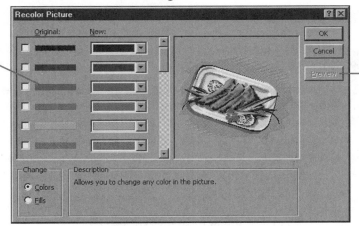

Click to preview the effect of the change on the slide

FIGURE B-7: Background of picture complements background of slide

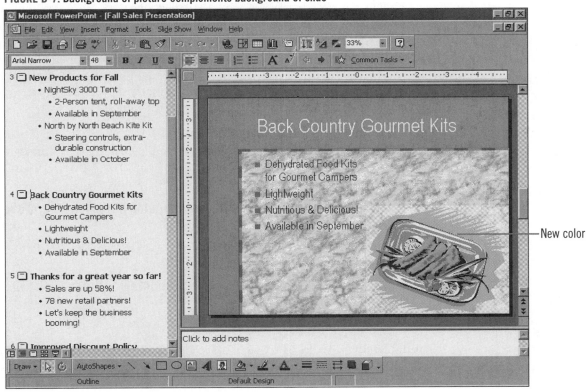

New color

TABLE B-1: Picture toolbar buttons

button	function	button	function
	Insert Picture from File		Crop
	Image Control		Line Style
	More Contrast		Recolor Picture
	Less Contrast		Format Picture
	More Brightness		Set Transparent Color
	Less Brightness		Reset Picture

Unit B

PowerPoint 2000

Running an Online Slide Show

PowerPoint lets you run an online slide show on any compatible computer. You can use the keyboard or mouse to control the progression of slides, annotate the current slide, and navigate among slides in any order, so you can tailor the presentation to your current audience. An online slide show is often a good alternative to printing transparencies or slides because you don't need any equipment other than a computer to run the presentation. ✐ You practice running the slide show so you can make suggestions to Kim about how to run her presentation effectively.

Steps 1234

1. Click the **Previous slide button** ⬆ on the vertical scrollbar three times to go to slide 1, then click the **Slide Show View button** ☐ to the left of the horizontal scroll bar
   The first slide in the sales presentation fills the screen.

2. Move the mouse anywhere on the screen to display the **Slide Show menu icon** (the semi-transparent icon in the lower-left corner of the screen), then click it
   The Slide Show menu opens. You can move the mouse anywhere on the screen to display the Slide Show menu button or right-click anywhere on the screen to open the pop-up menu at the location of the mouse pointer button. This menu offers several choices for running the slide show, including navigating through slides, annotating your presentation with an on-screen pen, displaying speaker's notes, and ending the slide show.

3. Point to **Go**, then click **Slide Navigator**
   The Slide Navigator dialog box opens, as shown in Figure B-8. In this dialog box, you can move to any slide using the title of the slide. This dialog box is especially useful when working with a presentation that contains a large number of slides.

4. In the Slide titles list box of the Slide Navigator dialog box, click **6. Improved Discount Policy**, then click **Go To**
   Slide 6 fills the screen. Now you'll use another tool to annotate this slide by circling important information.

5. Right-click anywhere on the screen, point to **Pointer Options** on the pop-up menu, then click **Pen**
   You can use the pen to highlight important information as you're delivering the presentation.

6. When the pointer changes to ✎, drag a circle around the last bulleted item in the list
   As shown in Figure B-9, the last bulleted point is now circled with a pen. This mark lasts only until you move to a different slide.

7. Press [←]
   Slide 5 fills the screen.

8. Press **[B]**, note the effect, press **[B]** again to restore the screen, press **[W]**, then press **[W]** again
   You can use these shortcut keys to change the screen to black or white; this can be helpful when you want to direct attention away from the screen for a moment to discuss something with the audience, then move back when finished.

9. Press **[Home]** to return to the first slide, then press **[Spacebar]** to progress through the presentation slide by slide

> **QuickTip**
> To remove a Pen mark immediately, press [E].

> **QuickTip**
> To view a list of keyboard shortcuts to use during a slide show, right-click anywhere on the screen during an online slide show, then in the pop-up menu click Help.

FIGURE B-8: Slide Navigator dialog box

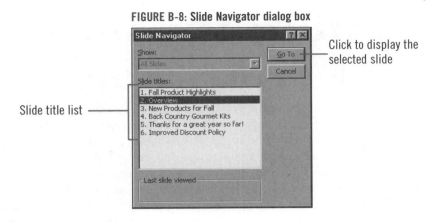

Click to display the selected slide

Slide title list

FIGURE B-9: Annotating a slide

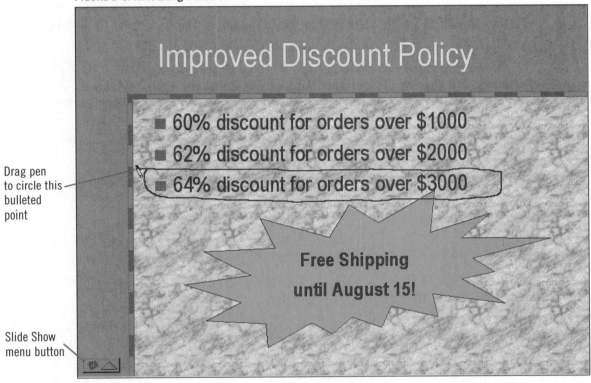

Drag pen to circle this bulleted point

Slide Show menu button

CLUES TO USE

Using PowerPoint Viewer when PowerPoint isn't installed

Sometimes you want to run a PowerPoint slide show on a computer that does not have PowerPoint installed. You may have a laptop computer without enough free disk space to install PowerPoint, or need to run a presentation on someone else's computer. You can run a PowerPoint presentation on any compatible computer as long as the computer can run a small program called PowerPoint Viewer. To use PowerPoint Viewer, you copy the program onto the disk where you save your presentation, then use it when you insert the disk in the other computer. PowerPoint contains a wizard that makes this process easy. Click File on the menu bar, then click Pack and Go. If the Pack and Go feature is not installed on your system, insert the appropriate Office 2000 CD before proceeding. When the Pack and Go Wizard opens, proceed through the steps to prepare your presentation.

PowerPoint 2000

PowerPoint 2000

Setting Preset Timing and Transitions

Sometimes you want to run a presentation without manually controlling the progression of slides. PowerPoint makes it easy by letting you set timing and transition effects ahead of time in Slide Outline, Normal, or Slide Sorter view. Working in Slide Sorter view is easiest because you can see icons that represent your settings, and preview them before you run the slide show. Then, once in Slide Show view, you can let the presentation run itself, or make manual moves only when you wish to. You can set timing and transitions in Slide Sorter view, Slide view, or Normal view. ✎ You decide to set timing and transitions so Kimberly can focus on her customers instead of on running the slide show. First, you set the timing for all slides in the presentation to 20 seconds, but also enable Kimberly to advance a slide manually to move more quickly.

Steps

1. Click the **Slide Sorter View button** 🔡 to the left of the horizontal scroll bar

QuickTip

You can also open the Slide Transition dialog box by right-clicking any slide while in Slide Sorter view.

2. Click **Slide Show** on the menu bar, then click **Slide Transition**
   The Slide Transition dialog box opens, as shown in Figure B-10. In this dialog box, you can set **timing**, the amount of time each slide appears before the next is displayed, and also set **transitions**, which controls how a slide appears, such as whether it appears to fade in or expand like a box.

3. In the Advance area, click the **Automatically after check box** to select it if necessary, then type **20** in the text box below the check box
   You leave the On mouse click check box selected so Kimberly has the option of advancing to the next slide using the mouse if she finishes speaking in less than 20 seconds.

4. Click **Apply to All**
   This applies the transition to all slides in the presentation. You can also apply timing or transition effects to only the current slide or selected slides.

5. With the first slide selected, press and hold [Shift], click **Slide 2**, click **Slide Show** on the menu bar, then click **Slide Transition**

QuickTip

Be careful not to click Apply to All at the end of this step. If this happens, press [Ctrl] [Z], then repeat Step 6.

6. In the Slide Transition dialog box click the **Effect list arrow**, click **Blinds Horizontal**, click the **Medium option button**, then click **Apply**
   This transition effect causes the first two slides in the presentation to appear in a blind-like design, making it look like you are closing the blinds to show a new slide. See Table B-2 for a description of popular transition effects.

7. Right-click **Slide 3**, then click **Slide Transition** in the shortcut menu

QuickTip

To preview any transition setting in Slide Sorter view, click the transition icon under the slide.

8. Click the **Effect list arrow**, click **Box Out**, click the **Slow option button**, type **30** in the text box below the Automatically after check box, then click **Apply**
   This sets a timing of 30 seconds for this slide and a transition effect that makes the slide appear as a small box that slowly expands to fill the screen.

Trouble?

If you do not have a sound card installed, you will not be able to hear the sound effects during the presentation.

9. Click **Slide 4**, press and hold [Shift], click **Slides 5** and **6**, click **Slide Show** on the menu bar, click **Slide Transition**, click the **Effect list arrow** in the Slide Transition dialog box, click **Dissolve**, click the **Sound list arrow**, click **Whoosh**, then click **Apply**
   Kimberly has a sound card on her PC, so these sound effects will be a great addition. In Slide Sorter view, the timing for each slide appears below it, along with an icon if a transition has been preset for the slide, as shown in Figure B-11.

FIGURE B-10: Slide Transition dialog box

Previews effect of transition

Leave selected so you can advance manually with mouse when necessary

When selected, the slide will advance automatically to the next slide

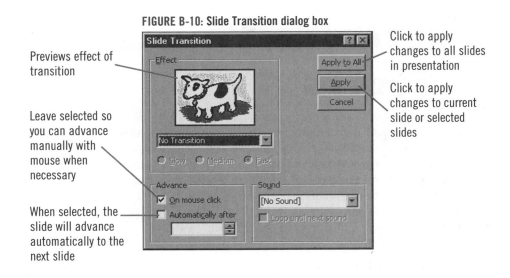

Click to apply changes to all slides in presentation

Click to apply changes to current slide or selected slides

Displays current transition effect

Slide Sorter toolbar

FIGURE B-11: Transition and timing effects appear in Slide Sorter view

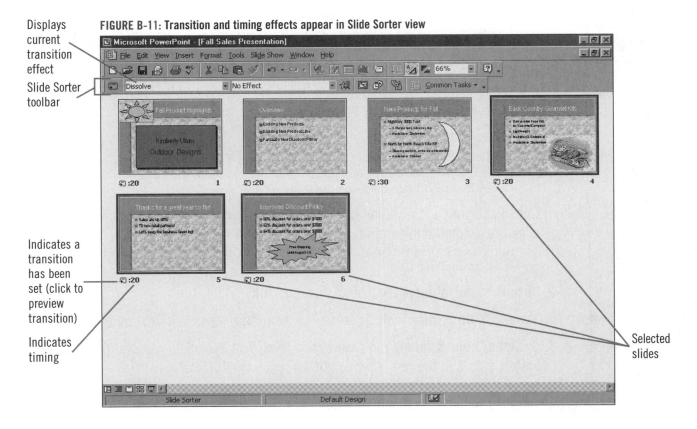

Indicates a transition has been set (click to preview transition)

Indicates timing

Selected slides

TABLE B-2: Popular transition effects

effect	description
Box In	Edges of slide appear first and fill in toward the center
Box Out	Slide appears as a small box that expands to fill the screen
Dissolve	Previous slide appears to dissolve into the current slide.
Random Transition	Sets a different transition effect for each selected slide, or for all the slides in a presentation if you click Apply to All
Wipe Left	Slide appears to move in over previous slide from right to left
Wipe Right	Slide appears to move in over previous slide from left to right

PowerPoint 2000

Setting Animation Effects

Animation effects are special transition effects and graphics effects you can set to make elements on a slide appear more interesting. You can set all the elements on a slide to animate, or select items such as the title or a picture. You can even specify the order in which you want the elements to animate. You can make all animation choices in the Custom Animation dialog box, or you can select one or more elements on a slide and use the Preset Animation command on the Slide Show menu. The Custom Animation dialog box is available only in Normal View and Slide View, so you need to switch to one of these views before adding custom animation effects. You decide to add some animation effects to selected slide elements.

Steps

1. Click **Slide 1**, click **Slide Show** on the menu bar, point to **Preset Animation**, then click **Laser Text**

   The title appears as if it were being printed on a laser printer and an accompanying sound effect reinforces the effect. Notice that beneath Slide 1 is now an icon indicating that an animation effect has been set for this slide.

2. Click **Slide 2**, press and hold **[Shift]**, click **Slides 3** and **4**, click **Slide Show** on the menu bar, point to **Preset Animation**, then click **Flying**

   Observe the new effects in Slide Sorter View.

3. Click the **Slide View button** □, move to **Slide 6**, click **Slide Show** on the menu bar, click **Custom Animation**, then click the **Order & Timing tab**

   The Custom Animation dialog box opens, as shown in Figure B-12. In this dialog box, you can customize individual objects on the slide to create specific effects.

4. Click **Explosion 3**, press and hold **[Shift]**, click **Text 4**, in the Start animation area click the **Automatically option button**, then type **2** in the text box

   The Animation order list box shows the two selected items listed in the order in which they are set for animation.

5. Click **Preview**, observe the effect, then click **OK**

6. Move to **Slide 5**, click **Slide Show** on the menu bar, then click **Custom Animation**

7. Click the **Order & Timing tab** if necessary, click **Text 2**, click the **Automatically option button**, type **2** in the text box, click **Title 1**, click the **Automatically option button** and type **2** if necessary, then click **OK**

   Now that you have set the animation order to list the text element before the title element, the message of thanks will appear after the bulleted text.

8. Click the **Slide Sorter View button** ▦ to the left of the horizontal scroll bar

   You have now set timing, transitions, and animations for each slide, as shown in Figure B-13.

9. Move to **Slide 1**, then click the **Slide Show View button** ▭ to view the entire slide show

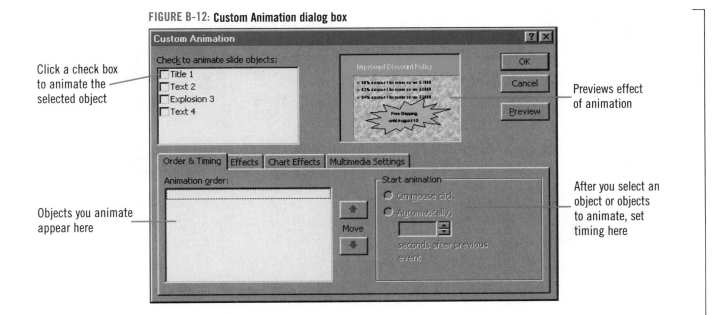

Click a check box to animate the selected object

Previews effect of animation

Objects you animate appear here

After you select an object or objects to animate, set timing here

FIGURE B-13: Slide Sorter View showing timing, transitions, and animation effects

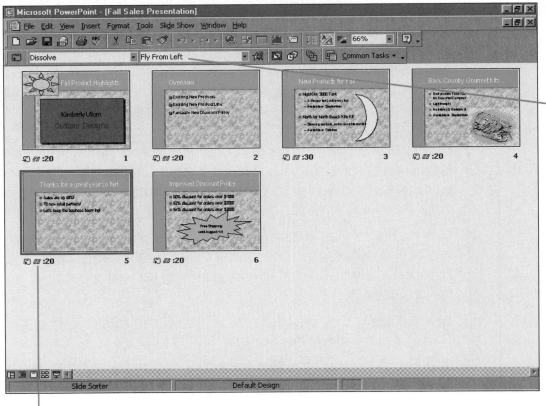

Displays current animation effect

Indicates an animation effect has been set (click to preview effect)

PowerPoint 2000

PowerPoint 2000

Creating Speaker's Notes and Printed Materials

Speaker's notes accompany slides to help you remember important information that you do not want to appear on the slides. You can use speaker's notes on-screen or print them out. You can create and work with speaker's notes in either Normal View or Notes Page View. ✎ Kimberly will need some notes to help her remember important information as she makes her sales presentation.

Steps 1 2 3 4

1. Press **[Home]** to move to Slide 1, click **View** on the menu bar, then click **Notes Page**

2. Click the **text placeholder** below the slide
   The insertion point appears in the placeholder.

3. Click the **Zoom list arrow** on the Standard toolbar, then click **75%**
   The view is enlarged, as shown in Figure B-14, making it easier to enter text.

4. At the insertion point, type **Thanks for taking the time to meet with me today. I have been an inside sales representative for Outdoor Designs for three years, and I'm very excited to be working directly with you now as a field rep. At Outdoor Designs, our goal is to get out into the field as much as possible, to answer questions and help solve problems as well as to tell you about our exciting line-up of products. My goal today and every day is to help you increase your business, so don't hesitate to ask questions or make suggestions. You can call or e-mail me at any time. Before we get started, are there any issues you would like to address?**
   As you type, text wraps automatically.

5. Move to **Slide 3**, click the **Click to add text placeholder**, then type **Both of these new products are manufactured by El Jardin, a major European manufacturer of outdoor products based in Barcelona, Spain. We hold exclusive distributorship of El Jardin products in North America.**

6. Click the **Normal View button** 🔲 to the left of the horizontal scroll bar, move to Slide 1, click in the Notes pane, scroll down in the Notes pane vertical scroll bar as shown in Figure B-15, select all the text from **My goal today** to **e-mail me at any time.**, then click the **Cut button** ✂

7. Move to **Slide 6**, click in the Notes pane, then click the **Paste button** 📋
   The text is pasted into the new location.

8. Click **File** on the menu bar, click **Print**, click the **Print what list arrow**, as shown in Figure B-16, click **Notes pages**, then click **OK**
   A copy of your notes prints with the slide attached to make it easy to refer to.

9. Save your changes to the presentation, then click the **program window Close button** to close the presentation and exit PowerPoint

FIGURE B-14: Adjust zoom size to make typing easier

Zoom list arrow

Note text
placeholder

FIGURE B-15: Working with speakers notes in Normal View

Click to scroll
down in Notes
pane

FIGURE B-16: Working in the Print dialog box

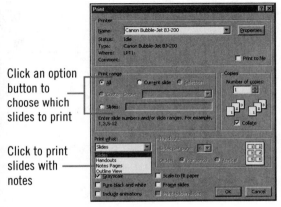

Click an option
button to
choose which
slides to print

Click to print
slides with
notes

Preparing for an off-site presentation

When preparing for an off-site presentation, do as much information-gathering and planning as possible to ensure your success. If you plan to use an overhead projector or a slide projector, set up the equipment ahead of time so you can test it with your materials. If you plan to use a PC, make sure that PowerPoint or PowerPoint Viewer is installed, and that the audience will be able to see the screen; you may want to arrange to connect the PC to a projection device if the audience is larger than three or four. Find out where the light switches are for the room, and make sure that you or someone you designate can turn off or dim the lights so that the audience can see the monitor or projection screen more clearly. If you plan to use handouts or refer to notes during the presentation, be aware that the altered lighting may not allow you or your audience to read printed handouts easily. If possible, arrange time for a rehearsal at your presentation site. Sight-lines and acoustics vary from space to space and can greatly affect the success of your presentation.

Practice

▶ Concepts Review

Label each of the Picture toolbar buttons shown in Figure B-17.

FIGURE B-17

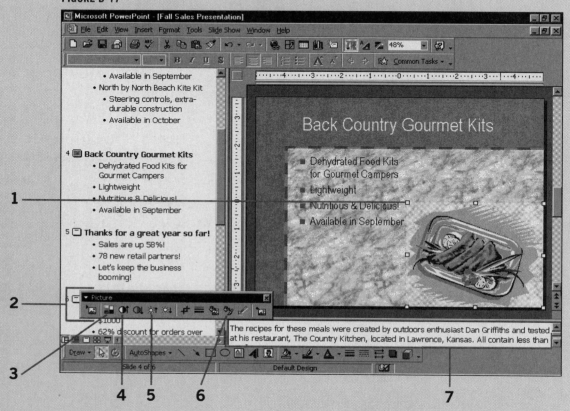

Match each of the following tasks with the dialog box and tab best used to complete it.

8. Change one color in a presentation.
9. Change a picture's fill and line colors, position, and size.
10. Change one color in a picture.
11. Change all the colors in a presentation.
12. Insert a piece of clip art in a slide.

a. Recolor Picture dialog box
b. Standard tab in the Color Scheme dialog box
c. Microsoft Clip Gallery
d. Format Picture dialog box
e. Custom tab in the Color Scheme dialog box

Select the best answer from the list of choices.

13. **A color scheme is**
    a. The combination of colors in a piece of clip art.
    b. A combination of three colors applied to a presentation.
    c. A combination of eight colors applied to a presentation.
    d. The combination of design elements in a presentation.

14. **Annotating a slide with the Pen tool causes which effect?**
    a. The slide displays the marks you create until you move to a different slide.
    b. The slide is printed with whatever marks you create.
    c. The slide text is highlighted in yellow.
    d. The slide is deleted from the presentation.

15. **When you preset the transition in a slide, you are controlling**
    a. The size of the slide when it displays.
    b. The manner in which objects on the slide display.
    c. The manner in which the slide displays.
    d. The color scheme of the slide.

16. **In Slide Show view, what happens when you point anywhere on the screen?**
    a. The slide show ends.
    b. You move to the next slide.
    c. You move to the previous slide.
    d. The Slide show menu button appears.

17. **When you preset the timing of a slide, you are controlling**
    a. How long it remains on-screen before advancing to the next slide.
    b. How long it remains on-screen before changing to a black screen.
    c. How long it remains on-screen before changing to Slide Sorter view.
    d. How long it remains on-screen before ending the slide show.

PowerPoint 2000

18. **In Slide Show view, what key can you press to move to the previous screen?**
    a. [Spacebar]
    b. [Enter]
    c. [N]
    d. [←]

19. **What is the best way to run a PowerPoint presentation on a compatible computer that does not have PowerPoint installed?**
    a. Convert the slides to .GIF files, and open them on the compatible computer.
    b. Use PowerPoint Viewer on the compatible computer.
    c. Install Microsoft Office on the compatible computer.
    d. Try opening the presentation in a different presentation graphics program installed on the compatible computer.

▶ Skills Review

1. **Change the color scheme of an existing presentation.**
   a. Start PowerPoint if necessary.
   b. Click the Open an existing presentation option button, or if PowerPoint is already running, click File on the menu bar and then click Open.
   c. Open the file PPT B-2 from your Project Disk.
   d. Click File on the menu bar, then click Save As.
   e. Save the file as "Fall Company Meeting."
   f. Click Format on the menu bar, then click Slide Color Scheme.
   g. Click the Standard tab if necessary, then click the first color scheme box in the row.
   h. Click Apply to All.
   i. Save your changes.

2. **Use clip art.**
   a. Move to Slide 7.
   b. Click in the title placeholder and type "1st Annual Employee Volunteer Contest!".
   c. Click the text placeholder, type "Log your volunteer hours with Human Resources", press [Enter], type "1st prize is a weekend getaway in Aspen", press [Enter], then type "Support your favorite cause!".
   d. Double-click the clip art placeholder.
   e. In the Microsoft Clip Gallery, click the Sports & Leisure category, right-click the picture of the downhill skier, then, in the Shortcut menu, click Insert (or click Insert on the menu bar, point to Picture, click From File, then insert the file Skier_ on your Project Disk).
   f. Drag the upper-right corner sizing handle of the inserted picture until the skier's hair just covers the title text.
   g. Save your changes.

3. **Work with a picture.**

   a. If necessary, click the picture to select it, then click the More Contrast button ⬚ on the Picture toolbar three times.

   b. Click the Format Picture button ⬚ on the Picture toolbar.

   c. In the Format Picture dialog box, click the Colors and Lines tab, click the Color list box in the Fill section, then in the color palette click the fourth box in the top row, the color that follows the Title Text Scheme Color.

   d. Click the Semitransparent check box, then click OK.

   e. Move the picture down by clicking in the center of the image and dragging down so that it is directly below the title text and the right edge of the fill does not obscure the bullets.

   f. Click the Recolor picture button ⬚ on the Picture toolbar, then click the third color checkbox, click the New list arrow in the third row, click the fourth color in the first row, the color that follows the Title Text Scheme Color, then click OK.

   g. Save your changes.

4. **Run an online slide show.**

   a. Move to Slide 1.

   b. Start the Slide Show.

   c. Press [Spacebar] three times to move to the third slide, titled "Secrets of Our Success".

   d. Right-click on the screen, point to Pointer Options, then click Pen.

   e. Drag to circle the bulleted point, "Emphasis on Quality of Life".

   f. Right-click, point to Go in the pop-up menu, point to By Title, then click "Goals for Fall Quarter".

   g. Press [Spacebar] to move to the next slide.

   h. Press [←] to move to the previous slide.

   i. Press [End] to move to the last slide.

   j. Press [Spacebar] twice to return to Slide view.

5. **Use preset timing and transitions.**

   a. Change to Slide Sorter view.

   b. Click Slide Show on the menu bar, then click Slide Transition.

   c. Click the Automatically after check box to select it, then type 10 in the text box.

   d. In the Effect area, click the list arrow, then click Split Horizontal In.

   e. Click Apply to All.

   f. Click Slide 5, right-click, then click Slide Transition in the pop-up menu.

   g. Change the timing to 15, and change the effect to Uncover Up, then click Apply.

   h. Save your changes.

PowerPoint 2000

6. Use animation effects.

a. Change to Normal view.

b. Move to Slide 1.

c. Click Slide Show on the menu bar, then click Custom Animation.

d. Click the Effects tab if necessary, in the Custom Animation dialog box, click the Title 1 checkbox, then press and hold Shift and click the Text 2 checkbox.

e. Click the top list arrow under Entry animation and sound, click Fly, then in the list box to the right click From Right.

f. Click OK.

g. Move to Slide 2.

h. Click the slide text to select it, then click Slide Show on the menu bar, point to Preset Animation, and then click Drive-in.

i. Save your changes.

j. Move to the first slide.

k. Switch to Slide Show view, and view the presentation.

7. Create speaker's notes and print materials.

a. Change to Notes Page View.

b. Move to Slide 5.

c. Click the Zoom list arrow on the Standard toolbar, then click 75%.

d. Click in the text placeholder, then type "Frasier implemented two co-marketing ventures with major retailers and also designed a direct mail campaign that drew a 12% return."

e. Press [Enter].

f. Type "Kimberly increased orders in her new sales region by 70%, a company record."

g. Move to Slide 7.

h. Click in the text placeholder, and type "In this annual contest, we will recognize the Outdoor Designs employee who donates the most hours to volunteer service. The winner will receive a weekend ski package for two at a luxury spa in Aspen. In addition, the charity of his or her choice will receive a $1000 donation!"

i. Save your changes.

j. Click File on the menu bar, then click Print.

k. In the Print dialog box, print the presentation as Notes pages.

l. Close the Fall Company Meeting file, and exit PowerPoint.

► Independent Challenges

1. At Stuff for Pets, you are preparing to present your expansion plan to potential investors. You have completed a marketing plan presentation that outlines the goals and projections for the establishment of a new retail outlet on the south side of town. You decide to enhance your presentation before producing the 35mm slides needed for your slide projection presentation.

To complete this independent challenge:

a. Start PowerPoint if necessary.

b. Open the file PPT B-3.

c. Save the presentation as "Final Stuff For Pets Presentation."

d. Enhance the presentation by changing the color scheme or individual color elements.

e. Add clip art to the presentation. (*Hint:* Remember that you can add clip art to any slide by clicking Insert on the menu bar, pointing to Picture, then clicking Clip Art.)

f. Add speaker's notes to help remember key points.

g. You do not need to set transitions, timing, or animation effects for this slide show because you plan to output it on 35mm slides. Instead, take this opportunity to learn about how to output a presentation for a film-processing bureau. Start PowerPoint Help, and search for information on 35mm slides. You plan to send your files to Genigraphics to produce the slides.

h. Run the Genigraphics Wizard if it is installed on your system by clicking File on the menu bar, pointing to Send to, and then clicking Genigraphics. (If the Genigraphics Wizard is not installed on your system, follow the prompts to install it using your Office 2000 CD. If you need help, ask your Instructor or Technical Support person for assistance.)

i. When you are finished, print the slides as Notes pages.

j. Close the presentation, saving changes when prompted, and exit PowerPoint.

PowerPoint 2000

2. The Literary Loft is starting a book club. To encourage customers to join the book club, staff members will take turns leading the first several meetings. To lead the book club meeting, you must choose a book and create a brief presentation raising issues or questions that encourage discussion about the book. You have been asked to lead the first book club meeting. You anticipate attendance at the first meeting to be small, so you plan to use your PC to make your presentation.

To complete this independent challenge:

a. Choose a favorite book.
b. Plan your presentation by thinking about what you like best or least about the book and the author. Think about the tone you want to establish and the types of discussion questions that would encourage a greater appreciation of the book. If the author is a favorite of yours, you might want to include information about the author or other books she has written.
c. Start PowerPoint if necessary.
d. Use the AutoContent Wizard or another template to create your presentation.
e. Save the presentation using the title of your chosen book.
f. Use your skills and your imagination to create interesting slides that complement the tone of the book and the goals of your discussion.
g. Enhance the presentation with colors, clip art, transitions, and animation effects.
h. If you wish, create speaker's notes to help you remember key points.
i. Run the slide show, pressing [S] to pause the presentation as necessary. Use the Pen pointer to annotate key points. Press [S] again to resume the presentation.
j. When you are finished, print the presentation as Notes pages, save and close the presentation, and exit PowerPoint.

3. The Wacky Words Card Company is preparing sales representatives to create several presentations while they are on the road. The presentations will instruct retailers on stocking and inventory during special promotional seasons. The sales representatives travel with PCs and black and white printers. They plan to make group presentations to the entire staff of one or more stores, so they will not be able to use their PCs. They will need to print black and white transparencies to use with overhead projectors. You have volunteered to help the reps achieve the best results with their limited resources.

To complete this independent challenge:

a. Start PowerPoint if necessary.
b. Start the Office Assistant.
c. Ask how you can work best in black and white.
d. Browse through the topics Office Assistant offers, and learn how to work and print in black and white. Find out how text and objects in a color presentation will be printed on a black and white printer, and how to work in black and white so that what you see on the screen is what you get when you print.
e. Create a black and white presentation that summarizes and conveys the information you learned. Use the Design Template of your choice to start the presentation, then change the slide color scheme to black and white. Use the information you learned in Help to make design and formatting decisions.
f. Add at least one piece of full-color clip art to the presentation, then convert it to black and white (*Hint*: Use the Image Control button on the Drawing toolbar). Use tools on the Drawing toolbar to enhance the appearance of the image in black and white.
g. When you are finished, print the presentation as Slides, then save and close the Help system and exit PowerPoint.

4. The Microsoft Clip Gallery makes it easy to organize and use clip art. In addition to the clip art in the gallery, you can access additional clip art on the Microsoft Office CD-ROM and from other sources, including the World Wide Web. Add a new piece of clip art to one of the presentations you created in this unit.

To complete this independent challenge:

a. Start PowerPoint if necessary.

b. Open one of the presentations you created in this unit.

c. Change to Slide view if necessary.

d. Insert a new slide that contains a clip art placeholder, or move to a slide where you would like to add clip art. (*Hint:* Remember that you can add clip art to any slide. If the slide does not contain a clip art placeholder, simply click Insert on the menu bar, point to Picture, then click Clip Art.)

e. Double-click the clip art placeholder.

f. In the Microsoft Clip Gallery, click Import Clips.

g. Browse your hard drive to find other folders that contain clip art. If you have access to the Microsoft Office CD-ROM, insert it and change to the drive that contains it.

h. When you return to the Microsoft Clip Gallery, click the Clips Online button.

i. Connect to the Internet if necessary.

j. Read and accept the terms of the end-user agreement.

k. Use the Browse by category list box to choose a clip art category of interest to you, then browse the clips to find a picture you like.

l. Scroll through the available choices to find clip art you want to download.

m. When you find a piece of clip art you want, click it. A large preview of the clip appears in the lower left corner of the screen, along with keywords links to related pictures.

n. Click the preview of the clip to download it.

o. Disconnect from the Internet if necessary.

p. In the Insert ClipArt window, locate the clip in the Downloaded clips category, then insert it in the desired slide. Move and resize the clip as necessary.

q. Print the slide that contains the clip art, close the presentation, then exit PowerPoint.

PowerPoint 2000

▶ Visual Workshop

Use the skills you have learned in this unit to create the presentation slides shown in Figures B-18 and B-19. To begin, open the file PPT B-4, and save it as "Star Gazers Club". Print each slide, and save the presentation as "Star Gazer Announcement".

FIGURE B-18

FIGURE B-19

Unit
A

Integrating
Office 2000 Programs

Objectives

- ► **Embed an Excel chart into a PowerPoint slide**
- ► **Send a PowerPoint presentation to Word**
- ► **Insert a file in a Word document**
- ► **Link an Excel worksheet to a Word document**
- ► **Update a linked Excel worksheet**
- ► **Insert Access fields into a Word form letter**
- ► **Merge Access data with a Word form letter**
- ► **Save a Word document as a Web page**

So far you've created many documents, worksheets, databases, and presentations using the individual Office programs. Sometimes, however, you may want to create documents that contain elements created with different Office programs, such as a newsletter you create with Word that also contains a chart created with Excel. You also can save any Office document as a Web page for use on the Internet or an intranet. The staff at Outdoor Designs would like your help in creating a report for investors that will include information from a PowerPoint presentation and an Excel workbook. They want you to send the report as a form letter to each investor, and have provided an Access database of the investors' names and addresses so that you can accomplish this quickly. Finally, you need to convert the final report to a document that can be published on the company's Web site.

Embedding an Excel Chart into a PowerPoint Slide

Office 2000 enables you to easily combine information from its different programs. For example, inserting an Excel chart into a PowerPoint slide takes just a few steps. The Excel chart becomes an **embedded object**, which is a separate copy of the original file (called a **source file**) that you can edit using the menus and toolbars of the program in which it was created. Sue Ellen has prepared her six-month sales summary presentation for the sales staff, except for a slide showing the total sales by region for the previous two quarters. You need to embed an Excel chart with this information into a slide for her.

Steps 1234

1. Start PowerPoint, open the presentation **INT A-1** on your Project Disk, then save it as **July Presentation**

   The PowerPoint presentation opens in Normal view with two slides.

2. Click **View** on the menu bar, point to **Toolbars**, click **Customize**, click the **options tab** if necessary, click to deselect the **Standard and Formatting toolbars share one row checkbox** if necessary, click the **Reset my usage data button**, click **Yes** in the message box, then click **Close**

3. Click the **Next Slide button** [▼] on the Slide pane scroll bar to move to Slide 2, click the **Common Tasks button** on the Formatting toolbar, click **New Slide**, click the **Blank layout** (row 3, column 4), then click **OK**

   A new, blank slide appears as the third slide in the presentation.

4. Click **Insert** on the menu bar, then click **Object**

   The Insert Object dialog box opens as shown in Figure A-1. You can create the embedded object by choosing a new object to create from the Object type list or by inserting an object from an existing file.

5. Click the **Create from file option button**, click **Browse**, double-click **INT A-2** on your Project Disk, then click **OK**

   The embedded Excel chart appears in the slide as a selected object, as shown in Figure A-2.

6. Double-click the **chart object**

   The Excel menu bar and toolbars replace the PowerPoint menu bar and toolbars, giving you access to these features so that you can work with the chart just as you would in Excel.

Trouble?

If you don't see the Chart toolbar, right-click any toolbar to open a shortcut menu, then click Chart.

7. Click **View** on the menu bar, point to **Toolbars**, click **Customize**, click the **options tab** if necessary, click to deselect the **Standard and Formatting toolbars share one row checkbox** if necessary, click the **Reset my usage data button**, click **Yes** in the message box, then click **Close**

8. Click the **Chart Objects list arrow** on the Chart toolbar, click **Chart Title**, click the **Font Size list arrow** on the Formatting toolbar, then click **28**

   Because the chart is an embedded object, the title size changes only in the copy on the PowerPoint slide, not in the original Excel chart. See Figure A-3.

Trouble?

If an Excel toolbar appears as you try to drag the object, click in the Presentation window outside the chart object, then try Step 9 again.

9. Click anywhere outside the chart object to return to PowerPoint, click the **chart** to select it, then drag it up until the title is slightly above the black line and the plot area is just below the line, then save your changes to the presentation

FIGURE A-1: Insert Object dialog box

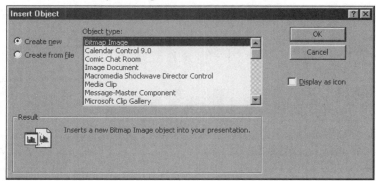

FIGURE A-2: Embedded Excel chart object

Selected embedded chart object —

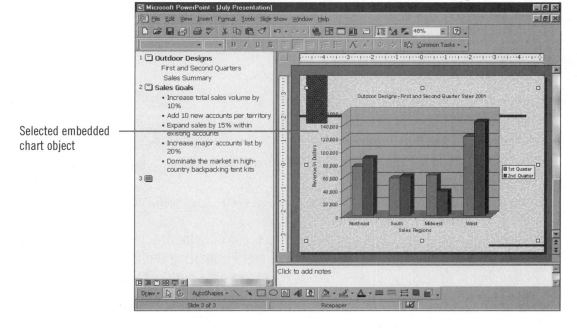

FIGURE A-3: Embedded Excel chart with source file commands

Excel menu bar and toolbars available in PowerPoint —

Chart toolbar —

Excel sheet tabs —

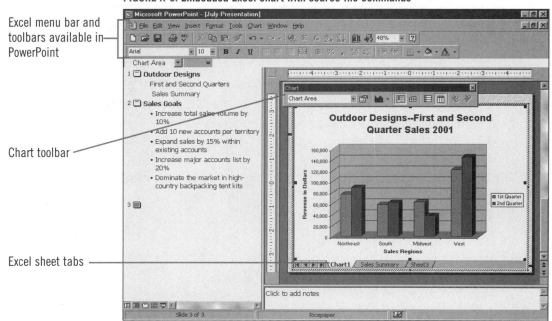

Sending a PowerPoint Presentation to Word

Sometimes you want to **export** a document, or change it from one file type to another. For example, you can easily save an existing PowerPoint presentation as a Word document. You can choose from five layout styles for your new Word document. Four of the layout styles include slides, and the other includes only the text outline. After you export the presentation to Word, you can save, edit, and format it just as you would any other Word document. Derek wants to incorporate the sales goals from Sue Ellen's sales presentation into a report he is working on. He asks you to export an outline of Sue Ellen's six-month sales summary presentation to a Word document.

Steps

QuickTip

When you choose an option other than Word document on the Send To menu, such as Mail Recipient or Genigraphics, you are choosing an actual recipient, not a different file type for the presentation.

1. Click **File** on the menu bar, point to **Send To**, then click **Microsoft Word**
   The Write-Up dialog box appears.

2. Click the **Outline only option button** as shown in Figure A-4

3. Click **OK**, maximize the Word program window, if necessary, then switch to Print Layout View
   Word starts, and the PowerPoint slide outline appears in a new Word document. This might take a minute or two. See Figure A-5.

4. Click **View** on the menu bar, point to **Toolbars**, click **Customize**, click the **options tab** if necessary, click to deselect the **Standard and Formatting toolbars share one row checkbox** if necessary, click the **Reset my usage data button**, click **Yes** in the message box, then click **Close**

5. Click the **Show/Hide button** ¶ on the Standard toolbar

6. Delete the top four lines of text from **Outdoor Designs** through **Sales Goals** including the paragraph mark, and also the blank line below the bulleted text, then apply the **Normal style** to the five sales goals
   The text changes to 12-point Times New Roman and the bullets are removed.

7. Click **File** on the menu bar, click **Save As**, change to the folder and drive location of your Project Files, click the **Save as type list arrow** and click **Word Document** if necessary, then save the document as **Sales Goals**

8. Close the **Sales Goals** document

9. Maximize the **PowerPoint program window**, close the **July Presentation** file, then exit **PowerPoint**
   Word remains open.

FIGURE A-4: Write-Up dialog box

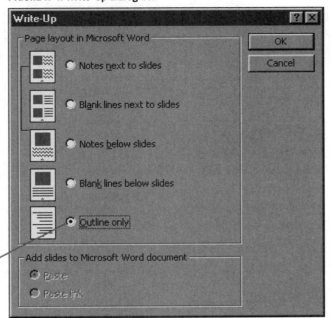

In Step 2, click this option button

FIGURE A-5: Word document with exported PowerPoint outline

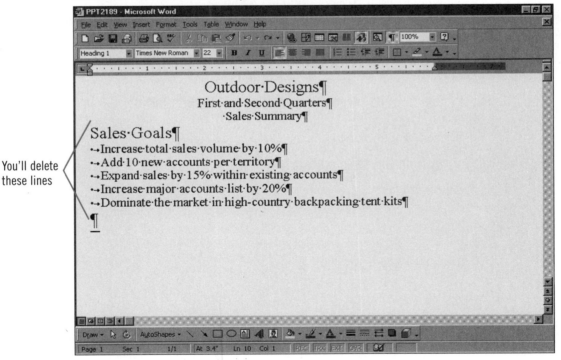

You'll delete these lines

Inserting Word text into a PowerPoint slide presentation

You can create a PowerPoint presentation outline in Word using the built-in heading styles. Type your outline in Word using the Heading 1 style for slide titles, Heading 2 for the first level of indented text, and so on. When the outline is complete, save and close the Word document. Open PowerPoint, click Insert on the menu bar, then click Slides from Outline. Select the Word file with your outline, then click Insert. You can edit the outline and design your slides as usual.

Inserting a File in a Word Document

As you work, you might want to combine two files into one, or insert someone else's document into your own. Although you can easily copy and paste information between open documents, it's sometimes easier to **import**, or insert, the entire contents of a closed file into an open document. ✐ Derek wants to include Sue Ellen's Sales Goals document in a report that will be sent to the company's investors. He asks you to import the Word document containing the sales goals into the report, which is also a Word document.

Steps 123 4

1. Open the file Word **INT A-3** on your Project Disk, and save it as **Investors Report**
This is Derek's report.

2. Move the insertion point to the blank line after the first paragraph in the body text
This is the location where you want to insert the Sales Goals document.

QuickTip

The Insert File dialog box works the same way as the Open dialog box, with which you are already familiar.

3. Click **Insert** on the menu bar, then click **File**
The Insert File dialog box appears. This dialog box looks and functions similarly to the Open dialog box. See Figure A-6.

4. Click **Sales Goals** on your Project Disk, then click **Insert**
The entire Sales Goals document appears in the report.

5. Select the entire list of goals, then click the **Bullets button** ▤ on the Formatting toolbar
The sales goals are formatted in a bulleted list. See Figure A-7.

6. Click away from the selected text to deselect it

7. Save your changes

CLUES TO USE

Using Drag and Drop to Insert an Access table into Word

You can insert an Access table into a Word document using drag and drop. Open the Access database containing the table you want to insert, and then click the Tables button in the Objects list, but don't open the table. Start Word and open the document you want to insert the table in, and then minimize the Word window. In the Access window, select (but don't open) the table in the Objects list, then drag it from down to the Word button on the taskbar; when the Word window opens, drop the table into the document. The table is inserted as a regular Word table, not as an Access object, so you can edit it as you would any Word table.

FIGURE A-6: Insert File dialog box

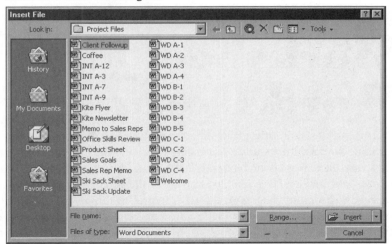

FIGURE A-7: Sales goals formatted as a bulleted list

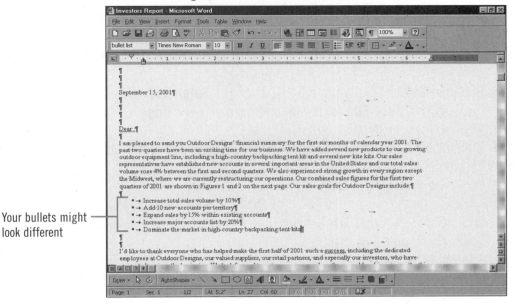

Your bullets might look different

CLUES TO USE

Inserting Excel data in a Word file

It takes just a few steps more to insert all or part of an Excel worksheet or an entire Excel workbook into a Word document. Move the insertion point to where you want to insert the worksheet. Click Insert on the menu bar, click File, click the Files of type list arrow, click All Files, click the Excel file to import, click Range and enter a range in the Set Range dialog box if you only want to insert part of the worksheet, then click Insert. If prompted to install this feature, insert your Office 2000 CD and click OK. In the Open Worksheet, dialog box, shown in Figure A-8, click the Open document in Workbook list arrow, click the worksheet you want to import, then click OK. The Excel data appears in the Word document as a table, which you can edit and format as usual using the table commands in Word.

FIGURE A-8: Open Worksheet dialog box

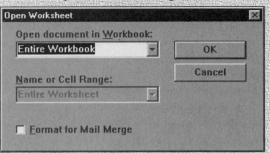

Linking an Excel Worksheet to a Word Document

Another way to share information between files is to link them. A **link** displays information from one file called the **source** in another file called the **destination**. In a document, linked data looks just like inserted or embedded data; the difference is that if you edit linked data, any changes you make in one file also appear in the other file. ▰▰▰ Derek asks you to link the Excel worksheet and chart with the sales figures to the Investors Report so if Sue Ellen updates a number, the change will be made automatically in the report. He suggests that you tile the Word and Excel program windows to make it easier to work in both programs.

Steps 1234

1. Start **Excel**, open **INT A-2** on your Project Disk, then save it as **July Sales Summary** on your Project Disk
   Both Word and Excel are now open.

2. Right-click the **taskbar** to open a shortcut menu, then click **Tile Windows Vertically**
   Now you can see both program windows at once.

3. Click in the Excel program window, click the **Sales Summary sheet tab**, select the range **A3:C8**, click **Edit** on the menu bar, then click **Copy**
   The cells are copied to the Clipboard.

4. Click in the Word program window, then click in the **blank line** below the Figure 1 caption near the end of the document
   See Figure A-9.

5. Click **Edit** on the Word menu bar, click **Paste Special**, click the **Paste link option button**, click **Microsoft Excel Worksheet Object**, click **OK**, then save your changes to the **Investors Report** document
   The Excel cells appear in the Word document as a selected object, as shown in Figure A-10.

6. Click in the Excel program window to make it active, click the **Chart 1 Sheet tab**, click the **chart area** to select the entire chart, then click the **Copy button** 📋 on the Standard toolbar
   A copy of the chart is stored on the Clipboard.

7. Click in the Word program window, click in the **blank line** below the Figure 2 caption, click **Edit** on the Word menu bar, click **Paste Special**, click the **Paste link option button**, click **Microsoft Excel Chart Object**, then click **OK**
   The Excel chart appears in the document, but is much too large.

8. With the chart object selected, click **Format** on the Word menu bar, click **Object**, then in the Format Object dialog box click the **Size tab**

9. In the Scale area click the **Lock aspect ratio check box** to select it if necessary, type **55%** in the Height text box, click **OK**, drag the chart down and to the right until the left object border is even with the left page margin, then save your changes to the document
   See Figure A-11.

FIGURE A-9: Excel worksheet cells copied to Clipboard

Inactive program
window (title bar
is gray)

Copied cells

You'll paste the
copied selection
here

Active program
window (title bar
is blue)

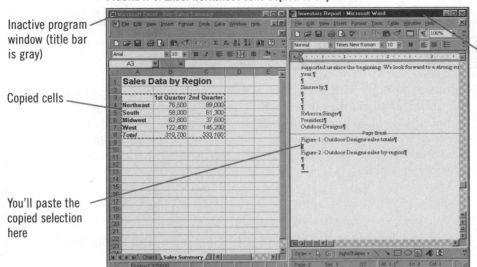

FIGURE A-10: Excel cells pasted to Word document

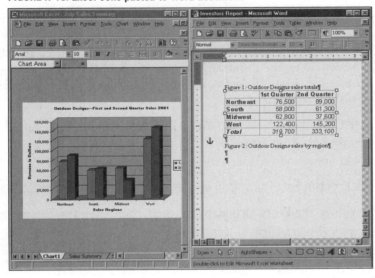

FIGURE A-11: Linked objects in Word document

Linked objects

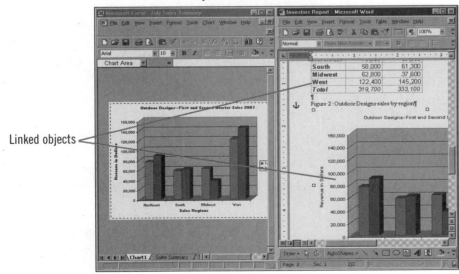

Integration 2000

Updating a Linked Excel Worksheet

The beauty of working with linked files is that if you change the information in one file, it is updated automatically in the other file. You can also update a linked object manually by selecting the linked object and pressing [F9]. ✐ Sue Ellen just determined that the second quarter sales total for the Midwest region should be $39,200, not $37,600, as recorded in both the July Sales Summary and the Investors Report. Because the two files are linked, you only need to make the change once.

Steps

1. Click in the Excel program window, then click the **Sales Summary sheet tab**

2. Click cell **C6**, type **39200**, then press **[Enter]**
   The new figure appears in the Excel worksheet and also in the Word document. See Figure A-12.

3. Save **July Sales Summary**

4. Click the **Chart 1 sheet tab**, then point to the second quarter bar for the Midwest
   A ScreenTip appears, showing the new value of the bar, 39,200, as shown in Figure A-13. Because the chart is linked to the worksheet cells, the chart is updated whenever data in the worksheet changes.

Trouble?
If the linked worksheet cells and chart are not updated, click the linked worksheet cells in Word to select them and press [F9]. Repeat to update the chart.

5. If necessary, click in the Word program window and scroll until you can see the updated chart in Figure 2
   The change is also made in the linked chart.

6. Click in the Excel program window, close **July Sales Summary**, then exit Excel

7. Maximize the **Word program window**, then save the file as **Investors Report Letter** on your Project Disk
   You'll use this document to create form letters in the next lesson.

FIGURE A-12: Updated Excel worksheet reflected in Word document

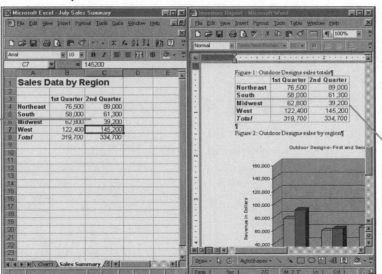

New data entered here

Linked cell updated here

FIGURE A-13: Excel chart with updated value

Excel charts and worksheets are automatically linked, so data is updated here

Unlinking files

If you decide that you no longer want changes you make in one file to affect another file, you can break the link between them. The linked object in the destination file will become an embedded object. You can still edit the embedded object using the source file's menus and commands, but the changes you make won't appear in the source file. Click the linked object in the destination file to select it. Click Edit on the menu bar, then click Links to open the Links dialog box. See Figure A-14. Click the name of the source file, click Break Link, then click OK. The object in the destination file is now an embedded object.

FIGURE A-14: Links dialog box

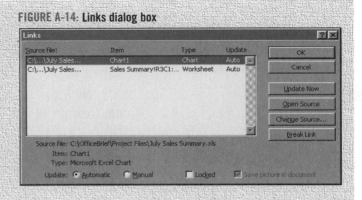

Inserting Access Fields into A Word Form Letter

A **form letter** is a document that contains standard body text and a custom heading for each recipient. The letter itself is usually written in Word, and the data for the custom headings usually are compiled in a table, worksheet, or database such as Access. ✐▬▬ Derek wants to send the Investors Report to all of Outdoor Designs' investors. He asks you to set up a form letter using Investors Report Letter as the standard body text. You use names and addresses from a database compiled by Elizabeth.

Steps

1. **Click Tools on the menu bar, then click Mail Merge**
   The Mail Merge Helper dialog box opens.This dialog box leads you through the three basic steps involved in creating a form letter: choosing the **main document**, the document that contains the text that should appear in each letter; the **data source**, the file that contains the variable information, such as names and addresses; and the **merged document**, the file or printout that contains all the personalized letters.

2. **Under Step 1 click Create, click Form letters, then click Active Window to use the Investors Report Letter as the main document**
   The Mail Merge Helper dialog box reappears so you can specify a data source, the location where the variable information is stored, as shown in Figure A-15.

3. **Under Step 2 click Get Data, click Open Data Source, click the Files of type list arrow, click MS Access Databases, then double-click INT A-4 on your Project Disk in the Open Data Source dialog box**
   Access starts, and a link containing the investors' names and addresses is established between the Word document and the Access database.

4. **Double-click Investors in the Tables in INT A-4 list on the Tables tab of the Microsoft Access dialog box**
   Because the Investors Report Letter main document doesn't contain any **merge fields**, field names from the specified data source, you are prompted to add them.

QuickTip

If the Mail Merge toolbar is floating, drag it below the Formatting toolbar to dock it.

5. **Click Edit Main Document in the Microsoft Word dialog box**
   The Mail Merge toolbar opens in the document window. This toolbar contains buttons for inserting merge fields in your document, and for working with all three files involved in creating a form letter or other merged document.

6. **Scroll to and click in the second blank line below the date, click the Insert Merge Field button on the Mail Merge toolbar, then click First_Name**
   The merge field appears in the document.

Trouble?

To see nonprinting symbols, click the Show/Hide ¶ button ¶.

7. **Press [Spacebar], click the Insert Merge Field button on the Mail Merge toolbar, click Last_Name, then press [Enter]**
   This comprises the first line of the return address. The space you inserted will separate the first and last name of each investor.

QuickTip

Double-check the spacing and punctuation around the merge fields for accuracy.

8. **Insert merge fields for the rest of the address and the salutation, as shown in Figure A-16**
   The merge fields in the main document will be replaced with names and addresses from the data source when the two are merged.

9. **Save the Investors Report Letter document**

FIGURE A-15: Mail Merge Helper dialog box

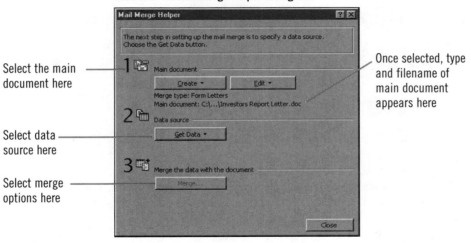

Select the main document here

Once selected, type and filename of main document appears here

Select data source here

Select merge options here

FIGURE A-16: Main document with merge fields

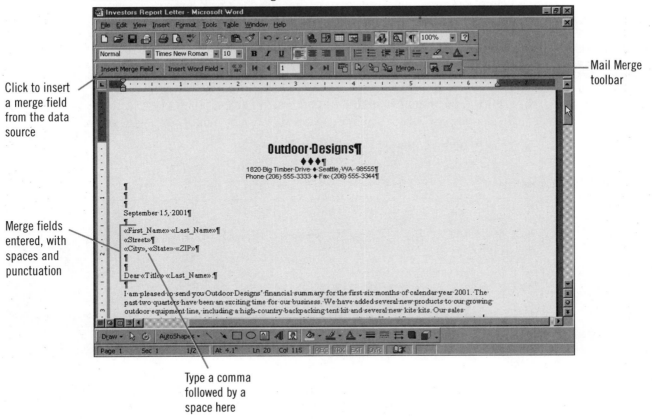

Click to insert a merge field from the data source

Mail Merge toolbar

Merge fields entered, with spaces and punctuation

Type a comma followed by a space here

Merging Access Data with a Word Form Letter

After you set up a main document, specify a data source, and insert merge fields, you can **merge**, or combine, the custom information with the standard text to create the personalized form letters. See Table A-1 for buttons on the Mail Merge toolbar. ✒ Investors Report Letter is a main document complete with merge fields that will pull information from the Access data source. You merge the main document and data source, then print the letters for Derek.

Steps 1 2 3 4

1. **Click the View Merged Data button ≪»ABC on the Mail Merge toolbar**

   The merge fields in the main document show the first record from the data source, which looks accurate. See Figure A-17. You can merge the main document and the data source in several ways. The Mail Merge button allows you to specify certain records from the data source to merge with the main document. The Merge to Printer button merges the main document with the data source and prints the results. Most often, however, you will want the merge results to appear in a new document, which you can save, preview, modify if necessary, and print.

2. **Click the Merge to New Document button ▣ on the Mail Merge toolbar**

   The mail merge runs, and the four personalized form letters appear in a new document.

3. **Save the document as Investors Report Form Letters on your Project Disk**

   Before you print, preview it to make sure you don't have any corrections to make.

4. **Click the Print Preview button ▣ on the Standard toolbar**

   As you scroll through the letters, you can see that in each letter the merge fields were replaced with data from the Access database. Each letter is two pages long, and there are four records in the Access table, so the merged document is eight pages long.

5. **Print the document Investor Report Form Letters, then close it**

   The letters now await a signature before they can be mailed. See Figure A-18.

6. **Save Investors Report Letter, then close it**

   Access closes when you close the main document.

TABLE A-1: Mail Merge toolbar buttons

button	name	description
≪»ABC	View Merged Data	Shows how merged data will look in main document
◁◁ , ◁ , ▷ , ▷▷	Record Navigation buttons	Move between records
▣	Mail Merge Helper	Opens the Mail Merge Helper dialog box
▣	Check for Errors	Reports errors in main document or data source that prevent a successful mail merge
▣	Merge to New Document	Merges main document and data source to new document
▣	Merge to Printer	Merges main document and data source to printer
Merge...	Start Mail Merge	Opens the Mail Merge dialog box, where you can isolate certain records from data source to merge
▣	Find Record	Locates a specific record in data source
▣	Edit Data Source	Opens data source for editing

FIGURE A-17: First record viewed in main document

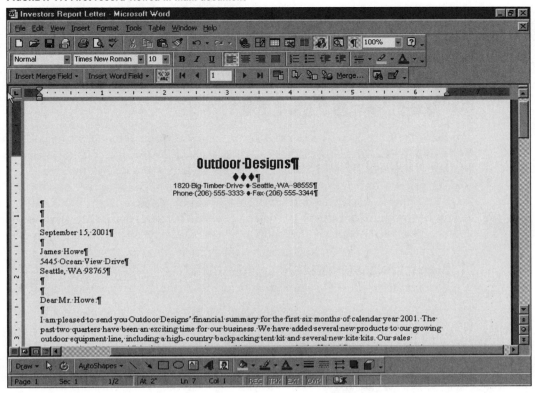

FIGURE A-18: First page of printed form letter of last record

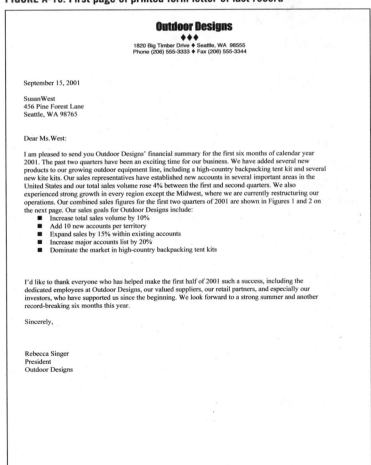

Saving a Word Document as a Web Page

In Microsoft Office 2000, you can save any file as a Web page so that it can be posted to the World Wide Web. When you save an Office 2000 document as a Web page, you are saving it as **HyperText Markup Language (HTML)**, the file format for documents posted on the Web. The file extension for Web pages is .htm. A browser program, such as Internet Explorer, interprets the HTML codes to determine how to display the document on your screen. Derek wants to post the Investors Report on the Outdoor Designs Web site so potential investors can see the latest sales figures for the company. He asks you to save the report as a Web page so he can publish it on the Web.

Steps

1. Open **Investors Report** on your Project Disk
   The version of the report you saved before inserting merge fields appears.

2. Type **Investor** in the salutation after "Dear"

3. Click **File** on the menu bar, then click **Save as Web Page**
   The Save As dialog box opens.

> **QuickTip**
> When saving a document as a Web page, any linked or embedded objects are saved as independent graphic images in a GIF format.

4. Save the file as **Investors Report Web Page** on your Project Disk
   An information dialog box opens, showing you a summary of features in the original document that are not supported by Web browsers, and which will appear differently or not at all in the Web page. See Figure A-19.

> **QuickTip**
> In order for a Web page to display properly, the Web page file must be located in the same folder that contains the Web page files folder, so if you move a Web page file, always move the folder along with it.

5. Click **Tell me more**, read the Microsoft Word Help screen that opens, close Microsoft Word Help, then click **Continue** in the Information dialog box
   Word saves the document as a Web page, with the modifications. When you save a document as a Web page, Office creates a new folder in the folder where you saved the Web page. The folder contains all the supplementary files created as part of the Web page, including graphics files, frame files, and other essential files. The folder name is based on the Web page filename and contains the additional text "_files." For example, when you save the Investors Report Web Page file, a folder called "Investors Report Web Page_files" is created.

6. Click **File** on the menu bar, click **Web Page Preview**, then scroll through the document
   The Web page opens in Internet Explorer (or the browser installed as the default browser on your computer) so that you can see how it will look when posted to the World Wide Web. Notice that the spacing of the body text and bullets has changed. Depending on your Web browser, the chart now may appear above the Figure 2 reference instead of below it.

7. Click **File** on the Internet Explorer menu bar, then click **Close**
   You are returned to the Word document window.

8. Click **View** on the menu bar, then click **HTML Source** (If prompted, insert your Office 2000 CD and install this feature)
   The coded document appears in a new document window as shown in Figure A-21. If you know HTML, you can edit the codes in this window.

9. Click **File** on the Microsoft Development Environment menu bar, click **Exit**, close the Web page, then exit **Word**

FIGURE A-19: Information dialog box alerts you to
potential changes in the Web page

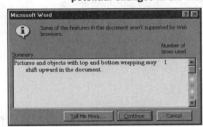

FIGURE A-20: Web Page preview

Report in Internet
Explorer window
(your Web browser
might be different)

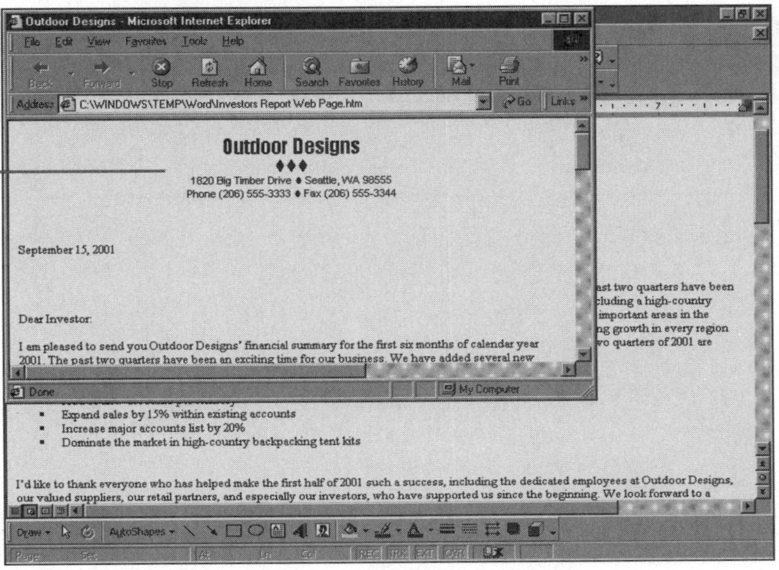

FIGURE A-21: Microsoft Development Environment window

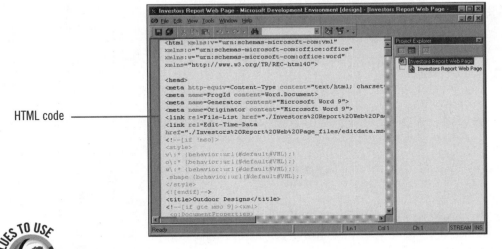

HTML code

CLUES TO USE

Understanding the World Wide Web

The **Internet** is a worldwide network that connects computers and computer networks from all over the world. The **World Wide Web** (also known as the **Web**) is a part of the Internet that contains Web pages that are linked together. Web pages contain highlighted words, phrases, and graphics called **hyperlinks**, that open other Web pages when you click

them. **Web browsers**, such as Microsoft Internet Explorer or Netware Navigator, are software programs that allow you to access and view Web pages in a graphical, easy to navigate format. The World Wide Web was first created in Switzerland in 1991 to allow links between documents on the Internet.

Practice

▶ Concepts Review

Label each element of the window shown in Figure A-22.

FIGURE A-22

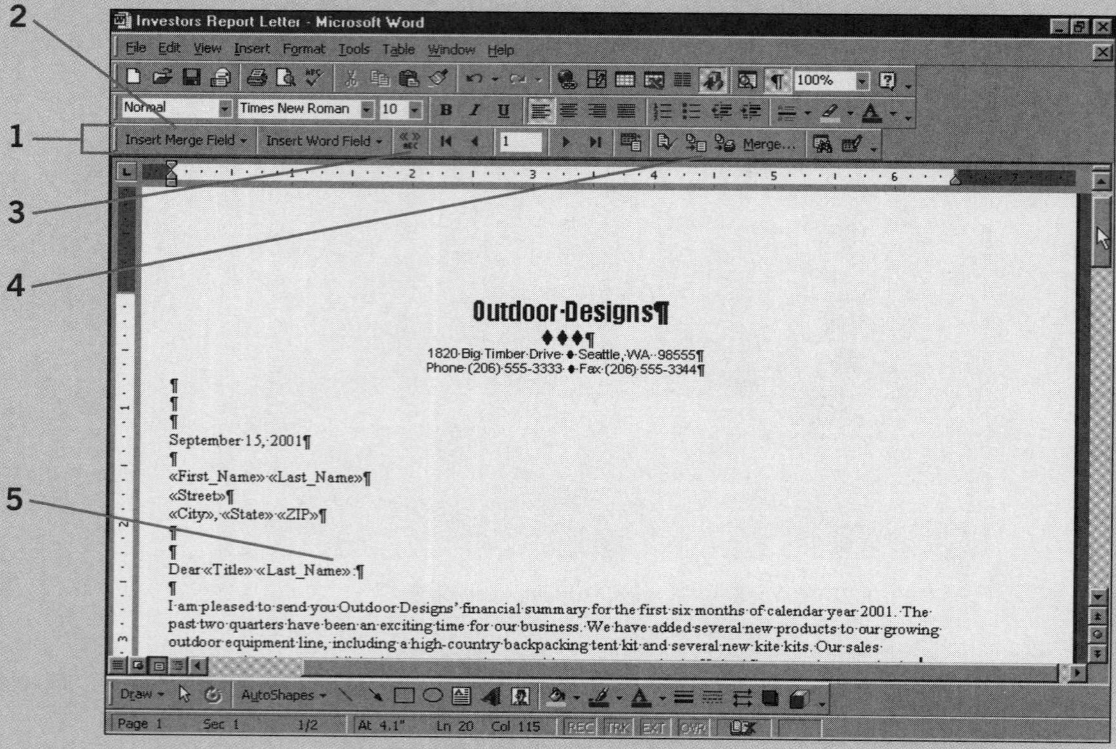

Match each of the descriptions with the correct term.

6. Display information from one file in another
7. A document with standard body text and a custom heading for each recipient
8. A file that stores variable information for the mail merge
9. To change a file from one type to another type
10. The original file or program
11. Field names from a specified data source
12. Insert the entire contents of a closed file into an open file

a. source
b. export
c. form letter
d. link
e. data source
f. import
g. merge fields

Select the best answer from the list of choices.

13. To edit an embedded object, you must
    a. click it.
    b. double-click it.
    c. right-click it.
    d. drag it.

14. You can embed an object by using the
- **a.** File command.
- **b.** Edit command.
- **c.** Insert command.
- **d.** Embed command.

15. Sending only the outline of a PowerPoint presentation to Microsoft Word is an example of
- **a.** importing.
- **b.** exporting.
- **c.** embedding.
- **d.** linking.

16. Inserting the entire contents of a closed file into your open document is called
- **a.** importing.
- **b.** exporting.
- **c.** embedding.
- **d.** linking.

17. If you want to insert an Excel chart in a Word document so that the contents of the chart are updated in the Word document whenever changes are made to the Excel file, you should
- **a.** Link the Excel chart to the Word document.
- **b.** Embed the Excel chart in the Word document.
- **c.** Create a new Excel chart object in Word that contains the same data as the chart you want to insert.
- **d.** Send the Excel chart to Word using the Write-Up dialog box.

18. To update linked files, you must make the change in
- **a.** the source file.
- **b.** the destination file.
- **c.** both the destination file and the source file.
- **d.** either the destination or the source file.

19. If you break a link, the object in the destination file becomes a(n)
- **a.** source file.
- **b.** embedded object.
- **c.** data source.
- **d.** merge field.

20. The file that stores variable information is the
- **a.** main document.
- **b.** source file.
- **c.** data source.
- **d.** merge field.

21. The file format for documents posted to the World Wide Web is
- **a.** HTML.
- **b.** DDE.
- **c.** styles.
- **d.** dynamic data exchange.

▶ Skills Review

1. Embed an Excel chart in a PowerPoint slide.
- **a.** Start PowerPoint if necessary, then open INT A-5 on your Project Disk.
- **b.** Create a new, blank slide at the end of the presentation (use the Blank Auto Layout).
- **c.** Open the Insert Object dialog box.
- **d.** Create an object from the existing Excel file INT A-6 on your Project Disk.
- **e.** Activate the embedded object for editing.
- **f.** Enlarge the table title to 22 points.
- **g.** Return to the Presentation window.
- **h.** Use the Format Object dialog box to increase the height of the object to 125% of its original size.
- **i.** Reposition and resize the table as needed to center it horizontally.
- **j.** Save the file as "Investors Presentation" on your Project Disk.

2. Send a PowerPoint presentation to Word.

   a. Click File, point to Send To, then click Microsoft Word.

   b. Send only the presentation outline.

   c. Save the new document as "Confidential" in Word format on your Project Disk.

   d. Delete the first three lines and any extra blank lines at the end of the document.

   e. Apply the Normal style to the remaining lines.

   f. Save the Confidential document, then close it.

   g. Close the Investors Presentation presentation.

   h. Exit PowerPoint.

3. Insert a Word file in a Word document.

   a. Open the file INT A-7 on your Project Disk.

   b. Save the file as "Confidential Investor" on your Project Disk.

   c. Scroll down until you see "[Insert Word file here]" in the document.

   d. Delete the placeholder from the document, and the paragraph mark that follows it.

   e. Insert the Confidential file at this location in the document.

   f. Select the inserted text.

   g. Format the selection as a bulleted list.

   h. Deselect the selected text.

   i. Save the document.

4. Link an Excel worksheet to a Word document.

   a. Start Excel.

   b. Open INT A-6 on your Project Disk, and save it as "Confidential Data."

   c. Tile Word and Excel vertically on your screen.

   d. Copy the range A1:F5 to the Clipboard.

   e. Activate the Word program window.

   f. Delete the bracketed text "[Link Excel table here]" and the paragraph mark that follows it.

   g. Open the Paste Special dialog box.

   h. Link the Excel cells to the Word document.

   i. Save the Confidential Investor document.

5. Update a linked Excel worksheet.

   a. Activate the Excel program window.

   b. Change the value in cell E4 to 950000.

   c. Save the Confidential Data workbook.

   d. Activate the Word program window.

   e. Scroll until you see the linked cells.

   f. Verify that the value changed in the Word document. If necessary, update the link manually (*Hint:* Click the linked object and press [F9]).

   g. Save the Word document.

   h. Activate the Excel program window.

   i. Close the workbook.

   j. Exit Excel.

6. Create a form letter.

a. Maximize the Word window, and save the file as "Confidential Investor Letter" on your Project Disk.

b. Open the Mail Merge Helper dialog box.

c. Specify that you want to create form letters and set the Active Window as the main document.

d. Open the Access file INT A-4 on your Project Disk as the data source.

e. Select the Investors table as the data source.

f. Switch to the main document.

g. Replace the bracketed text in the document with the appropriate merge fields.

h. Check the spacing and punctuation around the merge fields for accuracy.

i. Create the form letters by merging to a new document.

j. Save the document as "Confidential Form Letters" on your Project Disk.

k. Preview, then print the letters.

l. Save, then close all the files.

7. Save a Word document as a Web page.

a. Open the file Confidential Investor on your Project Disk.

b. Replace all the bracketed text after the word "Dear" in the salutation with "Investor."

c. Delete the bracketed text between the date and the salutation.

d. Click File on the menu bar, then click Save As Web Page.

e. Save the file as "Confidential Investor Web Page."

f. Preview the Web page in your browser program, then close the Web Page Preview.

g. View the HTML source code.

h. Save and close the Web page.

i. Exit Word.

▶ Independent Challenges

If you complete all of the exercises in this unit, you may run out of space on your Project Disk. To make sure you have enough disk space, please copy the files INT A-8, INT A-9, INT A-10, INT A-11, INT A-12, and INT A-13 onto a new disk and use the new disk to complete the rest of the exercises in this unit.

1. As the owner of Stuff for Pets, a store catering to the needs of pet owners, you are always on the lookout for new products. You are very excited about a new eye medication for miniature poodles that you have just begun to stock. Because miniature poodles tend to have chronic eye problems, you decide to send a letter to all customers who purchased that breed of dog to inform them of the new eye medication. The sales representative for the product left you his PowerPoint presentation, so you decide to include some information from his slides in your letter.

To complete this independent challenge:

1. Start PowerPoint, open INT A-8 on your Project Disk, and save it as "Poodle Presentation."

2. Send the outline only from Poodle Presentation to Word.

3. Delete the top line and any extra blank lines at the bottom; apply the Normal style to the remaining lines of text.

4. Save the document as "Clear Eyes" in Word format (click the saves as type list arrow, then click Word document) then close the document.

5. Open INT A-9 on your Project Disk, and save it as "Poodle Letter."

6. Delete the bracketed text "[Insert Clear Eyes here]," then insert the Clear Eyes document to that location.

7. Change the inserted text to a numbered list.

8. Start Excel, open INT A-10 on your Project Disk, then save it as "Poodle Data."

9. Tile Word and Excel on your screen.

10. Delete the bracketed text "[Link chart here]," in the Word document, then link the chart from Poodle Data to that location.

11. Format the linked chart in Word so it is easier to read.

12. Change cell B3 to 45% on the Numbers worksheet, then verify that the Word chart reflects the revision.

13. Set up Poodle Letter as a main document; use the Customers table in the file INT A-11 as the data source.

14. Replace the bracketed text in the letter with the appropriate merge fields.

15. Perform a merge to a new document, and save it as "Poodle Form Letters."

16. Print only the first letter.

17. Close any open files, and exit all programs.

2. You are an editor at a small, start-up publishing company. You just received a book proposal from an author who wants to write a book about the history of the environmental movement. The proposal seems good, but you want to see what has already been published on the subject. You find out what other books exist, then write a report about the competition.

To complete this independent challenge:

1. To find out about the competition, log on to the Internet, and use your browser to go to www.course.com. Click the link for Student Online Companions, select the link for this book, then click the link for Integration Unit A. This link brings you to Amazon, an online bookstore. Search for any books related to environmental history, the environmental movement, and so forth.

2. Create an Excel spreadsheet with the following information: book title, author, publisher, copyright date, page count (if the books you choose include this information), and price. Include at least four books in your spreadsheet. Save the workbook as "Competition" on your Project Disk.

3. Write a report to the editorial team that includes a description of the proposed book and the competition you found.

4. Embed the data from Competition in the appropriate place in your report.

5. Edit the embedded object by adding an appropriate title and formatting it in 18-point.

6. At the top of your report, add today's date, a To: line, a From: line with your name, and a Re: line with "Environmental History Competition."

7. Save your report as "Environmental History Competition" to your Project Disk.

8. Use the active window as the main document of a form letter.

9. Use INT A-12 on your Project Disk as the data source.

10. Add the appropriate merge field or fields to the To: line. Be sure to include the first and last name, and the position of each recipient.

11. Merge the document to the printer.

12. Close any open documents, and exit any open programs.

3. Val Enjo plans to start Software Galore, a computer software mail-order company. He has written his business plan and put together an estimate of expenses and sales for the first five years. He needs a $50,000 loan to cover start-up and operating costs. He asks you to help him write a letter with his financial information to send to several banks requesting the loan. He also asks you to create a document with this information that he can post on the Web to attract potential investors.

To complete this independent challenge:

1. Start Word and open a new, blank document.

2. Write a letter that Val can send to banks requesting a loan. Include the following information in your letter: the date; a salutation; body text with the name and type of company Val plans to start, three reasons you think the company will be successful, and a reference to financial information; and a complimentary closing.

3. Start Excel, open INT A-13 on your Project Disk, then save it as "Business Loan."

4. Tile Word and Excel on your screen.

5. Embed the worksheet in the appropriate place in your letter. (*Hint:* In the Paste Special dialog box, click the Paste option button.)
6. Double-click the embedded object to edit it.
7. Change the title to "Financial Analysis for 2001-2005."
8. Save the letter as "Business Loan Letter" on your Project Disk.
9. Create an Access database called Software Galore Finances on your Project Disk, and then create a table with the names, addresses, and loan officers of at least four banks. Use real or fictional information.
10. Make Business Loan Letter the main document of a form letter.
11. Insert appropriate merge fields to address the letter from the Access database you created.
12. Merge the data to a new document. Save the document as "Bank Letters."
13. Delete the merge fields from Business Loan Letter, and type "Potential Investor" in the salutation.
14. Save the document as a Web page with the name "Potential Investors Web page" on your Project Disk, then print it.
15. Close any open files, and exit any open programs.

4. Theatre in the Park is a stage company established in 1980 that performs Broadway plays in San Francisco's Golden Gate Park every year from May through September. This year's season features the plays **Hamlet**, **Art**, **Rent**, and **The Cherry Orchard**. The group consists of local professional actors and actresses; national stars appear in special engagements. In order to promote the performances, the troupe performs show excerpts at local schools, then gives a presentation about their upcoming shows using PowerPoint. Tara Martin, the manager of Theatre in the Park, asks you to put together a presentation for this season that includes the information explained above.

To complete this independent challenge:

1. Start Word, open a new, blank document, then save it as "Theatre Outline" on your Project Disk.
2. Using the outline tools or the heading styles, create text for at least three slides. Include information about Theatre in the Park, the upcoming season, and special appearances by national stars (real or made up).
3. Open a new, blank document, and save it as "Theatre Schedule" on your Project Disk.
4. Create a Word table that includes the four plays the company will perform this season. Include the play titles, special appearances, and dates of the performances.
5. Use the Send To command to send Theatre Outline to PowerPoint as a new presentation.
6. Switch to the new PowerPoint file, apply a design template and design, and edit the slides as necessary.
7. Link Theatre Schedule to a new slide to add the upcoming schedule of events to your presentation.
8. Switch to Microsoft Word, open Theatre Schedule, and change one of the dates in the table. Switch to PowerPoint and verify that the change was made in the linked table. If necessary, update the link manually by right-clicking the table, then clicking Update Link in the shortcut menu.
9. Save the presentation as a Web page using the name "Theatre Web Page."
10. Print the presentation as Handouts.
11. Close any open files, then exit all programs.

▶ Visual Workshop

Create the form letter and data source shown below. (*Hint:* You must create a data source, as shown in Figure A-24, in order to have merge fields to insert.) Merge the form letter with the data source to a new document. Save the document as "Runners Thanks," then print the letters.

FIGURE A-23

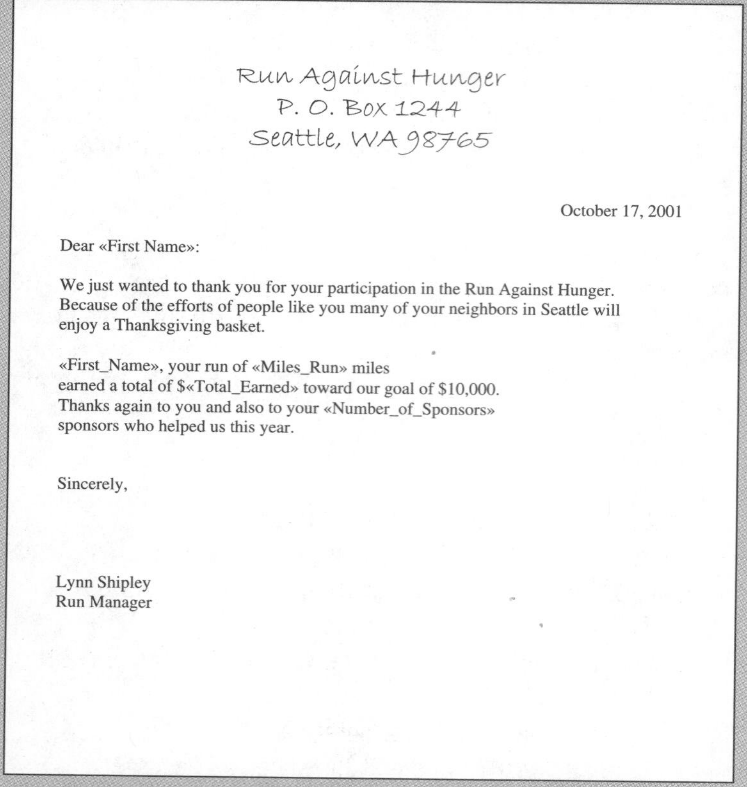

Run Against Hunger
P. O. Box 1244
Seattle, WA 98765

October 17, 2001

Dear «First Name»:

We just wanted to thank you for your participation in the Run Against Hunger. Because of the efforts of people like you many of your neighbors in Seattle will enjoy a Thanksgiving basket.

«First_Name», your run of «Miles_Run» miles earned a total of $«Total_Earned» toward our goal of $10,000. Thanks again to you and also to your «Number_of_Sponsors» sponsors who helped us this year.

Sincerely,

Lynn Shipley
Run Manager

FIGURE A-24:

ID	First Name	Last Name	Miles Run	Total Earned	Number of Sponsors
1	Preston	Hyde	12	690	17
2	Rebecca	Van Thorre	15	1200	20
3	Marie	Jamison	17	1300	23
4	Mark	Faro	16	800	14
5	Bina	Edwards	18	1400	19
(AutoNumber)			0	0	0

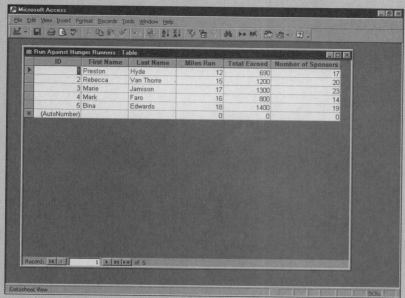

Glossary

Absolute cell reference In Excel, a cell reference that does not change when copied to refer to cells relative to the new location. For example, the formula "=B5*C5" in cell D5 does not change to "=B6*C6" when copied to cell D6. *See also* relative cell reference.

Accessories Built-in programs that come with Windows 98.

Active cell The current location of the cell pointer.

Active desktop Windows desktop where you can organize information and tools for accomplishing computer tasks seamlessly, whether they reside on your computer, a network, or the Internet.

Active program The program that is running (that is, open).

Active window The window that you are currently using. If a window is active, its title bar changes color to differentiate it from other windows and its program button is highlighted on the taskbar.

Address Bar An area in a program that you can use to open and display a drive, folder, or Internet location.

Alignment The horizontal or vertical position of numbers or text, relative to the page margins. Text can be right-, center-, left-, top-, and bottom-aligned, or justified between the margins.

Animation effects Special transition effects and graphics effects that cause elements on a PowerPoint slide to display in a more interesting way.

Annotation Temporary marks or writing on a PowerPoint slide during an onscreen slide show which disappear when you move to the next slide.

Area chart A line chart in which each area is colored or patterned to emphasize the relationships between pieces of charted information.

Argument A value, cell reference, or text used in a function. Commas separate arguments and parentheses enclose them; for example, AVERAGE(A1,10,5).

Ascending order A sort in which fields are ordered numerically from 0–9 or alphabetically from A–Z.

Auto fit A feature that automatically resizes a worksheet column so that it is slightly wider than the longest item in the column.

AutoContent wizard A wizard that designs and creates a PowerPoint presentation based on information you provide in a series of dialog boxes.

AutoCorrect A feature that automatically corrects certain words as you type.

AutoNumber field A data type that assigns a unique sequential number to each record.

AVERAGE function Calculates the average value of the arguments.

Back up To save files to another location in case you have computer trouble and lose data.

Bar chart A chart that displays worksheet data as a series of horizontal bars.

Bold A font style that makes text appear in darker type; used to emphasize text in a document.

Bound control A control in Access that has a table or query as its data source.

Browser program A program, such as Microsoft Internet Explorer, that allows you to access, view, and interact with pages on the World Wide Web.

Calculated control A control in Access that uses an expression as its data source, which may include a bound control.

Cell The intersection of a row and a column in an Excel worksheet or any table.

Cell reference The name of a worksheet cell; for example, A1.

Channel bar Bar on the Windows active desktop that contains buttons you use to access the Internet.

Chart A graphic representation of selected worksheet data.

Chart title The name assigned to a chart.

Chart Wizard An Excel wizard that helps you to create or modify a chart.

Check box A square box in a dialog box that turns an option on or off.

Click   To press and release the left mouse button quickly.

Click and Type   A feature that allows you to begin typing in almost any blank area of a Word document simply by clicking in the desired location.

Clip art   Ready-to-use electronic artwork.

Clipboard   A temporary storage area for items that have been cut or copied and may be pasted.

Close   To quit a program or remove a window from the desktop. The Close button usually appears in the upper-right corner of a window.

Color scheme   A set of coordinated colors for each element in a PowerPoint presentation.

Column   A vertical block of text in a document.

Column chart   A chart that displays worksheet data as a series of vertical columns.

Column width   A cell's horizontal dimension.

Combination chart   A chart that displays worksheet data in both line and bar graphs in a single chart.

Command   Direction that provides access to a program's features.

Command button   In a dialog box, a button that carries out an action. A command button usually has a label that describes the action, such as Cancel or Help. If the label is followed by an ellipsis, clicking the button displays another dialog box.

Common Tasks button   Toolbar button that lists common PowerPoint tasks.

Context-sensitive help   Information related to your current task.

Control   An object on an Access form or report that displays data, performs calculations, or is used for decoration. Examples include fields, text boxes, and graphic images. *See also* bound control, unbound control, *and* calculated control.

Control Panel   A Windows utility for changing computer settings, such as desktop colors or mouse settings.

Copy   A command that copies selected text in a document to the Clipboard.

COUNT function   Calculates the number of values in the argument list.

Criteria   Conditions or qualifications that determine whether a record is chosen for a filter or query.

Currency format   A type of worksheet formatting that adds a dollar sign ($) and decimal places to selected cells.

Cut   A command that removes a text selection or selected object from a document and places it on the Clipboard.

Data form   In Access, an electronic form you can use to enter data in a database, one record at a time, and in a layout that is easy to navigate.

Data source   The file that stores the variable information for a form letter or other mail merge document.

Data types   Determines the kind of data a database field contains, such as text, dates, or numbers.

Database   An organized collection of data related to a particular topic or purpose and stored electronically in a file.

Datasheet view   A view in Access that displays records in a grid format, making records easy to compare and edit.

DDE link   *See* dynamic link.

Decrypting   Reverses the encryption process. *See also* encrypting.

Default   A setting that is preset by the operating system or program, such as desktop color or font size.

Descending order   Sort in which fields are ordered numerically from 9–0 or alphabetically from Z–A.

Design templates   PowerPoint templates that contain suggested design and formatting but no content. *See also* presentation templates.

Design view   A window that shows the structure of a table, form, query, or report. Use this view to modify the object by editing or moving the controls or to change the structure of a table by adding, deleting, or editing fields and field properties.

Desktop   An on-screen version of a desk that provides a workspace for different tasks.

Destination file   When linking and embedding data between documents the target file or program.

Detail section   In Access, the section of a form or report that displays the field labels and data for each record.

Dialog box   A place in which you enter information needed to carry out a command. Many commands display dialog boxes in which you must select options before Windows can carry out the command.

Disk label Name that you assign to a disk using the Properties dialog box.

Document window Displays the current document.

Double-click To press and release the left mouse button twice quickly.

Double-spacing A document (or paragraph) that has one blank line between each line of text.

Drag and drop The action of moving or copying selected text in a document by dragging it with the mouse and depositing it at a new location.

Drive Device which reads and saves files on a disk. Floppy drives read and save files on floppy disks. Hard drives read and save files on your built-in hard disk.

Dynamic data exchange link *See* dynamic link.

Dynamic link Also called a dynamic data exchange link or DDE link; displays information from one file (called the source) in another file (called the destination).

Edit To modify the contents of a file without having to recreate it.

Embedded object A separate copy of a file inserted in a file in a different program that you can edit using the menus and toolbars of the program in which it was created.

Encrypt To compact and scramble a database file so that it is difficult to decipher for security purposes. *See also* decrypting.

Endnote A note or citation that corresponds to a number or symbol in the document and appears at the end of the document. *See also* footnote.

End-of-cell mark The mark in each cell in a table; all text entered in the cell is entered to the left of the end-of-cell mark.

End-of-row mark The mark at the end of each row in a table.

Enter To type information in a document or dialog box.

Exclusive mode A database opened in exclusive mode is only available to the user who has opened it.

Explorer A Windows 98 program you use to manage files, folders, and shortcuts; allows you to work with more than one computer, folder or file at once.

Export Change a file from one file type to another.

Expression Provides additional information about the data in a database; expressions can include field names and mathematical functions as well as built-in functions.

Field description In a database table, a descriptive comment that helps document the database by explaining the purpose of a field.

Field label/field name In Access, the control that describes the contents in the field value text box.

Field list List that contains all the fields in a database table; used to add fields to forms or reports.

Field properties Settings and characteristics that determine the way data is stored, displayed or manipulated in a field, such as the length of a text field or the decimal places in a number field.

Field properties pane In Access, a tabbed pane that provides complete information about the currently selected field.

Field value text box The control that contains the data in a field.

Field Specific category of information in a database such as name, address, or phone number. Usually organized in the smallest possible unit to facilitate organization, such as last name and first name.

File An electronic collection of data that has a unique name, distinguishing it from other files.

File management The process of organizing and keeping track of files and folders on a computer system.

Fill handle A box that appears on the lower right corner of a worksheet cell that you can drag to the right or down to copy the cell's contents into adjacent cells.

Filter Displays only the data that you want to see in an Excel worksheet or an Access database based on criteria you set.

Find A command that searches for a word, phrase, or format in a document.

Folder A file management tool you can use to store files and other folders in order to organize them.

Font A set of characters in a particular design; for example, Arial or Times New Roman.

Font style Attribute that changes the appearance of a font when applied; bold and italic are two common font styles.

Fontography The process of creating new fonts.

Footer Text that appears just above the bottom margin of every page in a document.

Footnote A note or citation placed at the bottom of a document page.

Footnote reference mark The mark next to a word in a document that indicates a footnote or endnote is associated with the word.

Form A database object that is used to enter, edit, or display information in a database one record at a time.

Form footer A section of a database form that appears at the bottom of each form and can contain totals, instructions, or command buttons.

Form header A section of the form that appears at the top of each form and can contain a title or logo.

Form letter A merged document that contains standard body text and a custom header for each recipient.

Format To enhance the appearance of text in a document but not the content; also to prepare a disk so it can store information.

Formula An equation that calculates a new value from existing values. Formulas can contain numbers, mathematical operators, cell references, and built-in equations called functions.

Formula bar The place in a worksheet where you enter or edit the formulas of the selected cell.

Function A prewritten formula you can use instead of typing a formula from scratch. Each function includes the function name, a set of parentheses, and function arguments separated by commas and enclosed in parentheses. *See also* formula.

Goal Seek An Excel command that lets you calculate the value in a target cell by changing the values in another cell.

Graphical user interface (GUI) An environment made up of meaningful symbols, words, and windows in which you can interact with a computer and computer programs.

Gridlines Horizontal and vertical lines connecting to the X-axis and Y-axis in a chart.

Handles Black boxes that appear around the perimeter of a selected control or object and are used to resize it.

Hanging indent A type of paragraph indent in Word where subsequent lines of text in a paragraph indent further than the first line.

Header Text that appears just below the top margin of every page in a document.

Horizontal scroll bar Moves the window view from side to side.

HyperText Markup Language (HTML) The file format for documents posted on the World Wide Web.

Icon Small pictures intended to be meaningful symbols of the items they represent.

Image properties Properties of a picture that can be modified using the Image Properties button on the Picture toolbar, such as brightness, contrast, and colors.

Import Insert the entire contents of a closed file into an open document.

Indent A set amount of space between the edge of a paragraph and the right or left margin.

Input mask Optional property that controls the format in which users must enter data in a database field.

Insertion point In a document, a blinking vertical line indicating the point where text will be inserted when you type.

Internet A worldwide collection of over 40 million computers linked together to share information

Italic A font style that makes text appear slanted; used to emphasize text in a document.

Justified text Text aligned at both the right and left margins.

Keyboard shortcut A keyboard alternative for executing a menu command; for example, [Ctrl][X] for Cut.

Label Descriptive text used to identify worksheet data in Excel, and titles or brief description in Access.

Landscape Layout orientation for a document so that it reads down the length rather than across the width of the page. Used when you want a rectangular page to be wider than it is long.

Legend Area that explains what the labels, colors, and patterns in a chart represent.

Line chart A graph of data mapped by a series of lines. Because line charts show changes in data or categories of data over time, they are often used to document trends.

Link When sharing data between files and programs, displays information from the source file in the destination file. *See also* source file *and* destination file.

List box A box in a dialog box containing a list of items. To choose an item, you click the list arrow and then click the desired item.

Main document A document that stores the standard body text for a form letter or other mail merge document.

Main text Bullet points under a title on a slide.

MAX function Calculates the largest value in the argument list.

Maximize To enlarge a window so that it takes up the entire screen. The Maximize button is usually located in the upper-right corner of a window.

Menu A list of available commands in a program.

Menu bar Set of menus available in a program for the tasks you need to perform; changes depending on the active window.

Merge To combine custom information with the standard text to create personalized form letters or other mail merge documents.

Merge fields Field names from the specified data source that act as placeholders for variable information in a form letter or other mail merge document.

MIN function Calculates the smallest value in the argument list.

Minimize To reduce the size of a window to an icon on the taskbar or to a smaller size. The Minimize button is usually located in the upper-right corner of the window.

Mouse A hand-held device that you roll on your desk to position the mouse pointer on the Windows desktop. *See also* mouse pointer.

Mouse buttons The two buttons (right and left) on the mouse that are used to make selections and issue commands.

Mouse pointer The arrow-shaped cursor on the screen that corresponds to the movement of the mouse as you roll it on your desk. The shape of the pointer depends upon the program and task being executed.

Multi-user environment Permits more than one user to modify the same set of data at the same time.

My Computer Windows 98 program you can use to view the files on your computer and how they are arranged. The icon appears on the desktop.

Name box Displays the name or reference of the currently selected cell in the worksheet.

Normal view A view in Word that displays the text and some graphic elements in a document without showing exactly how all the elements in the document will print. A view in PowerPoint that displays the presentation in three panes-Outline, Slide, and Notes.

Notes Page view View in PowerPoint that displays a slide and a designated area for typing speaker's notes to accompany the slide.

Number format A format applied to numbers in cells that represents different number types, such as currency, decimal, date, or percent.

Numeric value A number in a worksheet cell.

Object A graphic or other item or set of items that can be moved and resized as a single unit. In Access, also one of seven principal program components you can create and modify—tables, queries, forms, reports, pages, macros, and modules.

Office Clipboard An electronic clipboard that can hold up to 12 items at once, and which is accessible from any Office program. *See also* Clipboard.

Onscreen presentation A PowerPoint slide show run from a computer.

Open Starting a program or displaying a window that was previously closed; a program that is currently running, but not necessarily displayed in an active window; or the act of loading an existing file into an Office program.

Operating system Computer program that controls the basic operation of your computer and the programs you run on it.

Option button A small circle in a dialog box that you click to select an option.

Order of precedence The order in which Excel calculates a formula; the order of precedence is exponents, multiplication and division, addition and subtraction. Calculations in parentheses are evaluated first.

Orphan The first line of a paragraph that appears by itself on the bottom of a page.

Outline view A view that shows the structure of a Word document or a PowerPoint presentation in selected text levels.

Page break The point at which text in a document flows to the top of a new page.

Paint A Windows 98 accessory you can use to draw simple pictures and diagrams.

Password A string of characters that must be typed correctly in order to access a file.

Paste A command that copies information from the Clipboard into a document at the location of the insertion point.

Paste function A series of dialog boxes that guides you through entering a function into a worksheet.

Pie chart A circular chart that displays data in one data series as slices of a pie. A pie chart is useful for showing the relationship of parts to a whole.

Placeholder A line of text in a document template used to reserve space for text the user will insert in its place.

Point A unit of measurement used to measure characters; a point equals 1/72 of an inch.

Popup menu A menu of common commands that opens when you right-click an item for which a popup menu exists.

Portrait Layout orientation for a document so that it reads across the width rather than down the length of the page. Used when you want a rectangular page to be longer than it is wide.

PowerPoint Viewer Program included with PowerPoint that you can use to run a PowerPoint presentation on a computer without PowerPoint installed.

Presentation graphics Software designed for creating onscreen slide shows, 35mm slides, overhead transparencies, and other business presentation materials.

Presentation templates PowerPoint templates that contain suggested design, formatting, content. *See also* Design templates.

Presentation window The area of the PowerPoint program window in which you work with the text or graphics of a presentation.

Primary key field In Access, a field that ensures that each record is unique in a table.

Print Layout view A view in Word that displays layout, graphics, and footnotes exactly as they will appear when printed.

Print Preview A view in several other programs that shows exactly how a document will look when it is printed.

Printer port A special connector on the back of a computer that connects the computer to the printer.

Program Task-oriented software that you use for a particular kind of work, such as word-processing or database management.

Program button A button that appears on the taskbar, representing a running program.

Properties Those characteristics of a specific desktop or program element (such as the mouse, keyboard, or printer, or a document, database field, or object) which you can customize.

Property sheet In Access, a window that displays a control's name and source; can be used to edit the control's properties.

Query A set of criteria specified to retrieve data from a database. Queries may be saved as objects for later use.

Radar chart A chart that displays worksheet data frequency relative to a center point.

RAM (random access memory) The memory that programs use to perform necessary tasks while the computer is on. When you turn off the computer, all information in RAM is lost.

Range A selected area of adjacent cells.

Range reference The name of a selected range; for example, C5:E15.

Record A collection of related fields that contains all information for an entry in a database such as a customer, item, or business.

Recycle Bin An icon that appears on the desktop which represents a temporary storage area for deleted files.

Relational database A database which is actually a collection of one or more related tables that can share information. Access is a relational database program.

Relative cell reference In Excel, a cell reference that changes when copied to refer to cells relative to the new location. For example, the formula "=B5*C5" in cell D5 changes to "=B6*C6" when you copy the formula to cell D6. *See also* absolute cell reference

Repaginate To recalculate the page numbers in a document.

Replace A command used to search for a word or format in a document and insert another word in its place.

Report A summary of database information designed specifically for printing.

Report footer Information or images that appear at the bottom of the last printed page of a report.

Report header Information or images that appear at the top of the first printed page of a report.

Restore To resize a program or document window to its previous size before it was minimized or maximized. The Restore button is usually located in the upper-right corner of a window.

Right-click To press and release the right mouse button once quickly.

Row height A cell's vertical dimension.

Screen saver A moving pattern that fills your screen after your computer has not been used for a specified amount of time.

ScreenTip A brief description of a toolbar button or other screen element that appears when you point to the item.

Scroll bar A bar that appears at the bottom or right edge of a window for which the contents are not entirely visible. Each scroll bar contains a scroll box and two scroll arrows that can be clicked or dragged to display the additional contents of the window.

Select To click or highlight an item in order to perform some action on it.

Select query A commonly used query in which records are collected and displayed in a datasheet and can be modified.

Selection handles *See* handles.

Serial number A number used in a worksheet that represents a date or time that is used in calculations.

Shading A pattern of dots, lines, or color applied to a worksheet cell, paragraph, page, or other bordered area in order to emphasize it.

Sheet tab In Excel, displays the names of a worksheet in a workbook.

Shortcut A link that you can place in any location that gives you instant access to a particular file, folder, or program on your hard disk or network.

Shut down The action you perform when you have finished your Windows session. After you perform this action it is safe to turn off your computer.

Single spacing A document (or paragraph) that does not have any blank lines between lines of text.

Slide miniature A small window that displays a reduced view of the current PowerPoint slide.

Slide Sorter view Displays all slides in a PowerPoint presentation in reduced size so that you can reorganize them easily.

Slide view Displays text and graphics of a presentation slide in WYSIWYG format.

Solver An Excel add-in program that is used to solve complex problems. Solver automatically calculates a maximum or minimum value of a cell by changing the values in other cells in the worksheet using a formula that you specify.

Sort A feature that organizes records in an Access database or columns in an Excel spreadsheet or a Word table numerically or alphabetically, and in ascending or descending order.

Source file When linking or embedding data between two files, the original file or program.

Speakers notes In PowerPoint notes that accompany slides; used to help remember important information that should not appear on the slides themselves.

Spelling and Grammar Checker A tool that checks the spelling and grammar in a document and offers suggestions for fixing possible errors.

Stacking Layering an object on top of another object on a PowerPoint slide. The first object placed in a stack is at the bottom of the stacking order; the last is at the top.

Start button A button on the taskbar that you use to start programs, find files, access Windows Help, and more.

Statistics Descriptive calculations used in worksheets, such as sum, average, or count.

Status bar Appears at the bottom of the program window and displays information such as the current page or record number, and important messages, such as the status of the current print job.

Style A defined set of formatting commands for a paragraph; can include the font, font size, font style, paragraph alignment, spacing of the paragraph, tab settings, and anything else that defines the format of the paragraph.

SUM function Calculates the sum of the arguments.

Tab A set position where text following a tab character aligns.

Tab stop A location on the ruler where a tab is currently assigned.

Table A collection of related records in Access; also, information displayed in rows and columns.

Table of authorities List of references in a legal document, such as cases or statues, and their location in a Word document.

Table of contents List of headings in a document and their location in a Word document.

Table of figures List of figures in a document and their location in a Word document.

Taskbar A bar at the bottom of the Windows desktop that contains the Start button and icons for all open programs and files.

Text box Text object that automatically wraps text and can be resized or moved.

Text label Text object that does not automatically wrap text and can be moved or resized.

Text placeholder A designated area on a PowerPoint slide for entering text.

Timing The amount of time a slide displays during an onscreen presentation.

Title In PowerPoint, the title or first line of text in a slide.

Title bar The horizontal bar at the top of the window that displays the program name and the name of the active file.

Title slide The first slide in a PowerPoint presentation.

Toolbar Contains buttons that allow you to activate commands quickly.

Transition The way a slide first appears in a slide show and obscures the previous slide.

Triple-click To press and release the left mouse button three times quickly. In some programs including Word, this action causes an entire line to be selected.

True Type font A font that appears on screen exactly as it will appear on the printed page.

Unbound control In Access, a label or graphic image with its data source outside the database; used to identify or enhance a database object.

Underline A font style that underlines text; used to emphasize text in a document.

Vertical scroll bar Moves your view of a document or form up and down through a window.

View A preset configuration that determines which elements of a document are visible onscreen; does not affect the actual content of the document.

Web Layout view A view that shows how a document will look if you save it as a Web page.

What-if analysis Using a worksheet formula to determine different outputs for the same formula using different values.

Widow The last line of a paragraph that appears by itself at the top of a page.

Window A rectangular c-shaped work area on a screen that might contain icons, the contents of a file, or other usable data.

Wizards Features that guide you through step-by-step options in dialog boxes to assist you in the process of creating documents and accomplishing tasks.

WordPad A Windows 98 accessory you can use to create and edit simple documents.

Word processor A program that used to create and manipulate text-based documents, such as memos, newsletters, or term papers.

Word wrap In a document, when a word being typed moves down to the beginning of the next line as necessary without the user pressing [Enter].

WordArt A type of stylized text created in Word with sophisticated text formatting features.

Workbook A collection of related worksheets saved in a single Excel file.

Worksheet An electronic spreadsheet that is used for performing numeric calculations for a variety of purposes.

Worksheet window The area in the Excel program window which contains worksheet data.

World Wide Web A part of the Internet that contains Web pages that are linked together. *See also* Internet.

X-axis The horizontal line in a chart that contains a series of related values from the worksheet.

X-axis label A label that describes the X-axis of a chart.

XY (scatter) chart A chart that shows the relationship between two kinds of related worksheet data.

Y-axis The vertical line in a chart that contains a series of related values from the worksheet.

Y-axis label A label that describes the Y-axis of a chart.

Zoom The percentage of normal size at which you view a document on-screen.

Index

special characters

$ (dollar sign), 155
() (parentheses), 153
* (asterisk), 153
+ (plus sign), 38, 39, 153
- (minus sign), 38, 39, 153
/ (slash), 153
^ (caret), 153

▶ A

absolute cell references, 155
Access, 50, 51
    databases. *See* database(s)
    exiting, 232, 233
    merging Access data with Word form letters,
        350–351
    starting, 220–221
    tables. *See* database tables
accessories, 6, 7
Access Snapshot Viewer, 50
Active Desktop, 2, 3
active window, 10
Add button, Spelling and Grammar dialog box, 85
addition operator (+), 153
Address Bar, 34, 35
Airbrush button, 29
alignment
    text in documents, 102–103
    worksheets, 156–157
Angle Text Downward button, 200
Angle Text Upward button, 200
animation effects, presentations, 324–325
annotating slides, 320, 321
area charts, 195
arguments, functions, 170, 171
    within another function, 176
asterisk (*), multiplication operator, 153
AutoContent Wizard dialog box, 290, 291
AutoCorrect button, 85
AutoCorrect dialog box, 127
AutoCorrect feature, 79
AutoFormat As You Type tab, AutoCorrect dialog box, 127
AutoFormat feature
    Excel, 158
    Word, 109
AutoForm button, 226
AutoLayouts, PowerPoint, 296
AutoNumber data type, database fields, 223
AutoNumber fields, databases, 228–229
AutoShapes, 300, 301
AutoSum button, 172, 173
AVERAGE function, 173
axis labels, charts, 202, 203

▶ B

background, charts, 206, 207
Background Color dialog box, 314, 315
bar charts, 195
Bold button, 55
boldfacing type, 100, 101
borders
    Excel worksheets, 158, 159
    Word documents, 125
bound controls, forms, 244
Box In effect, presentations, 323
Box Out effect, presentations, 323
Break dialog box, 110, 111
browsers, 2, 30, 352, 353
Brush button, 29
Business Planner, 50
buttons. *See also specific buttons and toolbars*
    displaying, 82
    toolbars, 55
By Column button, 200
By Row button, 200

▶ C

calculated controls, forms, 244
calculated expressions, database reports, 274–275
calculations, order in Excel, 153
caret (^), exponent operator, 153
cascading menus, 7
CD Player, 7
cell(s), 146
    deleting contents, 154
cell references, 155
Cells command, Format menu, 157
centering text, 102, 103
Change All button, Spelling and Grammar dialog box, 85
Change button, Spelling and Grammar dialog box, 85
Channel Bar, 2, 3
chart(s), 193–209
    axis labels, 202, 203
    background, 206, 207
    changing type, 200–201
    colors, 204, 205
    creating, 196–197
    embedding into PowerPoint slides, 338–339
    fonts, 204, 205
    formatting, 206, 207
    gridlines, 194, 202, 203
    labels, 194
    legends, 194
    moving, 196, 198, 199
    planning, 194–195
    previewing, 208, 209
    printing, 208, 209
    sizing, 198, 199
    titles, 196, 197
    types, 195
    X-axis, 194
    Y-axis, 194
Chart toolbar, 200, 204
Chart Type button, 200
Chart Wizard, creating charts, 196–197
check boxes, 13
Check for Errors button, 350
check marks, menus, 10
Classic style mouse, 5
Click and Type feature, 81
clicking, 4, 5
clip art, 130–131
    database reports, 278–279
    forms, 248–249
    presentations, 316–317
    sizing, 316, 317
Clipboard. *See* Office Clipboard; Windows Clipboard
Clip Gallery, 130, 131
closing
    files, 62, 63
    programs, 18, 19
Collapse button, Outline view, 295
colors
    borders in worksheets, 158
    charts, 204, 205
    pictures, 318, 319
    presentations, 298, 299, 314
    printing worksheets, 160
Color Scheme dialog box, 314, 315
Colors dialog box, 300, 301
column(s). *See* table columns; worksheet columns
column charts, 195
command(s), dimmed, 11
command buttons, 12, 13
Comma Style format, numbers in worksheets, 157
complex problems, solving using Solver, 181
context-sensitive help, 16, 17
control(s)
    formatting using property sheet, 247
    forms, 244
Control Panel, 10, 11
Copy button, 30
copying
    files, 32, 36–37
    folders, 32
    linking Excel worksheets to Word documents,
        344–345
    text in documents, 82, 83
correcting errors. *See* error correction

Index

COUNT function, 173
criteria, filtering databases, 250
Currency data type, database fields, 223
Currency Style format, numbers in worksheets, 157
Curve button, 29
Custom Animation dialog box, 324, 325
Customize dialog box, 54, 55
customizing
    filters, 185
    menus, 54, 55
    Recycle Bin, 40
custom marks, footnotes and endnotes, 132
Cut button, 30
cutting text in documents, 82, 83

►D

database(s), 217–233, 241–257
    adding clip art to forms, 248–249
    changing fonts and styles on forms, 246–247
    data entry forms, 226–227
    editing, 230, 231
    entering data, 228–229
    existing, opening, 242–243
    filtering, 250–251
    merging Access data with Word form letters,
        350–351
    modifying layout, 244–245
    multiple, opening at same time, 242
    planning, 218–219
    printing, 232, 233
    protecting, 256–257
    queries. See queries
    records. See records
    reports. See database reports
    saving, 242
    sorting, 252–253
    tables. See database tables
database reports, 265–281
    adding clip art, 278–279
    adding expressions, 274–275
    adding summary information, 272–273
    creating, 266–267, 270–271
    creating mailing labels, 280–281
    modifying, 268–269
    previewing, 276–277
    sections, 267
database tables, 51
    creating, 222–223
    inserting into Word, 342
    modifying, 224–225
data entry. See entering data
data entry forms, 226–227
data forms, 222
Datasheet view, 226
Data Table button, 200
date(s), calculating using serial numbers, 175

date and time functions, 171, 174–175
Date Style format, numbers in worksheets, 157
Date/Time data type, database fields, 223
decryption, databases, 256, 257
default settings, 2
deleting
    cell contents, 154
    files, 40, 41
demoting text, Outline view, 294, 295
Design templates, PowerPoint, 291
Design view, 226, 227
    formatting mailing labels, 281
desktop, creating shortcuts, 42–43
destination file, 344
Detail section
    database reports, 267
    forms, 245
dialog boxes, 12–13. See also specific dialog boxes
dimmed commands, 11
Direct Mail Manager, 50
disks, 26
displaying
    buttons, 82
    documents, 86–87
    reports, 276–277
    slide show keyboard shortcuts, 320
Dissolve effect, presentations, 323
division operator (/), 153
documents, 26, 51. See also file(s)
    borders around text, 125
    centering text, 102, 103
    clip art, 130–131
    editing, 80–81
    entering text, 78–79
    footers, 134, 135
    footnotes, 132–133
    formatting. See formatting documents
    headers, 134, 135
    importing files, 342–343
    inserting Access tables, 342
    inserting Excel data, 343
    lengthy, 133
    linking Excel worksheets, 344–345
    moving insertion point, 81
    moving text, 82–83
    multi-page, headers and footers, 135
    planning, 74–75
    printing, 88–89
    replacing text, 112–113
    saving as Web pages, 60, 352–353
    text alignment, 102–103
    verifying page layout, 136–137
    viewing, 86–87
document window, Word, 77
dollar sign ($), absolute cell references, 155
double-clicking, 4, 5
down scroll arrows, 14, 15
drag and drop technique, 82, 83
    inserting Access tables into Word, 342
dragging, 4, 5

Drawing toolbar
    opening, 76
    PowerPoint, 293, 300–301
    Word, 77
drawn objects, inserting in documents, 131

►E

Edit Data Source button, 350
editing
    database records, 230, 231
    database tables, 224–225
    documents, 80–81
    footers, 134
    headers, 134
    Paint files, 28, 29
    worksheets, 154–155
Edit menu
    Excel, 154
    Word, 113
Edit WordArt Text dialog box, 128, 129
Ellipse button, 29
ellipsis, 11, 12
embedded objects, 338
embedding Excel charts into PowerPoint slides,
    338–339
Encrypt/Decrypt dialog box, 256
encryption, databases, 256, 257
endnotes, 132
end-of-cell marks, 122, 123
end-of-row marks, 122, 123
entering data
    databases, 228–229
    worksheets, 148, 149
entering text
    Outline view, 294–295
    Slide view, 296–297
    Word documents, 78–79
    worksheet labels, 148, 149
Eraser button, 29
error correction
    AutoCorrect feature, 79
    spell checking presentations, 304, 305
    Spelling and Grammar Checker, 84–85
Excel, 50, 51
    charts. See chart(s)
    functions. See functions
    inserting data in Word files, 343
    templates, 179
    workbooks. See workbooks
    worksheets. See worksheet(s)
exclusive mode, opening databases, 256
exiting programs, 62, 63
    Access, 232, 233
Explorer Bar, 38, 39
exponent operator (^), 153
exporting PowerPoint presentations to Word, 340–341
expressions, database reports, 274–275

► F

field descriptions, database tables, 224, 225
field labels, forms, 244
field list, 244
Field List button, 244
field names, databases, 228–229
field properties, database tables, 224, 225
Field Properties pane, 220, 221
field stat types, databases, 223
field value(s), databases, 228–229
field value text box, forms, 244
file(s), 1, 25
  closing, 62, 63
  copying, 32, 36–37
  creating, 26, 27, 58–59
  deleting, 40, 41
  destination, 344
  importing into Word documents, 342–343
  linked. See linked objects
  moving, 32, 36–37
  multiple, selecting, 37
  names, 60, 61, 76, 77
  opening, 76, 77
  renaming, 32
  restoring, 40, 41
  saving, 26, 27, 60–61, 76, 77
  shortcuts for accessing, 32
  source, 338, 344
  viewing using My Computer, 34, 35
file hierarchies, 32, 33
file management, 32–33
  Windows Explorer, 38–39
File menu
  Access, 232, 233
  Excel, 179
filenames, 60, 61
file sizing buttons, 9
Fill With Color button, 29
filter(s), customizing, 185
filtering
  databases, 250–251
  data in worksheets, 184, 185
Filter window, 250, 251
financial functions, 171, 178–179
Find and Replace dialog box, 112, 113
Find command
  Excel Edit menu, 154
  Word Edit menu, 113
Find record button, 350
first line indents, 106, 107
floppy disks, 26
folders, 32
  copying, 32
  creating using My Computer, 34, 35
  moving, 32
  multiple, selecting, 37
  renaming, 32
font(s)
  charts, 204, 205
  forms, 246, 247
  size. See font size
  styles. See font styles

TrueType, 99
  types. See font types
fontography, 99
font size
  Excel worksheets, 158, 159
  Word documents, 98, 99
font styles
  Excel worksheets, 158, 159
  Word documents, 100–101
Font tab, Format Cells dialog box, 158
font types
  Excel worksheets, 158, 159
  Word documents, 98, 99
footers
  database reports, 267
  documents, 134, 135
  Excel worksheets, 161
  forms, 245
footnote(s), 132–133
Footnote and Endnote dialog box, 132, 133
footnote reference marks, 132
form(s), Access, 226–227
  clip art, 248–249
  fonts and styles, 246–247
  footers, 245
  headers, 245
  modifying layout, 244–245
format, numbers in worksheets, 157
Format Axis button, Chart toolbar, 204
Format button, Chart toolbar, 200
Format Cells dialog box, 156, 157, 158, 159
Format Data Series dialog box, 204, 205
Format menu, 150, 157
Format Painter button, 55
Format Picture dialog box, 318
formatting
  charts, 206, 207
  documents. See formatting documents
  mailing labels, 281
  pictures, 318, 319
  reports, 268–269
  tables, 126–127
  text. See formatting text
formatting documents, 97–113
  alignment, 102–103
  font style, 100–101
  font type and size, 98–99
  manual page breaks, 110–111
  margin settings, 104–105
  replacing text, 112–113
  ruler use, 106–107
  styles, 108–109
formatting text, 26
  presentations, 298–299
Formatting toolbar
  PowerPoint, 293, 299
  Word, 53, 54, 77
Form Footer section, 245
Form Header section, 245
form letters
  inserting Access fields, 348–349
  merging Access data, 350–351
formula(s), worksheets, 152–153

formula bar, worksheets, 146, 147
Form view, 226, 227
Form Wizard dialog box, 226, 227
forward slash (/), division operator, 153
Free-Form Select button, 29
functions, 169–181
  date and time, 171, 174–175
  financial, 171, 178–179
  Goal Seek command, 180–181
  information, 171
  logical, 171
  lookup and reference, 171
  math and trig, 171
  mathematical, 172–173, 177
  planning for use, 171
  statistical, 171, 176–177
  text, 171
  worksheets, 152

► G

Goal Seek command, 180–181
graphical user interfaces (GUIs), 1
graphics. See clip art; pictures
gridlines, charts, 194, 202, 203
Group footer section, database reports, 267
Group header section, database reports, 267

► H

hanging indents, 106, 107
hard disks, 26
header(s)
  database reports, 267
  documents, 134, 135
  forms, 245
  worksheets, 161, 182
Header and Footer command, View menu, 161
Help pointer, 17
Help system, 16–17, 56–57
Help window, Word, 56, 57
horizontal scroll bars, 15
  Word, 53
Hypertext Markup Language (HTML), 352

► I

Ignore All button, Spelling and Grammar dialog box, 85
Ignore button, Spelling and Grammar dialog box, 85
image properties, changing, 318, 319
Imaging, 7
importing files into Word documents, 342–343
inactive programs, 10
indents, setting using ruler, 106, 107
Index and Tables dialog box, 133
Index tab, Windows Help dialog box, 16, 17

Index

information functions, 171
input devices, 4
input masks, database tables, 224
Insert ClipArt window, 130
Insert File dialog box, 342, 343
Insert Hyperlink button, 55
inserting
    Access tables into Word, 342
    Excel data in Word files, 343
insertion point, 78
    moving in documents, 81
Insert Object dialog box, 338, 339
Insert Picture dialog box, 249
integrating programs, 337–353
    embedding Excel charts into PowerPoint slides, 338–339
    exporting PowerPoint presentations to Word, 340–341
    importing files into Word documents, 342–343
    inserting Access fields into Word form letters, 348–349
    linking Excel worksheets to Word documents, 344–345
    merging Access data with Word form letters, 350–351
    saving Word documents as Web pages, 352–353
    updating linked Excel worksheets, 346–347
Internet, 2. *See also* Web *entries*
    accessing from Active Desktop, 2
Internet Explorer, 3
Internet style mouse, 5
Italic button, 55
italicizing type, 100, 101

▶ J

justifying text, 102, 103

▶ K

keyboard, moving insertion point in documents, 81
keyboard shortcuts, 10, 11, 12
    data entry forms, 229
    slide shows, viewing, 320

▶ L

labels
    charts, 194
    entering in worksheets, 148, 149
Label Wizard dialog box, 280, 281
layout
    forms, modifying, 244–245
    pages, verifying, 136–137
Layout option, Page Setup dialog box, 104
legend(s), charts, 194

Legend button, Chart toolbar, 200
letters, form. *See* form letters
Line button, 29
line charts, 195
line spacing, 102
linked objects
    linking Excel worksheets to Word documents, 344–345
    unlinking files, 347
    updating worksheets, 346–347
linking Excel worksheets to Word documents, 344–345
Links dialog box, 347
list arrows, 13
logical functions, 171
Log Off command, 19
long documents, 133
lookup and reference functions, 171

▶ M

Magnifier button, 29
mailing labels, creating, 280–281
Mail Merge Helper dialog box, 348, 349
Mail Merge toolbar, 350
manual page breaks, 110–111
margin settings, Word, 104–105
Margins option, Page Setup dialog box, 104, 105
mathematical functions, 171, 172–173, 177
mathematical operators, 153
MAX function, 173
maximizing windows, 8, 9
Memo data type, database fields, 223
Memo Wizard, 58, 59
menu(s), 10, 11, 54, 55
    cascading (submenus), 7
    check marks, 10
    items, 11
    personalizing, 54, 55
    pop-up, 4, 5
menu bar, 10, 11
    Access, 220
    Word program window, 53
Merge to New Document button, 350
Merge to Printer button, 350
merging. *See* form letters
Microsoft Clip Gallery, 278, 279, 316, 317
Microsoft Word Help button, 55, 56
Mil Merge Helper button, 350
MIN function, 173
minimizing windows, 8, 9
minus sign (-)
    subtraction operator, 153
    Windows Explorer, 38, 39
mistakes. *See* error correction
Modify Style dialog box, 108, 109
More button, Find and Replace dialog box, 112
mouse, 4–5
    Classic style and Internet style, 5
    techniques, 4–5

mouse buttons, 4, 5
mouse pointer, shapes, 4
Mouse Properties dialog box, 12, 13
Move Up button, Outline view, 295
moving. *See also* navigating
    charts, 196, 198, 199
    drag and drop technique. *See* drag and drop technique
    files, 36–37
    files and folders, 32
    insertion point in documents, 81
    slides in Slide Sorter view, 304
    text in documents, 82–83
    windows, 8, 9
multi-page documents, headers and footers, 135
multiple files and folders, selecting, 37
Multiple Pages button, Print Preview toolbar, 86
multiplication operator (*), 153
multitasking, 10, 30–31
My Computer, 3
    browsing using multiple windows, 32
    copying files, 36–37
    creating folders, 34, 35
    moving files, 36–37
    viewing files, 34, 35
My Computer toolbar, 35
My Documents folder, 3

▶ N

name(s)
    files, 32, 60, 61
    folders, 32
name boxes, worksheets, 146, 147
navigating
    presentations, 292–293
    between slides, 296
    workbooks, 146–147
    worksheets, 148
navigation buttons, Word, 77
Network Neighborhood, 3
New button, 55
New dialog box, 58, 59
New Office Document dialog box, 53
New Record button, 230
New Report dialog box, 266
New Slide dialog box, 296, 297
Normal view, 86, 87
Notes Page view, 293
Notes pane, 293
number(s)
    entering in worksheets, 148, 149
    mathematical functions, 171, 172–173, 177
    serial, calculating dates using, 175
Number data type, database fields, 223
number format, worksheets, 157

▶O

objects, 128
    embedded, 338
    linked. See linked objects
    PowerPoint, 296
    presentations, 300–301
    stacking presentations, 303
Office 2000, 49–63
    closing files, 62, 63
    creating files using wizards, 58–59
    editions, 49
    exiting programs, 62, 63
    Help system, 56–57
    menus, 54, 55
    saving files, 60–61
    starting programs, 52–53
    toolbars, 54, 55
Office Assistant, 56, 57
    turning off, 58
Office Assistant button, Standard toolbar, 146
Office Clipboard, 83
Office Language Settings, 50
Office Shortcut Bar, 50
off-site presentations, preparing for, 327
One Page button, Print Preview toolbar, 86
online presentations, 320–321
on-screen presentations, 290
Open button, 55
Open dialog box, 28, 29, 76, 77
opening
    Drawing toolbar, 76
    files. See opening databases; opening files
opening databases, 242–243
    exclusive mode, 256
opening files, 76, 77
    databases. See opening databases
    Paint files, 28, 29
    presentations, 314
    shortcuts, 32
Open Worksheet dialog box, 343
operating systems, 1
option buttons, 13
order, calculations in Excel, 153
orphans, 111
Outline pane, 293
Outline pane scroll bar, 293
Outline view, 86, 87
    PowerPoint, 293, 294–295
Outlook, 50
Outlook Express, 3

▶P

page breaks, manual, 110–111
Page footer section, database reports, 267
Page header section, database reports, 267
page layout, verifying, 136–137
page number indicator, Word, 77
Page Setup command, File menu, 160
Page Setup dialog box, 104, 105, 135, 161

Paint, 7, 28–29
    toolbar buttons, 29
panes, 16
    PowerPoint, 293
    Windows Explorer window, 38, 39
paper size option, Page Setup dialog box, 104
paper source option, Page Setup dialog box, 104
paragraph(s), indenting first line, 106, 107
Paragraph dialog box, 111
paragraph styles, 108–109
parentheses (()), formulas, 153
passwords, databases, 256, 257
Paste button, 30
Paste Function dialog box, 170, 171
pasting
    linking Excel worksheets to Word documents,
        344–345
    text in documents, 82, 83
Patterns tab, Format Cells dialog box, 159
Pencil button, 29
Percent Style format, numbers in worksheets, 157
personalizing. See customizing
Phone Dialer, 7
Pick Color button, 29
pictures
    documents, 131
    modifying, 318–319
    presentations, 316
    reports, 279
Picture toolbar, 319
pie charts, 195
placeholders, 78, 79
    PowerPoint, 296
planning
    charts, 194–195
    databases, 218–219
    documents, 74–75
    for function use, 171
plus sign (+)
    addition operator, 153
    Windows Explorer, 38, 39
PMT dialog box, 178, 179
point(s), 98
pointer trail, 12
pointing, 4, 5
Polygon button, 29
pop-up menus, 4, 5
PowerPoint, 50, 289. See also presentation(s); slide(s)
    AutoLayouts, 296
    Drawing toolbar, 300–301
    Formatting toolbar, 299
    objects, 296
    placeholders, 296
    running presentations without, 321
    scroll boxes, 292
    selection boxes, 296
    templates, 291
    views, 293
PowerPoint dialog box, 290, 291
PowerPoint program window, 292, 293
presentation(s), 289–305, 313–327. See also slide(s)
    animation effects, 324–325
    clip art, 316–317

    colors, 298, 299
    color schemes, 314–315
    creating, 290–291
    designing, 315
    Drawing toolbar, 300–301
    entering text in Outline view, 294–295
    entering text in Slide view, 296–297
    exporting to Word, 340–341
    formatting text, 298
    inserting Word text, 341
    navigating, 292–293
    objects, 300–301
    off-site, preparing for, 327
    online, 320–321
    on-screen, 290
    opening, 314
    pictures, 318–319
    preset timing and transitions, 322–323
    previewing, 304, 305
    printed materials, 326, 327
    running without PowerPoint, 321
    speakers notes, 326, 327
    spell checking, 304, 305
    text boxes, 302–303
    timing and transitions, 322–323
presentation graphics programs, 289. See also
    PowerPoint; presentation(s); slide(s)
Presentation Options dialog box, 290, 291
Presentation templates, PowerPoint, 291
previewing
    charts, 208, 209
    presentations, 304, 305
    reports, 276–277
    Web pages, 352, 353
    worksheets, 160, 161
Print button, 55, 88
Print command, 232
Print dialog box, 88, 89
printed materials, presentations, 326, 327
printing
    charts, 208, 209
    databases, 232, 233
    documents, 88–89
    worksheets, 160, 161, 184, 185
Print Layout view, 86, 87
Print Preview, 86. See also previewing
programs. See also Access; Excel; PowerPoint; Word
    active, 10
    exiting, 62, 63
    inactive, 10
    integrating. See integrating programs
    starting, 6–7, 52–53
    suites, 49
program sizing buttons, 9
promoting text, Outline view, 294, 295
properties, 12, 13
Properties button, 244
property sheet
    formatting controls, 247
    forms, 244
protection, databases, 256–257

Index

▶Q

queries
  creating, 254–255
  creating reports, 270–271
  filters, 250–251
Quick Launch toolbar, 2, 3
Quick View command, 32

▶R

radar charts, 195
random access memory (RAM), 26, 60
Random Transition effect, presentations, 323
range references, functions, 170
Recolor Picture dialog box, 318, 319
records
  adding to databases, 230, 231
  editing, 230, 231
  sorting, 252–253
Rectangle button, 29
Recycle Bin, 3, 32, 40, 41
  customizing, 40
references, functions, 170
relative cell references, 155
renaming. See name(s)
repagination, 104
replacing text, 112–113
report(s). See database reports
Report footer section, database reports, 267
Report header section, database reports, 267
Report Wizard dialog box, 266, 267
resizing. See sizing
Restart in MS-DOS mode option, 19
Restart option, 19
restoring
  files, 40, 41
  windows, 8, 9
right-clicking, 4, 5
right indents, 106, 107
Rounded Rectangle button, 29
rows
  Word tables, inserting and deleting, 124–125
  worksheets. See worksheet rows
ruler, Word, 77, 106–107

▶S

Save As dialog box, 26, 27, 60, 61, 222, 223
Save button, 55
saving
  database objects, 242
  documents as Web pages, 60, 352–353
  files, 26, 27, 60–61, 76, 77
  Paint files, 28, 29
scatter charts, 195
ScreenTips, 10, 11, 56, 57

scroll bars, 14–15, 53
  Field List window, 244
  PowerPoint, 293
scroll boxes, 14, 15
  PowerPoint, 292
  Word, 77
Search tab, Windows Help dialog box, 16, 17
sections, database reports, 267
Select button, 29
selecting
  multiple fields at same time, 244
  multiple files and folders, 37
  objects in slides, 300
  text, 26, 78, 79
  worksheet cells, 147
selection bar, 82
selection boxes, PowerPoint, 296
selection handles, 128
select queries, 254, 255
Server Extensions Administrator, 50
Set Database Password dialog box, 256, 257
shading, worksheet cells, 159
shapes, presentations, 300–303
  adding text, 302–303
shortcuts
  accessing files, 32
  adding to Start menu, 43
  creating on desktop, 42–43
  keyboard. See keyboard shortcuts
Shrink to Fit button, 136
Shut down option, 19
Shut Down Windows dialog box, 18, 19
shutting down Windows, 18, 19
single-clicking, 4, 5
size
  fonts. See font size
  Recycle Bin, 40
  worksheets, 146
sizing
  charts, 198, 199
  clip art, 316, 317
  windows, 8, 9
sizing buttons, 8, 9
slash (/), division operator, 153
slide(s). See also PowerPoint; presentation(s)
  annotating, 320, 321
  embedding Excel charts, 338–339
  moving in Slide Sorter view, 304
  navigating between, 296
Slide Navigator dialog box, 320, 321
Slide pane, PowerPoint, 293
Slide pane scroll bar, PowerPoint, 293
slider, 12, 13
Slide Show view, PowerPoint, 293
Slide Sorter view, PowerPoint, 293
Slide Transition dialog box, 322, 323
Slide view, entering text, 296–297
Small Business Customer Manager, 50
Small Business Financial Manager, 50
Solver, 181
Sort dialog box, 182, 183

sorting
  database records, 252–253
  by multiple worksheet columns, 183
  worksheet rows, 182–183
sounds, inserting in documents, 131
source file, 338, 344
spacing, lines of text, 102
speaker's notes, 326, 327
Spelling and Grammar button, 55
Spelling and Grammar Checker, 84–85
Spelling Checker, PowerPoint, 304–305
Spelling dialog box, 304, 305
spin boxes, 13
Spreadsheet Solutions tab, File menu, 179
stacked objects, 303
Standard toolbar
  Excel, 146, 154
  PowerPoint, 293
  Word, 53, 54, 77
Start button, 2, 3, 52, 53
starting programs, 6–7, 52–53
  Access, 220–221
Start Mail Merge button, 350
Start menu, 52, 53
  adding shortcuts, 43
  categories, 6
statistical functions, 171, 176–177
statistics, summary calculations in database reports, 273
status bar
  Access, 220, 221
  PowerPoint, 293
  Word, 77
  Word program window, 53
styles
  fonts. See font styles
  forms, 246, 247
  paragraphs, 108–109
submenus, 7
subtraction operator (-), 153
suites of programs, 49
SUM function, 172–173, 173
summary information, reports, 272–273
Summary Options dialog box, 272, 273

▶T

table(s). See database tables; Word tables
Table AutoFormat, 126–127
Table AutoFormat dialog box, 126, 127
table columns, 123
  adjusting width, 126, 127
  inserting and deleting, 124, 125
Table Design toolbar, 220, 221
table rows, inserting and deleting, 124, 125
tables of authorities, 133
tables of contents, 133
tab order, forms, 229

tabs (in dialog boxes), 12, 13
  Windows Help dialog box, 16, 17
tabs (positions), 106, 107
tab stops, setting using ruler, 106, 107
taskbar, 2, 3
templates, 58
  Excel, 179
  PowerPoint, 291
text
  adding to shapes in presentations, 302–303
  entering. *See* entering text
  formatting, 26
  Outline view, 294–295
  promoting and demoting in Outline view, 294, 295
  selecting, 26, 78, 79
  Word. *See* documents; Word
  WordArt, 128–129
text boxes, 13
  presentations, 302–303
Text button, 29
Text data type, database fields, 223
text functions, 171
timing presentations, 322–323
title(s), charts, 196, 197
title bar, 8, 9
  Word program window, 53
toolbars, 10, 11, 54, 55. *See also specific toolbars*
  available, listing, 54
  buttons, 55
Toolbox button, 244
totals, calculating using SUM function, 172–173
trackpoint, 5
transitions, presentations, 322–323
triangle, menus, 11
trig functions, 171
TrueType fonts, 99

► U

unbound controls, forms, 244
Underline button, 55
underlined letters, menus, 11
underlining type, 100, 101
Undo button, Standard toolbar, 154
unlinking files, 347
updating linked Excel worksheets, 346–347
up scroll arrows, 14, 15

► V

vertical scroll bars, 15
  Word, 53
videos, inserting in documents, 131
view(s), PowerPoint, 293

view buttons
  PowerPoint, 293
  Word, 77
viewing. *See* displaying
View menu, 54, 55
View Merged Data button, 350

► W

Web browsers, 352, 353
Web page(s), 16
  previewing, 352, 353
  saving documents as, 60, 352–353
Web Page Layout view, 86, 87
Web style mouse, 5
Widow/Orphan control box, Paragraph dialog box, 111
widows, 111
windows, 1. *See also specific windows*
  active, 10
  moving, 8, 9
  panes. *See* panes
  sizing, 8, 9
Windows, shutting down, 18, 19
Windows Clipboard, 30
Windows Explorer, file management, 38–39
Windows Help dialog box, 16, 17
Wipe Left effect, presentations, 323
Wipe Right effect, presentations, 323
wizards
  creating files, 58–59
  creating reports, 266–267
Word, 50, 51
  documents. *See* documents
  exporting PowerPoint presentations to Word, 340–341
  form letters. *See* orm letters
  Help window, 56, 57
  inserting Word text into PowerPoint presentations, 341
  merging Access data with form letters, 350–351
  opening files, 76, 77
  program window, 53
  saving files, 76, 77
  Spelling and Grammar Checker, 84–85
  tables. *See* table columns; Word tables
  WordArt, 128–129
WordArt, 128–129
WordArt Gallery dialog box, 128, 129
WordPad, 6, 7
Word tables, 122–127
  columns. *See* table columns
  creating, 122–123
  formatting, 126–127
  inserting and deleting rows, 124, 125
workbooks, 145
  inserting in Word files, 343
  navigating, 146–147

worksheet(s), 51, 145
  adding shading to cells, 159
  alignment, 156, 157
  borders, 158, 159
  charts. *See* chart(s)
  columns. *See* worksheet columns
  editing, 154–155
  entering numbers and labels, 148–149
  filtering data, 184, 185
  font type and style, 158, 159
  footers, 161
  formulas, 152–153
  headers, 161, 182
  inserting in Word files, 343
  linked, updating, 346–347
  linking to Word documents, 344–345
  navigating, 148
  number format, 156, 157
  previewing, 160, 161
  printing, 160, 161, 184, 185
  row height, 150, 151
  rows. *See* worksheet rows
  size, 146
  updating linked worksheets, 346–347
worksheet columns, 147
  changing width, 150, 151
  selecting, 147
  sorting by multiple columns, 183
worksheet rows, 147
  changing height, 150, 151
  selecting, 147
  sorting, 182–183
World Wide Web (Web; WWW), 2, 353
Write-Up dialog box, 340, 341

► X

X-axis, charts, 194
XY charts, 195

► Y

Y-axis, charts, 194
Yes/No data type, database fields, 223

► Z

zooming, Print Preview window, 276, 277